Cross Dressing, Sex, and Gender

Cross Dressing, Sex, and Gender

Vern L. Bullough and
Bonnie Bullough

UNIVERSITY OF PENNSYLVANIA PRESS   Philadelphia

Library of Congress Cataloging-in-Publication Data
Bullough, Vern L.
  Cross dressing, sex, and gender / Vern L. Bullough and Bonnie
Bullough.
     p.   cm.
  Includes bibliographical references and index.
   ISBN 0-8122-3163-5. — ISBN 0-8122-1431-5 (pbk.)
   1. Transvestism.   2. Transvestites.   I. Bullough, Bonnie.
II. Title.
HQ77.B785   1993
306.77—dc20   92-32030
                                                        CIP

Contents

Introduction

Cross dressing is a simple term for a complex set of phenomena. It ranges from simply wearing one or two items of clothing to a full-scale burlesque, from a comic impersonation to a serious attempt to pass as the opposite gender, from an occasional desire to experiment with gender identity to attempting to live most of one's life as a member of the opposite sex. Early researchers, most of them physicians or psychiatrists, tended to utilize a medical model that conceptualized variations from the norms of sexual behavior as an illness or, in more recent years, as a behavior problem. Such definitions have been emphasized in an effort to arrive at the causes of a "disease" or "problem" and, once having achieved this, to take steps to "cure" the patient or client.

One of the first steps in this process was to name and label the phenomenon. The term *transvestism* (Latin for "cross dressing") was coined by Magnus Hirschfeld in 1910.[1] Havelock Ellis, his contemporary, felt that the term was much too literal, and that it overemphasized the importance of clothing while failing to include the "feminine" identity factors present in male cross dressers. More or less ignoring the possibility of female cross dressers, Ellis coined the term *eonism* based on a historical personage, the Chevalier d'Éon de Beaumont (1728–1810), who spent much of his life living as a woman.[2] Since that time other terms have been advanced, including *gynemimesis* (literally, "woman mime") and its counterpart *andromimesis*,[3] *gender dysphoria*, *female* or *male impersonation*, *transgenderist*, *femmiphile*, *androphile*, *femme mimic*, *fetishist*, *crossing*, *transsexual* (both preoperative and postoperative), and many others. Some of these terms are used in this book, particularly in the later chapters where we discuss the phenomenon from a more scientific point of view. Since these terms, however, tend to imply more than simple cross dressing, and the reasons for cross dressing in the past are not always clear, we generally have used the term *cross dressing*.

Cross dressing, moreover, has not necessarily been the same in different time periods or different cultural settings as it is in our own society. The historical view, which is strongly emphasized in the first part of this book, is crucial to understanding the phenomenon. In some eras and in some cultures, cross dressing is primarily associated with homosexuality or lesbianism, while in others it is seen as both a homosexual and heterosexual phenomenon. Dress traditionally has been a ubiquitous symbol of sexual differences, emphasizing social conceptions of masculinity and femininity. Cross dressing, therefore, represents a symbolic incursion into territory that crosses gender boundaries.

Sometimes these gender boundaries are more strict than at other times. For example, gender differences have come to be emphasized at an earlier age in twentieth-century America than they were in previous periods. Boy babies are dressed in blue and girls in pink, boys wear pants, girls dresses, and we assume that this has always been the case. Actually, babies in the past were dressed in unisex clothing, although if we are forced to give a gender identity to the clothing, it would be one associated with girls rather than boys: both boys and girls wore dresses which were usually white. Gender-based color schemes were adopted only at the outset of the twentieth century, as plumbing, cloth diapers, and color-fast fabrics became more available. However, different countries adopted different color schemes. In fact, there were heated arguments in the American popular press that pink was a more masculine color than light blue. Despite such arguments, pink came to be adopted for girls and blue for boys in the United States, primarily because of the publicity given Thomas Gainsborough's painting *Blue Boy* and Sir Thomas Lawrence's *Pinkie* when the American Henry Edwards Huntington paid a small fortune to bring these works to his San Marino museum early in the twentieth century.

Color schemes and other conscious or unconscious markings of gender difference seem important to most societies. Researchers have found that Western parents usually handle boy babies differently from girls, treating the girls as if they were much more delicate. They also tend to worry more if their boy acts feminine than if their girl is a tomboy. But what the girls gain by having slightly more freedom in crossing gender boundaries as children they lose as their opportunities and role expectations as women become much more restricted.

One of the questions our examination of cross dressing attempts to deal with is how much a behavior associated with one gender or another may be biologically programmed and how much is socially and culturally determined. We believe that both forces are at work, but we also believe that not everyone who belongs to the same sex or has the same gender identity is programmed in the same way. There are wide variations which, if plotted on a graph, would leave two overlapping bell-shaped curves with males in one hump and females in the other but with some females more toward the male side than many males are, and vice versa. This does not mean that there is any confusion about their sexual organs but only that some women are more masculine than others and some men are more feminine. Generally, however, society has tried to ignore this overlap and define behavior in black-and-white terms while in reality there are only different shades of gray.

Inevitably, many individuals violate these socially defined norms; cross dressing, in our opinion, represents a symbolic excursion across these boundaries for a wide variety of reasons. Thus, an examination of people who violate traditional gender norms by crossing these symbolic lines should enrich our understanding of the concept of gender. It is not only important to understand why some individuals cross dress but why so many do not. What is it that encourages people to stay within the defined gender boundaries?

We hold that cross dressing, even in its most burlesque and comic aspect, allows an individual to express a different facet of his or her persona. Some want to do so more than others and for a greater variety of reasons than commonly assumed. Most want to experience for themselves what it would be like to adopt a different or untraditional gender role. One of us (V.L.B.) has often asked freshmen students in Western Civilization courses to pick a historical period and culture and social class in which they would be willing to live, other than the twentieth century, and to justify their choice. Over the nearly two score years this question has been used, many women have chosen to live in past cultures on condition they could be a man, but never has a man chosen to live in the past as a woman. Many women in the past agreed with the women students since history records much larger numbers of women who have not only cross dressed but lived and worked as men than of men who cross dressed or lived as women. One reason for this discrepancy is that men traditionally have been dominant over women and have imposed numerous restrictions on them. Thus, a woman who somehow broke through the barriers found herself praised for having a masculine mind or in other ways following the masculine model.[4] On the other hand, men who expressed a feminine side were regarded as somehow weak, since femininity was socially defined that way. This also helps explain why men who cross dressed often burlesqued women's conduct rather than seriously enacting it, since comic impersonations left no question that they were males.

A variety of explanations have been posited for why people do or do not cross dress, ranging from the physiological to the psychological, from the sociological to the cultural. In this book we review various explanations and evaluate them, ultimately presenting our own synthesis. Interestingly, throughout much of history, cross dressing was not viewed as an aspect of sexual conduct at all. It is a topic excluded from medical discussions of sex until the nineteenth century. It was also not regarded as a mental illness, which was one way our predecessors labeled phenomena we now call psychological. In fact, many so-called primitive cultures simply regarded it as one variation in human behavior. Often cross dressing had religious connotations, and it formed a major element in some religious cults. The biblical prohibition against cross dressing (*Deuteronomy* 22:5) seems to have been an effort to condemn rival belief systems to Judaism. During the Middle Ages, it was sometimes associated with heresy and witchcraft, but as many festivals and masquerades demonstrate, the impersonation was usually regarded as relatively harmless. Cross dressing was not regarded as a sign of lesbianism or homosexuality until the eighteenth century and then, for men, it became associated with effeminate homosexuality. At the beginning of the twentieth century, Magnus Hirschfeld, who was the most descriptive and analytical of the early researchers into the topic, attempted to point out some of the complexities of what he called transvestism and emphasized the heterosexuality of both the men and women involved. From Hirschfeld the subject crossed over into psychiatric literature, where it remained until the last twenty years, during which there has been renewed study of the phenomenon by professionals in various disciplines.

This book is a comprehensive examination of cross dressing. We want to force attention on the complexity of the phenomenon and to emphasize that there are no simple explanations for it, as some of the psychiatric literature of earlier years has argued. We want to demonstrate that, within limits, cross dressing is a normative aspect of human behavior. It may often be an attempt to experience vicariously how the other gender lives. It may also be for many (both men and women) a sexual experience. It can also become such a compulsion that it weakens and sometimes destroys families. It can even lead to depression and suicide. We believe there are no simple solutions to the problems of those who are driven to cross dress, although if they lived in a different society, their behavior might not be viewed as problematic. The cross dressing individual whose conduct is distressing to other family members and who wants to remain involved with them but still cross dress has to involve the family directly, which usually results in the intervention of professional counselors. Even those who want to withdraw from their families in order to pursue a new gender identity should involve a family therapist, so the transition can be done with the least trauma both to the individual and to the family. Anyone involved in serious cross dressing needs to know the limitations of the new role he or she wants to enter. The second part of this book thus examines clinical and scientific issues.

In sum, our intended audience is a large one: the general public, in order to acquaint them with what cross dressing is all about; individual cross dressers and their families, so that they may better understand themselves or a loved one; and professionals in multiple disciplines, so that they can have an overview of the topic, which in the past has been so sadly lacking, and a list of treatment and other options, which will hopefully allow them to make wise decisions if they deem intervention necessary.

Acknowledgments

A book like this could not be published without the help of numerous friends and colleagues. Our professional colleagues in the Society for the Scientific Study of Sex have often discussed the subject with us, and are cited extensively in the notes. Particularly valuable have been the insights of the various cross dressers with whom we have discussed our ideas over the years including Virginia Prince, Ariadne Kane, Carol Beecroft, JoAnn Roberts, Dallas Denny, Merissa Sherill Lynn, Lou Sullivan, Rupert Raj, and Christine Jorgensen. Special thanks are due to Patricia Smith, acquisitions editor of the University of Pennsylvania Press, who had faith in the book, as well as to David Prout, copyeditor, Carl Gross, production and design manager, Mindy Brown, project editor, and Kathleen Moore, marketing manager. The index was prepared by Janice Fulton.

Notes

1. Magnus Hirschfeld, *Die Transvestiten: Eine Untersuchung über den erotischen Verkleidungstrieb mit anfangreichem casuistischen und historischen Material* (Leipzig: Max Spohr, 1910). For an English translation, see *Transvestites: The Erotic Drive to Cross Dress*, trans. Michael Lombardi-Nash (Buffalo, NY: Prometheus Books, 1991).

2. Havelock Ellis, *Eonism and Other Supplementary Studies*, vol. 6 in *Studies in the Psychology of Sex* (Philadelphia: F. A. Davis, 1926). D'Éon is examined in greater detail in Chapter 6.

3. John Money, *Love Maps: Clinical Concepts of Sexual/Erotic Health and Pathology, Paraphilia, and Gender Transposition in Childhood, Adolescence, and Maturity* (Buffalo, NY: Prometheus Books, 1988), 103–4.

4. For an analysis of this kind of behavior see Vern L. Bullough, Brenda Shelton, and Sarah Slavin, *The Subordinated Sex* (Athens, GA: University of Georgia Press, 1988).

Part I
Cultural and Historical Background

Chapter 1
Cross Dressing in Perspective

Cross dressing implies different things in different cultures and has been viewed historically in widely varying ways. Some societies, perhaps influenced by the existence of hermaphrodites, believed in a third sex that combined qualities of the other two.[1] Anthropologists, influenced by early Spanish observers in the New World, and reluctant to use such terms as *homosexual,* referred collectively to such individuals as *berdaches.*[2] Some scholars, aware that berdache originally was a term describing male conduct, adopted the term *Amazons* to describe the female counterparts.[3] In either case, the terms have been extended far beyond their original meaning to describe individuals who did not conform to the standardized bipolar model of the sexes so long established in Western culture.

Status and the Social Implications of Cross Dressing

Recently, as distinctions have emerged between sex and gender, the term *supernumerary gender* has been used by many to describe individuals who adopt the role and many of the customs of the opposite sex. Still others hold that it is not so much an extra gender as a blending together of the masculine and feminine.[4] The male berdache has recently been referred to as being in a gender-transformed status or adopting an alternative or cross-gender role.[5] This is because in many Native American religions the berdaches often have special ceremonial roles.[6] Male berdaches also do some of the work attributed to women and mix together much of the behavior, dress, and social roles of women with those of men. They gain social prestige by their spiritual-intellectual or artistic contributions, as well as by their reputation for hard work and generosity. The berdaches often serve a mediating function between women and men precisely because their character is seen as distinct from either sex. In their erotic behavior such individuals generally, but not always, are homosexual or lesbian. Some are asexual and others heterosexual.

The distinction between status and role is regarded by the anthropologist Anne Bolin as a "critical one" for understanding gender. She questions whether the berdache was just another social role or one that enhanced status or position; Bolin concludes that it gave additional status.[7] Status, as emphasized later in this book, is a key concept in defining how a society accepts cross dressing or gender transformation. An illustration of status gain is the so-called manly hearts, a special class of North Piegan women (a Blackfoot-speaking group in Canada). Such women were characterized as aggressive, independent, bold, and sexual,[8] all terms normally reserved for the male. In her study of the fieldnotes and texts of the original investigators, Bolin concludes that these women did not constitute a supernumerary gender but rather had a variant role similar to that of the Western tomboy but without the age restrictions. This role variation was accepted because the North Piegan society, as was the case with most Plains Indians, placed a higher value on "masculine" characteristics than "feminine" ones. Among the North Piegans masculine characteristics were defined in terms of ownership, manipulation, and disposition of property. Though men dominated in this field, women were not prohibited from accumulating property, whether by inheritance or their own efforts, and as a result, some women excelled in this traditional masculine field. These women became known as *ninauposkitzipspe,* or "manly hearted women," since simply by their achievement they demonstrated behavioral traits usually attributed to the males and different from the stereotypical behavior of most women. Both within the tribe and in the home, they had greater say than other women.[9]

Status gain, however, is not the only possible explanation. Gregory Bateson hypothesizes on the basis of his study of the naven rituals practiced by the Iatmuls in New Guinea that when one gender found itself in a unique circumstance that demanded behaviors of the other, they simply adopted a "bit" of the other gender's culture.[10] Margaret Mead suggested that cross dressing represented a mismatch between individual temperaments and socially demanded requirements of particular cultures. When bravery in warfare was expected, some by temperament would not be able to perform, hence the berdache, the cross dresser, or similar individuals.[11] Alfred Kroeber held that the abnormal individuals needed a social niche in a culture, just as everyone else did. The berdache was an example, and customs evolved to accompany the personal needs of the deviant's nature to culture.[12]

Cross-Cultural Views of Gender-Crossing

Gender-crossing is so ubiquitous, that genitalia by itself has never been a universal nor essential insignia of a lifelong gender.[13] Gender instead is an achieved status rather than an ascribed biological characteristic and is based on tasks performed and the significance of clothing as well as anatomical and other factors.[14] Some look to socialization variables as most important,[15] while others look to biological variables whether genetic, prenatal, hormonal, or fetal metabolic.[16] Some, like John Money, who at one point in his career heavily emphasized the socialization variables, have begun to modify their original suppositions and argue for multicausal relationships. In some of his later writing Money integrates naturalistic, cultural, phylographic (species shared), and ideographic (individually unique) developments of gender identity and maintains that prenatal hormones are a key factor.[17] At times, he even seems to argue that the distinction between nature and nurture is more or less irrelevant.[18]

One way of determining attitudes about gender is to examine those whose status in society is ambiguous because of their genitalia. This is particularly true of pseudohermaphrodites and hermaphrodites.[19] Among the Pokot of Kenya, where both males and females are circumcised, there is a class of pseudohermaphrodites known as *Sererr* whose genitals are too small for circumcision. This results in a denial of either male or female status and assignment to a third category that is more or less genderless.[20] The Navajos of the southwest United States recognize three different sexes: males, females, and Nadles, that is, hermaphrodites, but there are even more gender assignments than sexual ones, since physiologically "normal" men and women may pretend to be Nadles. Nadle sex partners may include either males or females but not other Nadles or Nadle pretenders.[21] In contemporary India, the hijras constitute a special religious community and include not only hermaphrodites but "men" who undergo emasculation and effeminate homosexuals who are hijra impostors.[22]

In this brief discussion, three different solutions have been explored: the Pokot establish a supernumerary gender, the Navajos emphasize the independence of sexual preference from the question of gender, and the hijra allow for a variety of gender identities within a special category. These examples can be expanded even more but serve only to emphasize that a number of variations from traditional Western practice of recognizing only two sexes and two forms of gender behavior exist in a number of societies.

In fact, the realization of the potentially androgynous nature of the sexes and the possibility of various gender behaviors is not confined to those groups studied by contemporary anthropologists. It is an inherent part of many non-Western religious traditions and exists in the mythologies of many peoples. Among major religions, it probably remains most strongly entrenched in Hinduism where some forms of Hindu esoteric belief still hold androgyny as an ideal to be pursued.

According to some forms of Hindu belief the Supreme Being is of one complete sex, possessing both female and male principles and having the qualities attributed to both genders. Śiva, one of the three major gods of the Hindu pantheon, for example, is sometimes represented in sculpture and painting as Ardhanārīśvara, a hermaphroditic god fused halfway into the form of his spouse Pārvatī or, alternatively, as a hermaphrodite with female elements on his left side and male on his right. Vishṇu, another member of the triad of great gods, is shown the same way as Kṛishṇa, the most celebrated deity of the Hindu pantheon. There are many legends in which the male gods take on female form. Vishṇu, for example, became a ravishing beauty known as Mohinī in order to settle a dispute among the gods and demons over whom he had precedence. So enchanted was Śiva with the charms of Mohinī that he begged Vishṇu to revert to his female form again; when he obliged, they engaged in intercourse, giving birth to Harihara, a hermaphroditic deity.

In legend, what was possible for the gods was also possible for mortals with the assistance or intervention of the gods. When the prospective parents of Śikhaṇḍin who as yet lacked a son requested Śiva to give them a son, the god had replied: "You will have a male child who is a woman." When a daughter was born, the parents, following the will of the gods, proceeded to raise her as a boy, and she, not knowing any different, assumed she was a boy. Ultimately, she was married to the daughter of a powerful king. On the wedding night, however, the bride discovered her husband's true sex and fled to her father's house, where she revealed the hoax that had been played on her. Her father, regarding the masquerade as an insult, declared war. In the meantime Śikhaṇḍin, forced to recognize her true sex, fled to a forest determined to end her life over this disgraceful turn of events. There she encountered a kindhearted *yaksha* (supernatural being) who, after seeking out the cause of her distress, offered to change sex with the princess if she would promise to exchange back in the not too distant future. The princess agreed, whereupon Śikhaṇḍin returned home and proclaimed that he now had male genitalia to his father, who in turn, communicated this fact to the bride's father. Eunuchs and old women were sent by the father-in-law to inspect his would-be son-in-law, and they reported that he was a male in all detail and that his daughter had probably been hallucinating. The war ended and the marriage was consummated. When Śikhaṇḍin returned to the *yaksha* to change back, he found that the supernatural being had been cursed to remain a woman until the death of the prince, when an exchange of sex could again take place.[23] The king then lived happily in his new male gender until his death.

Though this last incident deals with a change of sex, and in Hindu mythology this is most often a woman changing into a man, cross dressing is also common in Hindu mythology. Cross dressing, however, more often involves a man donning the clothes of a woman and acting the feminine role than the reverse. Males are much more valued in Hindu society, and therefore, it is understandable that females would want to become males or that a family without a male child would want one. Males, on the other hand, seem fascinated by what it is like to be a woman and though perhaps envious of some aspects of the female role, are still conscious of men's higher status in society. Thus female impersonation often had erotic connotations because the cross dressing either led to sexual arousal or gave access to the company of women, which might not have been possible otherwise. It also often included an aspect of adventure, as if the male were saying, Look what I can do, though I am a man, I can make myself into an enchanting woman.

Śāmba, the son of Kṛishṇa, was notorious for his gluttony, drunkenness, and sexual adventures. He seduced the wives of other men and then, dressed as a female (usually a pregnant woman) went about mocking the other gods. As Śāmbalī, his name became a synonym for eunuch.[24] Arjuna, a mortal hero, disguised himself as a eunuch, dressed in women's clothing, and taught a young princess and her companions the arts of dancing, singing, and music.[25] Kauṭilya, a mortal, whose book on statecraft dates from about the third century of the modern era, held that cross dressing was a nonpunishable activity,[26] some indication of the prevalence of the custom in ancient India.

One of the major teachings of Hinduism is that every man and woman contained within himself or herself both male and female principles. A man was a man only because of the excess of the principle of masculinity, while a woman had an excess of femininity. This maleness or femaleness remained in conflict within the individual and could only be harmonized for very brief periods during sexual intercourse, something which allowed the couple to realize the absolute. Such a realization occurred when each had lost consciousness of his or her own sex and found the other. Interestingly, it was believed to be more possible for the male to do this than the female since the nature of her additional orifices (*yoni*) and her breasts complicated matters. On the other hand, a traditional Hindu belief says that women derive greater pleasure from sex than men.[27]

Male cross dressing is often a part of Śakti worship, those Hindu sects that consider the godhead to be essentially feminine. Śakti is the wife of Śiva, although both are also known under many different names. Her worshippers are broadly divided into two groups: "right-handed" adherents who worship the god in public and "left-handed" ones who worship her in secrecy. The left in Hindu mythology is associated with the female. The worship of Śakti can also be classified as a form of Tantrism, so called because its adherents follow scriptures known as tantras. Essentially, tantric cults are antinomian, that is, they teach that men and women are not always bound by moral law but can reach a state that takes them so far beyond its purview that they can cease to obey its precepts. The Sanskrit equivalent for the term *antinomianism* (a Greek term also applied to certain Christian and Buddhist sects) is *nirdharma* ("unrighteousness"). This implies a disregard for societal conventions. Hindu tantrics believe that the goddess Śakti is particularly gratified by prohibited and reprehensible acts that either ignore or transgress the established laws of society, morality, and religion; a key teaching is that spiritual union with the god can best be attained through sexual union in the flesh.

Since, despite the gods' androgyny, the major gods are male, believers often seek to achieve union with them through becoming like their wives; to achieve this, they worship the goddess most associated with the male god. One such cult, the Sakhībhāva, holds that only the godhead, Kṛishṇa, was truly male, while every other creature in the world was female, subject to the pleasure of Kṛishṇa. They worship Rādhā, the favorite consort of Kṛishṇa, and the object of their devotion is to become a female attendant upon her. Female followers of the sect grant sexual favors freely to anyone since they conceive of their sexual partner as Kṛishṇa himself. Male followers dress like women and affect the behavior, movements, and habits of women, including imitation menstruation, during which they abstain from worship. Many of them in the past emasculated themselves, and all were supposed to play the part of women during sexual intercourse (allowing themselves to be penetrated) as an act of devotion.[28]

The technical term *hijra* ("eunuch" or "transvestite") is applied to these men, and they serve an institutionalized third-gender role since they are regarded as neither male nor female. Some observers have called them homosexual, but it is probably better to regard the hijra role as asexual, even though many, if not most, engage in homosexual activity as the passive partner. The center of the community is located in Bombay, where seven houses, or subgroups, are located. The most significant relationship in the hijra community is that of the *guru* ("master" or "teacher") and *chela* ("disciple"). When an individual decides to join the hijra community, he is taken to Bombay to visit one of the seven major gurus, whom he agrees to follow, and the guru gives the novice a new female name and some gifts. The relationship thus formed is a lifelong bond of reciprocity in which the guru is obliged to help the chela, and the chela is obligated to be loyal and obedient to the guru. Hijras live together in communes ranging from five to fifteen members, and each of these local groups also has a local guru. There is also a fictive kinship relationship. Rituals exist for "taking a daughter" by a local guru and the "daughters" of the same "mother" consider themselves "sisters"; there might also be a "grandmother" and various "aunts."

Hijras regard themselves as "separate," neither men nor women, although they recognize they were born as men. To be admitted to the sect, however, they had to be castrated, although some individuals pretend to be hijras and do not undergo castration or initiation. Hijras dress as women, wear their hair long, pluck their facial hair (they do not shave it), adopt feminine mannerisms, take women's names, and use female kinship terms and a special, feminized vocabulary. They demand to be seated as women in those areas reserved for women, and on one recent occasion they demanded to be counted as women in the census. Most hijras, however, do not necessarily pass as women, although there is great variation, and some are far more feminine than others. Many burlesque feminine behavior and dress, doing things not considered appropriate for ordinary women. Some hijras or hijra pretenders also act as prostitutes.

Although Indian belief and often the hijra's own explanation commonly attribute the reason for becoming a hijra as due to hermaphroditism, this is true only in some cases. Serena Nanda did fieldwork among the hijras and quoted one such hermaphrodite:

From my childhood I am like this. From birth my organ was very small. My mother tried taking me to doctors and all but the doctors said, "No, it won't grow, your child is not a man, this is God's gift and all . . ." From that time my mother would dress me in girl's clothes. But then she saw it was no use, so she sent me to live with hijras. I am a real hijra, not like those others who are converts; they are men and can have children, so they have the [emasculation] operation, but I was born this way.[29]

The existence of the hijras allows a wide variety of individuals with a number of different motivations to have a place in an organized subgroup. Quite clearly, many survive through homosexual prostitution, but others are more clearly transsexual, and some are clearly heterosexual, perhaps acting as hijras and doing the womanly tasks in order to survive economically. The only common ground is that all are impotent by Hindu standards, that is, unable to beget children, but even this provision is violated by the pseudohijras. Some men don women's clothing and style their hair like women in order to make their living performing as women, even though they might be married and have children of their own.[30]

In some ancient tantric sects, particularly those worshiping Durga, another wife of Śiva (usually equated with the goddess Kālī), male votaries tried to accustom themselves to thinking they were women since the goddess implies female power. In order to understand this power they believed they had to transform themselves into a woman; only by doing this could they understand the women within themselves, and only when this occurred could they experience true love.[31]

The ability to express both the feminine and masculine sides of one's personality is important to many Hindus, not only to those who belong to the tantric cults. Chaitanya (1485–1534), a Bengali religious reformer of the sixteenth century, taught that Rādhā and Krishna, who symbolize erotic love, were one soul in two bodies whose delight lay in experiencing each other's love. Chaitanya himself dressed as both Krishna and Rādhā in order to do both male and female devotions.[32] Though somewhat unusual, other holy men have done the same. For example, Rāmakrishna (born Gada-har Chattopādhyāya), the founder of a nineteenth-century sect within Hinduism, emphasized the continuity of this belief. In order to achieve a vision of Krishna, he took to wearing women's clothing and imagined himself as Rādhā. He is regarded as one of the reformers of modern Hinduism.[33]

The Hindu belief in androgyny and the widespread existence of cross dressing make it much easier and more acceptable for men to adopt women's gender roles and patterns as well as clothing. Any major religious figure in the West who dressed as a woman in order to get closer to God predictably would have been treated quite differently than the Hindu prophets who have done so. In fact, it is quite possible they would have been institutionalized. This difference between Hinduism and Western religions serves to emphasize that cross dressing is a much more complicated phenomenon than the diagnostic categories so favored by Western psychologists and psychiatrists. What is so contradictory about the Hindu cults, which to some extent still emphasize the necessity of understanding the existence of two genders within one's self, is that in most cases men cross dress and attempt to seek the feminine. Women are expected to achieve their dualism in other ways, which leads one to wonder what there is in the male psyche or male role that makes men feel that only through cross dressing can they gain this insight.

Performing a function similar to the hijras in India are the xaniths in Islamic Oman. *Xanith* in Arabic means "impotent," "effeminate," or "soft." Though the xaniths are biological males and, unlike the hijras, are not castrated, they are regarded by Oman society as neither male nor female but as having the characteristics of both. They have masculine names, are referred to in the masculine grammatical form, and under Islamic law have all the rights of a man. They also worship in the mosque with men and support themselves economically. They are like women in that they perform household work and feel flattered by compliments about their cooking and housekeeping abilities. The standards of female beauty are also applied to them, and they are encouraged to have light skin, shiny black hair, large eyes, and full cheeks. Unlike women in Oman, however, they do not have to follow purdah, although for many social purposes they are classed as women; that is, they join the women in singing and dancing during festivals, are allowed to visit and gossip with women, may walk in public arm in arm with a woman, and are allowed to eat with women, which in Oman is considered an intimate act and which purdah would not permit.

One thing they cannot do, however, is give any public verification of their ability to have sex with a woman. This is demonstrated in Omani society on the marriage day when a bloodied towel is displayed publicly as proof that the marriage has been consummated. Penetration of the female in sexual intercourse, in short, is the ultimate sign of one's manhood, something the xanith does not have. He is recognized as a homosexual and, by definition, must take the passive or female role in sexual intercourse.

One of the interesting consequences of this definition of what constitutes maleness is that the xanith can change his status in society and become a man by marrying and demonstrating in the publicly approved way (displaying the bloodied towel) that he is a potent male. Xaniths technically also are not cross dressers since they are forbidden by Omani law from wearing women's clothing. Rather, they are defined and classed as prostitutes (a male occupation, since by definition women in Omani society cannot be prostitutes). Although it is known that some female prostitutes do exist, they are not officially recognized.

Despite being forbidden to wear women's clothing, the xanith manages to appear feminine. He wears the ankle-length *gallabeja* of the men but belts it tightly at the waist as a woman would do. While men generally wear white clothing and women bright-colored patterned clothes, xaniths wear colored, unpatterned clothes. They oil their hair in the manner of a woman but comb it forward from a side part instead of diagonally from a center part as women do. This style, however, is different from that worn by most men. In sum, the xanith has cultivated a careful intergender role for himself. The fact that xaniths can leave this role and become men by marrying a woman only emphasizes how much of their role is a cultural one.[34]

The Oman case is not unique to the Islamic world. Though Muhammed stated that certain things were only appropriate to men and others to women, this has not prohibited cross dressing. Al-Bukhāri, the famous ninth-century commentator on the Koran, devoted an entire section to "men who wish to resemble women, and women who wish to resemble men." Such men were called *mukhannathūn*, while the women were *mutarajjulat*.[35] Al-Bukhāri devotes little space to the women cross dressers but much to men, many of whom were singers who imitated women in their clothing and external appearance, painted their hands with henna, had their hair combed and braided, and wore loose, brightly colored women's clothes. Like men and boys who used to act the female parts in Elizabethan drama because women were forbidden on the stage, these cross dressers were tolerated because men acting women's roles in public allowed the Muslims to keep women in purdah.

In some Islamic areas these female impersonators were called *khäal* ("dancers"), a term by which they were still known in nineteenth-century Egypt. These were described by W. E. Lane, a nineteenth-century traveler to Egypt, as favored by people who thought it indecent for a woman to appear unveiled and uncovered in public:

They are Muslims and natives of Egypt. As they personate women, their dances are exactly of the same descriptions as those of the ghawazee [female dancers]; and are, in like manner, accompanied by the sounds of castinets; but, as if to prevent their being thought to be really females, their dress is suited to their unnatural profession; being partly male and partly female: it chiefly consists of a tight vest, a girdle, and a kind of petticoat. Their general appearance, however, is more feminine than masculine; they suffer the hair of the head to grow long, and generally braid it, in the manner of the women; their hair on the face, when it begins to grow they pluck out, and they imitate the women also in applying kohl and henna to their eyes and hands. In the streets, when not engaged in dancing, they often even veil their faces, not from shame, but merely to affect the manners of women. . . . There is, in Cairo, another class of male dancers, young men and boys, whose performances, dress, and general appearance are almost exactly similar to those of the khä-wals, but who are distinguished by a different . . . [term] which is "Gink"; a term that is Turkish, and has a vulgar signification which aptly expresses their character.[36]

Obviously, it was difficult for the Victorian Englishman to write about homosexuality (indeed, the term had not yet been coined) or to describe any sexual act, but what Lane is talking about here are male prostitutes, similar to those in Oman. In addition to the *ghawazi* (spelled various ways) and the *gink,* there were also the *mohabbazin,* who performed in public places or in the houses of the wealthy at festivals preceding weddings and at circumcisions, and they continue to do so as of this writing.

Boys in female garb often formed a part of rich men's harems in Afghanistan, at least as late as the nineteenth century. Sir Richard Burton reported:

The Afghans are commercial travellers on a large scale and each caravan is accompanied by a number of boys and lads almost in woman's attire, with kohl'd eyes, and rouged cheeks, long tresses and hennaed fingers and toes, riding luxuriously in *Kajawas* or camel-panniers; they are called *Kuch-i safari* or traveling wives and the husbands trudge patiently by their sides.[37]

In addition, there was a kind of psychic transvestism among Muslim dervishes, those members of a Muslim religious order who took vows of poverty and austerity and lived in monasteries or wandered about as holy men. One of the aims of the dervish was to become the perfect man, one who had realized his essential oneness with the divine being, in whose likeness he had been made. This experience was the foundation of Sufi theosophy and was possible only to those who were the elect. These dervishes became *awilya* (plural of *wali,* meaning "near"). The *wali,* or "saint," was considered a model of the perfect man, and this implied nothing less than divine illumination, immediate vision and knowledge of things unseen and unknown, and the overwhelming glory of the "One True Light." The purpose of the Path or Sufi discipline was to predispose and prepare the disciple to receive this incalculable gift. Among some sects of dervishes the protégé became a female saint (*walyeh*) and sat "among the women," because he had been for the "moment changed into a woman." This was because saintliness and femininity were regarded as somewhat related, since women were the mothers of men, carried no arms, often suffered beating and humiliation, and baked bread, all of which were proper conduct for a *wali.*[38]

Not all orders of dervishes emphasized this "feminine state," nor did they equate God with both male and female. Still when the Sufi poet Ibun al-Fārid wished to express the transformation of the soul in his poetry, he referred to it with the feminine pronoun. The feminine is also used to denote the Universal Self.

Until then I had been enamoured of her, but when I renounced
   my desire, she desired me for herself and loved me.
And I became a beloved, nay, one loving himself; this is not like
   what I said before, that my soul is my beloved.

Through her I went forth from myself to her and came not back
to myself; one like me does not hold the doctrine of return.[39]

More restricted in their gender-crossing than the Sufis are the *mahu*
in Tahiti, although this role also has much historical precedent behind
it. A mahu is a man who publicly takes on the activities and dress of a
woman; that is, he performs household activities, takes care of babies,
and braids coconut palm leaves into thatching plaits.[40] Each district in
Tahiti has only one mahu, although every district has one. When the
position becomes available, it is voluntarily filled. Mahu engage in
fellatio with other men and by Western standards would be described
as homosexual. Not all effeminate men, however, would be described
as a mahu. Also it was possible to stop being a mahu and adopt a male
role again. Robert Levy, who studied the mahu, held that a boy might
be "coached" into the role of mahu by his elders by dressing him in
girl's clothes, particularly if he had a persistent desire to do so. Some
mahu are not supercised (an incision on the shaft of the penis at the
traditional coming-of-age ceremony for boys), although it is not clear
that this is the case with all.

Mahu were reported by Captain Bligh, the famed commander of
the *Bounty*, as well as other eighteenth-century visitors who reported
that mahu never cohabited with women but lived instead as women,
plucked out their beards, danced and sang with women, and were very
effeminate in voice and action. Bligh examined the genitals of a mahu
and found both the penis and testicles very small, but this is not the
case with all mahu.[41]

On Madagascar, some parents in the past raised boys as girls. Among
the Hovas, one of the island tribes, such children were called *sekrata.*
They were biological males who came to be treated as females because
they were regarded as too gentle and weak to be men. One observer reported that "autosuggestion" was so effective that the sekrata reached
the point where they considered themselves women, totally forgetting
their "true" sex. They assumed the apparel, customs, and character of
women, wore long clothes and long hair in decorative knots, placed
silver coins in their pierced ears, and adorned their arms and ankles
with bracelets, just as women did. Through long practice, they were
able to acquire voices that sounded like women's. They did all things
appropriate to a woman and none of the traditional tasks of the man.
Their behavior was regarded as totally natural, although they also had
special powers since it was believed that those who attacked a sekrata
would bring injury upon themselves.[42]

Frederick L. Whitam and Robin M. Mathy studied homosexuality in
Brazil, Guatemala, Peru, the Philippines, and the United States, and

observed that cross-dressing behavior was widespread, particularly among homosexuals.

Cross-gender behavior is manifested in many different ways in the homosexual world and is one of the elements which gives the homosexual world its distinctive qualities. Homosexuals and heterosexuals all live in the same world and share much in common, but the homosexual world has distinctive qualities which are not a part of the everyday heterosexual world. For example, consider the cross gendering of pronouns and the use of female names. While all homosexuals do not engage in such behavior, enough homosexuals do so—usually in fun—as to give many conversations among homosexuals a cross-gendered twist which heterosexual conversations do not have.[43]

They also found that lesbians had similar cross-gendering words and names.[44]

Most of the societies they studied were considerably more tolerant of such cross-gendered behavior than had usually been the case in the United States. They reported that in Latin America, attitudes toward cross-dressing homosexuals were similar to the attitudes toward prostitutes, that is, they were part of ordinary social reality.[45] Similarly, in the Philippines parents openly acknowledge that one's child may be *bayot*, or a cross-dressing homosexual.[46]

In Myanmar (formerly Burma), male cross-gender behavior is interpreted in light of the animistic beliefs still engrained in Burmese Buddhism. Such males are referred to as *acault* and are revered as sacred beings with special ceremonial roles as shamans and seers. Their special powers are believed to have been derived from a spiritual marriage to one of the thirty-seven female *nats* ("spirit gods") named Manguedons. A Manguedon has the powers to demonize any male at any time, but she is more likely to begin this process at an early age; once invaded by her spirit, the boy or man has little choice but to accept his status as acault. There are both negative and positive consequences. Since the Therevada Buddhism of the Burmese emphasizes that only a man can reach nirvana, or freedom from suffering, an acault cannot reach nirvana in the next life. Some also believe that having a son become an acault is evidence of having led a disreputable life in a previous incarnation and therefore reflects upon them. Such families try to encourage their sons to become more manly, but most Burmese regard these efforts as fruitless endeavors, for there are positive aspects to acaults that counteract the negative aspects. A Manguedon is the spirit of success and good fortune, and for this the acault can act as intercessor. This gives acaults an important place in society, and they are often consulted by individuals of all classes in order to ensure good fortune.

Some acaults live the female role and express the wish to have the physical body of a woman. Since, however, a Manguedon is jealous if acaults have sexual activity with women (because this constitutes a betrayal), they often engage in homosexual activity. This is supposedly encouraged by the Manguedon since they then represent her, symbolizing her own desire to be sexual with men. The men who have sexual encounters with an acault, however, are not regarded as homosexual because of the spiritual connotation of the acault.[47]

Not all cross dressing in non-Western societies, or even historically, is associated with homosexuality, although in many societies heterosexual and homosexual cross dressers are lumped together. The matter is made even more complex because many societies have long held that every person was a combination of both male and female elements. Chinese-influenced cultures symbolized this by yin and yang. The sexual union of a man and woman in traditional Chinese belief mirrored on the microcosmic level the macrocosmic interaction of heaven and earth. The *I Ching,* the oldest Chinese classic, held that there was an intercommunication of seeds between male and female.[48] Though male and female are dominated by different essences, within the human body there is both yin and yang; the yin essence is more important in women, the yang in men. Life is dependent upon a balance of these elements.

C. G. Jung in his studies of myths held similar views. He hypothesized a shadow self, an "inner figure," within each of us. For a man, this represents the female personification of his unconscious; for a woman, a male one. Jung called the male and female forms animus and anima, respectively. The anima, he held, was a personification of all feminine psychological tendencies in a man's psyche, which he described in typical gender stereotypes as including vague feelings and moods, prophetic hunches, receptiveness to the irrational, capacity for personal love, feeling for nature, and a relationship with the unconscious. The animus within a woman represented a sacred conviction that often expressed itself in loud, insistent attempts to impose one's views on others. The animus, he said, never believed in exceptions.[49]

Though the ancient preservers of myths did not put things the way Jung did, there was a widespread belief in the individual's potential to intermix gender, which was often emphasized in the initiation rites and coming-of-age ceremonies. The uninitiated boy is considered to be a child, similar to a young girl, but once initiated, he becomes accepted into the clan as a man. Sometimes this is done by emphasizing the bisexuality of the person, for example, as among the indigenous Australian tribes. They make a subincision on the penis, a procedure that some commentators believe gives the new initiate a "female sex organ so that he will resemble the divinities" who are always bisexual. Not all accept this view, but as Mircea Eliade commented, there is a widespread belief in a variety of tribal religions of the existence of a divine totality that implies the coexistence of all the divine attributes, and the coalescence of sexes.[50]

Invariably, this belief is expressed at initiation ceremonies through various cross-dressing ceremonies. For example, among the Masai, Nandi, Nuba, and other African tribes, boy initiates are dressed as girls; similarly, the boy novices to be initiated into the Arioi society in Tahiti are dressed as women. Among the South African Sotho, girls who are being initiated wear men's clothing. Ritual transformation of men into women is practiced in New Guinea and in the Torres Strait.[51] Cross dressing, symbolizing androgyny, is often also thought to be a sign of spirituality. Yahutian shamans in Siberia wore women's clothes in everyday life. Similarly, shamans among the Chuckee in Siberia threw away their rifle, lance, lasso, and harpoon and accepted a woman's needle and skin scraper.[52] In Chile, Araucanian sorcerers were required to dress as women.[53] In Southeast Asia among the Dyaks, priests dressed as females and were treated as women although it was known they were males. In other places as well, cross dressing became an acceptable way of life because it is believed to have been ordered by the gods.[54]

Sometimes a change of clothing takes place either to fool the gods or to change one's luck. One way in which Egyptian peasants of today protect their young boys from the evil eye is to dress them as girls. Since the evil eye is especially interested in pretty boys (not girls), this disguise protects them, particularly if they also do not wash or keep themselves clean.[55] At a different stage in life, a man of the Bangalan tribe in the upper Congo who found himself troubled by an evil spirit secretly left his house and donned women's clothes in order to deceive the spirit.[56] In other areas of Africa, men attempted to fool the devil (or the evil eye) by disguising themselves as women, since they believed evil forces did not regard women as being as important as men.[57] Zulu men dressed in female girdles when drought threatened their land, in the belief that a change in their outward appearance might bring about a change in nature and bring about rain. Toward the same goal, girls and unmarried women dressed themselves in their brother's clothes and herded cattle for a day.[58] In Java, certain tribal groups changed the dress of a child when it fell ill on the assumption that this act would remove the disease. Similarly, when men prayed with urgency for a particular goal, they wore women's clothes in the hope that the gods would grant their wishes more quickly.[59] Among the Gond of Central India, men are required to put on women's jackets as part of the ceremony associated with entering into a prophetic trance. In the same society women dress as men before a hunt is undertaken.[60]

Summary

The point of all these references (and many more could be given) is to emphasize that cross dressing has been ubiquitous. It is an important element in many religions and serves to emphasize that male and female are somehow incomplete standing alone, and that there is some element of both sexes in everyone. Male coming-of-age ceremonies are often marked by a recognition of leaving feminine things and ideas behind. It seems, however, much easier for men to understand a goddess changing into a god than vice versa, since the latter might challenge traditional male prerogatives. At the same time, it is much more likely for men to have a religious justification for taking on the role of women than vice versa. Women, however, sought to cross dress for other reasons, a theme which will be developed later in this book.

Notes

1. For a brief illustrated overview see Elémire Zolla, *The Androgyne: Reconciliation of Male and Female* (London: Thames and Hudson, 1981). The concept of a third sex was popularized in English by Edward Carpenter, *The Intermediate Sex: A Study of Some Transitional Types of Men and Women* (London: Sonnenschein, 1908), and *Intermediate Types Among Primitive Folk* (London: George Allen and Unwin, 1918).

2. The word is derived from a Persian term, *bardag,* that spread to Europe in the sixteenth century (Spanish *bardaxa* or *bardaje,* French *berdache*). It meant a boy or young man who was kept by a man as his male courtesan. When such individuals were encountered among American Indians, a French explorer called them "berdaches." While the emphasis of the European observers was clearly on the homosexual aspects, American Indian cultures focused on the gender role of the androgynous male. See Walter Williams, *The Spirit and the Flesh: Sexual Diversity in American Indian Culture* (Boston: Beacon Press, 1986). For a bibliography on the topic, see Will Roscoe, "Bibliography of Berdache and Alternative Gender Roles Among American Indians," *Journal of Homosexuality* 14 (3/4, 1987): 81ff.

3. For a study of the myths of Amazons, see William Blake Tyrrell, *Amazons: A Study in Athenian Myth Making* (Baltimore: Johns Hopkins Press, 1984). Williams, *The Spirit and the Flesh,* used the term *Amazons* in his work to refer to women who assumed masculine roles or attire.

4. See M. K. Martin and B. Voorhies, *Female of the Species* (New York: Columbia University Press, 1975), 101, which argues for a supernumerary sex. Walter Williams in *The Spirit and the Flesh* (p. 268), stated they represented a blending together. Still others have held them to be neither man nor woman. See, for example, Serena Nanda, "The Hijras of India: Cultural and Individual Dimensions of an Institutionalized Third Gender Role," *Journal of Homosex-*

uality 11 (1985): 35–55; see also Serena Nanda, *Neither Man Nor Woman: The Hijras of India* (Belmont, CA: Wadsworth Publishing Co., 1990); P. Fry, "Male Homosexuality and Spirit Possession in Brazil," *Journal of Homosexuality* 11 (1985): 137–54; R. Parker, "A Report from Rio," *Anthropological Research Group on Homosexuality Newsletter* 5 (1–2, 1984): 12–21; and cited in D. L. Davis and R. G. Whitten, "The Cross Cultural Study of Human Sexuality," *Annual Review of Anthropology* 16 (1987): 69–98. For an early account, see Ferdinand Karsch-Haack, *Das Gleichgeschlectliche Leben der Naturvölker* (Munich: Ernst Reinhardt, 1911), which was reprinted by Arno Press (New York) in 1975.

5. Evelyn Blackwood, "The Cross Cultural Dimensions of Lesbian Relations," unpublished M.A. thesis, Stanford University, 1984, 78.

6. A good example is the case of We'wha, a Zuni berdache, who was introduced to Washington, DC, society in 1886. See Will Roscoe, *The Zuni Man-Woman* (Albuquerque: University of New Mexico Press, 1990).

7. Anne Bolin, "The Transition from Physical Sex to Gender: A Cultural Process," unpublished papers, AAAS, New Orleans, 18 February 1990.

8. Martin and Voorhies, *Female of the Species*, 103.

9. Oscar Lewis, "Manly-hearted women among the North Piegan," *American Anthropologist* 43 (1941): 173–87.

10. Gregory Bateson, *Naven*, 2d ed. (Palo Alto, CA: Stanford University Press, 1958), 200.

11. Margaret Mead, *Sex and Temperament in Three Primitive Societies* (New York: William Morrow, 1935), 294–96.

12. Alfred Kroeber, "Psychosis or Social Sanction," *Character and Personality* 8 (1940): 204–15.

13. Anne Bolin, "Transsexualism and the Limits of Traditional Analysis," *American Behavioral Scientist* 31 (1987): 41–65.

14. See, for example, Gilbert Herdt, "Representations of Homosexuality: An Essay on Cultural Ontology and Historical Comparison, Part 1," *Journal of the History of Sexuality* 1 (3, 1991): 481–504. His examination of homosexuality has many similarities to the findings reported in this chapter about cross dressing. Among the examples he cites are George Devereux, "Institutionalized Homosexuality Among the Mohave Indians," *Human Biology* 9 (1937): 498–527, whose interpretation was heavily influenced by psychoanalytic thinking. Clifford Gertz, *The Interpretation of Cultures* (New York: 1973), explained some of the differences in terms of insider/outsider accounts and structuralist versus subjective interpretative frameworks.

15. John Money and A. A. Ehrhardt, *Man and Woman, Boy and Girl* (Baltimore: Johns Hopkins University Press, 1972); John Money and P. Tucker, *Sexual Signatures* (Boston: Little, Brown, and Company, 1975); Robert Stoller, *Presentations of Gender* (New Haven: Yale University Press, 1925).

16. James D. Weinrich, "Is Homosexuality Biologically Natural?" in W. Paul, J. D. Weinrich, J. C. Gonsiorek, and M. E. Hotvedt eds., *Homosexuality: Social, Psychological, and Biological Issues* (Beverly Hills, CA: Sage Publications, 1982), 183–95; Weinrich, "A New Sociological Theory of Homosexuality Applicable to Societies with Universal Marriage," *Ethology and Sociobiology* 8 (1987): 34–47; Weinrich, *Sexual Landscapes: Why We Are What We Are, Why We Love Whom We Love* (New York: Charles Scribner's Sons, 1987); Michael Ruse, "Are There Gay Genes? Sociobiology and Homosexuality" *Journal of Homosexuality,* 6 (4, 1981): 5–34.

17. John Money, *Love and Love Sickness: The Science of Sex, Gender, and Pair Bonding* (Baltimore: Johns Hopkins University Press, 1980).

18. David Gerlman and Mary Hager, "Body and Soul," *Newsweek*, 7 November 1988.

19. The terms *hermaphrodite* and *pseudohermaphrodite* are used here to describe a large category of individuals, including those with both testicular and ovarian tissues and individuals born with gonads matching their chromosomal sex but a genital appearance resembling the opposite sex. Part of the difficulty is that until recently distinctions about the variations in hermaphroditism were not made.

20. R. B. Edgerton, "Pokot Intersexuality: An East African Example of the Resolution of Sexual Incongruity," *American Anthropologist* 66 (1964): 1288–89.

21. W. W. Hill, "The Status of the Hermaphrodite and Transvestite in Navajo Culture," *American Anthropologist* 37 (1935): 273–79.

22. Nanda, "The Hijras of India," 149, and Nanda, *Neither Man Nor Woman*, 11–12, passim.

23. Wendy Doniger O'Flaherty, *Women, Androgynes and Other Mythical Beasts* (Chicago: University of Chicago Press, 1980), 306; P. Thomas, "Kāma Kalpa or the Hindu Ritual of Love" (Bombay: D. B. Taraporevala Sons and Co., 1959), 113–14.

24. Benjamin Walker, *The Hindu World* (New York: Praeger, 1968), 2:343.

25. O'Flaherty, *Women, Androgynes*, 298.

26. Pratap Chandar Chunder, *Kauṭilya on Love and Morals* (Calcutta: Janyanti, 1970), 190.

27. Vern L. Bullough, *Sexual Variance in Society and History* (Chicago: University of Chicago Press, 1976), 254–55.

28. R. B. Bhandarkar, *Vaiṣṇavism, Śaivism and Minor Religious Systems* (Varanasi, India: Indological Book House, 1965), 86–87.

29. Nanda, "The Hijras of India," 38.

30. Nanda, *Neither Man Nor Woman*, 11.

31. Ibid., 146–47; Walker, *Hindu World*, 1:44.

32. Walker, *Hindu World*, 1:214–16.

33. Ibid., 2:282–84.

34. Unni Wikan, "Man Becomes Woman: Transsexualism in Oman as a Key to Gender Roles," *Man*, n.s., 12 (1977): 304–19.

35. Abu ab Allah Muhammad ibn al-Būkhari, *Sahih*, translated from the Arabic by Muhammad Assad (Lahore, Pakistan: Awafat Publications, 1938), 7:159. According to Sunni Muslims, *Sahih* ranks second only to the Koran as a source of Muslim law and tradition.

36. W. E. Lane, *Manners and Customs of the Modern Egyptians* (reprinted, London: Everyman's Library, [1860] 1962), 388–89.

37. See Richard Burton's edition of the *Book of the Thousand Nights and a Night*, 6 vols. in 3, translated and annotated by Richard F. Burton ([1885] reprinted, New York: Heritage Press, 1934). This quotation is found in the terminal essay entitled "Pederasty," 3748–82. (The quote is on p. 3769.) It is available only in some of the editions of Burton's translation but has often been reprinted. It also can be found in *Homosexuality: A Cross Cultural Approach*, ed. Donald Webster Cory (New York: Julian Press, 1956).

38. Philip J. Baldensperger, "Orders of Holy Men in Palestine," *Palestine Exploration Fund Quarterly Statement* (1894), 38. See also Frederick J. Bliss, *The Religions of Modern Syria and Palestine* (New York: C. Scribner's Sons, 1912), 254,

and Raphael Patai, *Sex and Family in the Bible* (Garden City, NY: Doubleday, 1959), 173.

39. Reynold Alleyne Nicholson, *Studies in Islamic Mysticism* (Cambridge: University Press, 1921), 217. The translation is by Nicholson.

40. Robert Levy, *Tahitians: Mind and Experience in the Society Islands* (Chicago: University of Chicago Press, 1973), 140. See also Robert Levy, "The Community Function of Tahitian Male Transvestism," *Anthropological Quarterly* 44 (1971): 12–21.

41. Levy, *Tahitians*, 130–31.

42. Magnus Hirschfeld, *Transvestites: The Erotic Drive to Cross Dress*, translated by Michael Lombardi-Nash (Buffalo, NY: Prometheus Books, 1991), 257.

43. Frederick L. Whitam and Robin M. Mathy, *Male Homosexuality in Four Societies: Brazil, Guatemala, the Philippines, and the United States* (New York: Praeger, 1985), 82.

44. Frederick L. Whitam and Robin M. Mathy, "Childhood Cross-Gender Behavior of Homosexual Females in Brazil, Peru, the Philippines, and the United States," *Archives of Sexual Behavior* 20 (1991): 151–70.

45. Whitam and Mathy, *Male Homosexuality in Four Societies*, 73.

46. Ibid., 77. See also Frederick L. Whitam, "A Cross Cultural Perspective on Homosexuality, Transvestism and Transsexualism," in *Variant Sexuality*, ed. Glen D. Wilson (London: Croom Helm, 1987), 176–200.

47. See the unpublished paper by Eli Coleman, Philip Colgan, and Louis Gooren, "Male Cross-Gender Behavior in Burma (Myanmar)," Society for the Scientific Study of Sex, Toronto, Canada, November 1990. See also J. Stevenson, "The Southeast Asian Interpretation of Gender Dysphoria: An Illustrative Case Report," *The Journal of Nervous and Mental Disease* 165 (1977): 201–8; Stevenson, "Twelve Cases in Thailand and Burma," in *Cases of Reincarnation Type*, 4 vols. (Charlottesville: University Press of Virginia, 1983). See also M. MacIntyr, "The Spirit of Asia: Film Documentary," British Broadcasting Corporation, 1980.

48. There are numerous translations of the *I Ching*. See James Legge in *Sacred Books of the East*, ed. F. Max Müller, 2d ed. (Oxford: Clarendon Press, 1899), vol. 16, sec. II, chap. 5, par. 43, p. 393, for the citation; a more modern edition is by Cary F. Baynes, which is based on a German translation by Richard Wilhelm in the Bollingen series (Princeton, NJ: Princeton University Press, 1967), sec. II, chap. 5 and 13, pp. 342–43.

49. See Carl G. Jung, ed., *Man and His Symbols* (New York: Doubleday, 1964), 31; Chapter 3 by M. L. von Franz, "The Process of Individuation," 158–229, deals with this in more detail.

50. Mircea Eliade, *Rites and Symbols of Initiation: The Mysteries of Birth and Re-Birth*, trans. Willard R. Trask (New York: Harper Torchbooks, 1965), 25.

51. Ibid., 26.

52. M. Czaplicka, *Aboriginal Siberia* (Oxford: Clarendon Press, 1914), 199.

53. Iwan Block, *Anthropological Studies on the Strange Sexual Practices of All Races and Ages* (New York: Anthropological Press, 1933), 121.

54. Mircea Eliade, *Shamanism* (Princeton, NJ: Princeton University Press, 1964), 158.

55. For the implications of this on Egyptian health care, see Bonnie Bullough, "Malnutrition Among Egyptian Infants," *Nursing Research* 18 (Spring 1969): 172–73.

56. J. H. Weeks, "Anthropological Notes on the Bangala of the Upper

Congo," *Journal of the Royal Anthropological Institute of Great Britain and Ireland* 40 (1901): 370–71.

57. R. Brasch, *How Did Sex Begin?* (New York: David McKay, 1973), 48.

58. E. Crawley, *The Mystic Rose: A Study of Primitive Marriage* (London: Macmillan, 1902), 269.

59. J. Modi, "A Note on the Custom of the Interchange of Dress Between Males and Females," *Man in India* 5 (1925): 115–17.

60. Verrier Elwin, *The Muria and Their Ghotul* (Bombay: Geoffrey Cumberledge, 1947), 441, 445, 461.

Chapter 2
Mythology and History in the Ancient World

One of the earliest references to male cross dressers in the ancient world occurs in a moralistic tale about Sardanapalus (Ashurbanipal), the last of the Assyrian kings. The story is told by Ctesias, a fifth century B.C.E. Greek writer who was for a time a physician in the court of the Persian king, where he copied the royal archive records that he used as a basis for his history. Though the story is now seen as mythical, it was widely believed in the ancient world and accepted as fact until the nineteenth century, when modern studies of Assyria began.

In the story, Sardanapalus was described as spending much of his time in his palace dressed in women's clothing and surrounded by his concubines. When his secret life became known to some of his key nobles, they used his cross dressing to justify a revolt against him. Sardanapalus, forced to abandon his feminine finery, mounted a campaign against the rebelling nobles. Though he twice defeated them in battle, the war continued until only his capital city of Nineveh remained under his control. After a two-year siege, realizing his cause was hopeless, he collected his treasury, wives, and concubines into a room and then set fire to the remains of his palace, killing himself and his companions.[1] The message of the story quite clearly is a mixed one: cross dressing is a sign of feminine weakness and justified a revolt, but beneath all the finery there was strong male potential, since Sardanapalus mounted a strong counterattack.

If a man's cross dressing as a woman was a sign of weakness, would a woman cross dressing as a man be regarded as having greater "strength" than other women? This issue is raised by the case of Hatshepsut, an Egyptian ruler of the eighteenth dynasty (fifteenth century B.C.E.). Hatshepsut, the daughter of Thutmose I and his Great Wife, was married to her half-brother Thutmose II, perhaps to legitimate his rule since he was the son of a lesser wife. When he died shortly after the marriage, she was married to another half-brother who took the name Thutmose III. Apparently, neither Thutmose II nor Thutmose III were of an age to rule effectively or else they lacked the ability to do so, since Hatshepsut acted as the real ruler and she did so with the support of the temple community of Amun. To maintain their support, she built magnificent monuments in honor of the god Amun, notably one at Deir el Bahari (near Luxor), where the queen's reign was commemorated. In her statues and pictures she is usually portrayed as a man with a symbolic royal beard.

After her death Thutmose III tried to obliterate her memory, and later the Amun-hating Amenhotep IV (Ahknaton) tried to complete the task by removing all references to the god. These reactions, however, were apparently not due to the fact that she was a woman but for dynastic and religious reasons. The case of Hatshepsut emphasizes a theme that appears throughout this book: namely, that women cross dressed and impersonated men to gain what they could only achieve if they acted like men, while male cross dressers, as personified by the legends surrounding Sardanapalus, were portrayed as doing so for "erotic" or other reasons. Though men also cross dressed to disguise themselves in order to infiltrate enemy lines or achieve other short-term goals, repeated incidents of cross dressing seem to have stronger sexual connotations in men than in women. Some have argued that Hatshepsut's cross dressing involved more than adopting the necessary symbolism to rule and expressed her desire to change her sex, since some surviving representations of her portray her with a penis. Still, the fact that the pronouns accompanying the text are feminine make it clear she was a woman, and it seems to imply that the male clothing and appearance was a prerequisite to rule.[2] The implicit lesson in the two stories is that for those who told them men lost status by cross dressing, at least if they did so in any serious way, while women who cross dressed overcame many of the barriers that handicapped them.

The Greeks wrestled with this problem of status when they described cross-dressing customs of other peoples they encountered, most notably the Scythians. Herodotus, the Greek historian of the fifth century B.C.E., reported that among the Scythians were individuals known as *Enarëes,* who had the gift of foretelling the future but who also dressed as if they were women.[3] He explained that these cross dressers were descendants of men who had been cursed with the "feminine disease" by the goddess Aphrodite for pillaging her temple at Ascalon in Palestine.[4] A more skeptical writer in the Hippocratic corpus (those writings attributed to Hippocrates) rejected this supernatural explanation for a more "natural" one, claiming that cross dressing was brought on by a temporary impotency caused by spending so much of their time on horseback. He added that the Scythians, rather than looking for a natural explanation, believed that their impotency came about because they had somehow sinned against the gods. In order to expiate the sin, which Herodotus had attributed to Aphrodite, they put on women's clothing and devoted themselves to feminine occupations. He added that the illness usually attacked only the most powerful and richest men, who after they took up cross dressing became powerful shamans.[5] Aristotle offered still another explanation, holding that the "disease" involved in cross dressing was hereditary. He agreed, however, that the Enarëes were both respected and feared.[6]

Since there is a long tradition of cross-dressing shamans in many cultures, it might well be that the Greeks were just trying to find some sort of justification for a custom that seemed foreign to them. One way of coping with individuals who do not conform to traditional gender roles is to attribute special powers, either negative or positive, to them. Negative power is associated with violation of taboos or defined as being polluting, as witchcraft or as sin, and the individuals involved are often seen as a threat to society. This concept became secularized in the nineteenth century as perversion. Another way of dealing with such individuals, however, is to remove them from the realm of threat and to sanctify them. This seems to have been the case with the Scythians.[7]

Cross Dressing as Ritual

Though the Greeks (and for that matter the Romans) did not have cross-dressing shamans, cross dressing often was a part of the ceremonies that symbolized life's transitions. In Greek and Roman cults, as well as other religious groups, the

symbolism of initiation corresponds to the sense of an essential opposition between the male essence, personified in the community of young men, and the female element. So it is not uncommon for novices, at the beginning of the initiation rites, to put on clothing resembling that worn by women, and for the culmination of the ceremonies to be the donning of the masculine garb.[8]

Or similarly:

The practice of disguise and of exchange of clothing from one sex to the other expresses a symbolism inspired by the same preoccupation. The feminine principle in the candidate is affirmed in the initiation at the very moment when he is about to cast it aside.[9]

During special festivals when societal barriers are relaxed, cross dressing tends to equalize and temporarily destroy the inequality of gender and the rigid barriers established by many societies. Similar gender-blending occurs in our society during holidays such as Mardi Gras or Halloween.

Greek history and literature is full of illustrations of both types of cross dressing. In Sparta, for example, it was the custom to shave the head of the young bride and then dress her in male attire. Dressed as a boy she was then sent to lay on the marriage bed alone until her husband came secretly to her.[10] She was not allowed to fully resume her place among the women until she had become pregnant, thus acquiring the true sign of womanhood. At Argos, the bride wore a false beard on the wedding night,[11] while in Cos the husband put on the dress of a woman to receive his new bride.[12] The meaning of these cross-dressing ceremonies was probably not quite clear to the people at the time but represented survivals from times long past that were kept alive by myths.[13]

An example in Phaestos of such a mythical justification is the story of Leucippus. The story has two versions, one of them indicating a change of sex. In the transsexual version, Lampros, a citizen of Phaestos, told his pregnant wife Galatea that he would not rear a child unless it was a boy. A girl was born, but Galatea, unwilling to expose her, dressed the baby as a boy and gave it the masculine name Leucippus. When the child's sex could no longer be easily concealed, Galatea appealed to the goddess Leto (in Latin, Latona) to change its sex, and the goddess complied. This event was commemorated by a feast called *ekdysia,* the divestment (a term later adopted to describe a striptease artist). It also became the custom for a bride in Lampros to sleep beside an image of Leucippe (the feminine form of Leucippus) before her nuptials took place.[14] In the other version of the story, which had nothing to do with the festival, Leucippus, who was born a male, fell in love with the fair Daphne, who hated men and had dedicated herself to chastity. To ingratiate himself with her, Leucippus disguised himself as a girl. Ultimately, his disguise was discovered and he was killed.[15] Perhaps this version of the myth was later preferred to emphasize to the ardent male lover the dangers of cross dressing for deception.

Often the Greek (or Latin) reporters, puzzled by why cross-dressing customs existed, attempted to come up with "rational" answers, although how valid these are is debatable. Plutarch, for example, reported that the Lycians wore women's clothing while in mourning, and he claimed that this was to remind themselves to cut short the kind of lamentations in which women alone should indulge.[16] The temporary assumption of the opposite gender by men was clearly acceptable to society if the aim was laudable or if the alternatives to the impersonation were considered more socially undesirable than the disguise itself.

For example, Hymenaeus, a youth from Argive, disguised himself as a girl in order to follow the young Athenian maid he loved; while he was disguised, both he and his beloved were captured by pirates. Fortunately, he was able to assert his "superior" masculine strength and save her.[17]

Disguise was also permissible if it led to the capture or defeat of an enemy. Solon is said to have defeated the Megarians by disguising part of his troops as women and infiltrating the enemy forces.[18] Cross dressing was justified when men had to perform activities usually done by women because of religious or other reasons. For example, men played female roles on the Greek stage because the alternative, to have women exhibit themselves in public, was something "decency" would not permit. This kind of female impersonation has been a tradition in many cultures.

Such "officially" tolerated impersonation was given "scientific" sanction by the belief that women were not meant to expose themselves by performing in public. Proof of this was the "fact" that their sex organs were hidden and mysterious. On the other hand, the male reproductive organs, particularly the "noble" penis, was easily visible. Such a belief certainly was translated into social policy when it was argued that women were designed for inner activity, keeping the home, raising the children, and doing other things that did not expose them to public gaze. Men, for their part, were designed to perform outside chores and appear publicly.[19] Cross dressing on the stage within such a belief system was justified as being protective of women.

Men, however, did cross dress at various festivals probably for very similar reasons to those associated with initiation, a sort of unconscious reminder of the existence of a feminine element within themselves, although the observers of such customs tried to offer more rational explanations. For example, each year in Sparta men dressed as women marched in a procession to Mount Taygetos. Herodotus explained that the custom derived from a historical incident when the Spartans had seized and imprisoned the adult males of the Minyae, a neighboring people. While their husbands were awaiting execution at sundown, the women of Minyae were allowed to visit them, and while doing so they exchanged clothes with their husbands, who then walked away as mourning and bereaved women, leaving their wives behind in prison. When the Spartans discovered what had happened, they allowed the women to leave as a reward for their bravery and ingenuity.[20] Modern scholars have argued that this romantic story was nothing more than a pseudohistorical explanation for an archaic initiation ceremony involving cross dressing that had lost its meaning and thus forced the Spartans to invent another story.[21] It is also possible that clothing was exchanged in various religious ceremonies to deceive malignant powers, such as the evil eye, whose hostility was to be particularly feared at such critical times.[22]

Cross dressing figured most prominently in the various festivals associated with the god Dionysus. According to legend Dionysus had been reared as a girl by King Athamas (of Orchomenus) and his queen, Ino.[23] He also impersonated a girl at various stages of his career.[24] The association of cross dressing and Dionysian festivals appears at a fairly early date since a number of sixth-century lyrical poems assume the existence of cross dressing as a matter of routine.[25] Several vases depicting scenes from the Dionysian festival of *Lenaia* in Athens show men dressed as women and women dressed as men.[26] In some of the vase depictions, women also wear a beard or are portrayed with a phallus.[27] The Athenian festival of *Oskhophoria,* a public procession marched from the sanctuary of Dionysus in Athens to the shrine of Athena Skiras in Phaleron, was led by two young men of noble birth and wealthy families who were dressed as women.[28] In the fourth-century B.C.E. Egypt, men arrayed themselves as women in the Dionysian procession, and this cross dressing continued down to the first century.[29]

Unfortunately, we have no documentation of the key rituals of this early Greek religion except for depictions recorded on vase paintings, although Euripides' play *The Bacchae* deals with it in part. In this play, Dionysus makes his first appearance in Greece in the city of Thebes disguised as an effeminate young man with long hair. Rejected by the city's ruling clan and the young King Pentheus, he inspired the women of Thebes to abandon their housework and worship him with wild rites in the mountains at night. Men were not excluded from the rites but were only permitted if they wore the fawnskin hides that were viewed as a form of women's clothing. A stranger tells Pentheus, the young king who fears the rites might be a prelude to the destruction of his reign, where the rituals are taking place, and, with Pentheus disguised as a woman, the two set out to witness the revels. While there, Pentheus is unmasked and torn apart by the women who, in the madness or ecstasy of the rites, think he is a lion. Critics are uncertain whether the playwright is denouncing the religion of Dionysus or all religion as barbaric and irrational. Was he branding opposition to an established cult as sacrilegious, or was he promoting a toned-down version of a wild rite for the satisfaction of those people who needed emotional release?[30]

One of the more interesting modern interpretations of the Euripides play is that of Arthur Evans, whose translation of the *The Bacchae* was performed at the Valencia Rose Cabaret in San Francisco in 1984. In this version Pentheus is portrayed as an insecure new king of Thebes who had a constant need to prove his ability and his masculinity both to himself and others. He has an arrogant attitude toward women and contempt for femininity in men. In the Valencia Rose production this attitude was conveyed by a portrayal of Pentheus as a young, bullying, up-and-coming executive who wears a natty three-piece business suit and is fearful both of cross dressing and of showing a more feminine side to himself. Euripides may not have accepted this interpretation, but it does make the play more contemporary for Americans. It certainly emphasizes the gender-crossing that seems to be an important part of ancient religion.[31]

Other gods and goddesses also were worshipped by cross-dressing believers. At the feast devoted to Hera at Samos, men donned long white robes that swept the ground, encased their hair in golden nets, and adorned themselves with feminine bracelets and necklaces.[32] In Argos, during the festival commemorating the heroism of the fifth-century B.C.E. poet Telesilla, who had put herself at the head of an army of women to defend the city from the Spartans, women dressed as men and vice versa.[33] Like many other cross-dressing ceremonies, this was probably a pseudohistorical explanation for a long-standing custom invented after the real meaning and justification for cross dressing was lost.

In Amathus, on the island of Cyprus, where a male-female divinity was worshipped, a young boy pretended to lie in childbed imitating the pains of labor as part of the annual ceremonies to the god Aphroditos. Aphroditos was portrayed as having a female shape and clothing like Aphrodite's but also a beard and penis, and hence, a male name. At sacrifices to the god men wore female clothing and women wore male attire.[34] This seems to have been a Greek masculinization of Ishtar, the Sumerian-Akkadian goddess who was the most celebrated deity in the Middle East and who became identified with Aphrodite. Men also often worshipped Ishtar while dressed in women's clothing.

The ubiquity of such festivals (and there are others) might well indicate that the Greeks, who drew strict lines between sex roles and assigned a restricted role to women, needed periods during which the barriers were removed. Some of the ancients themselves seemed to imply such a need. Philostratus, for example, in describing the rituals involved in these festivals, said that the image or the impersonator of the god was accompanied by a large train of followers in which girls mingled with men because the festivals allowed "women to act the part of men, and men to put on woman's clothing and play the woman."[35] The widespread acceptance of cross dressing at such festivals is indicated by a chance remark of the second century (M.E.) writer, Artemidorus, in his *Interpretation of Dreams*. He stated that even though the best omen in a dream was for a person to see himself dressed in his usual clothes, it was not harmful for a man to be seen in a varicolored garment or a woman's garment, provided the dream seemed to take place during a festival.[36] Another indicator of the public acceptability of cross dressing on these occasions is the survival of at least fifteen vases depicting bearded figures in women's clothing, all seemingly bent on pleasure. Some of the individuals appear to be men in women's clothes, while others are women wearing false beards.[37]

Mythological Foundations

Giving further justification for cross dressing at festivals was the existence of cross-dressing episodes in the careers of several legendary heroes. Achilles was believed by the later Greeks to have lived part of his life as a girl. In this legend, Achilles' mother, Thetis, aware of a prophesy that he would be killed in the Trojan War, sent him to Lycomedus in Scyros, where, disguised as a girl, he went into hiding. The Greeks, anxious to have Achilles fight for them, sent out various individuals to track him down. Odysseus finally tracked him to Scyros but was unable to distinguish him from the other girls until he hit on a stratagem for exposing him. Disguised as a merchant, Odysseus was allowed entrance to the women's quarters, where he placed a pile of gifts including jewels, girdles, embroidered dresses, a shield, and a sword for the girls to examine. When one of them took the shield and the sword, Odysseus knew he had found his man.[38]

Heracles (Hercules, in Latin) is another mythical hero who donned feminine garb, in this case, as a sign of humiliation and degradation. Dressing himself in the clothing of Queen Omphale, he was clearly a burlesque character since her girdle was much too small for his waist, his shoulders split the sleeves of her gown, and the ties of her sandals were too short to cross his instep. When the god Pan tried to seduce him, Heracles kicked him across the room. Thereafter, Pan was so suspicious of clothing that he would have nothing to do with clothes and went nude.[39] As with Achilles, there are variant versions of Heracles as a cross dresser, some picturing him surrounded by girls, spinning wool, and being scolded when his fingers crushed the spindle.

Theseus also, according to tradition, passed some time as a woman when he first arrived in Athens. In fact, even as a man he appeared so effeminate that when he passed the temple of Apollo, a group of workers mistook him for a girl and demanded to know why he was allowed to go about unescorted. Theseus did not bother to reply but instead, after unyoking the oxen from a nearby cart, tossed one of the oxen in the air[40] and then went on his way.

Is there any significance in these stories beyond simple cross dressing or effeminacy? One authority has claimed that since Achilles, Heracles, and Theseus were the three men most successful in dealing with the Amazons, the point of the stories might be to emphasize that only a man who has experienced some of the things a woman experiences can deal with women warriors.[41] The legends can also be interpreted as implying that the Greeks, as well as the Romans who adopted many Greek legends, recognized that within each man there are some feminine elements, just as there are masculine ones within each woman; they thus chose to stress the dual nature of their strongest and greatest heroes. It was perhaps this same factor that encouraged the worship of the hermaphrodite Aphroditos on Cyprus mentioned above. Several other deities in ancient times seem to have also hesitated between the two sexes including Pales, Pomo-Pomona, and Tellumon-Tellurus-Tellus.[42] And it was to the legend of the Cyprian Aphrodite (Venus Castina, in Latin) that C. J. Bulliet dedicated his history of transvestism.[43]

The Greek legend of the Amazons, a society of women warriors who undermined traditional gender barriers, has long caught the Western imagination. Always pictured in classical sources as existing on the border of the known world, the Amazons, at one level, seem to be little more than the subject of the common traveler's tale of distant foreigners who do everything differently. Still, they figured strongly in the nineteenth- and early twentieth-century argument over the origins of matriarchy and patriarchy.[44]

The Amazon myths are symbolic of a weakness in the Greek patriarchy. Though many Greeks downgraded women's social importance by insisting that the male seed was the key to generation, the men still needed mothers if only as wet nurses. The Amazons had no such weakness: they produced daughters with only a casual dependence upon men, whom they met at certain seasons, coupled with, and then left behind, keeping their female children and getting rid of the boys. They shared in the strengths of both sexes and were stronger than either; still, perhaps in order to distinguish them from most women or otherwise lessen their femininity, the Greeks reported that the Amazons had their right breasts removed to prevent them from getting in the way of the bowstring during battle.[45] In order to defeat the Amazons in battle, the Greek heroes first had to overcome the Amazons' male side through combat and then subdue their female side by having intercourse with them, essentially by rape.[46] The Amazons figured strongly in Greek mythology and are often represented in Greek art; perhaps they serve as reminders that the women they relegated to the house and family had greater potential than they were allowed to express. In other words, the legends conveyed the message that the Greeks' gender constructs were highly artificial.

Greeks tended to fear powerful women. Indeed, many of the more powerful goddesses, particularly those who were believed to have originated elsewhere, were depicted in visual arts as having penises; in this way the patriarchal Greeks effectively transformed the potent goddesses into bisexual figures. This process of defeminizing and, accordingly, "masculinizing" the goddesses served to support the popular Greek belief that if women had their choice they would have been born men. The Amazons at best could only be imitation men, and the powerful goddesses became masculinized in order to emphasize this.

The Greeks were particularly intrigued by stories of women who changed their sex either for symbolic purposes or through godly intervention. One such story deals with Caenis, the daughter of the king of Lapithaei, who had the misfortune to come to the attention of the god Poseidon. Poseidon very much wanted to seduce Caenis and promised to fulfill any wish she might have if she granted his request. Caenis requested that she become a man, invulnerable to wounds.[47]

Procris, according to one version of the legend, had been rejected by her husband Cephalus, supposedly because she had been unfaithful to him by taking another lover, although she had known all along that her "secret" lover had been her husband in disguise. In disgrace, she fled to Crete where she met Diana, goddess of the hunt. Touched by Procris's misfortunes, Diana gave her a javelin that would always find its target and a dog from which no wild beast could escape. Disguised as a boy, Procris returned to the mainland, where she challenged and surpassed her husband in the hunt. Cephalus tried to purchase the dog and javelin from his vanquisher, even offering the disguised Procris a share of his kingdom, but Procris refused. Finally, after much pleading, Procris agreed to relinquish the javelin and dog if Cephalus would do to her that which "boys are wont to grant." Cephalus, eager to please, took the "young boy" to his bedchamber, whereupon Procris took off her tunic, revealing herself as his wife.[48]

Perhaps the most famous sex change in Greek mythology involves the soothsayer Tiresias, who was born a boy, changed into a woman, and then changed back into a man. According to a widespread version, after Tiresias witnessed two snakes copulating, the creatures attacked him. When he killed the female snake by hitting it with his staff, he was immediately turned into a woman, and later became a celebrated harlot. No male, godly or mortal, however, could permanently become a woman, and so Tiresias again became a man through the reverse process, this time killing a male snake coupling with a female one. Tiresias's experience in both female and male roles later served him well with the gods since he was able to see both sides of any gender issue. But this knowledge later led to difficulty when he became involved in a dispute between Zeus and Hera over the former's numerous infidelities. Although Zeus admitted his sexual promiscuity, he defended himself by saying that it did not matter, because women enjoyed sex much more than men. Hera denied this, and turned to Tiresias to settle the dispute with her husband. Tiresias replied:

> If the parts of love pleasure be counted as ten,
> Thrice three go to women, one only to men.

Hera was so exasperated by Tiresias's opinion that she blinded him. Zeus, unable to remove the spell of blindness, compensated Tiresias with inward sight and extended his life to seven generations.[49] Similar myths of women's greater enjoyment of sex are common in many other cultures and in fact, the Greeks regarded it as one of the few advantages of being a woman. The myth can also be interpreted as a male justification for keeping women subordinate, since it was only by such actions that their sexuality could be controlled. Cross dressing for men, in turn, could also be interpreted as a way to lessen this threat by asserting that they were not afraid of things feminine.

Gender and Power

In general, Greek society was very sex-segregated. Women were accepted for their biological function but were not recognized for their personalities or intelligence. Greek philosophic and scientific thought emphasized the subordination of women. Though Plato seemingly cast a slight dissenting vote early in his career,[50] even he ultimately turned against equality.[51] Biology, for him, was destiny:

The womb is an animal which longs to generate children. When it remains barren too long after puberty, it is distressed and sorely disturbed, and straying about in the body and cutting off the passages of the breath, it impedes respiration and brings the sufferer into extreme anguish and provokes all manner of diseases besides.[52]

One of the most moving descriptions of the gender restrictions put on women is Euripides' description of Medea, who is driven to the madness of killing her own children:

> We women are the most unfortunate creatures.
> Firstly, with an excess of wealth it is required
> For us to buy a husband and take for our bodies

A master, for not to take one is even worse.
And now the question is serious whether we take
A good or bad one, for there is no easy escape
For a woman, nor can she say no to her marriage.
She arrives among new modes of behavior and manners,
And needs prophetic power, unless she has learned at home
How best to manage him who shares the bed with her.
And if we work out this well and carefully,
And the husband lives with us and we lightly bear his yoke,
Then life is enviable. If not, I'd rather die.
A man, when he's tired of the company in his home,
Goes out of the house and puts an end to his boredom
And turns to a friend or companion of his own age.
But we are forced to keep our eyes on one alone.
What they say of us is that we have a peaceful time.
Living at home, while they do the fighting in war.
How wrong they are! I would very much stand
Three times in front of battle than bear one child.[53]

Medea was portrayed as a bitter woman, discontented with her lot, but while murdering one's children was not considered a viable escape from the problems Greek women of ancient times faced, good women (as distinct from prostitutes) were also taught to be neither seen nor heard. It was only in their roles as mothers that they were honored, and it was only at the sometimes exuberant festivals that they could escape their regimented role. I. M. Lewis has gone so far as to argue that in rigidly male-dominated societies such as the Greeks', one of the main strategies throughout which women could find escape was demonic possession.[54] Only then could they be freed from inhibitions. Demonic possession, however, was defined by male observers, and it could be argued that women who escaped from most aspects of male control, even temporarily, were likely to be seen by men as demons or witches.

   In the patriarchal Greek society there was strong male bonding, with the entire male citizen population acting as a men's club. Homosexuality was institutionalized in the form of intimate relationships between an adolescent male and an older man who was usually younger than the boy's father. But there was also strong peer-group bonding, so much so that Plato argued that the most formidable army in the world would be one composed of lovers, with each inspiring the other to deeds of heroism and sacrifice.[55] This ideal came close to being realized in the fourth century B.C.E., when an elite fighting corps known as the Sacred Band was formed by Gorgidas at Thebes. The band was composed of three hundred men grouped together as pairs of lovers.[56]

Despite the emphasis on masculine power and influence, the Greeks recognized that some men had greater feminine components than others, and even that some women had more masculine ones. One of the writers in the Hippocratic corpus offered an explanation as to how this could come about. In his view, male and female characteristics can fuse together because both are nourished in all persons and because the soul is the same in all living creatures, even though the bodies are different. Though the female principle is weaker and smaller, the mechanism is fluid, and various mixtures occur, depending on which sex gains mastery. This is more or less determined in utero, since each sex can secrete either male or female substances; thus there could be male-males, female-females, or a mixture of mannish women or womanly men. Or if the male matter is secreted by a woman and the female matter by a man, the result would be men-women or hermaphrodites.[57]

The institutionalization of homosexuality in the Greek world can be described as the males' strategy to free themselves from females and their fears of being feminine. Anthropologists and others have detailed various strategies by which males in various cultures attempt to arrogate to themselves the power and prestige of female procreation, about which the Greeks were so concerned. These strategies range from ceremonial mutilation to couvade (mimicking by men of pregnancy, labor, and giving birth) and homosexuality. The most elaborate of what might be called a homosexual form of procreation takes place in New Guinea and was described by Gilbert Herdt. Here young boys are initiated into manhood by fellatio with an older male.[58] What such customs seem to emphasize is that men are not born but made, and that without the appropriate rituals boys do not become men. Greek ritualized pederasty could in this sense be a carryover representation of the procreation of males by males, claiming a reproductive capacity analogous to that of women.[59]

Our analysis perhaps draws stricter gender lines than may have existed. Only hints of gender-crossing not associated with festivals or transitions appear in Greek literature. One such hint is in Aristophanes' *Thesmophoriazusae*, which features Agathon, a character who sometimes dresses in women's clothes. When questioned as to why, Agathon states:

I chose my dress to suit my poesy
A poet, sir, must needs adapt his ways
To the high thoughts which animate his soul.
And when he sings of women, he assumes
A woman's garb, and dons a woman's habit.[60]

Certainly, Aristophanes seems to believe that cross dressing is a way to adopt the gender attributes of the other sex. For example, he uses the cross-dressing theme in his comedy *Ecclesiazusae* as the means by which women wrest control of the state by appearing and voting in the same way as men.[61]

Further Cultural Influences

Many, if not all, of the cross-dressing ceremonies and festivals described above were widespread in the Mediterranean world, including the non–Greek-speaking parts. In fact, many of the sources cited are from Latin writers such as Ovid and thus emphasize the continuation of the tradition in Rome. The Romans, however, were quite different from the Greeks if only because eventually they militarily and politically dominated all the Mediterranean civilizations. This domination led to a rapid interchange of ideas and beliefs among the various peoples of the empire, some of which were officially sponsored by Rome, but others of which, including Judaism and Christianity, appeared without such sponsorship. Whatever traditions entered the empire, which was a tremendous mixture of peoples and ideas, were not untouched by Roman concepts, although some things remained less Roman than others. Much of the scientific literature of Greece, for example, remained untranslated into Latin, and the Greek-speaking areas of the empire essentially remained the home of the scientific centers in the Roman Empire. Women generally had more power and influence in Roman life than they did in Greek life, and homosexuality was not institutionalized to the extent that it was in the Greek educational system. The older forms of Roman religion lacked the cross dressing that characterized so much of the imported Greek cults, although this tradition did not prevent the Greek cults from spreading once the Romans encountered them.

One of the few references to cross dressing in Roman traditional religion is a reference to Vertumnus, the god of the changing year. According to legend, Vertumnus loved Pomona, the goddess of fruit trees, who refused to have anything to do with him. In an effort to become intimate with her, he experimented with various disguises, but it was only when he finally dressed as an old woman that he was successful.[62]

Romans, however, took seriously the possibility of a sex change and there was a widespread belief that women could change into men. Pliny, a popularizer of both scientific and pseudoscientific concepts, wrote in the first century C.E.:

Transformation of females into males is not an idle story. We find in the Annals that in the consulship of Publius Licinius Crassus and Gaius Cassius Longinus [171 B.C.E.], a girl at Casinum was changed into a boy under the observation of the parents, and the order of the augurs was conveyed to a desert island. Licinius Macianus has recorded that he personally saw at Agros a man named Arescon who had been given the name of Arescusa and had actually married a husband, and had then grown a beard and developed masculine attributes, and taken a wife, and that he had also seen a boy with the same record at Smyrna. I myself saw in Africa a person who had turned into a male on the day of marriage to a husband; this was Lucius Constitus, a citizen of Thysdritium.[63]

Though there are few records of hermaphrodites that have come down to us, such people must have aroused considerable interest when they came to official attention to have their names inscribed in the official records of Rome. Awareness of an androgynous potential is also demonstrated by the myth of Hermaphroditus, son of Hermes and Aphrodite, who became joined with the body of the nymph Salmacis. And some indication of the fear that such individuals aroused is indicated by Pliny, who tells of the drowning of two hermaphrodites at birth so that no one would be defiled by their blood.[64] A woman who in 90 B.C.E. was reported to have changed into a man was burned alive.[65] The fact that the hermaphrodites mentioned above were women who turned into men is probably indicative of the Roman tendency to classify any child with sexual ambiguities as male, without having them undergo careful examination. This remains a common practice in many Third World countries today where males are prized more highly than females.

Cross dressing, however, was not regarded with the kind of fear that greeted the hermaphrodite. Almost all the recorded instances of Roman cross dressing take place in the imperial period at the beginning of the common era and usually involve members of the emperor's family. Julius Caesar, for example, found himself involved in an incident connected with the worship of the goddess Bona Dea. Bona Dea was considered a woman's goddess, and only women could worship her. By Caesar's time one of the ceremonies associated with her was held in the house of the pontifex maximus ("chief priest") under the supervision of his wife. In 62 B.C.E., when Caesar was pontifex maximus, the services in his house were attended by Clodius, who disguised himself as a woman. According to Caesar's critics, Clodius, a Roman politician, attended not so much to observe the ceremonies but to follow through on an assignation with Caesar's wife.[66]

Clodius was unmasked by the women and accused of sacrilege, but was acquitted, supposedly by bribing the jurors. Cicero gave evidence that destroyed Clodius's alibi, and Clodius later used his influence to force Cicero into exile. Caesar seized upon the occasion to divorce his wife Pompeia on the grounds that as Caesar's wife she had to be above suspicion. He also backed Clodius, who was extremely popular with the Roman electorate. Although Caesar eventually broke with Clodius, Clodius's cross-dressing affair continued to make and unmake Roman political careers for several years.

It was the Roman emperors, however, who—"born to the purple," and often indulged in their every whim since childhood—achieved the most notoriety for their sexual activities as adults. Cross dressing was often involved. Gaius Caesar Germanicus, better known as Caligula and who ruled briefly in the first century c.e., is said to have appeared in public as the goddess Venus. Caligula would dress in women's clothing, but retained some semblance of his masculine self by keeping his beard.[67] Though Suetonius, the source for much of this information, was a gossipy historian and no admirer of Caligula, there is enough independent evidence to verify his account.[68] Perhaps the most notorious cross dresser was the Emperor Nero (54–68 c.e.), although his cross dressing seemed incidental to other aspects of his personality. The scandal-mongering Suetonius wrote: "He castrated the boy Sporus and actually tried to make a woman of him; and he married him with all the usual ceremonies, including a dowry and bridal veil, and took him to his house attended by a great throng, and treated him as his wife." Later, he married his freedman Doryphorus, "in the same way that he himself had married Sporus," going so far as "to imitate the cries and lamentations of a maiden being deflowered."[69]

Nero became sort of grab bag for all kinds of incidents of "evil" in Roman and medieval literature, and the cross-dressing stories were certainly meant to disparage him. One of the more bizarre stories told about him was by thirteenth-century Dominican writer Jacopo da Voragine, who reported that Nero, after being reproached by the physicians for killing his mother, the woman who had borne him in pain and nurtured him with so much care and labor, replied: "'Make me conceive a child and then bear it, so that I can know what pain my mother suffered.' He had also conceived this wish to bear a child because, passing through the city, he had heard the cries of women in labour."

The physicians responded that this was not possible, but Nero replied that if they could not make him conceive and give birth, he would put them all to a cruel death.

Then the doctors gave him potions to drink, in which they secretly introduced a frog, and by artifice they made this frog grow in his belly; soon his belly, being unable to endure this unnatural state, began to swell, so that Nero believed himself with child; and the doctors made him follow a diet which they knew would be nourishing to the frog, claiming the child he had conceived made this necessary. At last, tormented by intolerable pains, he said to the doctors: "Hasten the moment of giving birth, for the anguish of my future labour scarcely lets me breathe." Then they made him take a potion which made him vomit and he brought up a frog hideous to behold, soaked in humours and covered in blood. And Nero, seeing the fruit of his womb, was appalled by it himself and wondered that such a monster should have appeared; but the doctors told him that he had produced a deformed foetus because he had refused to wait for the required time. And he said: "Was I thus when I came from the body of my mother?" "Yes," they replied. So he told them to feed his offspring and to keep it in a vaulted room, where it would be cared for.[70]

Though Nero came to symbolize perverted evil in the popular imagination, this was not true of all the cross-dressing emperors. One of the most enigmatic and perhaps most tragic Roman emperors was Elagabalus, who was proclaimed emperor as a fourteen-year-old boy in 218 C.E. He has been described as a particularly beautiful boy who detested Roman clothes, which he said were made of cheap wool. He refused to wear anything but silk. His grandmother Julia Maesa worried about his costume for fear that the Romans might think "it more suitable for a woman than a man." Her worries were perhaps justified, since Elagabalus was said to have requested castration so that he could be a true woman. This, however, was just one incident in his four years of rule which ended with his murder by the military.[71]

This discussion of imperial activities, however, can give a misleading view of what was taking place among the Roman populace. Increasingly, the intellectual outlook of Roman citizens was being influenced by ascetic philosophies that emphasized moderation as a way of life. Stoicism was particularly influential. The Stoic watchwords were nature, virtue, decorum, and freedom from excess. Moderation in sex if not abstinence was particularly desirable. Marriage was recognized, but passion in marriage was suspect because the only "true" justification for marriage was propagation of the race. The first-century (C.E.) Stoic teacher Musonius Rufus went so far as to argue that sexual pleasure even within the confines of marriage was reprehensible.[72] Tied in with this was the growth of Neoplatonism, based on the writings of Plotinus, who urged abstinence from all carnal pleasures, even from sexual intercourse.[73] Against this background Christianity appeared and incorporated much of the Roman ascetic teaching into its own theology.

Christianity also partook of the Jewish tradition, and in terms of cross dressing, this was particularly influential since Judaism strongly condemned any manifestations of gender confusion, both male and female: "The woman shall not wear that which pertaineth unto a man, neither shall a man put on a woman's garment; for all that do so are abominations unto the Lord thy God."[74] The reason for this early condemnation, however, was not because of the sexual overtones inherent in cross dressing; instead, it formed part of a campaign against the Syrian goddess Atargatis, who was probably a Syrian version of the Assyrian goddess Ishtar. In some of the worship ceremonies, the followers of Atargatis dressed in the clothes and assumed the role of the opposite sex, just as their Greek counterparts did.[75] Jewish men were also enjoined from using cosmetics, wearing brightly colored garments, donning jewelry or ornaments associated with women, and shaving the hair on the hidden parts of their body. Women were to keep their hair long, while men were to keep their hair short. Since simulated sex change was often a part of many of the fertility cults of the time,[76] the biblical writers were probably much more hostile to cross dressing at this time than were later commentators.

In fact, cross dressing in Judaism was far more frequent than such prohibitions would indicate. It was even encouraged when the motive was innocent or necessary to preserve honor. A woman traveling with an all-male caravan, for example, was encouraged to cross dress and act a man's role.[77] In short, it seems probable that the biblical prohibition against cross dressing started out as a condemnation of the practices of rival cults and only later came to be interpreted as having the erotic overtones that so many biblical commentators traditionally have imputed to it, and which has given Western cross dressers so much anxiety. Still, even with the biblical condemnation, the strict gender roles set for men and women could be eased in Judaism by cross dressing during festivals (which were often condemned as pagan), and during various events that were carried out on stage. Many of these exceptions will be examined later in this volume.

It was this combination of Greek, Roman, and Jewish traditions that influenced thinking on cross dressing in the medieval period. Also important in influencing the developing Christian culture was the Germanic tradition, which in some ways was also hostile to cross dressing, or at least to androgyny. This hostility is emphasized by some of the surviving Norse legends and is perhaps best illustrated by Ymir, a half-male and half-female creature who had been created by the influence of "fire" and "frost" from the primeval fluids. Ymir had the ability to generate life by himself/herself and initially gave birth to a set of twins, a boy and a girl. Since Ymir in the end was killed by the gods, however, the implication of this legend seems to be that androgyny is ultimately to be rejected and denigrated.[78] Actually, medieval Germanic prohibitions were not quite so severe because there was also a perceived sex difference by which women were given greater permission to cross dress than men. This medieval tradition is examined further in the next chapter.

Summary

Though the Christian transmitters of classical culture preserved much of the Greek and Roman mythology, their ideas about cross dressing were most influenced by Judaism. It was Judaism reflected through a Stoic, Neoplatonic mirror, however, which not only condemned cross dressing but often sexual activity itself. The Christian tradition also preserved much of the classical thinking about the differences between the sexes and not only accepted traditional male domination as normative but, influenced by anxieties over the dangers of sex, emphasized a kind of misogyny that went beyond the classical examples and emphasized woman as temptress. This concept created difficulties since a woman, Mary, was also the holy mother. Mary, however, was chaste and virginal, and though all women were potentially Mary, they were more likely to be seen as Eve, the temptress.

Notes

1. The writings of Ctesias are no longer extant. This fragment was preserved by Diodorus Siculus, *History*, trans. and ed. C. H. Oldfather (London: William Heinemann, 1933), II:21. Where possible in this chapter, we have used English translations to better enable the reader who is not able to consult the originals in Latin and Greek to verify the sources.

2. James Henry Breasted, *Ancient Records of Egypt* ([1906] reprinted, New York: Russell and Russell, 1962), 3:248; Edward L. Margetts, "The Masculine Character of Hatshepsut, Queen of Egypt," *Bulletin of the History of Medicine* 25 (1951): 559ff.

3. Herodotus, IV:67, *History*, trans. A. D. Godley (London: William Heinemann, 1946).

4. Ibid., 1:105.

5. Hippocrates, *Of the Airs*, XXII, in *Collected Works*, ed. and trans. W. H. S. Jones (London: William Heinemann, 1923).

6. Aristotle, *Nichomachean Ethics*, VII, 7 (1150b), ed. and trans. H. Rackham (London: William Heinemann, 1934).

7. Walter Williams, *The Spirit and the Flesh* (Boston: Beacon Press, 1986), 3. See also Mary Douglas, *Purity and Danger* (Baltimore: Penguin, 1966); and James Thayer, "The Berdache of the Northern Plains: A Socioreligious Perspective," *Journal of Anthropological Research* 36 (1980): 292–93.

8. Henri Jeanmaire, *Coiroir et couetes* (Lille: Bibliothèque Universitaire, 1939), 153. The translation is essentially that of Marie Delcourt, *Hermaphrodite: Myths and Rites of the Bisexual Figure in Classical Antiquity*, trans. Jennifer Nicholson (London: Studio Books, 1958), 5.

9. Jeanmaire, *Coiroir,* 321, and Delcourt, *Hermaphrodite,* 6.

10. Plutarch, "Lycurgus," XV:3, in *Plutarch's Lives,* ed. and trans. Bernadotte Perrin (London: William Heinemann, 1959).

11. Plutarch, *Virtue of Women*, 4:245, in *Moralia*, ed. and trans. Frank Cole Babbitt (London: William Heinemann, 1931). This is perhaps only one interpretation of this rather obscure passage.

12. Plutarch, *Quaestiones Graecae*, 58, in vol. 4, *Moralia*.

13. For a discussion of this, although in a different perspective, see Bernard Sergent, *Homosexuality in Greek Myth*, trans. Arthur Goldhammer (Boston: Beacon Press, 1984).

14. Antonius Liberalis, *Metamorphoses*, cap XVII, ed. Edgar Martin (Leipzig: Teubner, 1896). See also Marie Delcourt, *Hermaphrodite*, 60–66.

15. Pausanius, *Descriptions of Greece*, VIII, 20, 3–4, ed. and trans. W. H. Jones (London: William Heinemann, 1959); Parthenius, *Love Romances*, 15, ed. and trans. Stephen Gaselee (reprinted, London: William Heinemann, 1962). There are other versions of the story; cf. Hyginus, "Fabula XCV," in *Myths of Hyginus*, trans. and ed. Mary Grant (Lawrence: University of Kansas Press, 1960), 146–47.

16. Plutarch, *A Letter of Condolence to Appolonius*, 22 (112 F) in vol. 2 of *Moralia*. This statement is repeated by Valerius Maximus, *Factorum et dictorum memorabilius*, II, vi, 13, ed. Carolus Kempf (Leipzig: Teubner, 1888).

17. In another version of the story, Hymenaeus is said to have vanished or died on his own wedding night. See Catullus, *Carmina* LXII, LXIII, ed. and trans. F. W. Cornish (rev. ed., London: William Heinemann, 1962).

18. Plutarch, *Solon*, VIII, 4–6, in *Lives*.

19. For a medieval discussion with classical references, see Marie-Christine Pouchelle, *The Body and Surgery in the Middle Ages*, trans. Rosemary Morris (New Brunswick, NJ: Rutgers University Press, 1990), esp. 101–24.

20. Herodotus, *History*, IV, 145–46.

21. George Dumézil, *Crime des Lemniennes* (Paris: P. Geuthner, 1924), 51–54; Delcourt, *Hermaphrodite*, 81.

22. Jeanmaire, *Coiroir*, 352.

23. Euripides, *Bacchanals*, ed. and trans. Arthur S. Way (London: William Heinemann, 1919); Diodorus Siculus, *History*, II, 62. For a hostile account of some of the rituals, see Clement of Alexandria, *Exhortation to the Greeks*, ed. and trans. G. W. Butterworth (London: William Heinemann, 1953).

24. See, for example, Ovid, *Metamorphoses*, IV, ed. and trans. Frank Paul (London: William Heinemann, 1966), 399–415; Antonius Liberalis, *Metamorphoses*, chap. X; Plutarch, *Quaestiones Graecae*, 38, among other references.

25. W. J. Slater, "Artemon and Anacreon: No Text Without Context," *Phoenix* 32 (1978): 185–94, esp. 190ff.

26. Clara Gallini, "Il Travestismo Rituale di Penteo," *Studi e Materiali di Storia delle Religione* 34 (1963): 211–28.

27. Eva Keuls, *The Reign of the Phallus: Sexual Politics in Ancient Athens* (New York: Harper and Row, 1985), pl. 296, p. 359, for woman with a beard, and pl. 314, p. 372, for a woman with a phallus.

28. H. W. Parke, *Festivals of the Athenians* (Ithaca, NY: Cornell University Press, 1977), 77.

29. Philostratus, *Apollonius of Tyana*, IV, xxi, ed. and trans. F. C. Conybeare (reprinted, London: William Heinemann, 1948).

30. Keuls, *The Reign of Phallus*, 358.

31. Arthur Evans, *The God of Ecstasy: Sex-Roles and the Madness of Dionysos* (New York: St. Martin's, 1988). The translation of the play is in the appendix, 199–272.

32. Athenaeus, *The Deipnosophists*, XII, 525e–f, ed. and trans. Charles Burton Gulick (London: William Heinemann, 1927).

33. Plutarch, *Virtue of Women,* IV (245).

34. Plutarch, *Theseus,* 20, 304, ed. and trans. Bernadotte Perrin (London: William Heinemann, 1959); Macrobius, *Saturnalia,* III, viii, 2, ed. and trans. Percival Vaughn Davies (New York: Columbia University Press, 1969).

35. Philostratus, *Imagines,* I, ii, 9–10, ed. and trans. Arthur Fairbanks (London: William Heinemann, 1931).

36. Artemidorus Daldiana, *Oneirocriticon,* 3, 8, ed. Rudolph Hercher (Leipzig: Teubner, 1864), II, 3, 8.

37. Delcourt, *Hermaphrodite,* 12.

38. Ovid, *Metamorphoses,* XIII, 162–80; Hyginus, *Fabula,* CXVI; Apollodorus, *The Library,* II, xiii, 8, ed. and trans. Sir James G. Frazer (London: William Heinemann, 1921); Statius, *Achilleis,* ll. 560–674, ed. and trans. J. H. Mozley (London: William Heinemann, 1931).

39. Ovid, *Heroides,* IX, 57–120; Ovid, *Fasti,* II, 303–58, ed. and trans. Sir James C. Frazer (reprinted, London: William Heinemann, [1921] 1959); Lucian, *Dialogue of the Gods,* 15 (13), ed. and trans. M. D. Macleod (London: William Heinemann, 1931), 758E–F, in vol. 10 of *Moralia.*

40. Pausanius, *Descriptions of Greece,* I, xix, 1–2.

41. Delcourt, *Hermaphrodite,* 10–11.

42. Ibid., 27–29, and Lewis R. Farnell, *The Cults of the Greek States,* 5 vols. (Oxford: Clarendon Press, 1896–1900), 2:628, 2:755.

43. C. J. Bulliet, *Venus Castina* (reprinted, New York: Bonanza Books, [1928] 1956).

44. See, for example, J. J. Bachofen, "Mother Right," in *Myth, Religion, and Mother Right: Selected writings of J. J. Bachofen,* trans. Ralph Mannheim (Princeton: Princeton University Press, 1967); Emanuel Kanter, *The Amazons: A Marxian Study* (Chicago: Ker, 1926); for a different view, see Abby Wettan Kleinbaum, *The War Against the Amazons* (New York: McGraw-Hill, 1983). For the effect on patriarchy theory, see Berta Eckstein-Diener [Helen Diner], *Mothers and Amazons,* ed. and trans. John Philip Lundin (Garden City, NY: Doubleday, 1973). See also Marilyn French, *Beyond Power: On Women, Men and Morals* (New York: Summit Books, 1985); William Blake Tyrrell, *Amazons: A Study in Athenian Mythmaking* (Baltimore: Johns Hopkins University Press, 1984).

45. Diodorus Siculus, *History,* II, 45.

46. Tyrrell, *Amazons,* 90–93.

47. Ovid, *Metamorphoses,* XII, 458–531; Hyginus, *Fabula,* XIV.

48. Hyginus, *Fabula,* CXVI, CLXXXIX; Ovid, *Metamorphoses,* VII, 685–865; Antonius Liberalis, *Metamorphoses,* chap. XLI.

49. Ovid, *Metamorphoses,* III, 315–38; Hyginus, *Fabula,* LXXV; Apollodorous, *The Library,* III, vi, 6–7. Frazer, the translator of Apollodorous, saw this as part of a tradition that regarded it as unlucky to see snakes coupling.

50. See *The Republic,* ed. and trans. Paul Shoren, 2 vols. (London: William Heinemann, 1935). Even here, where he accepted women as potential philosopher kings, he held their capacity to learn was less than a man's. See Book 5.

51. Plato, *Laws,* ed. and trans. R. G. Bury, 2 vols. (London: William Heinemann, 1952).

52. Plato, *Timaeus* 91C, ed. and trans. R. G. Bury (London: William Heinemann, 1952).

53. Euripides, *Medea,* trans. Rex Warner in *Complete Greek Tragedies,* ed. David Grene and Richard Latimore (Chicago: University of Chicago Press, 1959), 3:67, ll. 231–51.

54. I. M. Lewis, *Ecstatic Religion: An Anthropological Study of Spirit Possession and Shamanism* (London: Penguin, 1971).

55. Plato, *Symposium*, 178C, trans. W. R. M. Lamb (London: William Heinemann, 1953).

56. Plutarch, *Pelopidas*, 18, in *Plutarch's Lives*, ed. and trans. Bernadotte Perrin (London: William Heinemann, 1959).

57. Hippocrates, *Regimen*, I, xxviii, ed. and trans. W. H. S. Jones (London: William Heinemann, 1931), vol. 4.

58. Gilbert H. Herdt, *Guardians of the Flutes: Idioms of Masculinity* (New York: McGraw-Hill, 1981).

59. This theory was amplified by David M. Halperin, *One Hundred Years of Homosexuality and Other Essays on Greek Love* (New York: Routledge, 1990). It might also explain the Greek men's need to keep women in their place and to relegate gender-crossing to special occasions when the fear of the female could be neutralized.

60. Aristophanes, *Thesmophoriazusae*, 147–52, ed. and trans. Benjamin Bickley Rogers (reprinted, London: William Heinemann, [1924] 1955).

61. Aristophanes, *The Ecclesiazusae*, ed. and trans. Benjamin Bickley Rogers (reprinted, London: William Heinemann, [1924] 1955).

62. Ovid, *Metamorphoses*, XIV, 623–97.

63. Pliny, *Natural History*, VII, iv, ed. and trans. W. H. S. Jones (reprinted, London: William Heinemann, [1942] 1963).

64. Ibid., XXXI, 12; XXVII, 37.

65. Diodorus Siculus, *Histories*, XXXII, 12.

66. There is a brief biography of Publius Clodius in *The Oxford Classical Dictionary* (Oxford: Clarendon Press, 1961), 203.

67. Suetonius, "Gaius Caligula," XXXVI, in *De Vita Caesarum*, ed. and trans. John C. Rolfe (revised and reprinted, London: William Heinemann, 1951).

68. See Dio Cassius, *Roman History*, LIX, ii, ed. and trans. Ernest Cary (reprinted, London: William Heinemann, [1924] 1955). Similar references appear in works by Juvenal and Tacitus.

69. Suetonius, "Nero," XVIII–XXIX, *De Vita Caeasarum;* Dio Cassius, LXII, xvii. There are similar references in Juvenal and Tacitus.

70. Pouchelle, *The Body and Surgery in the Middle Ages*, 81.

71. Herodian, *History of the Roman Empire*, V, ii, 9, and V, v, 3–5, viii, 1–2, ed. and trans. Edward C. Echols (Berkeley: University of California Press, 1959).

72. A. C. van Reytenbeck, *Musonius Rufus and Greek Diatribe*, trans. B. L. Hijamans, Jr. (Assen, Netherlands: Van Gorcum and Company, 1963), 71–72.

73. See Vern L. Bullough, *Sexual Variance in Society and History* (Chicago: University of Chicago Press, 1976), 151–52, 166–67, passim.

74. Deut. 22:5. The quotation is from the Authorized Version (King James), although we have consulted various editions and translations as well as numerous biblical commentaries.

75. S. R. Driver, *A Critical and Exegetical Comment on Deuteronomy*, 3d ed. (reprinted, Edinburgh: T. & T. Clark, 1951), 250–51.

76. L. R. Farnell, *The Cults of the Greek States* (Oxford: Clarendon Press, 1896ff), V, pp. 160–61.

77. Louis M. Epstein, *Sex Laws and Customs in Judaism* (New York: Bloch Publishing, 1948), 64–67.

78. Uli Linke, "Women, Androgynes, and Models of Creation in Norse Mythology," *Journal of Psychohistory* 16 (1989): 167–206.

Chapter 3
Cross Dressing and Social Status in the Middle Ages

From the discussion so far, it should be obvious that cross dressing is influenced by cultural and social-structural variables. Different attitudes and assumptions about sex and gender make for different attitudes about cross dressing. Thus a key to understanding transvestism today lies in examining basic Western attitudes as formulated in the Middle Ages. What assumptions were embedded in Western culture that were different from those of other cultures? Clearly, Greek and Roman mythology had a far more tolerant attitude toward cross-gender role playing than did later Christian culture, emphasizing that only certain aspects of classical culture were adopted by the later Christian West.

A major influence was the Jewish tradition. Biblical statements, such as "The woman shall not wear that which pertaineth unto a man, neither shall a man put on a woman's garment; for all that do so are an abomination unto the Lord thy God,"[1] seemed to have been highly influential. As indicated some scholars today see this prohibition as a direct challenge to some of the religious rivals of Judaism who engaged in cross dressing rather than as a universal prohibition of such behavior, but it is perhaps equally important to recognize just how this edict came to be interpreted by Christians in medieval Europe. Medieval authorities frowned upon male cross dressing (though they did not regard it as a sexual activity), except under rather rigidly prescribed circumstances. But these same authorities were far more tolerant of women cross dressers, emphasizing the ability of interpreters to read into the Bible that which conformed with their own prejudices.

Also modifying the Graeco-Roman heritage which passed into medieval Europe were Germanic customs and traditions. Traditional Germanic laws, if old Norse laws are an example, emphasized the necessity of gender distinction. Males and females who adopted the appearance of the opposite sex, whether in the way they dressed, cut their hair, or in the insignia they bore (such as on weapons), could be declared outlaws.[2] But as the Middle Ages progressed, this prohibition was also reinterpreted and, in much of Germanic culture, disappeared.

A major factor in the reinterpretation of the Germanic and Jewish prohibitions toward cross dressing was the recognition of a status differential between the sexes that distinguished women who dressed as men from men who dressed as women. Female cross dressers have not only been tolerated but even encouraged, if only indirectly, through much of Western history, since it was assumed they wanted to become more like men and, therefore, were striving to "better" themselves. Males who cross dressed other than in a comic burlesque, on the other hand, not only lost status but also aroused suspicions because others believed they either were trying to gain easier access to women for sexual purposes or were following pre-Christian or anti-Christian religious rituals.

How did such attitudes develop? Obviously, these tendencies are closely related to differing attitudes toward females and males. A good starting point for examining medieval values is Aristotle, who believed that he had scientific evidence of female inferiority and went on to claim that women were not only intellectually but morally inferior to men. Proof of such a conclusion, he said, could be observed in nature, where the male of each species was demonstrably more advanced than the female—larger, stronger, and more agile. He reasoned that what was true for animals was also the case with humans. From this he concluded that male domination was the will of nature. To try to challenge nature in the name of some imagined principle of equality was quite contrary to the interests both of the individual and of the community.[3]

For additional "proof" of male superiority, Aristotle pointed to the overwhelming importance of the male principle in reproduction. He held that the key to life was in semen, although he did admit that the female supplied the matter for "shaping": "If, then, the male stands for the effective and active, and the female, considered as female, for the passive, it follows that what the female would contribute to the semen of the male would not be semen but material for the semen to work upon."[4] Aristotle even went so far as to claim that the female was little more than an incomplete male.[5] Evidence for this came from the "fact" that the active force in semen tended to produce a perfect likeness in the masculine sex, while the production of the female came from a defect in the active force or from some material indisposition.[6]

Medieval theorists, even those deeply influenced by Aristotle, tended to reject the philosopher on this last point. Saint Thomas Aquinas, for example, argued that women could not be misbegotten since they were part of God's intention. This, however, did not mean that she was equal to man in power or status: "For good order would have been wanting in the human family, if some were not governed by others wiser than themselves. So by such a kind of subjection woman is naturally subject to man, because naturally in man the discretion of reason predominates."[7] Since the action of the male and female were distinct from each other in the matter of generation, there was a need for two sexes and two distinct operations, "that of the agents and that of the patient. Wherefore it follows that the entire active operation is on the part of the male and the passive on the part of the female. For this reason in plants, where both forces are mingled, there is no distinction of male and female." And since the generative power of the female is imperfect compared with the male, and since "in the arts the inferior art gives a disposition to the matter to which the higher art gives the form . . . so also the generative power of the female prepares the matter, which is then fashioned by the active power of the male."[8]

Such suppositions inevitably lead to the question of whether the nature of the female was essentially different from the male. Soranus (second century C.E.) in his *Gynecology* briefly listed some of the authorities who held that women were different from men if only because they were formed to be the mothers of men. Most of the authorities he cited, however, believed that women were not formed from any different materials than men despite the fact that they had different generative organs.[9] He concluded that the

female has her illness in common with the male, she suffers from constriction or from flux, either acutely or chronically, and she is subject to the same seasonal differences, to gradations of disease, to lack of strength, and to the different foreign bodies, sores, and injuries. Only as far as particulars and specific variations are concerned does the female show conditions peculiarly her own, i.e. a different character of symptoms. Therefore she is subject to treatment generically the same.[10]

Averroës, an Islamic physician (d. 1198) who was influential in Jewish and Christian thought, essentially agreed that women,

in so far as they are of one kind in respect of the ultimate human aim, necessarily share in it [the aim] and only differ in degree.

This means: man is in most human activities more efficient than woman; though it is not impossible that women are in some activities more efficient, as is thought in respect of the art of practical music. For this reason, it is said that melodies are perfect if men invent them and women perform them.[11]

Medieval Latin writers supported this assessment and, in fact, reinforced it with biblical statements emphasizing that woman, in the final analysis, had been made from the rib of man.

This agreement did not mean, however, that women did not have qualities different from those of men. Isidore of Seville (d. 636) believed he had found explanations for this divergence in the etymologies of the various terms applied to the sexes. A man, he claimed, was called *vir* because there was greater force (*vis*) in him than in woman; thus *vir* was used as the stem word for *virtus,* or strength, because men ruled over women by force. A woman, in contrast, was called *mulier,* a term he said derived from "softness" (*molites*), since "softer" (*mollier*), with one letter changed and one taken away, was "woman." Though we can poke fun at Isidore's etymologies today, they were widely believed and helped justify the different status roles of the sexes. According to Isidore, since man's strength was greater than woman's, woman should be subject to man. One reason a woman could be forced to submit was that if she could easily repel a man, his lust might lead him to turn to his own sex for satisfaction (i.e., engage in homosexual activity), and this, Isidore felt, was against the will of God.[12]

Women were also different from men by virtue of their monthly periods. Isidore reported that the menstrual flow was woman's superfluous blood, and it was called *menstrual* because of the phase of the moon by which it came about.[13] Though the connection between menstrual blood and pregnancy was recognized early, some Christian writers also believed that menstruation itself had been inflicted upon women as a consequence of Eve's sin, and almost all accepted the mosaic concept that a menstruating woman was "unclean" and that menstrual blood might be dangerous. They also accepted the idea advanced by early non-Christian writers that menstruation was a cleansing process for the whole body. Women needed this since their life-style was more sedentary than men's; thus, more digestive by-products accumulated in women than in men and had to be cleaned out. As a result, menstruation, though it might originally have come about through the curse of Eve, was essential to ensuring good health in women.[14] But writers like Aquinas held that the menstrual blood had a certain natural impurity or corruption (from Eve's sin) even though it also cleared away certain diseases.[15] Among these diseases was gout, which was believed to result from a poisoning of the "juices" of the body. In women menstruation eliminated such poisons, but in men they concentrated in the lower parts of the body, where they remained and hardened unless eliminated by vigorous exercise.

The Galenic view of women also focused on "imperfection":

The female is less perfect than the male for one, principal reason—because she is colder; for if among animals, the warm one is the more active, a colder animal would be less perfect than a warmer. A second reason is one that appears in dissecting. . . . Think first, please, of the man's [sexual organs] turned in and extending inward between the rectum and the bladder. If this should happen, the scrotum would necessarily take the place of the uteri [*sic*], with the testes lying outside, next to it on either side; the penis of the male would become the neck of the cavity that had been formed; and the skin at the end of the penis now called prepuce, would become the female pudendum itself. . . .

In fact, you could not find a single male part left over that had not simply changed its position; for the parts that are inside in woman are outside in man. You can see something like this in the eyes of the mole which have vitreous and crystalline humors and the tunics that surround these and grow out from the meninges . . . and they have these just as much as animals do that make use of their eyes. The mole's eyes, however, do not open, nor do they project, but are left there imperfect and remain like the eyes of other animals when these are still in uterus. . . . Now just as mankind is the most perfect of all animals, so within mankind the man is more perfect than the woman, and the reason for his perfection is his excess of heat, for heat is Nature's primary instrument. Hence, in those animals that have less of it, her workmanship is necessarily more imperfect, and so it is no wonder that the female is less perfect than the male by as much as she is colder than he. In fact, just as the mole has imperfect eyes, though certainly not so imperfect as they are in those animals that do not have any trace of them at all, so too the woman is less perfect than the man in respect to the generative parts. For the parts were formed within her when she was still a fetus, but could not because of the defect in the heat emerge and project on the outside, and this, though making the animal itself that was being formed less perfect than one that is complete in all respects, provided no small advantage for the race; for there needs must be a female. Indeed, you ought not to think that our Creator would purposely make half the whole race imperfect, and, as it were, mutilated, unless there was to be some great advantage in such a mutilization [*sic*].[16]

This idea of women being men turned outside in was common, and occasionally, one finds in popular folk literature—ancient, medieval, and early modern—that women who spread their legs very far would have their organs fall out and become men. Pliny recorded several changes of women to men under these circumstances.[17] This same concept of women having internally what men had externally appeared in much of the medieval medical literature, even to the extent that the writers often called the ovaries "female testicles."[18] Regarded as further proof of male superiority was the fact that when males were castrated and became eunuchs, the "male complexion" changed to a female one.[19]

Tied in with and overlying this view of women as subordinate creatures was a kind of mystic view of the intellectual inferiority of the females as well. This attitude was perhaps inevitable, given the male domination of science and philosophy and religion, but it too had a rationale behind it. It became very strong in Christian thinking and, in large part, was derived from Neoplatonic thinking, which was very influential as the theology of Christianity developed. The Alexandrian Jewish Neoplatonist philosopher Philo held that the reason the male was superior to the female was because he represented the more rational part of the soul, while the female represented the less rational. For Philo, progress in this world meant giving up the female attributes, the material, passive, corporeal world perceived by the senses, and embracing the active, rational male world of mind and thought. The easiest way for women to approach the male level of rationality was for women to deny their sexuality, to remain virgins; the words *virgin, virginity,* and *ever virginal* occur continually in Philo's references to the best kind of women.[20]

Christianizing this belief were some of the early Church Fathers, particularly Saint Jerome. Most of the early Church Fathers were celibate and also misogynistic, perhaps because women aroused in them feelings and emotions which they sometimes found difficult to control.[21] Women often were perceived as a temptation. In the litany of the dangers of women, Saint Jerome stands out because, despite his acceptance of much of these early beliefs, he was also supportive of women, arguing that there could be no cause for shame in associating with the sex from which the Virgin Mary had originated. Jerome enjoyed teaching the Gospel to women and had several women as close friends, but his admiration had limits: He restricted his admiration to virgins and widows, since only then, in his mind, could women be regarded as spiritual companions and not as sexual objects. He argued that as "long as woman is for birth and children, she is different from man as body is from soul. But when she wishes to serve Christ more than the world, then she will cease to be a woman and will be called man."[22] Jerome was repelled by women who seemed to be dominated by their sexual biology and said he found nothing attractive in mother-hood. He considered pregnant women a revolting sight and could not imagine why anyone would want a child, a "brat" to crawl upon a person's breast, soiling their neck with nastiness.[23]

A similar concept was expressed by Saint Ambrose, also in the fourth century C.E.:

She who does not believe is a woman and should be designated by the name of her sex, whereas she who believes progresses to perfect manhood, to the measure of the adulthood of Christ. She then dispenses with the name of her sex, the seductiveness of youth, the garrulousness of old age.[24]

The list of authorities making similar statements is a very long one, and on the basis of such assumptions, a female who wore men's clothes or in other ways adopted a male role might be perceived as trying to imitate a superior sex in order to make herself more rational, while the reverse would be true for men donning women's clothes or taking on female attributes. No such simple statement to this effect can be found in any of the Church Fathers, but practice demonstrates this assumption.

Medieval Cross-Dressing Legends

One illustration is the medieval legend that explains why Saint Jerome temporarily fled Rome. Jerome himself only indicated that "certain persons" had accused him of every sort of crime, but through amplification, this became a story about how Jerome's enemies had set a trap for him. The precipitating incident for his temporary "disgrace" came about when certain Roman "pseudopriests and monks," furious at Jerome for attacking their lasciviousness, had

placed near his bed a woman's garment. The saint, getting up in the dark to go to matins, reached out and put it on, mistaking it for his own; thus scandalously appareled he made his way to church. His enemies played this trick on him so that the people might think he had spent the night with a woman.[25]

This seems such a minor incident that it is difficult to see it as a cause for Jerome's temporary disgrace, but it emphasizes that Jerome's very willingness to consort with women, even if limited to virgins and widows, was perceived by some as a subterfuge to get into their beds. To avoid such gossip and innuendo, it would seem to be ideal if the real dedicated virgin or widow could somehow become a "man."

Jerome's cross dressing was seen as an effort to gain access to women, but male cross dressing was also considered evidence of homosexuality. For example, Saint Cyprian (d. 258 c.e.), concerned about effeminacy among Christian men, held that men who dressed as women or who used feminine gestures or accoutrements should be forced to cease these offensive displays.[26] Though the Church Council, of Gangra (before 341) had condemned pious women who disguised themselves as men in order to join male ascetic and monastic communities,[27] holy women who impersonated men remained much admired, particularly if their disguise was only uncovered after their death. Illustrating this point are the large number of female saints who lived and worshipped as men for all of their adult lives and whose true sex was neither known nor suspect until they were being prepared for burial.[28]

Probably the archetype for the female cross-dressing saints is Pelagia. According to one version of the legend, Pelagia was a beautiful dancing girl and prostitute in Antioch who was also called Margaritó because of the splendor of her pearls. She was converted to Christianity by the saintly Bishop Nonus, who acted as her patron. Not wishing to be identified with her past, Pelagia left Antioch dressed as a man, although under her outer garments she wore, with the permission of Nonus himself, a hair shirt to remind her of the sufferings of Jesus and of her human frailty. After much travel she found refuge on Mount Olivet in Jerusalem, where she lived as a man called Pelagius. As Pelagius, she became admired throughout the Holy Land for her asceticism and holiness, and it was not until after her death that her sex was revealed. When they discovered her to be a woman, her mourners are said to have cried out: "Glory be to thee, Lord Jesus, for thou hast many hidden treasures on earth, as well female as male."[29]

A second and differing version of Saint Margarita/Pelagius recounts that Margarita held marriage in such horror that following her betrothal she fled the nuptial chamber dressed as a man, cut her hair, and took refuge in a monastery under the name of Pelagius. Such was her devotion that she was elected prior of a convent. She acted this male role so well that when the portress of the convent became pregnant and accused Margarita/Pelagius of being the father, the charge was believed. The result was her expulsion from the convent in disgrace. Margarita/Pelagius then found refuge as a hermit in a nearby cave, and it was only after her death that her true sex was discovered, and she was proclaimed innocent of the crime of which she had been accused.[30]

A similar story is told about Marina, the daughter of a Bithynian named Eugenius. Eugenius, after being left a widower, decided to enter a monastery. No sooner had he become a monk than he began to worry about his little daughter Marina, whom he had left in the care of a relative. He went to his abbot with his worries but, in the process of telling his story, changed the sex of his child from a girl to a boy. The abbot invited him to bring his young son to the monastery with him. Eugenius immediately did so, and Marina continued to live there as "Marinus" long after her father's death. One of her jobs in the monastery was to drive a cart down to the harbor to fetch supplies, a job necessitating an overnight stay at an inn. After one such visit a pregnant girl accused Marinus of seducing her, and Marinus, true to the unwritten code for cross-dressing saints, suffered ostracism from the monastery rather than admit her true sex. After her expulsion she and the infant boy thrust upon her by her accuser lived as beggars at the gate of the monastery, begging to be readmitted. After some five years of this, the monks at the monastery pleaded with the abbot to readmit her, and Marinus and the child were both allowed to enter. The austerities that Marina had imposed upon herself soon led to her death, and when the monks came to prepare her body for burial they discovered her true sex. The abbot of the monastery was overcome with remorse, while the woman who had falsely accused her became possessed by demons. The demons were only driven away when the woman confessed her sin and called upon Saint Marina for heavenly intercession.[31]

Though all of these stories have different elements, there is enough similarity that German scholar Herman Usener more than a hundred years ago argued that they represented survivals of the legend of Aphrodite of Cyprus, mentioned earlier, wherein women sacrificed to the goddess in men's clothing and men in women's. Usener, to support his argument, pointed out that Aphrodite was also sometimes known under the names of Pelagia and Marina,[32] although not all scholars accept this identification.[33] In terms of cross dressing, however, the issue is not whether the saints' stories were continuations of ancient legends but that they sanctioned cross dressing for women, and that women who did cross dress seemed to gain higher status.

Usually, the women who adopted the clothes of men did so when they were undergoing a crisis in their lives, and their new gender role marked a break with their former existence. Some of the saints went to such extremes as burning their old clothes and even visualizing themselves as males. Saint Perpetua, for example, saw herself in a dream being borne into an amphitheater stripped of all of her clothes and with the sex organs of a man.[34] This kind of visualization of a sex change for a woman was accepted with little comment and none of the hostility or fear that Pliny, for example, reported as existing in Rome.

Athanasia of Antioch represents still another variant on the standard story of cross-dressing saints. When her two children both died suddenly and unexpectedly on the same day, Athanasia began spending much of her time praying in a neighborhood church. One day during her prayers, she received a vision in which a stranger assured her that her children were both happy in heaven. When she told her husband, Andronicus, of her vision, the two decided to leave all their possessions behind in their house and to set out for Egypt to serve under Saint Daniel, famed for his ability to work miracles. Saint Daniel split up the couple, sending Andronicus to the monastery of Tabena, while Athanasia became an anchorite (a solitary monk) who wore the clothes of a man and was taken for a man. After some twelve years of isolation in the Egyptian desert, Athanasia decided to make a pilgrimage to Jerusalem and during her travels fell in with another monk—actually her husband Andronicus, who was also making the pilgrimage. The two traveled together, joined in religious exercises, visited the holy places, and in the process became so attached to each other that they both settled down in a monastery near Alexandria. Here they "joyously" carried out their monastic duties until Athanasius (her male name) felt death approaching and began to weep. When questioned as to why she was weeping when she was about to go to God, she said she grieved for her fellow monk Andronicus, who will "miss me." She asked the monks to give Andronicus some writing of hers, which they did, and at that point Andronicus suddenly realized that his friend and fellow monk was really his wife.[35]

Similar stories have only slight variations including those of Saint Apollinaris or Dorotheus,[36] Saint Eugenia,[37] Saint Euphrosyne,[38] Saint Theodora,[39] and Saint Anastasia Patricia.[40] Such stories are not limited to the early Church but continue up into the twelfth century with Saint Hildegund. Her story is somewhat different, since it probably was based on a historical incident, but the theme is the same. Though there are conflicting accounts of Saint Hildegund, she is usually portrayed as the daughter of a knight of Neuss on the Rhine who, after the death of his wife, decided to make a pilgrimage to the Holy Land. Unable to find anyone with whom he could leave his twelve-year-old daughter Hildegund, he solved the problem by dressing her as a boy, calling her Joseph, and taking her with him. The two traveled together to Jerusalem, where the knight, just before he died, put his "son" under the protection of a fellow knight. The protector first robbed the "boy," then deserted "him," leaving her to find her own way back to Europe. On her return (still posing as Joseph) she became a servant to an old canon of Cologne and accompanied him on a visit to the pope in Rome. She went through another series of extraordinary adventures that resulted in her wrongfully being condemned to death as a robber. She proved her innocence by undergoing the ordeal of a red-hot iron, but she then fell into the clutches of robbers who decided to hang her. Their technique was so clumsy, however, that Hildegund/Joseph was rescued and cut down before she expired. After finally meeting with the pope, she returned to Germany, where she entered a monastery at Schönau, remaining there until her death. Only then was it discovered that the famous monk Joseph was actually a woman.[41] If this account, which actually had some degree of authenticity, could be so complex, it is easy to understand how the mythical stories themselves developed.[42]

A variation of the cross dressing saints are the stories of bearded female saints. The most famous of these, Wilgefortis, or Uncumber, was said to have been one of septuplets (some sources say nontuplets) born to a non-Christian ruler of Portugal and his Christian wife. Wilgefortis early on decided to devote herself to Christianity and to remain a virgin, but her father had different ideas. When her betrothal to the king of Sicily was announced, Wilgefortis protested, but her father ordered her to marry the king. In desperation Wilgefortis prayed for help; in answer to her prayer she began growing a long, drooping mustache and silky, curling beard. Though taken aback at this hirsutism in his daughter, the king, determined that the marriage go on, ordered Wilgefortis to wear a heavy veil. When the king of Sicily arrived, Wilgefortis managed to let her veil slip enough to reveal her beard and mustache to him, whereupon he refused to proceed with the marriage. In a fit of rage, her father had her crucified.

This story has been described as having the "unenviable distinction of being one of the most obviously false and preposterous of the pseudo-pious romances by which simple Christians have been deceived or regaled,"[43] but such a modern scholarly assessment did not prevent the spread of Wilgefortis's cult throughout much of the Christian world. Wilgefortis came to be known by a number of different names, many of them derived from the term *liberata*, "the deliverer." In France she was called *Livrade*, in Spain *Librada*, and at Beauvais *Debarras*, all of which share some of the same meaning. In Germany she was usually called *Ohnkummer*, possibly derived from the German *kummer* ("trouble") and which survives in English in such words as *encumber* and its antonym *disencumber*. In Flanders she was called *Oncommer* and in England, *Uncumber*, and she became identified as the patron saint of married women who wanted to rid themselves of their husbands. To encourage action by the saint, believers were to bring her offerings of oats, although the reason for this particular gift is not known.[44]

Uncumber is not the only bearded saint; there are at least two others. Saint Galla, according to legend, was left a widow after only a year of marriage. Though she was young and healthy, she refused to remarry because she felt that matrimony which "always begins with joy . . . ends with sorrow." Her physicians warned her that if she did not marry again she would grow a beard, but still she refused. Bearded, then, she joined a band of religious women who lived close to the Basilica of Saint Peter in Rome and spent her life taking care of the poor and needy.[45]

Another bearded saint is Paula, a virgin of Avila who, fleeing from a suitor she did not want, in desperation threw herself at the foot of a crucifix and implored Jesus to disfigure her. She immediately grew a beard, and her suitor passed by without noticing her.[46] Though a bearded saint is different than a cross-dressing saint, the fact that such women could become saints emphasizes both the protective nature of the masculine role as well as its higher status.

One of the most controversial of medieval legends, and the one that perhaps has caused the greatest anguish to Catholics, is the legendary Pope Joan, who supposedly ruled under the name of John Anglicus.[47]

Several thirteenth-century chroniclers wrote about her life in great detail, and during much of the later medieval period her existence was accepted as fact. A statue of her was included among the popes in the Cathedral of Siena in the fourteenth century, and in the fifteenth century John Hus, the Bohemian heretic, reproached the delegates at the Council of Constance (1415) because their predecessors had allowed a woman to be pope. It was not until the sixteenth century that her existence was seriously disputed, and she soon was relegated to legend rather than to history. Pope Joan still has an occasional supporter, although few scholars today accept her story as factual.

The legend of Pope Joan is fairly complicated and has several variant forms. Essentially, Joan is usually said to have been born in England (hence the descriptor Anglicus, which was often attached to her name). As a child she was taken by her father, a learned man, to Mainz, where she was taught to read and write. While there she fell in love with a monk by the name of Ulfilias, who was attached to the monastery of Fulda, a German center of learning. In order to remain with Ulfilias, she disguised herself as a man and entered the monastery, where they chastely lived together. Later, she and Ulfilias traveled as pilgrims to the Holy Land and, after a series of adventures, made their way to Athens, where they studied philosophy, theology, and humane letters for ten years. Both became known for their great scholarship.

Tragedy struck the couple with the death of Ulfilias, and Joan, heartbroken, decided to return to Mainz via Rome. Arriving in Rome, she found her reputation as a scholar had preceded her, largely due to a number of former students from Athens who now lived there. The ex-students persuaded her to give some lectures in Rome, and as her reputation spread, she decided to remain there. Her abilities led to her rapid rise in the Church hierarchy, first as notary, then as cardinal, and on Pope Leo's death in the 850s, as pope under the name of John VIII, Anglicus. Despite her rise to power, Joan still grieved for the loss of her beloved Ulfilias, and when she saw a young Benedictine monk from Spain who resembled her dead companion, she fell in love with him. This time, the love did not remain platonic, and she became pregnant. Since she was assumed to be a man, her pregnancy was not noticed. In the midst of a papal procession, she entered into labor and gave birth to a son. According to one version, she and the child died shortly after, while another version has her son eventually becoming pope under the name of Adrian III. So much scholarly research has been expended on this story, we cannot begin to examine it in detail here. Nowhere in the legends about her, however, are there any hints of censure for her donning men's clothing. The basic attitude is one of admiration for her success; moreover, her ultimate fall is explained in the stories as due to the reappearance of "womanly weakness." If she had managed to remain chaste and virginal, that is, more like a man, she would not have failed.

Impersonation and Power

None of the other cross dressers discussed so far seemed to have wanted a position of power. They were women content to live as men for various reasons but mostly in order to preserve their virginity and to become closer to god. "Pope Joan" is the exception, but she had achieved power without really seeking it, and it was her own "womanly weakness" that led to her exposure. When a woman cross dresser attempted to meet a man on his own terms and was public about her true sex, she usually encountered opposition, as is most obvious in the accounts of Joan of Arc (1412–31): her cross dressing was one of the major reasons for her execution. In the legal complaints filed against Joan, it was alleged that she had not only adopted the costume of men but had had her hair cropped, wore spurs and a breastplate, and carried a sword, dagger, and other manly arms.[48] Later, the various charges against her were summarized in twelve articles, two of which dealt with cross dressing, as did two of the six admonitions directed against her.

Joan eventually recanted and agreed to don female clothing. It was her resumption of male dress that led to her execution. When her inquisitors asked why she had resumed it, Joan replied that "she had taken it of her own will, under no compulsion as she preferred man's to woman's dress." She was reminded by her inquisitors that she had promised and sworn not to wear men's clothes again, and she answered that she never meant to take such an oath. When requested to explain why this was the case, she answered that it was more lawful and convenient for her to wear such clothes since she lived among men.[49] Though Joan was directly challenging males on their own turf, her cross dressing was simply a political excuse for her execution. Indeed, after her death, a change in popes led to a declaration of Joan's innocence in 1456, and, ultimately, she joined the other cross-dressing saints in being canonized (9 May 1920) as a holy maiden. She is one of the patron saints of France, and the only cross-dressing saint whose life is fully documented.

Though we have no other historical figure in the Middle Ages similar to the fighting Saint Joan, there is the significant fictional figure of the knight named Silence. Silence appears in *Le Roman de Silence,* a book written in the third quarter of the thirteenth century by Heldris de Cournuälle, but only rediscovered in the 1960s and finally published in 1972.[50] The romance is set during the reign of a mythical English king named Ebains who, as a result of a quarrel to the death between two counts over which twin heiress would inherit land around Chester, had ruled that no woman could inherit property during his reign. Cador, one of the king's knights, finds that his wife Euphemie is pregnant. Fearful that Euphemie would not become pregnant again and unwilling to give up the property to others, the two decide that, regardless of its sex, the child will be raised as a boy.

The inevitable happens, and the girl infant is named Silence (or Silentius as a male). Silence is raised jointly by a trusted seneschal, who has a son of his own, and Cador's aunt, a widow who recently lost her own infant daughter. As a child, Silence learns quickly and even teaches herself to read. She receives a strong moral upbringing from her aunt and under the seneschal's guidance becomes skilled in hunting, gymnastics, and the various chivalric arts. At the same time, she becomes one of Nature's most beautiful creatures. As she approaches adolescence, her father explains the reason and the need for her disguise. Silence accepts her lot but upon reaching puberty is torn by Nature, who urges her to be a woman, and Reason (what we might call nurture), who insists she remain a man. She is especially worried that, if her true sex is revealed some day, she would find herself entirely unskilled at all womanly pursuits. In the struggle, Reason prevails, and she continues to live as a man.

When two jongleurs spend some time in Cornwall, Silence, determined to learn more about the world, stains her face brown with nettle juice, and runs off with them to the Continent. There she soon surpasses her mentors in talent, skill, and popularity. Jealous of her increasing reputation, the two jongleurs plot to kill her, but she confronts them, takes half their earnings, and gradually works her way back to Cornwall.

In the meantime, her father, believing she had been kidnapped by the jongleurs, ordered that all jongleurs found in the county he governed be killed. Silence, unaware of this edict, is saved from execution because she is recognized by a birthmark on her right shoulder. Reconciled with her parents in Cornwall, she does not tarry there long before being called off to serve in the court of King Ebains, whose promiscuous queen, Eupheme, immediately falls in love with her and does her utmost to persuade Silence to become her lover. Silence repeatedly rebuffs the queen, and this so angers her that to gain revenge she tells the king that Silence had tried to seduce her. Apparently, Ebains was not unaware of what was going on but saves face by sending Silence off to the court of the king of France with a letter explaining what had happened. The queen intercepts the letter and changes it for one demanding Silence's immediate execution. But the king of France checks with Ebains about his intentions, and Silence is again saved. She is subsequently dubbed a knight and becomes one of the leading knights in Christiandom.

Ebains eventually recalls her to England to help him put down a rebellion, and though Silence does so, she again arouses the queen's passion, and the same scenario is repeated. This time, the queen persuades Ebains to send Silence into more or less permanent exile by sending her on a seemingly futile mission: to find the ancient sage Merlin, who is living as a wild man in the woods. But Silence succeeds in this task, where others before her had failed, because Merlin had declared earlier that only a woman would be able to capture him. Brought to the court by Silence, Merlin gives vent to outbursts of sardonic laughter on four different occasions: at a villein who has bought a new pair of boots, at a leper begging for alms, at a priest burying a child while the father laments, and, finally, at King Ebains, the queen, Silence, and a nun in the queen's entourage. The king demands that Merlin explain what humor he found in these situations or else face execution. Merlin replies that he laughed at the villein because he knew he would die before he reached home with his new shoes; he laughed at the leper begging for alms because he was sitting on a huge hidden treasure; he laughed at the father's grief because the priest burying the child had seduced the man's wife and was really the child's father. Finally, he laughed at Ebains' court because the nun, a man in disguise, was the queen's lover, and because Silence herself was a woman. The queen and the false nun are executed, while Silence is forced to explain the secret of her life to Ebains.

Silence, now called Silentia, is dressed as a woman, and:

On the third day after Nature
had regained her right,
she began to reembellish
Silence's whole body, and to remove
everything masculine about her.
She left no bit of weathered skin,
and she remarried together
the rose and the lily, beautifully.
The king then took her to wife
so says the story I find it in,
by the counsel of those princes
whom he loved and valued most.
And the count, Silence's father,
and Euphemie, her mother, came to the wedding.

> There was great joy, as there should be.
> Master Heldris says here and now
> that one should love a good woman more
> than one should hate or revile a bad one.
> And I would show you the true reason;
> for a woman has less opportunity
> to have the time and chance
> to be good than to be evil,
> if she works diligently against nature.[51]

The male impersonation theme elaborated with such complexity in the *Roman de Silence* ultimately becomes an increasingly popular one in folk literature.[52] But perhaps the ultimate put-down of women comes in the legends of sex changes, all of which involve changes from females to males. One such incident comes from the life of Saint Abban:

Now the king was old at this time, and he had no heir except a daughter whom his wife bore that very night. And he requested Abban to baptize her. And he [Abban] perceived the sadness of the king at having no heir. "If Gode pleases," said Abban, "thou shalt have an heir." "Nay," said the king, "that is impossible for me owing to my age." Abban took the infant in his hands, and prayed earnestly to God that the king might have an heir; and the girl that he immersed in the font he took out as a boy, and laid it in the king's bosom. "Here is thy son," said he. And the king was exceedingly glad.[53]

A similar miraculous change of sex was attributed to the intervention of Saint Gerald, Abbot of Lismore, while he was being held prisoner by a pagan king. In this case the king's only child, a daughter whom the king had raised as a son, had died. The king promised freedom to Saint Gerald as well as an abbey rich in lands and goods if he and his God could raise up his "son" from the dead. Gerald attempted to do so, requesting God to not only restore life but to raise up a male child. To the amazement of all, a real boy arose from the bier.[54] A similar miracle is attributed to Theodore of Appoldia.[55]

Cross dressing by men is treated differently than that among women, as the execution of the impostor nun in the *Roman de Silence* indicates. Significantly, there are no transvestite male saints. Not only did male cross dressers lose status, but it was generally believed that a man would impersonate a woman either in an attempt to insinuate himself into the confidence of women for sexual purposes or as part of a witchcraft ceremony. As indicated above, Saint Jerome's forced flight from Rome is an example of the former. So too is the case of a sixth-century group of nuns at the Frankish convent of Radegunde who charged the abbess with keeping a man in the convent by dressing him as a woman. Everyone knew, they claimed, that he "was most plainly of the male sex; and that this person regularly served the abbess." The investigation that followed found that, in fact, he was a male nun. He reported he had donned female garb because as a little boy he "had a disease of the groin" that was regarded as incurable. His mother had gone to the holy Radegunde (the founder of the convent), who had summoned a local surgeon, Reovalis, to deal with the case. Reovalis reported to the investigating committee that he "had cut out the testicles of the boy, an operation which in former days I had seen performed by surgeons at Constantinople." Apparently, the mother had then raised the boy as a girl, and he had later entered the convent where no one knew he was a man. The abbess was cleared of any misconduct, but the implication remained that the only reason a man might don female garb and live in a convent was to gain sexual favors from the nuns.[56]

Even more feared than attempts at seduction was the association of male cross dressing with witchcraft, perhaps a carryover of the association of paganism with cross dressing. One of the first indications of this is in the penitential of Silos, compiled in the ninth century at the Spanish monastery of the same name. Penitentials, as the term implies, specify the penances for various kind of sins.

Those who in the dance wear women's clothes and strange devices and employ jawbones and a bow and a spade and things like these shall do penance for one year.[57]

A Frankish penitential of the same period, that of Saint Hubert, includes a similar reference, but it stipulates a three-year penance.[58]

An incident of witchcraft was reported by an inquisitor in southern France around 1250. According to the report, a number of men disguised as women entered the house of a rich farmer, dancing and singing, "We take one and give back a hundred." The verse referred to a popular belief in the power of the "good people" (in Latin, *bonae*) to confer prosperity upon any house in which they had been given presents. The suspicious wife did not accept the claim of the female impersonators to be *bonae* and tried to end the revel, but despite her protestations, they carried away all the movable goods from her house. Perhaps for this as well as similar reasons bishops were requested to look out for throngs of demons transformed into women.[59]

Boundaries of Social Tolerance: Impersonation and the Theater

Though unauthorized male cross dressing was either feared as a sign of witchcraft or scorned, cross dressing was, if not officially permitted, at least tolerated under two conditions: when the person was clearly recognized as being a man or when the man performed a social function that, because of other prohibitions, women were not allowed to do. In effect, the status loss associated with male cross dressing was only allowed when other more dearly held values of society otherwise would have been threatened. An example of the first condition is the thirteenth-century report of Cypriot knights fighting in tournaments while dressed as women; although it was considered peculiar, it was not regarded as criminal.[60] The most detailed illustration of cross dressing that was clearly recognized for its impersonation, however, is the case of Ulrich von Lichtenstein, a thirteenth-century knight from Styria (now part of Austria). Ulrich is best remembered today for his narrative poem *Frauendienst,* or *Service of Ladies.*[61] Though the poem originally was regarded as a highly reliable autobiography, modern scholars are not so sure. Some regard it as a fictional comedy, perhaps a predecessor to Cervantes's *Don Quixote.* Certainly those scholars who have attempted to authenticate some of the events depicted in the poem have had difficulty documenting them. One of the most remarkable of Ulrich's adventures supposedly took place in 1226–1227. Ulrich, in order to honor his lady and all women, disguised himself as the goddess Venus and traveled from Venice through northern Italy and into Styria and Bohemia (modern Czechoslovakia). To begin his tour he traveled to Italy in the fall of 1226 where he spent the winter gathering a retinue of servants who did not know and, therefore, could not betray his identity. He set out on 15 April 1227, dressed in dazzling white raiment and accompanied by a splendidly attired retinue of twenty.

Supporters of the autobiographical theory have advanced several explanations as to how a nobleman could travel for a month through several countries dressed as a woman, even wearing long braids, without any of the hundreds of knights he met and jousted with thinking him ridiculous or finding the situation at all humorous. Many have argued that the thirteenth century, saturated with chivalry and Arthurian romance, would have accepted the symbolism of Ulrich's journey in much the same way as modern music lovers do not judge a romantic opera by the standards of everyday reality. Others believe that the masquerade was not taken seriously but would have been received as a carnival, a light entertainment, a magnificent stunt. Others who believe the journey is factual feel the author used poetic license in describing it.

Before setting out, Ulrich had announced his intention to joust as Venus and gave the dates of his planned appearances. He described himself:

My cloak was velvet and was white
as was my hat, but this was bright
with many pearls on every side.
My loving heart was filled with pride
that I should serve my lady now
with knightly deeds and keep my vow.

The braids I had were thick and brown
and were so long that they hung down
below my sash, just like a girl's.
They too were richly decked with pearls
and in a most artistic way.
My heart has seldom been so gay.
Nobody ever owned before
a fairer skirt than that I wore.

I had a white and glossy shirt
which was as long as was the skirt
with woman's sleeve of quality
that made me proud as I could be.
My gloves were silk and finely made.
Attired like this and unafraid
I left the sea, as I had vowed,
and soon collected quite a crowd.[62]

Apparently, some quickly perceived that Ulrich was not a woman.
Before one joust he was kissed by a countess, but had to remove his veil
for her to do so. When he did,

The charming lady then began
to laugh and said, "Why you're a man!
I caught a glimpse of you just now.
What then? I'll kiss you anyhow.
From all good women everywhere
I'll give a kiss. Because you wear
a woman's dress and honor thus
us all, I'll kiss for all of us."[63]

Another woman gave him a skirt to add to his wardrobe and wrote him
a letter addressed to Noble Venus.

All ladies everywhere should be
grateful that you in friendliness

have put on you a woman's dress
and thereby honored womankind.[64]

Most of the people on his tour got into the act, and women seemed to be particularly impressed. There is no question that Ulrich thoroughly enjoyed his adventure. Whether fictional or historical, his adventures seem to be unique for the time. Still, the poem's existence would seem to indicate that comedic cross dressing was probably more widespread than surviving historical records suggest.

One area in which men were given Church sanction to dress as women was on the stage. Theater was almost nonexistent during the early Middle Ages in the West. Its fierce denunciation by some of the early Church Fathers was a factor in its decline, but also important was the decline of the major urban centers. Undoubtedly, some wandering mimes or *histriones* (actors) continued to practice their theatrical craft, but their tradition merged into that of the wandering minstrel. When drama did appear again, it was through the agency of the Christian Church, just as religion had been the basis for Greek and Roman drama. As religious ceremonies and rituals grew more elaborate, symbolic ceremonies and representations came to form part of the service, particularly on special holy days. These representations began with simple tableaux, such as a crib with Mary and Joseph at the side of the altar during Christmas services, and then gradually became more elaborate, developing into mystery plays (dramatic presentations of biblical stories), miracle plays (depicting miracles of the saints), and passion plays (depicting the events of Passion week and culminating in a re-enactment of the crucifixion and resurrection at Easter).[65] Usually, boys or men played the women's parts since the roles originally were performed in the church by clergy or individuals in minor clerical orders (lector, porter, exorciser, acolyte). Women had no role in the services and offices of the church, and as nonclergy were not permitted beyond the railing of the altar.

There are occasional glimpses of some of these early actors. There was an adolescent boy at Metz who performed the role of Saint Barbara so "thoughtfully and reverently that several persons wept for pity; for he showed such fluency of elocution and such polite manners, and his countenance and gestures were so expressive when among his maidens, that there was not a nobleman or priest or layman who did not wish to receive this youth into his house to feed and educate him; among whom there was a rich widow . . . who wanted to adopt him as her heir."[66] The youth's reputation as a female impersonator, however, was short-lived because the next year, when he acted the part of another woman saint, his voice had changed and the audience was not as impressed. He soon abandoned his acting career and went off to Paris to study for the priesthood.

As the pageants became more popular and important to the public, they moved away from the Church, and responsibility for them was taken over by local guilds. The guilds tended to preserve the all-male character of the plays, since most guild members were men, although women were not entirely excluded, and there are occasional references to them. Each guild specialized in plays suitable to the crafts they represented. In many English cities, the vintners performed the Marriage at Cana (where wine was served), and the shipwrights presented Noah and his ark. Gradually, more stories from the Bible were dramatized.

Celebrations associated with special occasions also contributed to the development of drama. Seasonal changes were often marked by rituals involving dancing, feasting, mock weddings, mock fights, and impersonations in which boys played the role of bishops. Several popular folktales were also enacted, and some—including those associated with the Abbeys of Misrule in France and northern Italy, the French Feast of the Fools, and the English Saint Stephen's Day celebration—involved men who burlesqued women. Similarly, the English festivities associated with Maid Marian and others involved cross dressing.[67]

That the individuals involved took these plays seriously is indicated by a passing reference of Sir John Paston, a member of a Norfolk family whose letters have been preserved. In 1473, Paston wrote about the defection of a servant who had been with him for two years, because the man wanted to play "St. George, Robin Hood, and the Sheriff of Nottingham."[68]

Since the role of women in these early plays was mostly a passive one, boys could easily stand in for women. The three Marys, for example, are usually inactive or silent, and a choirboy could carry off the part. One or two women characters, however, had larger roles that demanded some skill in impersonation, but such roles usually involved burlesques of women, as in the case of Noah's wife, who was always represented as a nagging shrew and gossip. She disapproves of what her husband is doing and even refuses to board the ship at the crucial moment. Her reasons are usually trivial, although they seem to be of vital importance to her.[69] According to Roger Baker, in reading these parts,

it does not need much imagination to feel that here are the rudimentary beginnings of the pantomime dame tradition, and that continual theme of the tough normal man who enjoys dressing up as a grotesque woman—a phenomenon [still] found in improvised work shows, among rugger teams and regiments. Anywhere, in fact, where men are together.[70]

As the theater increased in popularity, more secular plays and professional actors emerged as well. These actors were usually wandering players (that is, vagabonds) who were more or less outcasts, and like the more organized minstrel companies, they were overwhelmingly male. Men thus continued to enact women's roles—in England almost exclusively—and they were not condemned for this, since actors were already regarded as low-status persons who existed outside the recognized caste system.[71]

Male cross dressing was also permitted during festivals or carnivals during which the usual standards of behavior were laid aside. Although few of these medieval carnivals have been studied in detail, we know that women often were allowed to act male roles and men were allowed to impersonate women. During the Nuremburg festivals of the late medieval period, a number of male dancers wore feminine masks and probably also dressed as women. In fact, it seems to be such a common phenomenon that one authority has said that, as mentioned earlier, disguising oneself as the opposite sex was a custom "peculiar to all carnivals." A standard feature of the Nuremburg carnivals, for example, was the "Wild Woman," a man who impersonated a deranged-looking woman; several fifteenth-century illustrations of such impersonations have survived.[72] Carnivals and festivals removed many social status inhibitions since they allowed for boy bishops and peasant kings, as well as cross dressers. The cross-dressing aspects of such festivals have continued down to present-day Mardi Gras festivals in New Orleans and elsewhere, the Mummer's Parade in Philadelphia on New Year's, and even the sanitized version of Halloween that many Americans celebrate.

Late Medieval Redefinition of Gender Ideals

Though no male cross dressers became saints, there was a reassessment of some of the stereotypical gender attributes in the later Middle Ages, particularly among the Cistercian monks. Their thinking is characterized by an elevation of the feminine aspect through emphasizing the compassionate and tender love of God. Churches everywhere in Europe were dedicated to the Virgin Mary, and the maternal imagery of medieval monastic treatises written by cloistered monks indicate that they idealized the mothering role. Rather than redefining masculinity, they grafted feminine qualities onto the male, and Jesus came to be visualized as a mother, as was the abbot of a monastery.[73] The Cistercians distinguished between female sexuality, conceived as a biological given, and femininity, a gender quality, thereby emphasizing what many current gender specialists stress: that "female" and "feminine" are not the same concepts and that so-called feminine qualities can be adopted and incorporated by males and vice versa. Although the theologians of late antiquity and the early Middle Ages were unable to separate the female from the feminine and had defined ideals in terms of masculine characteristics, many later medieval writers recognized the value of some feminine qualities and tried to incorporate them into their masculine personae. This modification had little effect on the roles or everyday lives of women or men, or even on clerical attitudes toward females, but it serves to emphasize that the separation of gender qualities from sexual aspects has a long history and tradition in the West.

Some of this idea was reflected in medieval attitudes toward cross dressing, particularly as they affected women. Only when cross dressing went beyond the tolerated levels and threatened the status quo, as happened with Joan of Arc, or when it took on too much of an erotic appeal, as in the case of a man disguising himself as a woman in order to live in a convent, was there public reaction to it. Male cross dressers, however, were treated differently from female ones. A female who might try to pass as a man was not considered abnormal. That a female might desire to be a male, in fact, seemed to be a healthy desire, a "normal" longing not unlike the desire of a peasant to become a noble. This did not mean that either women or peasants were allowed to cross the status lines in great numbers but that the desire to do so was accepted as a norm. Though men might dress as women at carnivals, and the lord might mix with the peasants at various festivals, the status loss in any real change along these lines was so threatening that anything more than play-acting was forbidden. Even the monks who emphasized the mothering qualities of the abbot were very conscious that he was a male. On the other hand, women who were successful in changing their female identities were not stigmatized but instead accepted, and not a few became saints. Throughout the literature of the time, even that written by such women as Anna Comnena in the twelfth century, the most desirable characteristics in a female, once the superficial aspects of appearance were dealt with, were masculine qualities, that is, the qualities of a masculine mind. Anna believed that women had valuable attributes—devotion, love, beauty, and so on— but that the woman who was most likely to succeed was the woman who acted and thought most like a man. In crises, women were supposed to act "manly" and not show any "womanly and cowardly feeling." In describing the death of her father, Anna wrote about the "manliness" of her mother:

Always in former perils also the Empress had a manly mind, but especially on this occasion did she play the man. Though deeply moved by the feeling of grief, she stood like an Olympic victor wrestling against those keenest pains. For she was pierced in soul and troubled in heart by the sight of the Emperor's state, yet she braced herself and stood firm against trials. And though she received mortal wounds and the pain of them entered into her marrow, yet she resisted.[74]

Summary

Quite clearly, manliness in women if not carried too far was much admired. Masculine qualities were considered admirable, although some feminine qualities were also much admired. Men could, at least if they were monks, strive to adopt some of the feminine attributes, but they did not need cross dressing to do so. Men who both cross dressed and acted feminine were stigmatized, and their actions were linked with deviant eroticism or, in more modern times, with psychopathology. In this view, such men were aberrant, while women who cross dressed were only striving to reach a higher status. This implies that at least one root cause of Western hostility toward male cross dressing is fear of status loss. It also explains why, since female cross dressers gain status, there are so few female cross dressers in the psychological literature.

Society, in fact, traditionally encouraged women to assume male roles as a sign of their superiority to other women and only rarely regarded such women as abnormal. Only when women threatened the male establishment by taking a too overtly masculine role have they been ostracized in the past. By implication, then, if an undercurrent of status loss in assuming a woman's role still prevails in Western society, and studies of women's occupations such as nursing indicate that it does,[75] then we must also take into account a desire for status loss, either permanent or temporary, as a possible factor in male transvestism today. It also helps to explain why women cannot only act the role of men but also adopt men's clothing, whereas men have much more difficulty adopting a woman's role or clothing.

Notes

1. Deut. 22:5. This is from the Revised Standard Version, but the verse is the same in most translations.
2. This appears in the *Grágás*, ll. 203–4, and is cited in Jenny Jochens, "Before the Male Gaze: The Absence of the Female Body in Old Norse," in *Sex in the Middle Ages*, ed. Joyce E. Salisbury (New York: Garland Publishing, 1991), 9. Though there are Scandinavian editions of these laws, only the first half of one of the collections has been translated: Andrew Dennis, Peter Foote, and

Richard Perkins, *Laws of Early Iceland: Grágás* (Winnipeg: University of Manitoba, 1980).

3. Aristotle, *Historia animalium* 608 B, trans. D'Arcy W. Thompson in *The Works of Aristotle* (Oxford: Clarendon Press, 1910), vol. 4. See also Aristotle, *Politics* 1.2 (1242 B), ed. and trans. H. Rackham (London: Heinemann, 1944).

4. Aristotle, *Generation of Animals*, 729 A, 25–34, trans. A. L. Peck (London: Heinemann, 1953).

5. Aristotle, *Generation of Animals*, 728A, 17ff.

6. Aristotle, *Generation of Animals*, 766A, 1935.

7. Thomas Aquinas, *Summa theologica*, trans. Fathers of the English Dominican Province (New York: Benziger Brothers, 1947), part 1, question 92, "The Production of Women," article 2.

8. Ibid., part 3, question 32.

9. Soranus, *Gynecology*, trans. Owsei Temkin (Baltimore: Johns Hopkins University Press, 1956), bk. 3.1.2.5.

10. Ibid., bk. 3.1.5.

11. Averroës, *Commentary on Plato's* Republic, trans. E. I. J. Rosenthal (Cambridge: Cambridge University Press, 1956), 164–65.

12. Isidoris, *Etymologiarum sive originum libri XX*, ed. W. M. Lindsay (Oxford: Clarendon Press, 1911).

13. Isidorus, *Etymologiarum*, 11.140.

14. Soranus, *Gynecology*, 1.6.27–29.

15. Aquinas, *Summa theologica*, part 3, question 31, article 6, *ad tertium*.

16. Galen, *On the Usefulness of the Parts of the Body (De usu partium)*, trans. Margaret Tallmade May (Ithaca, NY: Cornell University Press, 1968), 14.6 in 2:628–30.

17. Pliny, *Natural History*, trans. H. Rackham (London: Heinemann, 1968), 7.4, 31.23, and 17.37. See also Diodorus Siculus, *Histories*, trans. C. H. Oldfather (London: Heinemann, 1933), 32:12.

18. George W. Corner, *Anatomical Text of the Earlier Middle Ages* (Washington, DC: Carnegie Institution, 1927). For others, see Vern L. Bullough, "Medieval Medical and Scientific View of Women," *Viator* 4 (1973): 485–501.

19. *On the Properties of Things: John Trevisa's Translation of Bartholomaeus Anglicus. De proprietatibus rerum: A Critical Text*, ed. M. C. Seymour (Oxford: Clarendon Press, 1975), 5:48.

20. Philo, *Questions and Answers on Genesis*, trans. Ralph Marcus (London: Heinemann, 1961); *On the Creation*, trans. F. H. Colson and G. H. Whittaker (London: Heinemann, 1963); and esp. Richard A. Baer, *Philo's Use of the Categories Male and Female* (Leiden: E. J. Brill, 1970).

21. Vern L. Bullough, Brenda Shelton, and Sarah Slavin, *The Subordinated Sex* (Athens, GA: University of Georgia, 1988), 96–97.

22. Saint Jerome, *Commentarius in Epistolam ad Ephasios*, book 16, col. 567 in *Patrologia Latina*, ed. J. P. Migne, vol. 26 (Paris: Garnier, 1884). This particular letter is not in the Loeb Library English translation (St. Jerome, *Select Letters*, ed. and trans. F. A. Wright [London: Heinemann, 1933]). There is, however, a letter dealing with his views on marriage in that edition which more or less states the same thing. See ibid., 22:20.

23. Jerome, *Letters*, LIV and CVII, and also *Against Helvidus*, trans. John N. Hritz, *The Fathers of the Church* (Washington, DC: Catholic University of America, 1948), vol. 53.

24. Ambrose, *Expositionis in evangelius secundum Lucum libri X*, book 15, col.

1938 in *Patrologia Latina,* ed. J. P. Migne (Paris: Garnier Fratres, 1887), vol. 15.

25. Eugene F. Rice, Jr., *Saint Jerome in the Renaissance* (Baltimore: Johns Hopkins University Press, 1985), 28–29. There is an illustration of this incident by Jean de Limbourg, dating from 1408–9, which appears in the book.

26. James Brundage, *Law, Sex, and Christian Society in Medieval Europe* (Chicago: University of Chicago Press, 1987), 108.

27. G. D. Mansi, ed., *Sacorum conciliorum et monumentorum historicorum, dogmaticorum, moralium amplissima collectio,* 60 vols. (Paris: Hubert Welter, 1901–27), 2:1101; JoAnn McNamara, "Muffled Voices: The Lives of Consecrated Women in the Fourth Century," in *Distant Echoes,* vol. 1 of *Medieval Religious Women,* ed. John A. Nichols and Lillian Thomas Shank, Cistercian Studies Series, no. 71 (Kalamazoo, MI: Cistercian Publications, 1984), 23–24.

28. For two early discussions of this, see John Anson, "The Female Transvestite in Early Monasticism: The Origin and Development of a Motif," *Viator* 5 (1974): 1–32, and Vern L. Bullough, "Transvestites in the Middle Ages: A Sociological Analysis," *American Journal of Sociology* 79 (1974): 1381–94. This last was reprinted in Vern L. Bullough, *Sex, Society, and History* (New York: Science History, [Neale Watson] 1976). A more recent study is Valerie R. Hotchkiss, "Clothes Make the Man: Female Transvestism in the Middle Ages," unpublished Ph.D. dissertation, Yale University, 1990.

29. Her story is rather confused and contradictory, probably because her life incorporates several conflicting legends. She is known both as Pelagia and as Margaritó and is also confused with another saint, Margarita, who is also known as Pelagia. We have simplified the story here. Where possible, we have used English accounts of saints' lives so that the non-Latin specialist can follow the sources. For Pelagia, see A. Butler, *Butler's Lives of the Saints,* edited, revised, and supplemented by Herbert Thurston and Donald Attwater (New York: Kennedy, 1956), 4:59–61. See also Helen Waddell, *The Desert Fathers* (reprint, Ann Arbor: University of Michigan Press, [1936] 1957), 171–88.

30. *Butler's Lives of the Saints,* 4:59–61.

31. Ibid., 1:313–14.

32. H. Usener, *Legends der Heiligen Pelagia* (Bonn: A. Marcus, 1879).

33. H. Delehay, *The Legends of the Saints,* trans. V. M. Crawford (Notre Dame, IN: University of Notre Dame Press, 1961), 204–6.

34. Marie Delcourt, *Hermaphrodite,* trans. Jennifer Nicholson (London: Studio, 1956), 90–99.

35. *Butler's Lives of the Saints,* 4:69–70.

36. Ibid., 1:33.

37. Ibid., 4:612.

38. Ibid., 1:4–5.

39. Ibid., 3:623–25.

40. Ibid., 2:546–47.

41. Ibid., 2:135.

42. Ibid., 3:538, 623–25. For the cases of Saint Thecla and Saint Natalia, the transvestite experience is only incidental.

43. Ibid., 3:151–52.

44. Gillian Edwards, *Uncumber and Pantaloon* (New York: Dutton, 1969). A more scholarly, albeit unpublished, study has been done by Elizabeth Nightlinger, a professor of art history at Marymount University in Arlington, VA. She has a series of papers on women and hirsutism: "Medieval Manifestation

of the Survival of the Bearded Aphrodite and Other Androgynous Cults," "Some Contributions of Cross-Cultural Iconographic and Folkloric Tradition to Early Medieval Hagiography," "The Bearded Aphrodite and Other Androgynous Deities: Images of Divine Unity," and "Cross-Cultural Aspects of Androgyny and Sacred Female Hirsutism." She has kindly sent us copies of her papers, and those interested in the subject might write her. She has many illustrations. Hopefully, these will be part of a forthcoming book.

45. *Butler's Lives of the Saints*, 4:36–37.

46. *Acta Sanctorum*, February, vol. 3, col. 174. There are various publishers of this series, which began in 1643 in Antwerp and continued on at Paris, is still in progress.

47. Johann Döllinger, *Papstfabeln des Mittelalters*, 2d ed. (Munich: Cotta, 1863); Alexander Cooke, *Pope Joan* (London: Blunt and Barin, 1610); Clement Wood, *The Woman Who Was Pope* (New York: Faro, 1931).

48. W. P. Barrett, *Trial of Jeanne d'Arc* (London: Routledge, 1933), 152.

49. Ibid., 158.

50. The romance exists only in one manuscript, Mi.LM.6, deposited on loan in the Muniments Room of the University of Nottingham. *Le roman de Silence* comprises folios 181–223. It was first published in a series of articles by Lewis Thorpe in *Nottingham Medieval Studies* 5 (1961): 33–74; 6 (1962): 18–69; 7 (1963): 34–52; 8 (1964): 33–61; 10 (1966): 25–69; 11 (1967): 19–56. These articles were brought together in book form and amplified by Lewis Thorpe, *Le Roman de Silence: A Thirteenth-Century Arthurian Verse-Romance by Heldris de Cornuälle* (Cambridge: W. Heffer, 1972). Thorpe summarizes the romance on pp. 17–22. It was translated into modern English by Regina Psaki. See Heldris de Cournuälle, *Le Roman de Silence*, trans. Regina Psaki, Garland Library of Medieval Literature, vol. 63 (New York: Garland, 1991). We wish to thank William Jordan for sending us information about the manuscript.

51. For other accounts of Silence, see Kathleen J. Brahney, "When Silence Was Golden: Female Personae in the *Roman de Silence*," in *The Spirit of the Court: Selected Proceedings of the Fourth Congress of the International Courtly Literature Society (1983)*, ed. Glyn S. Burgess and Robert A. Taylor (Exeter: D. S. Brewer, 1985), 52–61; Peter Allen, "The Ambiguity of Silence: Gender, Writing, and *Le Roman de Silence*," in *Sign, Sentence, Discourse: Language in Medieval Thought and Literature*, ed. Julian N. Wasserman and Lois Roney (Syracuse, NY: Syracuse University Press, 1989), 98–112. There is a rapidly expanding literature on the *Roman*.

52. See Stith Thompson, *Motif Index of Folk Literature: A Classification of Narrative Elements in Folktales, Ballads, Myths, Fables, Mediaeval Romances, Exempla, Fabliaux, Jest-Books, and Local Legends*, revised and enlarged edition, 6 vols. (Bloomington: Indiana University Press, 1955–56). Thompson used subject categories such as transformations to persons of different sex (D10) and other kinds of transformation (D11, D11.1, D12, D624.3, D658.3, and D658.3.1), witchcraft (T332), cross dressing as punishment (Q551.5.1.1), seduction (K1321), and escape (K521.4.1). Some of these were examined by Hotchkiss, *Clothes Make the Man*.

53. *Bethada Náem nérenn: Lives of Irish Saints*, ed. and trans. Charles Plummer (Oxford: Clarendon Press, 1922), 2:8, xiii (28).

54. See G. G. Coulton, *Life in the Middle Ages* (Cambridge: Cambridge University Press, 1967), 1:8–9.

55. *Acta Sanctorum,* Augusti (4 August), 1:652. We are indebted to Jane Schulenberg for these three references.

56. Gregory of Tours, *History of the Franks,* trans. O. M. Dalton (Oxford: Clarendon Press, 1927), 2:449.

57. John T. McNeil and Helen Gamer (ed. and trans.), *Medieval Handbooks of Penance* (New York: Columbia University Press, 1938), 289, no. XI.

58. F. H. Wasserschleben, *Die Bussornungen der abendläischen Kirche* (reprinted, Graz, Austria: Akademische Druck-U. Verlagsanstal, [1851] 1958), 383, cap. 42. Interestingly, in this penitential there is also a prohibition against women cross dressing.

59. Jeffrey Burton Russell, *Witchcraft in the Middle Ages* (Ithaca, NY: Cornell University Press, 1972), 157, 292, 315.

60. Brundage, *Law, Sex, and Christian Society,* 473.

61. The narrative first appeared in print in 1812: Ulrich von Lichtenstein, *Frauendienst, oder: Geschichte und Liebe des Ritters und Sängers,* trans. Ludwig Tieck (Stuttgart, 1812). It was translated in condensed form into English verse by J. W. Thomas: *Ulrich von Lichtenstein's Service of Ladies,* University of North Carolina Studies in Germanic Languages and Literature, No. 63 (Chapel Hill: University of North Carolina Press, 1969).

62. Thomas, *Service of Ladies,* p. 102, quatrains 487–89.

63. Ibid., p. 110, quatrain 538.

64. Ibid., p. 122, quatrain 604.

65. For further amplification, see E. K. Chambers, *English Literature at the Close of the Middle Ages* (Oxford: Oxford University Press, 1947), and Karl Mantzius, *A History of Theatrical Art,* trans. Louise von Cossel (New York: Peter Smith, 1937).

66. Mantzius, *A History of Theatrical Art,* 2:89.

67. See Natalie Zemon Davis, "Women on Top: Symbolic Inversion and Political Disorder in Early Modern Europe," in *The Reversible World,* ed. Barbara Babcock (Ithaca, NY: Cornell University Press, 1978), 165–66; E. P. Thompson, " 'Rough Music': Le charivari anglais," *Annales: Économies, Sociétés, Civilisations* 27 (1972): 186–217; and Valerie Lucas, "*Hic Mulier:* The Female Transvestite in Early Modern England," *Renaissance and Reformation,* 24 (1988): 65–84.

68. *The Paston Letters,* ed. John Fenn and re-edited by Mrs. Archer Hind (London: J. M. Dent, 1924), 2:132–33, Letter CCCXXXVI, "Servant Troubles, etc.," dated 16 April 1473.

69. There are many editions of the Chester Plays, including several published at different times by the Early English Text Society. See *The Chester Plays,* ed. H. Deimling and G. W. Matthew (London: Kegan Paul, Trench, Trübner, 1893, 1916), vols. 61 and 115, and *The Chester Plays,* ed. R. M. Lumiansky and David Mills (London: Oxford University Press, 1974–76), SS vols. 3 and 9. The Wakefield Plays were often in the past called the Townley Plays. See *The Townley Cycle,* ed. G. England and A. W. Pollard for the Early English Text Society (London: Kegan Paul, Trench, Trübner, 1897), vol. 71. For a later edition, see *The Wakefield Mystery Plays,* ed. H. Rose (New York: W. W. Norton, 1969).

70. Roger Baker, *Drag: A History of Female Impersonation on Stage* (London: Triton Books, 1968), 58.

71. J. J. Jusserand, *English Wayfaring Life in the Middle Ages,* trans. Lucy Toulmin Smith (London: Unwin, n.d.), 177–218.

72. Samuel L. Sumberg, *The Nuremburg Schembart Carnival* (New York: AMS, 1966).

73. A number of scholars, from Henry Adams at the turn of the century to a number of modern feminists, have explored this in greater detail. A good starting point is Caroline Walker Bynum, *Jesus as Mother: Studies in Spirituality in the High Middle Ages* (Berkeley: University of California Press, 1982), 110–69.

74. Anna Comnena, *Alexiad*, trans. Elizabeth A. S. Dawes (London: Kegan Paul, Trench, Trübner, 1928), XV, ii.

75. Vern L. Bullough and Bonnie Bullough, *Care of the Sick: The Emergence of Modern Nursing*, 3d ed. (New York: Science History (Neale Watson) Prodist, 1978).

Chapter 4
Playing with Gender: Cross Dressing in the Sixteenth and Seventeenth Centuries

Cross dressing and impersonation, or playing with gender,[1] was an increasingly important theme in the sixteenth and seventeenth centuries, emphasizing that gender differences were more flexible than they appeared. Festivals and recreation in which women held authority, gender was masked, and the conventional rules of society were reversed, increased in number. The mythical Amazon, the genuine hermaphrodite, the playful impersonation became titillating topics, a form of erotic pursuit.[2]

The anthropologist Victor Turner in his study of preliterate societies argued that the "masking of the weak in aggressive strength" and the concomitant "masking of the strong in humility and passivity" are devices used to cleanse society of its structurally engendered "sins" or what in modern terms might colloquially be called hangups. Invariably, at the end of the festival or special occasion, there is a sober return to a now purged and reanimated structure.[3]

What is true for primitive societies has also proved to be true throughout Western culture. Halloween, an amalgam of a number of pre-Christian festivals marking the end of the harvest season, traditionally has been such a time in which barriers have been dropped. In both the Anglo-Saxon calendar and the Celtic calendar, 31 October also marked the end of the year and was closely associated with the dead and the hellish powers of witchcraft. Masques and revelries and gender-merging were part of the festivities. Similarly, the festivals at the beginning of spring, symbolized in much of the Christian world by Lent and Easter, represented another occasion during which role and status reversals could take place. In Western Christian culture, this dropping of the hierarchical structure is now associated with the pre-Lenten festival of Mardi Gras.

Ceremonies marking significant transitions, such as marriage, also involved gender experimentation, probably as a continuation of ancient fertility rituals. An example is the disguised bride ritual in early modern Wales: On the night before the wedding, a few of the bridegroom's friends

proceed to the bride's house to see if she is safe, where her friends conceal her for a time, either by dressing her in man's apparel, or by putting her in some obscure place; but after some pretended difficulty, she is at length discovered when they sit down, and after spending the evening merrily depart home.[4]

Mumming, which involved men dressed like women and women like men going from house to house, also remained common during the Christmas season in England.[5] Similarly, carnival festivals on the Continent tolerated considerable gender role reversal, although it did not always involve cross dressing. During the Feast of Saint Agatha (5 February), Spanish women were allowed to dominate, giving orders that men obeyed.[6] At carnival time in Nuremberg, men were relegated to the house and domestic chores while women were allowed greater freedom.[7]

Still there was concern over cross dressing, some of which is expressed officially in court cases involving cross-dressing women, even during carnival time. In 1578, a certain Susan Bastwick from Standon was forced to ask her father's forgiveness because on All Saints' Day she had disguised herself as a man on horseback and demanded that he give her good ale. In 1585, a woman servant in Littlebury was accused of wearing "man's apparel" in her master's house. In 1592 the wife of Jacob Cornwall of Terlin was accused of unchastity; part of the evidence against her was that she wore a young man's garters. Another woman was accused of going contrary to "God's law" by putting on men's apparel and going forth from one house to another.[8] Despite such cases, however, female cross dressing generally aroused less hostility than did male cross dressing.

The Stage Tradition Continues

A major exception to this hostility toward male cross dressing was the continued female impersonation on the stage, even after drama had moved outside the realm of the churches. At first, secular plays used movable stages which were dragged through the streets on festivals; performances occurred at certain places along the set route. Thus, an audience could settle in one place and watch a succession of episodes as first one and then another of the portable stages stopped to present its show. Most of the characters in these plays were essentially caricatures who adopted exaggerated gestures and received visual punishments or rewards. In these very broad dramas, men could easily play the female role.

As theater continued to develop in complexity, the custom of female parts being played by men continued, but with new justifications for maintaining the old tradition. It was argued that the stage was not a suitable place for a "proper" woman since no proper woman would make such a display of herself. Since female characters appeared in the plays, however, the choice was to have "improper" women or men in drag play the parts. In many areas, particularly in England, men continued to play these roles even after the stage developed into a separate and more permanent structure. However, in Spain, where both men and women played women's roles for a time in the sixteenth century, women became more prominent sooner than in England. And, although the women outside of England who appeared onstage were not generally regarded as "respectable," this did not prevent them from appearing onstage or becoming popular. Why, then, did males in England continue to play women for so long?

The hypotheses are many and varied. Stephen Greenblatt has argued that an all-male acting troupe was the natural and unremarkable product of a culture whose conception of gender was simply "teleologically male," that is, women were regarded as being imperfectly formed or incomplete men. This, according to Greenblatt, meant that in the sixteenth century there could really only be one sex—male—and that modern notions of sexual difference developed only later.[9] This theory, however, ignores the gender experimentation that was taking place during the same period, as well as the fact that on the Continent, women in the sixteenth century increasingly played female roles (even though most Europeans had much the same assumptions about women).

Lisa Jardine has argued that the public theater of the time was really designed for the gratification of male spectators and that the boy actors aroused homoerotic passions in their male audience.[10] The association of the male "actress" with homosexuality is not something that modern critics originated; it was also discussed by contemporaries, although sometimes in veiled and ambiguous terms. Still, the implication that all the males' homoerotic passions were aroused does not correspond with what we know about human nature. Most of them could more easily have been aroused by women actors.

Stephen Orgel claimed that the suggestion of homosexuality on the English stage by female impersonators was probably less threatening than heterosexuality since it was less likely to happen and, therefore, was easier to desexualize. In effect, men were more afraid of women's sexuality than they were of homosexuality.[11] This theory, however, ignores the fact that there was great anxiety in England about the consequences of cross dressing young boys. Laura Levine, for example, has pointed out that behind at least some of the criticism of the stage by Puritans and others was the fear that boy actors would be made effeminate by wearing women's clothing, that gender was not immutable and the male was vulnerable—a rather frightening thought to many males.[12]

It is more likely that the answer depends on how—or whether—theatrical practice was thought to represent real life. If theater is visualized as pure fantasy, the sex of the actors might well be irrelevant in any performance.[13] Conceivably, then, English actors played women's roles merely because it had become the custom; once established, it became difficult to change. As actors' organizations became more powerful, they had a strong vested interest in maintaining the custom in England but were less able to do so on the Continent, where there was greater outside pressure by the royalty and other powerful individuals to include women than existed in England.

And, certainly, many of the plays of the time allowed both men and women to fantasize about changes in gender identity without having to change genders themselves.[14] The gender-change fantasizing made possible by theatrical impersonations in England might well have allowed the gender roles to undergo change without seeming to threaten the status quo.[15] This is emphasized by the fact that almost all of the female characters who disguise themselves as men in the plays (and are known to be in disguise by the audience) willingly resume their true gender role by the end of the play, after having their fling at being more dominant in society. This allows the fantasy to approach what was perceived to be reality, that assertive and aggressive women are able (and willing?) to adapt themselves to traditional male expectations once they meet the right man.[16] Shakespeare's *Taming of the Shrew* is an obvious example of this theme, but surely the play's resolution would have been just as effective if a woman had played the part in its original performances.

The continuance of the English male "actress" effectively demonstrates that the meaning of cross dressing has changed according to the societal values of any given time. Certainly, playing a woman's role in a Shakespearean drama is quite different and more demanding for the male actor than appearing as a woman in a tableau or burlesquing a woman in a Noah play. In addition, the demands of these roles increased in relation to the growing professionalization of the actors. By the time of Queen Elizabeth at the end of the sixteenth century, first-rate female impersonation was required if the play were to be successful. Although it would have been far easier to allow women to play these roles, self-appointed community watchdogs, determined to see that female purity was preserved, made change difficult. But as Puritan hostility to the theater grew stronger, there was a real quandary among some as to whether women appearing on stage was as dangerous as having men play women's roles. Just how much a society's perception of proper gender roles is culturally created is emphasized by an incident during the reign of Charles I (1625–49). Charles's wife, Queen Henrietta Maria, invited a theatrical company from her native France to appear in England, and the female actresses scandalized the English audience. One Englishman who steadfastly opposed the theater, William Prynne, went so far as to write that the actresses were "unwomanish and graceless."[17]

Prynne, however, was simply hostile to any kind of theater, and it was just this atmosphere of animosity that made change so difficult. Prynne was the most vocal Puritan to denounce the stage, and his *Histrio-Mastix: The Players Scourge, or, Actors Tragaedie* (1633) is a one-thousand-page diatribe against it. Key to his attack was the belief that God's wrath would be provoked if actors were allowed to appear as women, since this was expressly forbidden by the Scriptures. But Prynne's invocation of scripture was simply a subterfuge by which he could continue to attack the theater. For him, the plays themselves were "evil" because the "wanton" gestures of the actors and the "ravishing" music kindled a "very hell of lusts" in the spectators; clearly, no good could come from attendance at the theater.[18]

Theater defenders dismissed Prynne's arguments outright, including his citation of Scriptures. Ben Jonson (1572–1637) in *Bartholamew Fair* referred to Prynne's biblical opposition to cross dressing as an old, "stale argument against the players."[19] Jonson's response also emphasized the defense of female impersonators on the English stage by the playwrights themselves.

But Prynne's criticism was also more than Puritan hostility toward theater; it was also a protest against the blurring of gender and status distinctions that he perceived to be taking place in England. Newly enacted repressive legislation in England and elsewhere regulated dress in order to keep people in their social places. Dress was perceived as a major way of distinguishing one social group from another, as well as one sex from another. In "a highly regulated semiotic system," dress had became a major battleground for the struggle "over the mutability of social orders."[20] Phillip Stubbes, the Puritan pamphleteer, for example, not only worried that class distinction broke down as rules of apparel were violated but that the distinctions between the sexes were obliterated if one sex wore some part of the clothing of another.[21] A man wearing a women's dress was deemed to have undermined the authority inherent in the superior sex, or in more crude terms, cross dressing would not only make a man weak, tender, and infirm but also encourage him to play the woman's role in sexual congress. On the other hand, women who cross dressed were accused by polemicists not so much of sexual perversion but of loose morals, of being prostitutes. Such an accusation logically followed from the belief that women by their nature needed to be controlled by men, and that effective male control led women to be silent, chaste, and confined to the home. It was only the bad women, those who evaded male control, who gadded about and exposed or asserted themselves. Wearing men's clothes not only symbolically lifted the restrictions put on them by the male-dominated society, but indicated that their husbands, fathers, or brothers were weak and effeminate. William Parkes in 1612 wrote:

How are our women (as it were) trans-formed into men, by degenerating from their sex, and from the vertue [sic], modesty, and civility thereof, by their mannish complements, and ruffianly attires: And how are our men (as it were) transformed into women, by their lascivious, effeminate, and wanton imitations, none being content with their owne estates and conditions.[22]

The impassioned author of *Hic Mulier*, which appeared in 1620, denounced the hordes of "Masculine-Feminines" who are

Masculine in their genders and whole generations from the Mother, to the youngest daughters, Masculine in Number, from one to multitudes: Masculine in Case, even from the head to the foot; Masculine in Moode, from bold speech, to impudent action; and Masculine in Tense; for (without redress) they were, are, and will be still most Masculine, most mankinde, and most monstrous.[23]

The accusations of this pamphleteer led to a reply by another in *Haec Vir*. The woman narrator argues that male attire is utilitarian and not immodest, that the traditions of attire were established by custom and not reason, and that social customs differed from place to place. Moreover, she argued that since men have taken to cosmetics and have robbed women of their ruffles, earrings, fans, feathers, busks, and so on, women had no alternative. She promised to return to her traditional costume when men once more become men in shape, words, and actions.[24] Put in such terms, the struggle over alleged female cross dressing can be seen as an effort during a time of change to keep women in their traditional subservient position. Keeping them off the stage was one way of doing so.

But allowing men to cross dress even on stage raised the issue of homosexuality. This was compounded by the fact that the actors who played male roles had a higher status than those who played females; the latter were usually apprentice actors, although a few continued to play both roles. This use of apprentices would seem, on the surface, to limit the kind of women's roles that could be portrayed onstage. One twentieth-century producer, however, has been quoted to the contrary, arguing that Shakespeare

turned a limitation to account, made loss into a gain. Feminine charm—of which the modern stage makes much capital—was a medium denied him. So his men and women encountered upon a plane where their relation is made rarer and intense by poetry, or enfranchised in an hour which surpasses more primitive love-making. And thus, perhaps, he has helped to discover that the true stuff of tragedy and of the liveliest comedy lies beyond sensual bounds. His studies of women seem often to be begun from some spiritual paces beyond the point at which a modern dramatist leaves off.[25]

Conversely, some of the more mature roles might well have been written for men playing women rather than for real women. This was the view of Kenneth Tynan, a late twentieth-century drama critic, who argued that Lady Macbeth is basically a man's (not a boy's) role, and claimed it would be a mistake to cast a woman in the role at all.[26]

As actors formed into different companies, each under the patronage of a wealthy member of the aristocracy, a training system developed within which boys were apprenticed to a leading actor from whom they learned their art. They were given special training in order to develop the voices and gestures of women. Some of the boys were better than others in the feminine role, and a few became noted for their ability. Nathaniel Field was one such boy, but as he grew up he took on more male roles and soon became a playwright himself. He continued to play women's roles until his retirement from the stage at age thirty-six. (Interestingly, Field was the son of John Field, one of the more hostile opponents of the stage.) Another popular player was Dickie Robinson who is described by Ben Jonson in his play, *The Devil Is an Ass*. One character states that Dickie Robinson "dresses himself the best, beyond Forty of your very ladies."[27]

There was so much demand for boy actors that some were recruited under rather dubious circumstances. During Shakespeare's time, Queen Elizabeth, a patron of music and theatricals, authorized Nathaniel Giles (d. 1634), master of her chapel choir, to take "well singing" children from cathedral, collegiate, and parish churches as well as chapels or any other place in her kingdom for the choir of her Chapel Royal and for acting in plays designed for her entertainment. Giles, who was apparently a pedophile, hunted through England for young boys whom he installed in the Blackfriars Theater. His troupe became the sensation of London, and audiences flocked there in such numbers that the other theaters suffered. In fact, Shakespeare and his company were forced to go on tour, temporarily closing the Globe theater. Some mention of their popularity occurs in *Hamlet,* where Rosencrantz tells Hamlet about the abilities of the youths in Giles' company and refers to them as an "aery of children, little eyases [young hawks recently taken from the nest]" whom even he admits are outstanding.[28]

The popularity of the company, combined with the queen's favor, encouraged Giles to throw all discretion to the winds in his recruiting sallies. He and his agents waylaid and captured the young son of Henry Clifton, a well-to-do gentleman of Norfolk. After brutally beating the boy, they spirited him off to Blackfriars. When Clifton finally found out what had happened to his son, he accosted Giles, who impudently said he had the queen's power to take any nobleman's son in the land. Clifton, not to be put off, appealed to the Privy Council in order to secure his son's return. Clifton continued his investigation even after the return of his son, ultimately laying his findings before the Star Chamber. As a result, Henry Evans, who held the lease on Blackfriars, as well as Giles were not only censored but prohibited from engaging in theatrical activities. Queen Elizabeth, shocked by the scandal, gave orders that children of her chapel should take no further part in theatrical activities. Though Giles and Evans managed to reopen their theater after the death of Elizabeth, they were closed down permanently in 1608 after several new scandals. Shakespeare and Richard Burbage took over the lease for Blackfriars, and along with it, the more talented child actors were added to their company for female roles.[29]

Other actors who played females roles for Shakespeare and other theater impresarios include Alexander Cooke (d. 1614) and Robert Goughe (or Goffe). Goffe's son Alexander was also known for playing women's roles and was doing so when the theaters were closed down, at the beginning of Puritan dominance, on 2 September 1642.[30] Since Oliver Cromwell did not himself agree with the closing of the theaters, enforcement was not always effective. Sporadic enforcement meant, however, that those actors caught violating the law against appearing on the stage were punished as rogues. Still, even before the formal restoration of Charles II to the throne in 1660, the theaters again began to function openly. Though the Cockpit in Drury Lane, the first theater to formally reopen in 1660, started with an all-male cast, women were soon allowed on the English stage, as they were on the Continent. This occurred despite the opposition of the actors' guilds, which referred to Continental actresses as "whores and common courtesans," emphasizing that the actors' guilds themselves had been a factor in keeping women off the stage. But the guilds were weakened after the Restoration, and the interference of powerful individuals prevented the guilds' restrictive policies from being effective. One of the first women to appear was Mrs. Hughest who, as if to prove the charges of the actors' guild, was the mistress of Prince Rupert, the grandson of James I. Rupert had supported the Stuart cause and returned to England with Charles II; no actor's guild remonstrances would prevent him from putting his mistress onstage. A special prologue was written for the occasion by Thomas Jordan:

> I come unknown to any of the rest,
> To tell you news: I saw the lady drest:
> The woman plays to-day; mistake me not,
> No man in gown, or page in petticoat
> . . . in this reforming age.
> We have intents to civilize the stage.
> Our women are defective so siz'd
> You'd think they were some of the guard disguis'd.
> For to speak truth, men act, that are between
> Forty and fifty, wenches of fifteen;
> With bone so large, and nerve so incompliant,
> When you call Desdemona, enter Giant.[31]

For a brief time, female impersonators and women competed for women's roles, and among the most notable of the former was the boy Edward Kynaston. Samuel Pepys reported that he had attended the theater on 18 August 1660, and saw Kynaston act the part of a woman: he "made the loveliest lady that ever I saw in my life, only her voice was not very good."[32] Pepys saw him again early in 1661 in a different play and reported that Kynaston appeared in three different roles:

first, as a poor woman in ordinary clothes, to please Morose; then in fine clothes, as a gallant, and in them was clearly the prettiest woman in the whole house, and lastly, as a man; and then likewise did appear the handsomest man in the house.[33]

It was not until the end of the seventeenth century that women had won out in the struggle to play female roles on the English stage. Although female impersonators did not entirely disappear, by 1690 the nature of their acting had changed. Roger Baker, in his study of female impersonation on the stage, argued that the roles now allowed cross-dressing male actors represented the difference between a "real" disguise and a "false" disguise, between a man playing a female role in all seriousness and expecting an audience to accept him as such, and a man playing a female part while the audience is expected to realize he is a man. This change put the female impersonator into a different category, as a sort of comic curiosity, and the result was a separation from the straight theater to the music hall, the comic show, the cabaret and pantomime.[34] It was here that the cross dresser could gain either a living or, by being in the audience, participate in his own fantasy (this aspect of the theater will be examined later in Chapter 9).

Similar to the sixteenth- and seventeenth-century English tradition of female impersonation on the stage is a Japanese theater tradition that continues to the present. It differs from the European tradition in that female roles are not enacted by apprentice actors, and Japanese female impersonators must play the woman's role not only onstage but offstage as well. In short, they are almost expected to become women. This was probably too openly a homosexual role for English and Western cultures to tolerate (the *oyama* was usually homosexual as well); perhaps if homosexuality had not been seen as threatening in Western society, cross dressing may have remained as in Japan, a major factor on the stage.

As was the case in Europe, the custom of males playing women's roles in Japan had originally developed from the religious plays in monasteries wherein males (usually boys) portrayed female roles. From the monastery, the plays and their female impersonators moved to the imperial court and eventually to the general public. The homosexual aspect attributed to these actors is indicated by the term *chigo* ("favorite," or later, "priest's favorite"), which came to be applied to them. Some also became favorites of emperors or shoguns. For a time, independent women's dance companies (*Onna Kabuki*) competed for public favor with the female impersonators, but in 1629 Japanese officials prohibited women from appearing on the stage, and all the women's roles were taken over by men in the *Wakashu Kabuki*.

The actors assigned to play women's roles increasingly followed the traditions set by the actor Yoshizaz Ayame (born in 1673). Forced to support himself at a very young age, he originally had turned to prostitution and often cross dressed for his clients. One of his patrons, impressed by his beauty and talent, encouraged him to become a professional female impersonator on the stage. Ayame did so and later wrote the standard guide for others who wanted to become an *oyama,* a male actor playing a woman's role. The key to success, he argued, was to live as a woman in everyday life. Unless the male threw himself entirely in the feminine role, living and thinking as a woman, his inherent masculinity would unconsciously appear in a stage portrayal.[35]

Ayame's concept became the standard for all the succeeding *oyama.* The male-women became so accepted as women in their private lives that there was even tacit approval for them to bathe at public baths reserved exclusively for women. The *oyama* went so far as to argue that since they studied and pursued femininity throughout their lives, their "artificial" femininity had become more convincing than the "natural" femininity of women. Though the idea that men make better women than women do seems unduly harsh, this complete devotion to the feminine role allowed the men to continue to play the role of women for a very long time.

The closest the West came to the Japanese approach was in opera, where the *castrati,* or castrated males, predominated in the women's roles. Although technically the Christian Church in the West had disapproved of castration (it was widespread in the Byzantine Empire), allowing males to be castrated seemed to be, for a time, a much lesser evil than allowing women themselves to appear onstage. Traditionally, the Catholic Church had held that women were not to sing in churches, and when high voices were required, boys or youths singing falsetto (falsettists) and an occasional eunuch were employed. When opera appeared as a new musical form at the end of the fifteenth century, the demand for individuals to sing female roles increased. This placed Church officials in an uncomfortable position, since they officially prohibited castration. The solution that evolved was for the Church to continue officially to condemn castration as well as the appearance of women on the stage, but it allowed individuals who "had become" castrated to sing, as it was the Church's duty to help such unfortunates. Though some popes spoke against the use of castrati, none prohibited their use. Formally, everyone connected with the operation was subject to excommunication, but once a person was castrated, no punishment was imposed on him, and there was little attempt to find out how this had come about. Since there were significant financial rewards for a boy with a good voice, his family might submit a son to castration in order to better the family fortune. Unfortunately, not all those castrated proved to have good voices as they matured. One contemporary remarked that the

cruel operation is but too frequently performed without trial, or at least without sufficient proofs of an improvable voice; otherwise such numbers could never be found in every great town throughout Italy, without any voice at all, or at least without one sufficient to compensate such a loss.[36]

Some of the castrati who achieved a wide reputation were possibly motivated by the same desire to modify their biological sex as transsexuals today, although it is difficult if not impossible to document this without much more evidence than we have. One of the most famous castrati was Carlo Broschi, best known by his pseudonym, Farinelli (1705–82), who exercised a great influence on Philip V of Spain and for many years sang nightly for that monarch. Another famous castrati was Girolamo Crescentini (1762–1846), who so enchanted Napoleon Bonaparte that he was invited to Paris to sing. Still a third singer was Gaetano Majorano, better known as Caffarelli or Cafariello (1710–83), who might well have insisted on his own castration to preserve his much admired, boyish soprano voice. Though some of the castrati lived more or less normal lives as men, and some even took wives, others liked to play the part of women offstage as well as on, and as such, they had powerful patrons. We can speculate that some castrati may have enjoyed playing the passive role in anal intercourse, since the prostate potentially is an erotic and sensitive area; anal intercourse thus would have allowed them to achieve orgasm despite their castration.

Justifications for continuing the practice of castration even as, at the same time, more women were attempting to be heard on the musical stage, were many and varied. Some argued that the castrati had better vocal training and greater endurance than women, but probably the real reason the practice continued was the cultivated musical taste of the period and the deadweight of custom. It has been estimated that 70 percent of all male opera singers as late as the eighteenth century were castrati, a ratio that began to change only in the last two decades of the century, owing both to the intellectual and attitudinal changes resulting from the French Revolution as well as to changes in musical tastes. Certainly it is possible that the fear and anxiety produced by the homosexual implications of the theater's female impersonators were lessened in the case of the castrati; perhaps because the castrati were known to have lost their manliness and, in effect, were more legitimately on their way to becoming true women, they posed less of a threat. Many gave remarkable impersonations of women; indeed, the illusion of femaleness that the castrati gave led Casanova to remark that Rome, "the holy city," forces every man to become a pederast, but "will not admit it, nor believe in the effects of an illusion" which "it does its best to arouse."[37]

As women started to appear on the stage more frequently in England and elsewhere, they also took to playing men's roles, thereby emphasizing just how much gender-changing play had become a part of the culture. Whereas men playing women were perceived as becoming dangerously feminine, women impersonating men proved an erotic attraction because they could show their legs and figures in ways that ordinary women could not. One of the first male impersonators to do so was Charlotte Charke (d. 1760?), the daughter of the English actor and playwright Colley Cibber. Because her first attempt was the role of Lord Foppington in Colley Cibber's play, *The Careless Husband,* he was very upset at his daughter's impersonation. He not only cut off her funds but also tried to use his influence to prevent her from getting any future acting parts. Charke, however, was persistent, and she went from playing men's roles on the stage to living as a man, even for a time running a grocer's shop in London while living with a young widow. At least two other women, mistaking her for a man, allegedly fell in love with her, ultimately "forcing" her to reveal her true sex to them. (Even then, she reported, one still refused to believe her.) It was probably the threat posed by her putative lesbianism that made her less popular than some of the other women who played what came to be called "breeches" roles.[38]

Between 1660 and 1700, nearly a quarter of the plays produced in London contained one or more roles for actresses to play in boys' parts (in about 90 plays), and women also played parts originally written for men in at least fourteen others. Almost every actress of the period appeared at one time or another dressed like a man, although few continued to impersonate men offstage, as Charlotte Charke had done. In effect, the wheel had come almost full circle, as the boys who impersonated women in Shakespeare's time were replaced in the Restoration wonderland "by raffish hoydens, breeched and periwigged with swords at their sides, and masculine oaths on their lips."[39] The contradictions involved in such role playing were noted by Bernard Mandeville:

If a woman at a merrymaking dresses in Man's clothes, it is reckon'd a Frolick amongst Friends, and he that finds too much Fault with it is counted censorious: Upon the Stage it is done without Reproach, and the most Virtuous Ladies will dispense with it in an Actress, tho' every Body has a full view of her Legs and Thighs, but if the same Woman, as soon as she has Petticoats on again, should show her Leg to a Man as high as her Knee, it would be a very immodest Action, and every body will call her impudent for it.[40]

Literary Play

Playing with gender also was a major theme in the literature of the sixteenth and seventeenth centuries. In Ariosto's (1474–1533) poetic masterpiece *Orlando Furioso,* Bradamante, a young Amazon whose exploits equaled and often excelled those of the male knights, is often mistaken for her twin brother because, after sustaining a head wound, her hair had to be cut short. Fiordispina, a Spanish princess, falls in love with Bradamante, who confesses that she is a woman. The princess takes her home with her anyway, all the time bemoaning her fate for cursing her to fall in love with a woman. When the two women go to bed together,

One sleeps, one moans and weeps in piteous plight
Because her wild desire more fiercely glows.
And on her wearied lids should slumber light,
All is deceitful that brief dreaming shows:
    To her it seems as if relenting heaven
    A better sex to Bradamante has given.[41]

When Bradamante returns home, she recounts her adventures to her twin brother, Ricciardetto. He, realizing that the princess is a beauty he had long admired, dresses himself in his sister's clothes and goes to visit the princess. The princess welcomes him with open arms, pleased at the return of "Bradamante." She gives him beautiful clothes to wear, and the two go to bed. There Ricciardetto tells her of his magical transformation and invites the princess to test the new equipment. The two live together as women for several weeks before the truth is discovered.

Invariably in such stories, the apparent homosexual or lesbian encounters eventually result in heterosexual intercourse. Obviously, cross dressing had erotic implications for both the authors and the readers of the time, so such plot resolutions were a safe way to deal with the more "dangerous" topic of homosexuality and lesbianism. Perhaps these plots also reflect the male response to a changing social order in which some men felt increasingly powerless, or, at least, in which the balance of power was perceived as being in flux. This explanation, for example, has been advanced for Ariosto's use of transvestism in his *Calandria,* written after the shock of a Venetian defeat. *Calandria,* however, can also be seen simply as another experiment with gender. In this work, the twins Lidio and Santilla change roles. Santilla, living as a man, acknowledges the superiority of the masculine lifestyle, which gives her greater freedom than she has ever had. Lidio, for his part, dresses like a woman for a specific purpose, namely, to keep his trysts with his lover Fulvia secret from Fulvia's husband Calandro, who is depicted as a fool. Role reversals dominate the play and emphasize the gender experimentation taking place between the sexes. While the men's greater physical strength remains a constant, the women's freedom is more limited, dependent in part on their economic status; the women can only truly achieve control over their lives by assuming masculine roles. Ultimately, however, honor and status quo are preserved by Ariosto, for when societal survival itself is threatened by the masculine behavior of women, he has them retreat behind male protection.[42]

In Sir Philip Sidney's *Arcadia,* the hero dresses as the Amazon Zelmane in order to gain access to a princess whose family is living in pastoral seclusion. His disguise is more successful than anticipated, and the heroine's father conceives a passion for this fair young "woman" who comes to his court. The princess's mother is not deceived but holds her peace since she, too, is interested in the handsome stranger. The daughter, innocent of the masquerade, worries about the passion Zelmane has for her as well as her own willingness to respond. Ultimately, of course, she discovers that Zelmane is really a man and that her passion is not "perverted or misplaced."[43]

Cross dressing was a minor theme in several of Shakespeare's plays, which included such roles as Rosalind in *As You Like It* and Viola in *Twelfth Night*. It must have taken considerable acting ability for the male actors who were impersonating women to also represent women impersonating men, and the continued incidence of such masquerades in plays of the time emphasizes the public appeal of such adventures.[44]

Sometimes, impersonation is the center of the story. A good example is a 1560 anonymous tale wherein Ambrose, a merchant of Jennen, boasts of his wife's fidelity to a friend. The friend bets that he can seduce her. Secreting himself in a chest, he is conveyed into her room; he stays there until night and then creeps out to steal three jewels and take note of a mole on her left arm. With this information, he convinces Ambrose of his wife's adultery, and a jealous Ambrose orders her slain. The wife manages to escape with the aid of a compassionate servant. Assuming the guise of a man, she travels to the court, where she becomes one of the officers of the king and the vanquisher of his enemies. Eventually, she meets her husband's friend, who boasts of his adventure. She requests the king summon her husband, and after exposing his friend, she is reunited with her husband and his former friend is put to death.[45] This kind of cross-dressing story carries a moral for both sexes, but the lesson seems to be that if a husband treats his wife well, she will be happy in her subordinate role.

Tied in with the gender-playing of the period was a concern with hermaphroditism. Ambroise Paré (1510–90), a Parisian surgeon, described hermaphrodites as drawing

the cause of their generation and conformation from the plenty and abundance of seed, and are called so because they are of both sexes, the woman yielding as much seed as the man. For hereupon it commeth to passe that the forming faculty (which alwaies endeavours to produce something like it self) doth labour the matters almost with equal force, and is the cause that one body is of both sexes.[46]

But there was also a fear that even one's established gender was not as secure as it seemed. For example, Baldassare Castiglioni (1478–1539), the Italian humanist, was concerned that men would gain a soft and womanish countenance by engaging in womanly pursuits or by consorting with women too much; even more threatening was the possibility that women could become like men.[47] One of Castiglioni's characters in *The Book of the Courtier* warns women against undertaking "manly exercise so sturdie and boisterous" or even playing instruments too vigorously for fear of becoming too masculine.[48]

The admonishments against "manly exercise" received emphasis in a sex change incident reported by Paré and others. In this case, Marie, a girl who had reached puberty, jumped across a ditch while chasing pigs and suddenly found that she possessed a penis. When Marie reported to her mother what had happened, physicians and surgeons were called in for consultation, and they agreed that her daughter had become a boy. The local bishop was consulted about a name change for this new male and agreed to name her Germain; and Germain began to wear men's clothing.[49] Paré utilized traditional medical theory to explain the sex change, namely, that women had as much hidden within their bodies as men had outside but the coldness of their bodies and temperament held it to the interior. In this case, the onset of puberty, combined with jumping or any similarly robust activity, increased the heat of the body; this led to the breakdown of the internal-external barrier and made the woman a man. While it was considered possible for women to become men, however, it was not possible for a man to be turned into a woman, since nature always tended toward that which was the most perfect,[50] and inevitably the male in a male-centered world was regarded as more perfect. In retelling the story, Michel de Montaigne (1533–92) added,

It is not so great a marvel that this sort of accident is frequently met with. For if the imagination has power in such things, it is so continually and vigorously fixed on this subject that in order not to relapse so often into the same thought and sharpness of desire, it is better that once and for all it incorporates this masculine member in girls.[51]

In short, we have a repetition of the medieval belief in the higher status of men, and that women can be excused for trying to be men and aspiring to manly wisdom and fortitude.[52]

Hermaphrodites and sex changes were also of concern to the emerging discipline of forensic medicine. In one of the first forensic studies, Paolo Zacchia (1584–1659) devoted some nineteen folio pages to trying to define who is to be called woman and who man. According to Zacchia, sex involved status, and males had a higher status; it was not impossible for a member of one sex to appear as the other. He attempted to draw up criteria to distinguish cases of ambiguity, all the while emphasizing male supremacy. Zacchia insisted that even in those rare cases where the sex organs of both sexes might be present, it was still possible to make a decision on anatomical or physiological criteria. In cases where two sets of conflicting organs appeared side by side, the genitalia on the right were to be used in determining the sex since the right side of the body was considered dominant. If the organs are aligned vertically, the organ on top was dominant, and the person belonged to that sex.[53]

Summary

The medieval idea of masculinity having a higher status than femininity remained strongly in force in the sixteenth and seventeenth centuries, despite the willingness of society to experiment with gender. Generally, however, experimentation was increasingly limited to women. But even as cross dressing for women continued to be tolerated, there were dangers. Ben Jonson, for example, accused one of his female critics of taking on masculine traits in order to attack him; he attempted to discredit her attacks by labeling her a *Tribade* (lesbian).[54]

There were limits on how much gender-crossing a woman could do, and everything supposedly remained right in the world if the women, after some play with role reversal, contentedly resumed their subordinated status. Though some have argued there was only one biological sex and that it remained theoretically possible for females to become males, there was a real concern that the biological differences between the sexes be clearly delineated. Regardless of biology, however, gender was not immutable, and there was a real fear that too much masculine behavior might actually transform a female into a male, at least during the onset of puberty. Though males could not change their sex, feminization could change their gender identity, and there was fear that this might lead to homosexuality. It was this fear which at least partly underlay the Puritan attack on the stage; after women began to appear on the stage, this perceived threat led to a gradual decline of female impersonators in the "legitimate" theater.

Notes

1. This term is taken from *Playing with Gender: A Renaissance Pursuit*, ed. Jean R. Brink, Maryanne C. Horowitz, and Alison P. Coudert (Urbana: University of Illinois Press, 1991).

2. See, for example, Natalie Zemon Davis, *Society and Culture in Early Modern France* (Stanford, CA: Stanford University Press, 1975), esp. pp. 97–189, as well as her study of gendered rhetoric, *Fiction in the Archives: Pardon Tales and Their Tellers in Sixteenth-Century France* (Stanford, CA: Stanford University Press, 1987). For hermaphrodites, see Elémire Zolla, *The Androgyne: Reconciliation of Male and Female* (New York: Crossroad, 1981). See also Eisaman Maus,

"Playhouse Flesh and Blood: Sexual Ideology and the Restoration," *English Literary History* 46 (1979): 595–617; and Laura Levine, "Men in Women's Clothing: Antitheatricality and Effeminization from 1579 to 1642," *Criticism* 28 (1986): 121–45. For the idea of self-fashioning, in this period, see Stephen Greenblatt, *Renaissance Self-Fashioning: From More to Shakespeare* (Chicago: University of Chicago Press, 1980), and esp. Stephen Greenblatt, "Fiction and Friction," in *Shakespearean Negotiations* (Berkeley: University of California Press, 1988), 66–93; and *Cannibals, Witches, and Divorce: Estranging the Renaissance*, ed. Marjorie Garber (Baltimore: Johns Hopkins University Press, 1987). For further bibliography, see the introduction by Maryanne Cline Horowitz in *Playing with Gender,* ed. Brink et al., ix–xxiv.

3. Victor M. Turner, *The Ritual Process: Structure and Anti-Structure* (Chicago: Aldine Publishing Co., 1969), passim, but esp. pp. 182–85.

4. Quoted from Theophilus Moore, *Marriage Customs and Modes of Courtship of the Various Nations of the Universe* . . . (London: John Bumpus, 1820), 37, by R. Valerie Lucas in *"Hic Mulier:* The Female Transvestite in Early Modern England," *Renaissance and Reformation*, 24, no. 1 (1988): 65. We are indebted to Lucas for several concepts in this chapter.

5. C. J. S. Thompson, *Mysteries of Sex: Women Who Posed as Men and Men Who Posed as Women* (London: Hutchinson and Co., 1938), 15–16.

6. Peter Burke, *Popular Culture in Early Modern Europe* (London: Temple Smith, 1978), 194.

7. Natalie Zemon Davis, "Women on Top: Symbolic Inversion and Political Disorder in Early Modern Europe," in *The Reversible World: Symbolic Inversion in Art and Society*, ed. Barbara Babcock (Ithaca, NY: Cornell University Press, 1978), 147–90, esp. 171.

8. See F. G. Emisson, *Elizabethan Life* (Chelmsford, U.K.: Essex County Council, 1973), 18.

9. Stephen Greenblatt, "Fiction and Friction," 66–93, esp. 88.

10. Lisa Jardine, "'As Boys and Women Are for the Most Part Cattle of This Colour': Female Roles and Elizabethan Eroticism," in *Still Harping on Daughters: Women and Drama in the Age of Shakespeare* (Totowa, NJ: Barnes and Noble, 1983), 9–36.

11. Stephen Orgel, "Nobody's Perfect: Or, Why Did the English Stage Take Boys for Women?" *South Atlantic Quarterly* 88, no. 1 (Winter 1989): 7–29.

12. Laura Levine, "Men in Women's Clothing: Antitheatricality and Effeminization from 1579 to 1642," *Criticism* 28 (1986): 121–43. We are indebted to Jean E. Howard, "Crossdressing, the Theatre, and Gender Struggle in Early Modern England," *Shakespeare Quarterly* 39 (1988): 181–210, for calling our attention to the controversies.

13. This is the view of Kathleen McLuskie, "The Act, the Role, and the Actor: Boy Actresses on the Elizabethan Stage," *New Theater Quarterly* 3 (1987): 120–30.

14. Juliet Dusinberre, *Shakespeare and the Nature of Women* (New York: Macmillan, 1975), 231–71.

15. See Phyllis Rackin, "Androgyny, Mimesis, and the Marriage of the Boy Heroine on the English Renaissance Stage," *PMLA* 102 (1987): 29–42; and Catherine Belsey, "Disrupting Sexual Difference: Meaning and Gender in the Comedies," in *Alternative Shakespeares*, ed. John Drakakis (London: Methuen, 1985), 166–90.

16. Clara Claiborne Park, "As We Like It: How a Girl Can Be Smart and Still

Popular," in *The Woman's Part: Feminist Criticism of Shakespeare,* ed. Carolyn Lenz, Gayle Greene, and Carol Neely (Urbana: University of Illinois Press, 1980), 100–116.

17. C. J. Bulliet, *Venus Castina: Famous Female Impersonators Celestial and Human* (reprinted, New York: Bonanza Books, [1928] 1956).

18. William Prynne, *Histrio-Mastix: The Players Scourge, or, Actors Tragaedie* (London, 1633), 63, 146, 374–75, 390–91, 909, as quoted by Godfrey Davies, *The Early Stuarts (1603–1660)* (Oxford: Clarendon Press, 1952), 393.

19. Act 5, scene 3. There are several editions of Ben Jonson's works. An easily available one is *The Complete Plays of Ben Jonson,* 3 vols. (reprinted, London: J. M. Dent, [1910] 1942). A more complete edition *Ben Jonson,* ed. C. H. Herford and Percy Evelyn Simpson, 11 vols. (Oxford: Clarendon Press, 1925–1952). The Biblical reference is Deut. 23:5.

20. Howard, "Crossdressing," 422.

21. Philip Stubbes, *The Anatomie of Abuses* (London: Richard Jones, 1583), C2v and F5v, and cited in Howard, "Crossdressing," 422.

22. William Parkes, *The Curtaine-drawer of the World* (London: for Leonard Beckett, 1612), 29, and quoted in Lucas, "*Hic Mulier,*" 69.

23. *Hic Mulier: or, The Man-Woman: Being a Medicine to Cure the Coltish Disease of the Staggers in the Masculine-Feminines of Our Times* (London: [G. Purslowe] f.J. T[rundle], 1620), A3(1), and quoted in Lucas, "*Hic Mulier,*" 71.

24. *Haec Vir: or, The Womanish-Man, Being an Answere to a Late Book intitled Hic Mulier* (London: J. Trundle, 1620), sig. B3(2). It was published just five days after *Hic Mulier*. Both pamphlets are reprinted in abridged form in *Half Humankind: Contexts and Texts of the Controversy about Women in England, 1540–1640,* ed. Katherine Usher Henderson and Barbara F. McManus (Urbana: University of Illinois Press, 1985), 264–89. There was also another response, *Muld Sacke: or, The Apologie of Hic-Mulier* (London: Richard Meighen, 1620), which extended the definition of masculine-feminine to include all unruly women. Muld Sacke is portrayed wearing trousers and having a moustache, and is much more mannish than the figures on the title page of the other two.

25. The statement was made by Harley Granville-Barker and is quoted in Guy Boas, *Shakespeare and the Young Actor: A Guide to Production* (London: Barrie and Rockliff, 1955), 1.

26. Kenneth Tynan, "Macbeth at Stratford on Avon," in *Tynan on Theatre* (Harmondsworth, U.K.: Penguin Books, 1964), 108.

27. Ben Jonson, *The Devil Is an Ass,* act 2, end of scene 3.

28. *Hamlet,* act 2, scene 22, ll. 336–57. The *Hamlet* in the Arden edition is edited by Harold Jenkins (London: Methuen, 1982).

29. See M. C. Bradbrook, *The Rise of the Common Player* (Cambridge: Cambridge University Press, 1979), 236–38, and Baker, *Drag,* 72–73.

30. For a discussion of some of the actors, see Gerald Eades Bentley, *The Profession of Player in Shakespeare's Time* (Princeton, NJ: Princeton University Press, 1984); and Bradbrook, *Rise of the Common Player.* For other aspects of the stage, see A. M. Nagler, *Shakespeare's Stage* (New Haven, CT: Yale University Press, 1958).

31. Quoted by Guy Boas, *Shakespeare and the Young Actor,* 1.

32. Samuel Pepys, *The Diary of Samuel Pepys,* ed. Henry B. Wheatley, 2 vols. (New York: Random House, n.d.), 1:161.

33. Ibid., 7 January 1661, p. 216.

34. Roger Baker, *Drag: A History of Female Impersonation on Stage* (London: Triton Books, 1968), passim.

35. Tsuneo Watanabe and Juńichi Iwata, *The Love of the Samurai: A Thousand Years of Japanese Homosexuality*, trans. D. R. Roberts (London: GMP Publishers, 1989), 86.

36. Angus Heriot, *The Castrati in Opera* (London: Secker and Warburg, 1956), 45–46.

37. Ibid., esp. 55. We are unable to find the quote attributed to Casanova in his works.

38. Charlotte Charke, *Narrative of the Life of Charlotte Charke Written by Herself* (London: W. Reeve, 1755).

39. John H. Wilson, *All the King's Ladies: Actresses of the Restoration* (Chicago: University of Chicago Press, 1958), 73.

40. Bernard Mandeville, *The Fable of the Bees*, ed. F. B. Kaye, 2 vols. (Oxford: Clarendon Press, 1924), Remark P., 1:172–73.

41. Ludovico Ariosto, *Orlando Furioso*. We are indebted to Valeria Finucci for some of the ideas here. She allowed us to examine an unpublished chapter, "Transvestite Love: Sexual Identity in the Fiordispina Story."

42. Linda L. Carroll, "Who's on Top? Gender as Societal Power Configuration in Italian Renaissance Drama," *Sixteenth Century Journal* 20 (1989): 531–57.

43. Philip Sidney, *The Countess of Pembroke's Arcadia* (Cambridge: Cambridge University Press, 1912), 174–75. A more recent edition is by Victor Skretkowicz (Oxford: Clarendon Press, 1987).

44. Jeanette Foster, *Sex Variant Women in Literature* (London: Frederick Muller, 1958), 38–39.

45. *Here begynneth a propre treatyse of a marchauntes wyfe, that afterwarde went lyke a man . . .* (London: Abraham Vele, 1560?). We are indebted to Lucas, *Hic Mulier*, for the reference.

46. Ambroise Paré, *The Works of Ambrose Parey*, trans. Thomas Johnson (London: Jos. Hindmarsh, [1691], reprinted, Ann Arbor, MI: University Microfilms, 1984), 973.

47. Baldassare Castiglioni, *The Book of the Courtier*, trans. Thomas Hoby (London: Everyman's Library, 1966), 39.

48. Ibid., 193–94.

49. Ambroise Paré, *On Monsters and Marvels*, trans. Janis L. Pallister (Chicago: University of Chicago Press, 1982), 31–32.

50. This is the view of Gaspard Bauhin, *Theatricum anatomicum* (Basel: 1605), and cited in William Harvey, *Lectures on the Whole of Anatomy*, translated into English from the Latin by C. D. O'Malley, F. N. L. Poynter, and K. F. Russell (Berkeley: University of California Press, 1961), 132, n.467. We are indebted to Thomas Laquer, *Making Sex: Body and Gender from the Greeks to Freud* (Berkeley: University of California Press, 1990), 127, for this reference.

51. See Michel de Montaigne, *The Complete Essays of Montaigne*, trans. Donald Frame (Stanford: Stanford University Press, 1965), I, 21, p. 69.

52. From George Sandys, *Ovid's Metamorphosis Englished, Mythologized, and Represented in Figures* (London: 1626), ed. Karl Hulley and Stanley Vandershall (Lincoln: University of Nebraska, 1970), 450.

53. Paolo Zacchia, *Questionum medico-legalium* (Leipzig: Eliae Rehefeldii, 1630), and quoted in Laquer, *Making Sex*, 140–41.

54. Ben Jonson, *Epigrammes*, in *Ben Jonson*, ed. C. H. Herford and Percy Simpson (Oxford: Clarendon Press, 1947), 8:76.

Chapter 5
Cross-Dressing Women and Men

Cross-dressing women were not only part of the fantasy of poems and plays but also very much part of reality. Changing social conditions had loosened some of the hierarchical ties and made it much easier for women to escape some of the confines of the female role by dressing like and passing as men. Most of these women were probably never uncovered, but hundreds of them are known.

One of the more interesting cases that has been preserved involves the Spanish woman Eleno/Elena de Cespedes (1545?–88). According to a contemporary chronicle, Eleno/Elena was a woman who had used magic to hide her true sex; she pretended to be a man and even married another woman. From what can be constructed of her case, she had been raised as a girl and taught weaving, a traditional task for women. Married at sixteen, she soon became pregnant, and was thereafter abandoned by her husband. After her son was born, she gave up the child to others and moved to Granada. There, she allegedly discovered she had a penis and had an affair with the wife of a merchant with whom she was lodging. Soon after, she began to dress like a man, and after a series of events she joined the army, was discharged, and then joined again. After serving for several years, she became an itinerant tailor, eventually ending up in Madrid. There Eleno/Elena lodged in the house of a surgeon who taught her his trade; she continued to practice as a surgeon for several years. Eventually, she ended up in a village where she fell in love with the daughter of a peasant family with whom she was staying. After obtaining permission from the father to marry the daughter, she went to Madrid to secure the necessary license. In Madrid the vicar, seeing that she lacked a beard, asked her if she was a *capón* ("eunuch"). She replied that she was a man and, to prove it, allowed an impromptu inspection by three or four men, who saw her only from the front, "as I never allowed anyone to look at me from behind in order to hide my female sex." After passing the inspection, she was given a license to marry.

At this point, a former lover challenged the marriage on the grounds that Eleno/Elena was really both a man and a woman. The Madrid vicar, anxious to do the right thing, ordered a proper inspection by physicians and surgeons. In order to pass this more intense inspection, "Eleno" said she applied certain ointments to herself in order to "close up her female sex." Again, the local physicians and surgeons studied her both from the front and behind. This time the inspection was carried out by day, and the physicians also used a candle to aid them in their close inspection. They reportedly saw a penis and testicles and no sign of a vagina, although they noted there was some kind of hard scar which, according to Eleno's account, was a result of a wound received during the war. The suspicious vicar demanded a second inspection by court physicians and surgeons, and Eleno, again after applying ointments and remedies, passed the inspection.

Soon after their marriage, the couple moved to a larger town that lacked a surgeon. The town's mayor, who knew Eleno from the army, reported that there were suggestions "he" was not a man but either a woman or a hermaphrodite. As a result Eleno was arrested and charged not only with impersonating a man but with mocking the sacrament of marriage. Eleno claimed in defense not to have committed a crime, since he/she was a hermaphrodite with both sexes, but also admitted that "his" male organs were now missing because a cancer had caused them to deteriorate and fall off. The physicians and surgeons who previously performed the inspection were summoned to do so again. This time they reported that although they had been visible previously, the male parts were no longer there; in fact, Eleno had a vagina. In their defense, the inspectors claimed that the change must have been due to the work of the devil.

The case of Elena, as she was now known, was transferred to the Inquisition. She was charged with being in league with the devil, because a sex change was believed to be impossible otherwise. Sentenced to receive two hundred lashes at a public whipping for her impersonation, Elena also had to serve ten years in a public hospital. During the trial she explained that she had discovered she had a penis following the birth of her son, when she was seventeen years old. At that time a piece of skin that had previously covered her urinary canal broke, revealing a "head" (probably an enlarged clitoris) about a half-inch long, like the head of a penis. The penis periodically disappeared, and it was only later, with the help of a surgeon, that it was more fully revealed. What had happened to this penis is unclear, since it was reported at her trial that she had a vagina and all the signs of being a woman, including breasts and the pitch of her voice. They also added that she was not a hermaphrodite. After the trial and conviction she more or less disappeared from the pages of history.[1]

Male Impersonation as Female Adventure

Though Elena's case was tragic, others were much less so. One of the more unusual male impersonators was another Spanish woman, Catalina de Erauso (b. 1592), who had a fantastic career, some of the details of which might well be fictional. Placed in a Dominican convent at an early age, de Erauso eventually took vows and became a nun. Increasingly unhappy with convent life, she cut her hair, and after making a male costume out of her habit, she fled. After a series of adventures, she changed her name to Alonso Diaz Ramérez de Guzman and joined a galleon crew bound for Latin America. Landing in Panama, she set out to make her fortune.

De Erauso's plans were set back when she killed a man in a brawl. She fled to Lima, where she enlisted in the army as a private. After serving in several campaigns against the Indians of Chile and Peru, she distinguished herself sufficiently to be promoted to the rank of ensign. For a time she served under her own brother, Miguel de Erauso, who had gone to America before she was born. Though she never identified herself to him, he considered her a fellow townsman and did what he could to advance her career. In battle, de Erauso earned a reputation for courage and daring, and when not on a campaign, she was known for her gambling and brawling. Once she was sentenced to death for killing an Indian chief who had surrendered, but just as the noose was being put around her neck, she was ordered transferred to another court and ultimately released.

Soon after this escape from death, she was arrested for killing another man in a gambling fight in which she herself had been badly wounded. Worried about what might happen to her, she confessed to the local bishop that she was actually a woman. After he made her secret public, she came to be popularly known as the "Nun Ensign," and people flocked to see her. In 1624, still in uniform, she returned to Spain as "Antonio de Erauso." After receiving a pension from the king, she set off for Rome, where Pope Urban VIII granted her special permission to continue to wear men's clothes. She kept her masculine role and appearance for the rest of her life.[2]

The cross-dressing adventures of Eleno/Elena and Catalina de Erauso perhaps helps explain why female cross dressing is such a major theme in early modern Spanish literature. Female bandits, adventurers, scholars, and hunters who disguised themselves as men furnish important subplots in many stories.[3] The same was true not only in Spain, where women adopted the masculine role, but throughout much of Europe. Even papal dispensation to wear men's clothes was not a singular event.

The most noteworthy instance was the case of Queen Christina (1626–89) of Sweden. Her father Gustavus Adolphus died when she was six years old, and while a regent ruled in her stead, she was educated in as masculine way as possible so that she would capably succeed to the throne when she reached the age of eighteen in 1644. Alex Oxenstjerna, the regent, had described her as a teenager as not like other women, but stout hearted and of a good understanding. As ruler, however, she did not get along well with her male advisers, who tried to treat her as "just" a woman. She refused to marry her cousin, Charles Gustavus, but was anxious to resolve dynasty problems and simply appointed Charles her successor; in 1654 she abdicated on the grounds that the burden of ruling was too heavy for a woman. Christina left Sweden in masculine attire under the name of Count Dohna and later joined the Catholic Church. She eventually settled in Rome, where she received permission to continue wearing men's clothes when she chose.

Contemporary accounts emphasize Christina's masculine appearance, and remark on her malelike voice and deportment. She also liked to appear as an Amazon. She had love affairs with both men and women, although only one of her female partners is known by name, the Countess Ebba Sparre, whom she met in Paris. In Rome she became a great patron of the arts, and her palace at Riario, now Corsini, contained the greatest collection of Venetian painting ever assembled as well as other notable paintings. She sponsored men-of-letters, philosophers, and musicians, established the Arcadia Academy, and was instrumental in the building of the first Roman opera house.[4]

Though none of the other known women cross dressers had the resources or notoriety of Christina, their cross dressing allowed them to live much more exciting lives than they might have otherwise. Examination of Dutch records of the seventeenth and early eighteenth centuries, for example, has so far disclosed more than a hundred documented cases of male impersonators who set out for the Dutch East Indies (Indonesia).[5] (Since discovery of their female identities was often accidental, it is assumed there were hundreds more whose cross dressing was never discovered because they never appeared in court or were never notorious enough to be mentioned in papers, diaries, or similar surviving sources.) The common theme running through the biographies of male impersonators is that they were usually born poor;

they often had unhappy childhoods, lost one or both parents while young, and had been forced to earn their living at a tender age. Many worked in the textile industry, others as maids, waitresses, or farmhands, virtually the only possible jobs for unskilled women at that time.

Most of the women were single at the time they assumed their male guises, although a few were attempting to follow their husbands to the East Indies. Most were discovered while they were between sixteen and twenty-five years old, but some were much older. The actual change of gender was not usually any sudden inspiration but took planning, since the poor seldom had more than one set of clothes, and they had to somehow find clothes that would allow them to pass as men. This usually involved an accomplice who could exchange clothes at a second-hand shop.

Lacking an accomplice, a woman fled to a town where no one knew her and hid, often in a churchyard, until they could somehow secure traditional male clothing. All cut off their long hair and took a new name, usually a male variant of their original one. Occasionally, two women joined together on the same venture. Since a woman passing as a man usually looks considerably younger than her years, it was not difficult for women in their twenties or even thirties to pass for a very young man whose voice had not yet broken and who had not yet grown a beard. Since boys could sign on as sailors at fifteen, the women cross dressers usually ended up in this group.

Some women posing as boys were discovered after a few days or even hours; others served as soldiers or sailors for many years. A record for attempts to pass might have been set by Maria van Spanje, who signed up as a man five different times but each time was exposed. The reasons for their being discovered varied. Some were immediately recognized or even betrayed by an accomplice. Others met someone who had known them as women. Sometimes it was their own lack of skills in impersonation that led to their exposure. Others were not careful enough when washing or changing clothes to escape detection, while some became so drunk that their disguise was recognized.

Still, a large number succeeded in reaching Indonesia where they could seek their fortune or in many cases find a husband. This seems surprising when one considers the total lack of privacy on Dutch sailing ships of the time. Dozens of men were packed into the forecastle, where they spilled over one another. When they were ill, wounded in battle, or suffered corporal punishment, they might be undressed by others. Some of the women carried off their impersonation so well that they were accepted everywhere as men. Some even married other women, and several were later denounced by their wives, who were upset after discovering the impersonation. It is likely that many more of the lesbian cross dressers' sympathetic female companions were natives of Indonesia.

In popular fiction, women often dressed like men and went through hardships in order to follow lovers and husbands. But many of the Dutch women who cross dressed seemed to want to escape the restrictions of the woman's role; like many of their male contemporaries, they wanted travel and adventure, and they also wanted to better themselves economically.

Most of the women in the records who reached the Indies ultimately resumed their feminine life-style and clothing and married, which is how their impersonations were eventually uncovered. One reason for their marriage was that European women in the colonies were in short supply. Although the Dutch East Indies, for example, had a reputation as a comparative paradise for European women, the policy of the company controlling passage to the Indies was to take as few women as possible on the ships. This policy encouraged impersonation since once the women reached the Indies they could expect to marry almost immediately and become mistresses of houses, complete with native servants or slaves. Not all married, however, and some ended up as pubkeepers.

Women from all areas of the Netherlands appear to have wanted to escape many of the restrictions imposed on them. In general, cross-dressing women who were unmasked after several years of faithful service as men could count on sympathy, their full wages, and even awards and presents. Women who were exposed after a few days or months or who were involved in a criminal offense were regarded more negatively. The most successful often became heroic figures in their own day, received by kings and popes; and if they went into business, they made every effort to make certain that everyone knew about their past. Many of them wrote of their adventures or told their stories to others, who then embroidered upon them.

Emphasizing just how much gender roles were socially and culturally constructed, many were able to adopt the masculine persona not only in appearance but in behavior. Several possessed true pugnacity and excelled in drinking and in telling sexually explicit jokes. Those who were most easily uncovered were those who could not do heavy work or who behaved in an "unmanly" fashion.

David Jans (née Maritgen Jens) told how she had traveled from the south of the Netherlands to Amsterdam to find work. She found a job making silk thread but only earned a pittance, hardly enough for her to survive. Unable to find anything better as a woman and unwilling to return to her family, she sold her clothes and bought others to transform herself into a man. She quickly worked her way up to foreman in another silk thread shop, a position denied her as a woman.[6]

Maria van Antwerpen became a soldier after a lackluster career as a maid, a position from which she had been fired several times. Finding herself without a job in the middle of the winter in Wageningen, a city where she knew no one, and without family resources to back her (her parents were dead), she decided to become a soldier. The only other alternative for her was prostitution. Lacking men's clothes to wear, she persuaded one farmer to give her an old pair of pants and another to give her a doublet. Thus disguised, she enlisted in the army.[7]

Many of the women put themselves at great risk, especially those who became part of a ship's crew, since if exposed they might become fair game for all the men. Somewhat surprisingly, however, the women often found support for their disguise, not only from other women but from men, indicating that the cross-dressing experience was not frowned upon by many segments of Dutch society. Not a few felt sympathy for the poor girl trying to better herself, even if she had to become a man to do it.

Several cross dressers became the subject of popular songs, some of which are quite bawdy. This was the case of Barbara Adriaens and Hilletje Jans, who married each other and inspired a ballad from 1632:

> For when the bride made free
> To feel if there might be
> Cock and balls, said she,
> "T'is most rare
> I perceive them not, yea, nothing there,"
> How may I then assay
> My heat with thee to allay
> In the nuptial bed where we two lay?[8]

Mary Frith, an Englishwoman popularly called "Moll Cutpurse" for her dexterity in picking pockets, was probably (and by her own description) a hermaphrodite. Born in London in 1584, she was raised as a girl by her parents, but as she grew up she began to act more like a boy than a girl, able to run and jump as well as any of her male contemporaries. She early decided she wanted to live and work as a man. For a time she simply abandoned her feminine clothes for more masculine ones, but later deciding that she was neither man nor woman, she devised a unique costume for herself which, though similar to one worn by men, allowed her to wear either skirts or breeches, depending on her mood. For her the world consisted of "cheats and the cheated," and she early resolved to be one of the former rather than the latter. Mary's story was told in 1662 in a chapbook, a pamphletlike publication available to a mass audience.[9] Moll's case attracted considerable attention among her contemporaries, and she was featured in a comedy, *The Roaring Girl* (1611), by Thomas Middleton and Thomas Dekker. She was also a character in Nathaniel Field's play, *Amends for Ladies* (1618).[10]

Somewhat different is the case of Long Meg, who became an English folk hero. Migrating to London from her native Lancashire, Meg became a serving maid in a tavern where she befriended soldiers and saved her newfound friends from robbers. According to several accounts, she disguised herself as a man in order to duel and defeat a braggart, Sir James of Castile, who as punishment had to wait on her at her supper. As his friends commiserated with Sir James for his humbling experience, Meg pulled off her hat, and with her hair falling about her ears revealed her identity. Similar adventures include serving as a laundress to the troops at Boulogne in France, where she defeated a Frenchman who challenged the English. Again after defeating him she revealed her true sex.

Returning to England, Meg became proprietor of an Islington tavern. When one of the customers attacked one of her maids, she beat him with a staff and forced him to dress like a woman. Dressing herself like a man, she paraded him through the streets. Ultimately, however, Long Meg became an obedient wife to a man who beat her; her fate thus reinforced the widespread belief that strong women who deviate from the norm only need strong men to keep them in check.[11] She also is referred to in many other works of the time.[12]

A male impersonator whose life had more than a little in common with the fiction of the time was Christian Davis, born in Dublin in 1667. Her father, loyal to James II, had rallied to the king's cause when he appeared in Ireland in 1690 after fleeing England. Soon after James II and his forces were defeated at the Battle of Boyne, Captain Bodeaux, her father's friend and companion at the battle, was killed at the siege of Limerick. When Bodeaux's uniform was removed, it was discovered that he was a woman. This masquerade apparently later exercised considerable influence on Christian.

After the death of her father, Christian moved in with an aunt who left all her property to her. Since women had to administer their property through a male guardian, it was overseen by a young man, Richard Welsh, whom she married and by whom she had two children. Welsh, however, disappeared for some twelve months after setting out on an errand. When he finally wrote to Christian, he said he had gone to a tavern after completing the errand and had become completely intoxicated. He awoke to find himself onboard a ship carrying recruits.

When the ship hit port, he reported that he could not find a ship back to Ireland, and lacking money, he enlisted in the army. Welsh's story, farfetched as it sounds, was probably true: this was a period of almost continual warfare between England and France, with this phase (1688–97) known as the War of the League of Augsberg, and the shanghaiing of recruits was not unknown.

Though Christian had some difficulty in understanding why her husband had been so long in communicating with her, she was not content to wait for her husband's return but decided to set out to find him. Recalling the case of Captain Bodeaux, she decided to disguise herself as a man, join the army, and go to Flanders, where she believed her husband to be. After placing her children under the care of her mother and a nurse, she cut her hair and dressed herself in her husband's suit (with added quilting in the waistcoat). She then bought a wig, a hat, some shirts, and a sword; after taking care to conceal some fifty guineas in the waistband of her breeches, she enlisted as Christopher Welch. She was then shipped to the Netherlands, where the fighting was centered. Christian was wounded, then taken prisoner, and ultimately exchanged for a French prisoner. She subsequently fought a sergeant for attacking another woman, but was then arrested for attacking a noncommissioned officer. When the fact that the sergeant had attacked the girl came out, Christian was pardoned by the king and released.

After being discharged from her regiment, Christian joined another regiment in time to participate in the siege of Namurs, which fell to the French in 1692. Again her regiment was disbanded, and she decided to return to Ireland. There, without revealing herself, she found that her children and her mother were faring well without her, and so decided to continue her life as a soldier. She again took a ship to Holland and reenlisted in the dragoons under her former commander, by now convinced that her husband must have been killed. In 1703 she was badly wounded, but despite the fact that her wound involved both her leg and thigh, her sex was not discovered. After being discharged from the hospital, she again engaged in battle, and it was in its aftermath that she saw her husband.

Christian took a private room in an alehouse and sent a message to her husband to come and see a "fellow Irishman." Richard did so, and after he had told the stranger that he had written to his wife more than a dozen times without hearing from her, she revealed to him that she was his wife. The couple's reunion, however, was interrupted by a Dutch woman who claimed to be Richard's wife. Richard admitted they had lived together as man and wife but had not actually married. After the woman had been persuaded to leave, Christian told her husband that she wanted to stay in the army; if he would pretend to be her brother and not claim her as his wife, nor reveal the secret of her sex, she would give him all that he wanted.

For a time the two saw each other every day, but at the battle of Ramilles, Christian was hit by a mortar fragment that fractured her skull. She was unconscious for several days, and it was during this time the surgeons discovered her true sex. Her commander was informed that his "pretty dragoon," as she had been called, was in fact a woman. Richard Welsh was summoned, and he confessed that he was not Christian's brother but her husband. Christian was given a silk gown, her pay was ordered continued, and all the officers of the regiment contributed money to buy her dresses. Christian continued to travel with the army, cooking for the regiment and acting as courier and nurse until her husband was killed in battle. She then obtained permission to return to Ireland. Nothing is known of the fate of her children, but it is known that she later became so impoverished that she opened up a small beer and pie house in Dublin in order to support herself. Christian Welsh died much later, at the age of 108, in Chelsea hospital and was buried among the old pensioners with military honors.[13]

Female Impersonation as Privilege of the Upper Class

In most of the cross-dressing accounts summarized here, as well as in many others, the women who successfully cross dressed were admired by others when they were finally unmasked. They had demonstrated that women could successfully compete with men and had for themselves, at least, removed many of the barriers that kept women in their place. Though some were lesbian, most of the women in these accounts seemed content to revert to their traditional feminine role once they found the "right" man. In short, they were nonthreatening to the male establishment. Cross dressing by men, outside of that reported in the theater and at festivals, seems much less common and is reported somewhat less charitably. It is also more often associated with homosexuality, or if the person is heterosexual, the accounts emphasize that the cross dressing is used as a way to gain access to women for sexual purposes. In effect, there are stronger sexual overtones associated with male cross dressing than with female cross dressing.

Probably both sexes found it exciting to get away with their impersonation, but since it was more difficult for society to accept the male cross dresser, if only because it was harder for men to understand why any man would want to be a woman except in jest, more sexual overtones were read into it. It is perhaps significant that all the male cross dressers we know about in this period belonged to royal or noble families and, in effect, were not worried about any loss of status that might have resulted from their cross dressing. Almost all the women in this chapter, on the other hand, came from lower socioeconomic groups, and cross dressing gave them not only freedom but increased status.

The most notable male cross dresser in this period is François Timoléon de Choisy, better known as the Abbé de Choisy (1644–1724). The Choisy family was well connected with the French court, which itself had been the scene of much cross dressing.

Earlier, Henri III of France (1574–89) had cross dressed frequently. He had appeared at parties, masquerades, and tourneys dressed as an Amazon or wearing a ball gown, makeup, earrings, and other jewelry, and attended by his so-called *mignons,* or homosexual favorites. Henri wore women's clothes and makeup much of the time, as did some of his favorites. Pierre de l'Estoile, who kept a journal of Henri's court, wrote in 1576 that the king's *mignons* wore their hair the way whores in a bordello did—pomaded, artificially curled and recurled and flowing back over small velvet bonnets. A contemporary critic, the Huguenot poet Agrippa d'Aubigne, accused Henri's mother, Catherine de Medici, of intentionally corrupting and feminizing Henri so that she could continue to rule France.[14]

In the seventeenth century, Philippe d'Orléans, the brother of Louis XIV, was both a homosexual and a cross dresser. On occasion, he even appeared publicly in the Palais Royal in womanly attire.[15] Though Choisy was closely connected with Philippe, his orientation was more heterosexual. Philippe d'Orléans and François de Choisy were childhood playmates, and both were raised in environments which, to the extent that environments are important to the development of cross dressing as adults, might encourage gender-crossing.

Choisy's father had been chancellor to Gaston d'Orléans, the brother of Louis XIII. His mother, Jeanne Olympe, was the oldest daughter of Monsieur de Belesbat of the House of Hurault and was herself well connected to the court. After the death of her husband, she was given a pension by Louis XIV. François had been born when his mother was already in her forties. He was her fourth and youngest son and was more or less raised as a girl, perhaps as the daughter she had never had. There is also speculation that he was raised as a girl to further ingratiate the family with Queen Anne, the queen regent of France and mother of both Louis XIV and Philippe.

Choisy wrote in his memoirs that the emasculation of Prince Philippe had been done on orders of the Cardinal Mazarin, who wished to render him so effeminate that he would not be a threat to Louis XIV, as his uncle, an earlier Prince d'Orange, had been.[16] This charge is denied by Philippe's biographer, who reported that Cardinal Mazarin deplored the effeminate ways of the young prince. Still, Philippe was raised in the company of women, and his pastimes were those of girls rather than boys. François de Choisy reported that they dressed

> me as a girl every time the little Monsieur [Philippe] came to play, and he came at least two or three times a week. I had my ears pierced, diamonds, beauty spots, and all the other little affectations to which one becomes accustomed so easily and that later are so difficult to do without. Monsieur, who liked all that, was always very friendly with me. As soon as he arrived, followed by the nieces of Cardinal Mazarin and the ladies of the queen, they began to dress him and arrange his coiffure. . . . His jacket was removed so that he could put on the coats and skirts of women.[17]

Occasionally, Philippe rebelled at his treatment, but the younger François apparently did not. Choisy reported that as an adult Philippe continued to cross dress, although not always completely, and he did not try to pass as a woman. Still in the evening Philippe would put on his long earrings, his beauty patches, his night cap, and gaze longingly and lovingly in the mirror. Even when he was dressed as a man, he appeared different from other men. One observer described Philippe at age fifty as "always adorned like any woman, covered with rings and bracelets and gems, with a long black, powdered wig brought very much forward, and ribbons wherever he could put them, exhaling perfumes of every kind, and cleanliness itself in all details." He took great care of his complexion, laughed prettily, minced, and "simpered in the most marvellous way." He also painted his face so that his "beauty was more suited to a princess than to a prince."[18]

Though Philippe married and even had a mistress, his erotic interests were probably predominantly homosexual. One historian particularly hostile to his life-style wrote that Philippe was the leading authority at court on female underclothing (which he often wore) and that he continued always to dress and admire himself in the mirror.[19] But Philippe amassed a fortune, was an effective general, and though a flamboyant homosexual and cross dresser, fathered a dynasty from Marie Antoinette to Italy's Victor Emmanuel, Austria's Franz Josef, and Spain's Juan Carlos.[20] Indeed, if France had a king today, it would be his descendants who would wear the crown.

Either Jeanne Olympe de Choisy went much further in feminizing her son than the queen of France with hers or else François de Choisy was much more pliable. The young Choisy was clearly brought up as a girl. Some indication of the strength of her determination is evidenced by the fact that her husband permitted her to do so, or at least did not prevent it. The boy apparently never rebelled against his cross dressing and was kept in constant attendance on his mother in her bedroom and even at her toilette. For a time after the death of his father, his mother even allowed him to live as a girl, and together mother and "daughter" attended the theater, receptions, and dances. So well did he carry off the impersonation that almost everyone took him to be the young girl he pretended to be.

Still, Choisy had some of the advantages of being a male. At the age of eighteen he attended the Sorbonne for his *tentative,* a public oral examination of candidates for the Bachelor of Theology degree. Though he had not prepared himself well for the examinations, he did not have to worry since he was told the nature of the questions in advance by the Archbishop of Paris; this gives some indication of the influence his family had at the court. Soon after, his family's influence led to his being awarded the income from the abbacy of Saint Seine. At this time (about 1663) he left Paris and went to Bordeaux, where he appeared briefly on stage as a woman and had male suitors.[21]

After a brief time, he returned to Paris, where he still dressed as a woman. Choisy himself reported that it was not until after his mother died in 1662 that he attempted to live completely as a man, but he was so often mistaken for a woman that he decided to revert to living full time as a woman. Choisy made careful plans for embarking on his new life away from people who knew him. Buying a house in Bourges where he was unknown, he pretended to be a rich young widow, the Comtesse des Barres. Choisy obviously received erotic satisfaction from his cross dressing and was particularly aroused when pubescent girls were attracted to him. When he became very enamored of one such young woman, he persuaded the girl's mother to allow her to stay with him for a week in order to teach her the Parisian style of hairdressing. The mother, much poorer than Choisy, was obviously flattered that a woman as rich as the "Comtesse" would be interested in her daughter, and she quickly consented. The young girl shared the same bed with Choisy, who spun out the lessons on hairdressing for several weeks.

One girl was followed by another. At first, Choisy was satisfied by being able to fondle and kiss them. He also found himself being courted by men, and though he enjoyed the attention, he turned them all down. He continued to invite young girls to share his bed, kissing them, often while their mothers' looked on, but was ever careful not to go beyond innocent embraces with the proper citizens of the town. He was less careful with others, however, and he got a young actress named Roselie pregnant. Choisy particularly enjoyed dressing Roselie as a man and had taken to pretending that she was his husband, a practice that ceased with her pregnancy. Choisy did not neglect the young woman and took her to Paris to be cared for by a midwife. He also assumed financial responsibility for the baby, a girl, and he later gave Roselie a dowry and married her off to an actor.

The pregnancy of Roselie, however, had precipitated his return to Paris and led him to abandon cross dressing for a time. Interestingly, this abandonment after a successful period of cross dressing is very similar to the purges that modern transvestites go through when, either because of guilt or because for a time they feel free of the compulsion to cross dress, they destroy their feminine clothes and try to be completely male.

Choisy later had another intense interlude of cross dressing, but since part of his *Memoirs* are lost, it is not always easy to piece together how one incident followed another. In this second period Choisy bought a house in Saint-Marceau (a suburb of Paris), had his ears repierced, had new corsets made, and gradually resumed his life as a woman, each day wearing more and more of the feminine dress until he dressed completely as one. Apparently his neighbors accepted him as a rich eccentric. Choisy self-analyzed his condition as follows:

I have carefully considered whence came such a bizarre taste and here is my explanation: the attribute of God is to be loved, adored; Man, as far as the weakness of his nature allows, wishes for the same but, as it is beauty that kindles love and since that is usually the lot of women, when it happens that men have, or believe themselves to have, certain traits of beauty, they try to enhance them by the same methods that women use, which are most becoming. They feel the inexpressible pleasure of being loved. I have felt this more than once during a delightful affair. When I was at the ball or the theatre, wearing my beautiful *robes de chambre,* diamonds and patches, and heard people murmur near me "There is a lovely woman," I experienced an inward glow of pleasure which is incomparable, it is so strong. Ambition, riches, even love do not equal it, because we always love ourselves more deeply than we love others.[22]

Like male cross dressers of today, Choisy was extremely interested in women's clothes. He recounted in one of the episodes of his memoirs how an uncle, knowing

that I dressed myself as a woman, came one morning to give me a good scolding. I was at my *toilette* and had just taken up my shift; I stood up. "No," he said, "sit down and dress yourself." So saying, he sat down opposite me. "Since you command me, dear Uncle, I said, I shall obey you. It is eleven o'clock and I must go to Mass." My servants brought me in a bodice laced behind, then a black cut velvet gown, a shirt of the same material over an ordinary petticoat, a muslin cravat and a gold and black steenkirk [ribbon or scarf worn around the neck that reaches down to the bosom]. Until then I had kept on my cornets [a ribboned night cap]. I put on a peruke [wig] which was well curled and powdered. My good uncle did not say a word. "I will soon be done, dear Uncle,"

I said. "I have to put on my ear pendants and five or six patches," which I did in a moment. "From what I have seen," he said, "I must now call you my niece, and, really you are very pretty." I flung my arms around his neck and kissed him two or three times; he made no reproaches to me, made me use his carriage, and took me to Mass and then to dine with him.[23]

Choisy was continually attracted to young women. Some of the girls who knew his secret were attracted to him because of it, and one told him that his cross dressing gave him an advantage: "The heart of a man is there, which has its effect on us [females] and on the other hand the charms of femininity transport us and quite disarm us."[24]

He particularly liked to have the young women dress up as men. His much poorer neighbors were flattered by his attention to their daughters and did not even mind them sharing his bed with them. When the family of one girl did object, Choisy reported the girl told them

"it is quite true that Madame [i.e., Choisy] loves me; she has given me a hundred little presents, and she can make my fortune; you know . . . that we are not rich. She invites me to come to see her on my own in her summer house; I have been there five or six times, but how do you think we pass the time? In clothing Madame, when she is going to make a visit, in dressing her hair, in putting on her ear pendants and patches, in admiring her beauty. I swear to you . . . that she thinks only of that; I never cease saying to her, 'Madame, how beautiful you are today!' and on that she hugs me, and says: 'My dear Charlotte, if you could always be dressed as a boy, I would love you even more and we would wed; we must find a way of sleeping together without giving offense to God.' My family would never agree to it, but we could have a marriage of conscience."[25]

Choisy even offered the relatives of one young girl an apartment in his house in order that the girl could be properly supervised. He soon realized the dream of many present-day transvestites by arranging a marriage ceremony in which he was dressed as the bride and the girl dressed as a groom, even to the point of having her hair cut in male style. The girl took the name of Monsieur de Maulny for the occasion, and the two lived together as man and wife, although apparently Choisy never had sex with her, or at least, she never became pregnant. (He did fondle and play with all the girls, however.) This relationship ended when his "husband" received a formal proposal of marriage from someone else and went off to become a bride herself. One reason Choisy did not object was that he was beginning to come under heavy criticism for sharing a bed with a young woman to whom he was not legally married.

Choisy next found a young servant girl to whom he grew attached, Mademoiselle Dany. He dressed her in luxurious clothes, sent her to learn the linen-draper's trade, and shared his bed with her. To win support from the cardinal for his activities, Choisy established an orphanage in the local parish, and the cardinal continued to tolerate his cross dressing, allegedly because of his good works.

Unfortunately, Choisy's absence from Paris and the court had been noticed, and fearful of the loss of royal favor if he did not keep up his contacts, he returned to Paris. There he turned to gambling and lost enough money that he had to sell his suburban house and give up his "poor little Dany," whom he sent off to a convent after paying her dowry entrance fee. He then purged himself of all his feminine clothing and possessions and stated that he had given up the thought of ever again dressing as a woman. This statement, however, like those of many of today's transvestites, did not ultimately translate into reality.

Choisy did, however, appear less frequently in public as a woman and tried to make a career for himself in other ways. He accompanied a family friend, the Cardinal de Bouillon (d. 1715), who had become part of Louis XIV's military entourage. When sufficient priests were not available, Choisy assisted the cardinal in serving Mass to the king. Choisy also accompanied the cardinal in 1676 to the consistory that elected Pope Innocent XI, and he apparently cross dressed during part of his stay in Rome.

In 1683 Choisy fell gravely ill. In his delirium, he saw a vision of a hell populated by sinners dressed as women. He became so alarmed that he resolved to live more devoutly if he recovered. Shortly thereafter, he became a priest and in 1685 was sent on a mission to Siam (Thailand), where part of his assignment was to convert the king of that country to Christianity. On his return from his unsuccessful mission, Choisy published the diary he had kept during the trip. Encouraged by its popular success, he followed it by a number of other books on religion and history. He was respected well enough to be admitted to the Académie française in 1687, which was as close as that body came to admitting a woman until the mid-twentieth century.

Choisy was a master of repartee, friendly, likable, and able to remain on the good side of most of the powerful people in France, despite his known fondness for dressing as a woman. In time, he became prior of Saint Lô de Rouen, of Saint Benoît de Sault near Bourges, and of Saint Gelais. He continued to gamble throughout his life, occasionally having to sell some of his property to pay his debts. He retained his desire to cross dress, though in later years he could not afford the elaborate dresses and ornaments he had worn in his youth. He died in 1724.[26]

Choisy's legacy of written works owes itself to the fact that he liked to amuse himself by writing stories about cross dressing. In addition to his historical and religious works, he wrote a novel, *La nouvelle Astrée*, which features a young shepherd who, in order to become closer to and more intimate with the shepherdess he loved, pretended to be a woman. He is also believed to be the author or coauthor of "The Story of the Marquise-Marquis de Banneville," which recounts the story of a boy raised as a girl.[27]

Many incidents in the life of Choisy have great similarity to the lives of male heterosexual transvestites today. Often the person is introduced to cross dressing as a child; he is erotically aroused by it and finds it exciting to pass himself off as a member of the opposite sex. He is erotically aroused by women and often has intercourse with women while cross dressed. Such actions are often followed by feelings of guilt or satiation, after which the transvestite purges his feminine wardrobe and promises never to cross dress again. Usually, the same process starts over again after a distinct interval.

Choisy apparently enjoyed being courted by men, although clearly his own sexual preferences were for girls and women. Even as he grew older, he continued to cross dress, and although he became less public with it (perhaps because it was more difficult to pass), he did not bother to keep it a secret since others knew about it. He also was aroused by reading transvestite fiction either authored by himself or others. In sum, he was a classic transvestite two hundred years before the term was coined or the condition described by Magnus Hirschfeld. He also quite clearly is different from the women cross dressers examined in this chapter.

Summary

Although homosexuality and lesbianism sometimes are involved, it seems that, both for men and women, the cross dresser can be heterosexual, homosexual, bisexual, or perhaps even asexual. (The nature of this difference will be explored in later chapters.) It is important to note, however, that there was a class and status difference between the male and female cross dressers: Women cross dressers, both in historical and fictional accounts, frequently came from the lower classes, and their cross dressing was perhaps perceived as a rational attempt to gain social status. Male cross dressers, however, more often came from a higher social class, and thus the converse perception—that of the male's loss of status—would be mitigated by the male's stable position as a member of a royal or noble family.

Notes

1. The story of Eleno/Elena was ferreted out by Richard L. Kagan of Johns Hopkins University and was reported at a seminar in Atlantic History and

Culture in April 1986. The full details of the trial, which give the necessary background information, are in the Archivo Historico Nacional (Madrid, Sección de Inquisición, *lejago* 234, *expediente* 24. It is approximately 150 folios in length. It was also reported by Henry C. Lea in *A History of the Inquisition in Spain*, 4 vols. (New York: The Macmillan Co., 1907), 4:187–88.

2. She wrote her own life story: Catalina de Erauso, *Relacion verdadera de las grandes hazañas, y valerosos hechos en veynte y quatro años que sirvio en al Reyno de Chile y otras partes al Rey nuestro señor, en abito de soldado . . . sacada de un original, que dexo en Madrid en casa de Bernardino de Guzman* (Madrid: Bernardino de Guzmán, 1625), although the date is misprinted as 1615. An enlarged edition appeared almost immediately after from the same publisher as *Segunda relacion de las mas copiosa y verdader que hal salido,* although the date is misprinted as 1615. A rival publisher released another edition at the same time as the second edition, *Segunda relacion de los famosos hechos que en el Reyne de Chile hizo una varonil muger sirviendo veynte y quatro años de soldado en servicio de su Magestad el Rey nuestro Señor, en qual tiempo tuvo muy onrosos cargos* (Sevilla: Juan de Cabrera, 1625). Her career was dramatized by Juan Pérez de Montalbán in 1626. Her life was translated into English under the title *The Nun Ensign* along with Montalbán's play, *La Monia Alférez,* by James Fitzmaurice Kelly (London: T. Fisher and Unwin, 1908). Her portrait was painted by Francesco Crescentio.

3. Melveena McKendrick, *Women and Society in the Spanish Drama of the Golden Age* (Cambridge: Cambridge University Press, 1974).

4. See Francis William Bain, *Queen Christina of Sweden* (London: 1890), and the popular biographies by Ruth Stephan, *The Flight* (New York: Knopf, 1956) and *My Crown, My Love* (New York: Knopf, 1960). Greta Garbo portrayed her in the film *Queen Christina*, made in 1933.

5. Rudolf M. Dekker and Lotte C. van de Pol, *The Tradition of Female Transvestism in Early Modern Europe* (London: Macmillan, 1989). The book was originally published in Dutch, *Daat was Laatst een meisje ioos: Nederlandse Vrouwen als matrozen en soldaten: een historish onderzoek* (Amsterdam: Uigerverij Ambo, 1982).

6. Dekker and van de Pol, *Female Transvestism,* 11, 13, 15, 16, 18–21, 33, 81–82, 91.

7. Ibid., 1, 3–4, 11, 19–23, 23–27, 30, 33, 62–69, 78–79, 82–84, 86, 89, 96–97.

8. Ibid., 84.

9. Chapbooks were broadsides folded into a convenient pamphlet of four or more pages. They often carried stories similar to those in the *National Enquirer* of today and were the chief reading matter for those masses of English who were just beginning to learn to read. There are special collections of them at various libraries, including the Huntington Library in California and the Harvard University Library. Charles Welsh and William H. Tillinghast compiled an early catalogue of the Harvard collection, *Catalogue of English and American Chapbooks and Broadside Ballads in the Harvard College Library* (Cambridge: Harvard University Bibliography Publications, No. 56, 1905), which was reprinted by the Singing Tree Press in 1968. The chapbook *The Life and Death of Mrs. Mary Frith* (1662) is in the British Museum.

10. See Thomas Middleton and Thomas Dekker, *The Roaring Girl,* in *The Work of Thomas Middleton,* ed. A. H. Bullen, 8 vols. (New York: AMS Press, 1964), vol. 4; Nathan [Nathaniel] Field, *Amends for Ladies,* in *Nero and Other Plays,* ed. H. P. Horne et al. (London: Vizetelly, 1888). This particular play was edited by A. Wilson Verity.

11. Four biographies were written about her: *The Life of Long Meg of Westminster* . . . (London: E. All.de f. E. White, 1620); *The Life of Long Meg of Westminster* . . . (London: [J. Beale], f.r. Bird, 1635); *The Life and Pranks of Long Meg of Westminster* (n.p. c. 1680); *The Life of Long Meg of Westminster* . . . (London: J. M. for G. Conyers [1690]).

12. R. Valerie Lucas, "*Hic Mulier*": The Female Transvestite in Early Modern England," *Renaissance and Reformation*, 24, no. 1 (1988): 76–77.

13. C. J. S. Thompson, *Mysteries of Sex: Women Who Posed as Men and Men Who Impersonated Women* (London: Hutchinson and Co., n.d.).

14. See Pierre de L'Estoile, *Journal des choses memorables advenues durant le regne de Henry III* . . . (Paris, Gallimard, 1943); and Agrippa d'Aubigné, *Les Tragiques*. Livre 2, *Les Princes* (Baltimore: Johns Hopkins University Press, 1953).

15. For a discussion of Philippe, see Nancy Nichols Barker, *Brother to the Sun King: Philippe, Duke of Orléans* (Baltimore: Johns Hopkins Press, 1989).

16. Abbé de Choisy, *Mémoires pour servir a l'histoire de Louis XIV* and *Mémoires de l'abbé de Choisy habillé en femme*, ed. George Mongrédien (Paris: Mercure de France, 1966), 219.

17. Ibid.

18. Quotations are from diaries of the time and can be found in Jacques Boulenger, *The Seventeenth Century in France* (New York: Capricorn Books, 1963), 180–81.

19. W. H. Lewis, *The Splendid Century: Life in the France of Louis XIV* (New York: Doubleday, 1957), 16.

20. See Barker, *Brother to the Sun King*, passim.

21. See Choisy, *Mémoires de l'abbé de Choisy habillé en femme*. This particular memoir has also appeared under other titles in its varied publication history, including *Histoire de Madame la comtesse des Barres, À Madame la marquise de Lambert; Histoire de Madame de Sancy*, and *Histoire de la marquise-marquis de Banneville*, and others. It has been translated as *The Transvestite Memoirs of the Abbé de Choisy*, by R. H. F. Scott (London: Peter Owen, 1973). See also one of the authors' (V.B.) translations, part of which was published in various issues of *Transvestia* magazine.

22. Choisy, *Transvestite Memoirs*, 30.

23. Ibid., 32.

24. Ibid., 36.

25. Ibid., 40.

26. In addition to the works cited above, see also O. P. Gilbert, *Men in Women's Guise: Some Historical Instances of Female Impersonation*, translated from the French by Robert B. Douglas (London: John Lane The Bodley Head, 1926), 3–102. See also Héctor Uribe Troncoso, "De Choisy . . . Prince of Transvestites," in *Transvestism: Men in Female Dress*, ed. D. O. Cauldwell (New York: Sexology Press, 1956), 40–50.

27. For a discussion of the story see Jeanne Roche-Mazon, "L'Abbé Choisy et Charles Perrault," *Mercure de France* (February 1920): 513–42.

Chapter 6
Challenges to the Hierarchy

Changes in the Patriarchy

Europe evolved as a hierarchical society in which being male gave one a higher status in the class to which one belonged. Hierarchical establishments, however, increasingly came under attack in the seventeenth and eighteenth centuries. Justification for a special noble class trained to fight grew more difficult with the development of canon, which resulted in a decline in the effectiveness of cavalry. Rebellious peasants attacked their landlords in the English Civil War, and the very basis of hierarchy had been undermined by the capture and execution of the English king in 1649; the French followed suit at the end of the eighteenth century.

Though the British monarchy was restored in 1660 with Charles II, kingship was never quite the same. James II, his brother and successor, was forced to flee in 1688 and formally deposed in 1689. As traditional hierarchies were under attack, the simple fact of being born male seemed to some men not enough of a guarantee of their dominance over women. It was necessary to be more aggressive, to wear masculinity as a badge of honor. Inevitably, many began to have fears about their own manliness. John Milton (1608–74), the great Puritan poet, wrote:

Why do I seem to those fellows [his fellow collegians] insufficiently masculine? . . . Doubtless it was because I was never able to gulp down huge bumpers [glasses filled to the brim as for a toast] in pancratic fashion. . . . But would that they could as easily lay aside their asshood as I whatever belongs to womanhood.[1]

One way for a man to overcome his anxieties about his manhood was to show his fellows he could be as vulgar as any of them, to be a jolly good fellow.[2] Still, males had to be ever watchful how they conducted themselves since all kinds of things could be defined as suggestive of femininity, and these changed with locality and region; the best safeguard was to watch other men and adopt their ways. Numerous behaviors were described as indicating feminine weakness. Lovesickness, that is, the mooning passion of a man for a woman, was a sign of feminine weakness.[3] Wearing one's hair too long was also suspect.[4] In some areas and increasingly in England, holding another man's hand was suspect.

Ideas of what constitutes masculinity also changed over time. For example, Martin Luther in the sixteenth century had regarded the elector John of Saxony as an authentic hero, the personification of the ideal male, and yet described him as crying out like a lion when he was in pain.[5] Such a lack of stoicism would later be described as feminine behavior.

A man, fearful of being labeled as exhibiting feminine weaknesses, could demonstrate his masculinity by asserting power over his wife and family. Tradition was the source of his power, and religion and law gave him the right to practice it; the Calvinistic premise of original sin gave fathers an added incentive to ensure their children's submission. And yet as time went on even this control was threatened, for in both Catholic and Protestant countries, the father's power had been considered similar to that of the monarch. Since subordination of the family to its head was analogous to (and indeed a direct contributing factor of) the subordination of subjects to the sovereign,[6] it was felt that rebellion against one would lead to rebellion against the other—both were under attack.

One of the more effective challenges to the concept of patriarchal family control occurred in John Locke's *Two Treatises of Government*, published in 1689 but written a decade earlier. In the second of the two treatises, Locke had emphasized that family power was invested in both the mother and the father, not in just one or the other.[7] Others agreed. William Wollaston emphasized that marriage involved not only the propagation of the species but the mutual happiness of the couple.[8] David Hume went so far as to hold that the subordination of women was a sign of a barbarian society.[9]

In general, the philosophers of the eighteenth-century Enlightenment believed that societies operated in accordance with natural law, which was as binding as the mathematical laws governing the function of the universe. The catchwords for the philosophes were *reason* and *nature*, terms they used to convey that people, unmolested by arbitrary authority and dependent on their own reason and observation, could not only discover the laws governing human nature but would act according to them in order to make a better world. All it took to find the truth was to gather knowledge, to challenge old assumptions, and to eliminate obstacles. The "defects" of women, which men had unhesitatingly elaborated upon in the past, were no longer to be regarded as imposed by the laws of nature but were believed to have been acquired as a result of the conditions under which women lived. To bring about change it was essential that women develop their own mental abilities, since it was only by becoming enlightened and knowledgeable that they could become virtuous and shun evil. Not all such discourse was "just talk." At least some of it carried over into the marriage relationship itself, where the concept of the companionate marriage and the domesticated family began to emerge.[10] Among other things these concepts also led to the foundation of utopian communities, particularly in the United States, where new ideas were being put into practice.

And yet the patriarchal idea strongly persisted. Jean-Jacques Rousseau (1718–78) emphasized in his work *Émile* that the true state of relations between the sexes was one in which men would be active and strong and women passive and weak. He believed that those who advocated equality of the sexes, with reciprocal duties and obligations, were indulging in ideal declamations that ran contrary to nature and reality. For a woman to cultivate so-called masculine qualities only led to the neglect of those qualities that were peculiar to her sex. Rousseau even went so far as to hold that women existed only by their connection to men; woman was created to please man and to obey him.[11]

Women writers of the time expressed ambivalence. Hannah More (1745–1833), one of the more famous of the English bluestockings, agreed with Rousseau that the goal of female education should not be equality with males but recognition of women as different. In her mind the essential differences were not so much physical but rather that women were more moral creatures than men. Women's education, then, had a higher purpose than that of men, for it raised the moral tone of society.[12] Though this concept proved attractive to many women (and men), not all women looked upon themselves as "finer" creatures. Mary Wollstonecraft (1759–97), for example, made passionate pleas that the education of women be improved so they could become the intellectual equals of men.[13]

The debates on the issue of emphasizing equality or difference have continued until the end of the twentieth century, but throughout this time a major result was the rethinking of the role of women. While the majority of women adopted the goal of working within a separate and more moral sphere than that of men (a view that proved politically potent), a minority, which over the years has waxed and waned in strength, has always argued for equality. Growing numbers of women also proved willing to challenge male domination in terms of their own personal lives. But although women's efforts to redefine their role and place in society had many male allies, most men proved unwilling to examine the male role itself, perhaps because an unexamined role assured them of continued dominance and influence.

Still, this does not mean that there were not more subtle, gradual changes in public perceptions. A good example of this change can be traced in the public attitudes toward the fop, whose interest in dress and manners came to be regarded as effeminate. Fops, from their first appearance, were caricatured unmercifully, but originally were assumed to be heterosexual males. Gradually, however, during the eighteenth century the fop came to be seen more stereotypically as a homosexual.[14]

From Fop to Rake: Libertinism in the Age of Scandal

In a sense, the eighteenth-century fop served an important role in preserving masculine self-esteem: a man could always rationalize that since the fop sought the passive role in a sexual relationship, he was not really a man at all. The fop's visible assertion of other feminine qualities was further evidence of this. Homosexuality was associated with being penetrated, not in being the penetrator, and a "real" man could penetrate both women and men without having his masculinity questioned.

One of the more fascinating counterdevelopments to the fop was the increasing prevalence of dueling. The prevailing belief that any offense to male honor needed a response found expression among gentlemen in the duel. That the duel served a role in preserving masculinity was clear from the fact that many of the duels were fought by male "protectors" to preserve a "lady's" honor, in a deadly revival of chivalry. Though officially most governments prohibited it, duelers were often not arrested and, if arrested, they were usually pardoned, since the male rulers and judges tended to sympathize with the importance of protecting honor. In the seventeenth century one Frenchman, Chevalier d'Andrieux, is said to have killed some seventy-two men in duels by the time he was thirty.[15] Men from the lower classes did not engage in dueling but fought with what was at hand, from knives to bare fists.

Another traditional way for a man to prove his masculinity was by his sexual conquests, which if word about them was carefully leaked out, removed all doubts about his ability to perform. Lawrence Stone has written that in the eighteenth century the two romantic heroes of the poor were the highwayman, who preyed exclusively on the rich, and the sexual athlete; the greatest hero of all was the man who was both. By the end of the seventeenth century, the term *libertine* was being used to describe a man who was not restrained by moral law, especially in his sexual relations.[16] David Foxon has traced the origin of libertinism to the Italian Pietro Aretino in the sixteenth century, dating its major flourishing from the 1650s to the 1750s.[17]

In England libertinism began with the restoration of Charles II and the rise of the rakes. *Rake* is a catchall term used to describe a man who not only made numerous sexual conquests but was also a skeptic in religion, republican in politics, and even suspected of engaging in sodomy with boys—in short, an individual who defied what might be called standard Christian conduct. The term is also reserved to certain classes, since the rakes came from a relatively small circle of aristocrats, and it was their power and influence that made them more or less immune to the ordinary standards of conduct, an immunity emphasized by the fact that much of their activity was either carried out in public or was widely known.

In a period when gender roles were being challenged, the rakes represent the ultimate extreme of masculinity. A real man had a penis and was willing to penetrate anything; he exhibited his sign of masculinity with pride. The rake Charles Sedley, for example, in a rather inebriated state, harangued a growing crowd from the balcony of an inn while he was naked. In acting out various postures of lust and buggery with his drunken companions, he continued to exhort the crowd as if "he had been a preacher."[18] Also to be listed among the rakes was Lord Rochester (John Wilmot), who wrote among other things a short play, *Sodom or the Quintessence of Debauchery*. Rochester, a bisexual, seemingly believed that almost anyone was fair game for his sexual conquests.[19]

England was not alone in its libertine activities. On the Continent kings and rulers set the example for their fellow nobles. The French court reached new heights of sexual activity under the reign of Louis XV who had succeeded to the throne as a five-year-old; Louis was notorious for spending much of his long reign (1710–74) hunting and fornicating. His most famous mistress was Madame de Pompadour who, in order to satisfy her royal suitor's demand for sexual variety, arranged a continuous supply of younger girls for him. The new recruits were set up at a special house in Deer Park (Parc aux cerfs) at Versailles where the king could visit them, supposedly without them knowing who he was. After some fifty-nine years of misrule, Louis is reported to have said on his deathbed in 1774: "I have governed and administered badly, because I have little talent and I have been badly advised."[20]

The king who fathered the most royal bastards was neither English nor French: he was Augustus the Strong (1670–1713), King of Poland and Elector of Saxony. His epithet almost surely came from his performance in the bedchamber, since his military abilities were not particularly notable. He fathered some 365 known children, only one of whom was legitimate (his successor Augustus III). Among the most famous of his illegitimate sons was Maurice de Saxe, who became a marshal of France.[21]

The successful seducer was exalted as a figure in the various versions of Don Juan, who originally was the hero in a seventeenth-century Spanish tragic drama, *El burlador de Sevilla* ("The rake of Seville"), attributed to Tirso de Molina (Gabriel Telléz). Many other versions followed, including one by Molière (1665), an unfinished one by Byron, and an operatic version by Mozart (1787). In Mozart's version, Don Giovanni is said to have had 700 mistresses in Italy, 800 in Germany, 91 in both Turkey and France, and 1,003 in Spain.

Adding verisimilitude to the fictional character was Giovanni Giacomo Casanova, Chevalier de Seingalt (1725–98), whose first recorded sexual experience consisted of coitus with two young sisters in one bed. He mentions some 116 mistresses by name and claims to have possessed hundreds more, ranging from chambermaids to noblewomen, with whom he made love standing, sitting, and lying down, in coaches, on boats, in beds, and even in alleys. He reported that after he had intercourse, his interest in the lady vanished, and he happily moved on to other conquests. He had sex with at least one of his own illegitimate daughters as well as with a nine-year-old girl. His oldest conquest was a seventy-year-old woman. Casanova's judgment of his life was contained in the words, "I regret nothing," although on his deathbed he reportedly said, "I have lived a philosopher and die a Christian." In his old age his chief regret seemed to be that he no longer retained his youthful vigor and potency. Though some of his stories might well have been his own fantasy running wild, many are accepted as genuine.[22]

Fiction kept up with reality and sometimes exceeded it, and in it women often gave as good as they received. In England the new eroticism was reflected in the pornographic novel *Memoirs of a Woman of Pleasure, or Fanny Hill* by John Cleland, which recounts the adventures of a young innocent in London using only the most modest of language. In France, Pierre Choderlos de Laclos (1741–1803) achieved similar fame with his more realistic novel, *Les Liaisons dangereuses,* which recounts how sexual conquests enhance one's sense of personal power.

It should be noted that this emphasis on new sexual conquests, even in fiction, was primarily associated with the upper classes, who as they were losing power took to asserting masculine privilege through rampant sexuality. In England especially, the disparity between the rich and powerful and the poor and helpless increased in almost geometric ratios. T. H. White labeled the first half of the eighteenth century "The Age of Scandal," and it was in this period that the aristocratic and privileged eccentric flourished. The lords knew one another, gossiped about one another, and recorded the latest scandals in their letters and memoirs.[23] As the turmoil between the upper and lower classes grew and disorder seemed to threaten, the ruling class increased the harshness of punishments meted out to the lower classes. In England, more than two hundred offenses were given the death penalty. Though there were probably greater disparities in England between the powerful rich and the average person than there were on the Continent, certainly the same ideals of erotic achievement existed on the Continent as well.

Moreover, the growth of major population centers such as London allowed the young and powerful to be somewhat anonymous, to escape from family supervision. Certainly in England, the upper-class male was given almost free rein to express his sexual inclinations, and special clubs grew up to cater to their different proclivities. In London, the activities of some of the clubs and affinity groups became notorious. One group known as the Mohocks went out nightly to beat up on people, standing lower-class women and girls on their heads so that their skirts would fall down, exposing their bare bottoms. Another of their favorite activities was to seize individuals they found walking about and roll them down hills inside casks. A group known as the Bold Bucks specialized in rape, the Sweaters in slashing people with swords, the Blasters in exposing themselves to passing women, while the Fun Club engaged in performing practical jokes. All the clubs had sexual overtones, and their bulletin boards listed famous madams and noted prostitutes. The aristocratic club members were so powerful that the authorities did not dare interfere.

Not all clubs of this period, however, conformed to the traditional masculine stereotype. One that was the most subversive of male tradition was the Molly club, whose members met in women's clothes to drink and party:

They adopt all the small vanities natural to the feminine sex to such an extent that they try to speak, walk, chatter, shriek and scold as women do, aping them as well in other aspects. In a certain tavern in the City, the name of which I will not mention, not wishing to bring the house into disrepute, they hold parties and regular gatherings. As soon as they arrive, they begin to behave exactly as women do, carrying on light gossip, as is the custom of a merry company of real women.[24]

In the Molly club mock marriages were performed between two men; births were enacted, complete with groaning "mother," midwife, and a wooden doll "baby." The name *Molly* (the familiar form of Mary and during an earlier period a term used for prostitutes) came to be applied to effeminate males during the early eighteenth century, and it was in this sense that the term *mollycoddle* developed, meaning to pamper or effeminize a male. Mollies used female names, perhaps to conceal their true identities, but these names probably also allowed them to take on a temporary feminine identity. Patronizing the Molly clubs were not only aristocrats but others, since the sources also mention butchers, fishmongers, garter sellers, and so forth. The aristocrats, however, set the pace, and their presence afforded the club's protection. Occasionally, a group of Mollies went dancing in public, with many members dressed as women. Some went to great lengths to acquire gowns, petticoats, headcloths, fine-laced shoes, furbelow scarves, and the newly introduced hoop petticoats. Others dressed in more specialized costumes, such as those of a shepherdess or milkmaid. Most had their faces painted and patched.[25]

One eighteenth-century writer reported that she had never known "Princess Seraphina" (a.k.a. John Cooper) by any other name. She described him as usually wearing "a white gown and a scarlet cloak with her hair frizzled and curled all around her forehead; . . . she would so flutter her fan and make such fine curtsies that you would not have known her from a woman; she takes great delight in balls and masquerades."[26]

Though the Molly clubs have traditionally been seen as the earliest appearance of organized homosexuals in England, they raise a whole series of questions about changes in sex and gender role as well as the self-identification of some of those who eventually came to be called homosexuals. Individuals who live under the threat of being identified as belonging to a stigmatized minority learn to cope in various ways. One coping strategy is to be the "gentleman deviant" who conforms to all societal norms, outwardly emphasizing that one is as "normal" and competent as anyone else. Such behavior serves as a mask that saves the individual from being publicly identified as a homosexual. At the other extreme is the person who most visibly and flagrantly flouts public reaction by dressing and acting as a woman, thereby assuming the stigma of the effeminate male.[27]

Some scholars of homosexuality look upon this cross dressing as the beginning of the social construction of the modern homosexual, marking a point when homosexuality changed from being a temporary aberration to a new life-style.[28] David Greenberg, for example, theorizes that it was at this time an identity based on exclusive homosex-

uality begins to be created in Western culture.[29] Randolph Trumbach
has a similar view:

Sodomy had traditionally meant any of three things: sexual intercourse between males, anal intercourse between men and women, or intercourse with
beasts. In the eighteenth century it came to refer increasingly to male homosexual relations alone. This sort of sodomite was presumed to have no interest
in women. By contrast, his seventeenth-century counterpart would have been
found with his whore on one arm and his catamite on the other. The new
exclusive adult sodomite was also supposed to be effeminate, and effeminacy
lost its seventeenth-century meaning of referring both to cross-dressing boys
and to men enervated by too great a sexual interest in women. The majority of
eighteenth-century men therefore constructed their masculinity around their
avoidance of the sodomite's role and, instead, fervently pursued women.[30]

The Molly club would tend to support Trumbach's argument for the
existence of more exclusive homosexual groups, although *sodomy* itself
continued to be a catchall term in the courts until the end of the nineteenth century. Even in popular usage, sodomy referred to anal intercourse, and some of the guidebooks to London nightlife referred to the
"black school of Sodom," individuals who patronized prostitutes for
anal intercourse. Similarly, not all "homosexuals" of the time were exclusively homosexual, and eighteenth-century writers emphasize that
wenching and wedlock did not prevent a man from being a sodomite.[31]

Changing Mores and the Rise of Privacy

Aside from the growth of the major cities, as mentioned above, several
factors seemed to have been at work to help bring about the more or
less organized interest groups of the eighteenth century. A major
factor in the changing sexual mores, heterosexual as well as homosexual, was the increase in personal privacy, at least for the well-to-do. The
great houses of the fifteenth and sixteenth centuries had been constructed of interlocking suites of rooms without corridors so that movement required one to move through other people's chambers. In the
late seventeenth century and afterward, corridors were built to allow
access to other areas of the house without going through another
person's room. Special rooms developed, and the concept of comfort
came to be looked upon as more important than it had been. Beds were
confined to the bedrooms, which in large houses were moved upstairs
and furnished with cupboards or alcoves that were often fitted with the
new toilette and hygienic equipment. In France and Italy the words
chambre and *camera* began to be used to denote the room in which one
slept, as distinct from *salle* or *stanza,* the room where one received
visitors and ate. In England, although this distinction was not made, a

prefix or adjective was added to *room* in order to specify its function, such as *dining* room or *bed*room.

Most importantly, specialized private rooms tended to remove the servants from underfoot. Sexual privacy had been almost impossible until architectural developments allowed assignations in the home without the servants watching. Though the servants were undoubtedly aware of what was going on, and probably gossiped about it, the actual activities were left to their conjecture. Certainly, the special clubs such as the Mollies not only offered even greater privacy than the home but made the crossing of class lines somewhat easier.

The architectural interest in privacy extended from the great houses to the well-to-do merchants and tradesmen. Gradually, apprentices and wage laborers moved out of the houses and shops (usually in the same building) of the tradesmen and smaller landowners. Though this gave the employers less control over their adolescent and young adult labor force, they apparently felt they were more than compensated by the greater privacy.

Removed from the continuous supervision of their masters, the apprentices and young journeymen also had greater freedom to move about. At the same time, the growing custom of giving wages in lieu of room and board gave apprentices and workers greater discretion over how they lived or spent their money. Among the working classes, however, privacy within one's home remained more or less nonexistent until the twentieth century since whole families were crowded together in one room or, in the case of those who were better off, in two- or three-room houses or flats. Most young men left the family as soon as they could, and being on their own gave them greater freedom to have sexual adventures.

This new privacy, combined with the rapid growth of urbanization in the eighteenth century, particularly in London and major cities on the Continent, also made it possible or at least easier to prevent one's family or work associates from learning of one's sexual proclivities. The city also allowed individuals with the same sexual inclinations to congregate because brothels and streetwalkers were confined to certain areas. As a result, homosexuals in such cities as London were able to establish a distinctive life-style.

Did such factors lead to new and different ways for individuals to explore new gender roles or sexual identities, and, in the process, to establish a new kind of homosexuality?[32] Not all investigators see the kind of changes in homosexuality in the eighteenth century that Greenberg, Trumbach, and others do. Instead, some hold that there was no real change until the nineteenth century.[33] Jeffrey Weeks, an avid social constructionist, agrees with those who questioned the changes in the eighteenth century and argues that a modern homosexual identity was not really possible until the nineteenth century. He feels the Molly clubs were merely an embryonic subculture and certainly had little in common with modern homosexuality, which he dates from the last part of the nineteenth century.[34]

Even though a majority of the current generation of researchers tend to see major changes in marriage and family and sexuality in the eighteenth century, the implications of these changes remain unclear.[35] Even among those who accept the concept that much of sexual behavior is socially constructed, there are differences over the meaning of the eighteenth-century changes, since behavior is continually being modified and reconstructed. If the eighteenth-century meaning of what it was to be a homosexual is different from that in the 1990s, then so is the meaning different in the last part of the nineteenth century. Still, similarities remain, if only because each new social construction draws upon past attitudes and assumptions.

Certainly, the Molly clubs tend to represent something different if only because in Western culture homosexuals had rarely cross dressed before in any consistent fashion, although the king of France or a brother of the king might have done so.[36] Certainly, fifteenth-century Italian "gay" cultures did not engage in cross dressing,[37] nor have current investigations disclosed any similar cross-dressing groups of homosexual men in fourteenth-century Toulouse, fourteenth-century Venice, or sixteenth-century Seville.[38]

Even in London there were many other ways for a man to find a male companion than by going to a Molly club. Brothels with male prostitutes existed, and a record of one such house has survived. The proprietress, Margaret Clap, popularly known as Mother Clap, was indicted in 1726 for keeping a house where she procured and encouraged persons to "commit sodomy." During her trial, a police constable gave evidence that he had visited the house on a Sunday evening and found between forty and fifty men, "making love to one another as they called it." Some, he reported, sat on other men's laps, kissing, and using their "hands indecently"; others would dance, curtsy, and mimic the voices of women. After deciding on a partner for the evening, they would go to another room on the same floor "to be married, as they called it [i.e., to have sexual relations]." Since no one came forward to defend Mother Clap, the judge asked her whether she had anything to state in her defense. She replied that since she was a woman, "it cannot be thought that I would ever be concerned in such practices." The judge did not accept this defense and, finding her guilty, sentenced her to stand in the pillory, pay a fine of twenty marks, and remain in prison for two years.[39]

Experimentation and Investigation

More males began to experiment with role reversal and cross dressing on a scale not recorded before outside of the theater. James Dalton, the source of some of our information about the Mollies, reported knowing several men who spent most of their time in women's clothes and were referred to by their acquaintances almost entirely with female pronouns. Certainly, the interest in gender ambiguity continued into the eighteenth century, and sexual experimentation and gender-playing was even more widespread. Hermaphrodites and other unusual sexual anomalies (including occasionally lesbians, homosexuals, and cross dressers) found in medical pathology were not only explained but used to teach and illustrate what was "normal."[40] Hermaphrodites in particular proved intriguing creatures to the eighteenth-century investigator. The Royal Society in England, for example, took up the phenomenon several times in the 1740s, and in 1750, Michel-Ann Drouart was exhibited before them as an example of hermaphroditism.[41] One result of this increasing medical interest was to give a more compassionate look at people with ambiguous genitalia instead of simply labeling them as monsters. Several physicians came to believe that hermaphrodites were simply women with enlarged clitorises that had been mistaken for penises at birth.[42]

These so-called clitoral penises proved fascinating to the writers of the time, for it was also believed to be the reason that some women became lesbians. A certain R. James, for example, wrote in the eighteenth century that all Tribades (a term for lesbians) had oversized clitorises "so shamefully large as to protuberate without the lips of the pudenda" and to resemble a penis.[43] Others added to this category by including individuals formerly classified as males who had a vaginal opening as well as a penis. Though there was strong commonsense evidence that many such individuals were really male (since the penis was fully functional for both voiding and ejaculation and an enlarged clitoris was not), there was a growing tendency to classify them as women, probably because they were imperfectly formed (something males were not supposed to be). George Arnaud, however, urged those medical practitioners called upon to determine the sex of a person with ambiguous genitalia to use extra caution since so many mistakes had been made and the standards for classification were unclear.[44]

Catharine Vizzani, a mid-eighteenth-century Italian woman cross dresser, was shot and killed during her attempt to elope with the niece of a minister; her body was dissected in an attempt to prove that hermaphroditism had brought about her actions. No signs of hermaphroditism were found, but John Cleland, the English translator of a book about her, argued that her irregular and violent inclinations proceeded either "from some error in nature or from some disorder or perversion in the imagination."[45] A French hermaphrodite, Anne Grand-Jean, was ordered not only to have her marriage with a woman annulled but to adopt female clothing, emphasizing the strong belief that a hermaphrodite was considered a deformed woman.[46]

Despite the travails of actual and suspected hermaphrodites, there was a very real interest by both men and women in impersonating the opposite sex, and such impersonations could be carried out at increasingly popular masked balls. During the eighteenth century, the London social season and parliamentary sessions coincided, and among the major events on social calendars were masked balls. These soon became so popular that entrepreneurs began staging them for people who would not be invited to the court events. So popular did the masked ball become both in England and on the Continent that Terry Castle has gone so far as to describe the eighteenth-century culture as "a culture of travesty."[47] In fact, it is cross dressing that distinguishes eighteenth-century balls from their earlier royal predecessors. Inevitably, the masked balls included a number of cross dressers of both sexes: some burlesqued the opposite sex but others took their impersonations more seriously.

The new popular masked balls of eighteenth-century England are descended from the masquerades and impersonations associated with festivals and carnivals that were mentioned in earlier chapters. The Venetian carnival, in particular, had attracted large numbers of English tourists before such events began taking place in London.[48] In London, the "Midnight Masquerade," an English version of the Continental masquerades, made its appearance in the second decade of the eighteenth century. The difference was that the London popular balls were run for profit by various entrepreneurs. One of the earliest to do so, and for a long time the dominant entrepreneur, was John James Heidegger, who organized his first masked ball in London in 1717 at the Haymarket Theater. The new venture was an instant success as well as a scandal. In the 1720s and 1730s, his Midnight Masquerades drew between seven and eight hundred people a week, and he continued to offer them until his death in 1749. Though the masked ball had pretensions of exclusivity (allegedly, George II and the Prince of Wales attended public masquerades), the appeal lay in its heterogeneous and carnival-like atmosphere. Anyone who could afford the ticket and put on a costume could come, and this meant that many of the new urban rich did. The anonymity of the scene encouraged unrestrained collective behavior, and it seemed so attractive to people at the time that a number of other entrepreneurs offered them as well.

One masquerade in May 1770 was attended by nearly two thousand persons.

Though public in nature, the masquerade still epitomized the clandestine sexual life of the city and gave free rein to some of its more secretive aspects, including transvestism. Social commentators of the time were aware of the masquerade as a means of expressing a hidden need among the participants. Henry Fielding, for example, wrote in 1728 that to "masque the face" was to "unmasque the mind." Joseph Addison noted that contemporary masqueraders invariably dressed as what they "had a Mind to be."[49]

Men could experiment in safety with gender reversal by dressing as women, primping in furbelows and flounces, while women could express a more masculine character, strutting about in jackboots and breeches. Horace Walpole (1717–97) reported passing as an old woman at a masquerade in 1742, while other males disguised themselves as witches, bawds, nursery-maids, and shepherdesses.[50] Though the cross dressing of the balls was equated by some with homosexuality and by others with hermaphroditism, most of the participants probably looked upon it as a chance to drop gender barriers, and for many it was also recognized as an erotic activity. Women and men could not only playfully belong to the opposite gender but could also engage in sexual play. Antimasquerade writers in fact found cross dressing a sure sign of depravity, perhaps because so many upper-class prostitutes attended the balls and found them advantageous to their business. In a sense, the balls represent an extension of the personal liberties the eighteenth century had begun to emphasize, perhaps even to invent, and often it was only in the masked balls that individuals could safely act out some of their fantasies.[51]

The Chevalier d'Éon

There was also a growing curiosity about cross dressing and impersonation in public, which reached a height in both England and France at the end of the eighteenth century with the case of Charles Geneviève Louis Auguste André Timothée d'Éon de Beaumont (1728–1810), known as the Chevalier d'Éon. It was from his case that Havelock Ellis derived the term *eonism* to describe transvestism. Ellis wrote that d'Éon was not a pseudo–cross dresser, but that the masquerade "fulfilled a deep demand of his own nature. He clearly had a constitutional predisposition, aided by an almost asexual disposition. In people with this psychic anomaly, physical sexual urge seems often abnormal.[52]

Born at Tonerre, France, on 5 October 1728, Charles d'Éon was the son of Louis d'Éon de Beaumont, a director of the king's *demesnes* ("private property"), and thus a man of some position. D'Éon received instruction from the local curé of the parish church until age twelve, when he was sent to Paris to complete his education at the College de Mazarin. Graduating as a doctor of civil and canon Law, he was called to the Bar of the Parlement, where he served as secretary to M. Bertier de Sauvigny, *intendant* (administrator) for the district of Paris.[53]

Described at this time as short in height with a slight, girlish figure and effeminate in appearance, his favorite recreation was fencing, in which he was highly proficient. There is an anomaly in this period in his life, however, namely, a portrait by Angelica Kauffman copied from the famous pastelist, Maurice Quentin de La Tour, painter to the king and the high nobility. It shows the young Chevalier d'Éon dressed as a young woman of quality, wearing a dainty lace cap, drop pearl earrings, a black velvet ribbon around the neck, a low, lacy *décolletage* revealing a full breast. Since La Tour commanded a high price for his work, there are questions as to why this portrait was painted and at whose request. Perhaps one of d'Éon's patrons sponsored the painting, but it seems clear that the chevalier might well have dressed as a woman early in his career.

Through his connections with de Sauvigny, d'Éon became known to Louis François Bourbon, the Prince de Conti (1717–76), an important military figure and patron of many French men-of-letters, including Jean-Jacques Rousseau. The influential prince recommended the special talents of d'Éon to Louis XV for a secret French mission to the Russian court. The king had his own secret service, separate from the other functions of government. This system, known as *Le secret du Roi,* was directed by his friend the Prince de Conti; it reported directly to the king and was not part of the French bureaucracy. The apparent purpose of d'Éon's secret mission was to lobby the Czarina Elizabeth to name the Prince de Conti as king of Poland, a policy officially opposed by the French government although favored by Louis XV. To keep up the secret nature of the mission, d'Éon was designated to accompany Douglas MacKenzie, a Scot in exile in France, to Saint Petersburg.

According to an undocumented tradition, the chevalier was introduced to Czarina Elizabeth as a young woman, the niece of the king's envoy. As such "she" was admitted to the society of the maids-of-honor, where she succeeded in presenting the Czarina with the private letter from Louis XV explaining the true object of the visit. This story, while intriguing, seems to have been made up by later writers, although the chevalier probably engaged in cross dressing in Russia.

If the purpose of the mission was to have the Prince de Conti named as king, d'Éon was unsuccessful. He did, however, receive a personal note from Elizabeth that she would welcome a renewal of diplomatic relations, and with this note he returned to Paris. D'Éon was sent back to Russia two more times in order to further the diplomatic opportunity he had initiated and to keep Catherine informed of the real intents of the king. D'Éon went to great lengths to keep the king informed. For example, on his second visit to Russia in 1757, he returned by way of Vienna and was in that city when the Austrian army won a victory over the Prussians at Prague. Since the Austrians were allies of France in what is known as the Seven Years' War (1756–63), news of the victory was important to the French king. D'Éon immediately set off for France, riding day and night in order to be the first to inform the king. Grateful for this dedication and information, the king gave him an ornamental snuffbox as well as a commission as lieutenant of the dragoons. During his third posting to the Russian court, d'Éon worked under the direction of the French ambassador, the Marquis de l'Hôpital, who affectionately referred to him as Lia, the girl's name he assumed when cross dressed (perhaps indicating that his cross-dressing activities were known to many). Ill health sent him back to France again in 1760, and Louis not only granted him a life pension of 2,000 livres a year but promoted him to the rank of captain of the dragoons. Recovered from his illness, he was sent as an aide-de-camp to the Comte de Broglie, then head of the *Secret du Roi* and second-in-command of the French forces on the Rhine. He ended up commanding a company of dragoons and distinguished himself in battle. As he wrote in his memoires, "No one ever questioned my sex when I was sent into battle, or to negotiate with the enemies of my country."[54]

In 1763, d'Éon was nominated as first secretary to the newly appointed ambassador to Great Britain. In this capacity, he was involved in the negotiations that led to the Treaty of Paris, which ended the war. Part of his job was to carry the dispatches to Paris, and again he was rewarded for his services by the king, who gave him 6,000 livres from the privy purse and conferred on him the Order of Saint Louis and the title of chevalier.

Though the Treaty of Paris cost France its territories in India, Canada, Nova Scotia, and much of the West Indies, its terms were better than Louis XV had expected. Still, soon after, the ever-conniving Louis, apparently without the knowledge of his ministers, began to plot an invasion of England. To aid in this, d'Éon returned to London as French resident and chargé d'affaires as well as secret agent of the king himself. Unfortunately for d'Éon, his old friend the ambassador had left London; until a new ambassador was appointed, d'Éon acted as minister plenipotentiary, which required living in a style he could not afford and he was forced to borrow money. When the new ambassador, the Comte de Guerchy (Claude Louis François Regnier), arrived, d'Éon found his hopes of recouping his expenditures dashed because of their disagreements. Their clash was perhaps to be expected, since the ambassador knew nothing of the secret missions d'Éon was conducting for the king. So antagonistic did the relations become that the ambassador requested d'Éon's recall. According to d'Éon, even when the new ambassador was in place, the king on 4 October 1763, sent d'Éon a letter stating:

You have served me as usefully in woman's clothes as in those you now wear. Resume them at once and withdraw into the city [London]. I warn you that the king this day signed, but only with the stamp and not with his hand, an order for your return to France. But I command you to remain in England with all your papers until I send you further instructions. You are not in safety at your residence and here you will find powerful enemies.[55]

When d'Éon refused to leave London (on the grounds the recall did not have an official signature), the struggle between the new ambassador and d'Éon became so heated that the chevalier believed the ambassador had hired assassins to kill him. This, in turn, led d'Éon to threaten to publish secret correspondence dealing with French plans for England, an action that made him *persona non grata* to the French ambassador and resulted in his being summarily discharged. Worst of all, his threat antagonized Louis XV and left him without allies. As part of the campaign against him, the French ambassador had spread the rumor that d'Éon was really a woman in disguise. Since d'Éon enjoyed the company of women but never made sexual overtures to them, several people seized on this rumor. Apparently, perhaps following the king's orders, he also had appeared in disguise as a woman, although these reports are only hearsay.

When the rumor about the chevalier being a woman began to gain momentum in London, there was wide-scale betting on his sex. When the French ambassador took to publicly denouncing d'Éon as either a woman or a hermaphrodite, his sex immediately became the subject of debate and wagers. D'Éon began to worry about his safety as the bets escalated, fearful that some of the gamblers would kidnap him in order to win their case, and if perchance his kidnappers had bet on the losing side he thought they might even kill him to repress the evidence.

The issue was complicated by the death of Louis XV, his old patron and by the concomitant collapse of his secret service. As conditions for the chevalier grew more desperate, he schemed to find a way to make his peace with the new administration. Ultimately, he came to believe that the only way to explain all of his actions was to proclaim he was a woman. The new king Louis XVI could then pardon d'Éon his excesses without losing face because as a woman in the sexist society of the eighteenth century, the chevalier would not be held accountable to the same standards as a man. D'Éon also gambled that the new king would give him a pension, thus relieving his financial crisis, and welcome him back to France if his "true" sex was revealed.

To aid him in this scheme, d'Éon took a fellow Frenchman, Pierre Augustin Caron (1743–99), then residing in England, into his confidence. Caron, better known as Beaumarchais, had a Rabelaisian joy for living and an interest in both sex and controversy. He is remembered today mainly as the author of *The Barber of Seville* and *The Marriage of Figaro*. Seeing an opportunity not only to help his countryman but to have some fun with the English and win some money, Beaumarchais encouraged d'Éon to "confess" he was a woman. Not satisfied with d'Éon's proclamation, two gamblers involved filed suit in London to get an official court opinion. The case of *Hayes* v. *Jacques* was heard at the Court of the King's Bench in July 1777. Two physicians testified at the trial; one claimed that he had treated d'Éon for "women's disorders," while the other implied that "she" had made suggestions of an amorous nature to him. The court ruled that d'Éon was a woman but only after the chevalier signed an affidavit swearing that he had no interest in the bets. Beaumarchais, however, was deeply involved in the betting and as it turned out, must have bribed the physicians for their testimony.[56] Moreover, through a technicality the winning claimant was unable to collect.

Soon after, d'Éon left for France where Louis XVI, perhaps not entirely knowledgeable about all the charges against d'Éon, and accepting d'Éon's statement that he was a woman, was willing to forgive the chevalier for his past indiscretions—they could be so easily explained by his "womanly" frailties. As d'Eon had anticipated, Louis also offered him a pension but stipulated, much to the chagrin of the chevalier, that he would have to continue to live as a woman. When d'Éon appeared hesitant to accept this condition, the king insisted that he either live as the woman he was or not only lose his pension but be subject to charges of treason. The chevalier found himself in a quandary: remain a man and lose a pension and possibly his life or don women's clothes and gain a sinecure? D'Éon felt he had no choice. He went into seclusion so that he could become accustomed to feminine clothing. He wrote:

In the seclusion of my apartment I am forcing myself to become accustomed to my melancholy fate. Since leaving off my uniform and my sword, I am foolish as a fox who has lost his tail! I am trying to walk in pointed shoes with high heels, but have nearly broken my neck more than once; it has happened that, instead of making a courtesy, I have taken off my wig and three tiered headdress, taking them for my hat or my helmet.[57]

When d'Éon finally appeared in public, he became a sensation in Paris, burlesquing the gestures and mannerisms of women. His notoriety eventually faded, however, and d'Éon grew increasingly unhappy at the restrictions of the woman's role. Using the excuse that he had business to complete, the chevalier was given permission by the king in 1785 to return to England and still receive his pension. But if he had planned his return to England in order to revert to his male self, he soon found that his continued income from the king was dependent on remaining in women's dress. He also realized that some of the losers of the bets on his true sex might do bodily harm to him if he turned out to be a man.

With the outbreak of the French Revolution, d'Éon's return to France became more problematic. He found himself increasingly beset by financial difficulties as the revolutionary government in France confiscated his estates and cut off his pension. As a result, he spent the rest of his life in England, where he continued to live as a woman. He survived by his swordsmanship, giving fencing exhibitions and lessons while dressed in proper women's attire. His notoriety brought him both students and exhibitions, but in 1796 he was seriously wounded during an exhibition. No longer able to support himself d'Éon was forced to live off the charity of friends. He died in poverty in 1810. While his body was being prepared for burial, it was conclusively proved that the chevalier was a perfectly formed male, a fact that proved somewhat shocking to the woman who had taken care of and lived with him for the last fourteen years of his life.[58] It also led to a vast outpouring of literature as the impersonation captured the popular imagination.

Indeed, d'Éon was the first male transvestite to become what at the end of the twentieth century might be called a media event, although the questions about his sex were only cleared up at his death. Still, the widespread gossip about him during his entire life emphasizes how fascinating the issue of gender was to many people of the period. Though the Abbé de Choisy represents a more classic case of transvestism, since he clearly received pleasure from it, he never had the widespread notoriety of d'Éon. Why d'Éon cross dressed is unclear. We do know he collected newspaper cuttings of even the slightest reference to cross dressing, hermaphroditism, and other such issues, which would indicate he was fascinated by the topic.[59] But often he seems to have been more the victim of events in his life as far as his cross dressing was concerned. When he was forced more or less to cross dress permanently, he did not make an effort to be particularly attractive as a woman, and this point, too, raises doubts about the nature of his transvestism. (The uncertainty surrounding d'Éon's cross dressing perhaps helps to explain why Havelock Ellis's term *eonism* was similarly fraught with ambiguity.) D'Éon wrote,

I am sufficiently mortified at being what nature has made me, and that the coolness of my natural temperament, having never led me into pleasure-seeking, should induce my friends to imagine in their innocence, in France as much as in Russia and in England, that I am of the female sex. The malice of my enemies has confirmed all this. . . . If the Great Master of the Universe has not endowed me with all the exterior vigour of manhood, He has amply made amends by giving me head and heart. . . . I am what the hands of God have made me; satisfied with my weakness, I would not change it . . . even if that were in my power.[60]

One reason the chevalier proved an object of fascination rather than disgust to the English audience of the eighteenth century is that they perceived him to be a woman cross dressing as a man. It was his cross dressing as a woman, however, which later generations have found so fascinating. Had his biological sex been known during his own lifetime, he probably would have experienced even more hostility, since he did not conform to what was considered the accepted way for men to act. In a novel of the same period, *The History of Henry Dumont* (written by Charlotte Charke in 1756), for example, the effeminate man impersonating a woman was a foreigner who, upon being unmasked, was subject to violent abuse and attack. The novel's hero, M. Dumont, justified his participation in the attack: "My behavior could not in any degree give the smallest hope to the unnatural passion of such a detestable brute. I therefore think it incumbent on me to make an example of the villain." Dumont gathered together a small mob, and as the cross-dressing male attempted to escape, he was snatched from his supporters and ducked in a fishpond.[61]

Challenges to Masculinity

Indeed, at this time any man's alleged cross dressing that went beyond the masquerade ball was popularly thought to indicate a weakness of character. A good example of such a stereotype is the case of Edward Hyde, Viscount Cornbury, who served as governor of New York and New Jersey from 1702 to 1708. Cornbury, later to become the Earl of Clarendon, was identified as a cross dresser by one of his steadfast opponents, Horace Walpole. Cornbury, as governor, had headed a rather corrupt administration, and his personal life so shocked his subjects that they denounced him for drunkenness, vanity, and oppression. His enemies also claimed that he dressed himself in women's clothing and, thus attired, paraded on the ramparts of the fort, the most conspicuous place in New York.

The facts about Cornbury's transvestism have been challenged by some but are generally accepted. What is fascinating about Cornbury's case is the attempt of some early commentators on his life to explain why Cornbury may have cross dressed. Others, including some modern investigators, have tended to dismiss any references to cross dressing as fictitious, if only because a man in his position could not conceivably do such a thing. The nature of the comments emphasize how difficult it was for many, not only in the eighteenth-century but also in later ones, to accept the fact that a man might gain enjoyment and satisfaction from cross dressing and not simply cross dress for a lark or because he belonged to a Molly club. One writer, for example, claimed that Cornbury cross dressed because of his likeness to his cousin Anne, and this led him to dress in elaborate and sumptuous female attire like a lady of the court. Another author suggested that Cornbury did not know what he was doing, since he was drunk when he dressed himself in his wife's clothes and paraded up and down in such a manner that he was arrested as an intoxicated vagrant by the officers of the watch. Still another writer said that Cornbury impersonated a woman to show people what the distant queen (in England) looked like. Quite clearly, a male cross dresser, unlike his female counterpart, seemed difficult to accept, even after the case of the Chevalier d'Éon. Though what is thought to be a portrait of Cornbury dressed in women's clothes now hangs in the New York Historical Society, it is not clear whether the portrait is authentic, just as it remains unclear whether Cornbury ever cross dressed. Such rumors might have been circulated to have him removed as governor (as eventually he was), but there were so many far graver offenses that could have been used against him for this purpose that it is difficult to understand why it was also necessary to accuse him of cross dressing unless he did so.[62]

Clearly, male cross dressing was an intriguing subject in the eighteenth century, but it seemed difficult for the people of the time to understand or explain it. The motives attributed to Cornbury, for example, seem to make little sense, and none of them seem to carry any sexual overtones. D'Éon's cross dressing was accepted because he was believed to be a woman, and thus "her" desire to be a man was understandable. What seems clear is that the eighteenth-century world was still male-dominated, and its society considered the effeminate male as somehow not quite a true, "masculine" man. And yet we know that male cross dressing existed, at least among some homosexual groups, that it was popular at masked balls and perhaps was more common than eighteenth-century observers (and, by extension, those of more modern times) realized.

When cross dressing was used in jest or to play a prank on someone, it was considered quite acceptable. For example, an unnamed eighteenth-century man was persuaded by one of the beauties of the day, Diana Davis, to cross dress and seduce the Duke of Grafton. The duke, greatly fascinated with the young cross dresser, invited him to his house, much to the delight of Diana and her co-conspirator, Annabella Parsons.[63]

Further Cases of Female Cross Dressers

If male cross dressers such as d'Éon were rare, women cross dressers were not. The *Annual Register,* a review of events that was founded in 1758, recorded a number of cases of women who lived or dressed and acted as men in its surveys for the years 1761, 1766, 1769, 1772, 1774, 1777, 1779, 1782, 1793, and so forth. Some of these women were clearly lesbian, attempting to find a way to survive in a male-dominated world; others were not. In a 1777 case, for example, one lesbian had married three different women who thought she was a man. Another woman, Hannah Snell, whose sexual orientation is unclear, was wounded in battle and later suffered some five thousand lashes for insubordination without revealing her sex.[64] In 1720, Mary Read and Anne Boney, two female cross dressers, were convicted and sentenced to death for piracy. Read died before her sentence could be carried out, while Anne Boney, whose execution was postponed, disappeared from the view of history.[65]

More complex was the case of Hannah Gray (1723–92) who, after being abandoned by her husband, joined the British army as James Gray in 1745. When one of her fellow soldiers told her of a scheme he had concocted against a local village girl, she managed to inform the girl, and afterwards, the two women continued to meet. Her jealous army comrade denounced her for neglect of duty, for which she was sentenced to receive six hundred lashes. Gray endured five hundred blows before the lashing was stopped without anyone discovering her sex. Still, she feared discovery, and when a new recruit turned out to be someone who had known her as a woman, she decided to desert rather than wait to be exposed. After wandering about for several months, she decided that the military life remained attractive to her and she re-enlisted, this time as a marine. Almost immediately, Gray was shipped off to India, where she fought against the French. She proved to be not only a brave warrior but a good drinking companion as well and was accepted by her mates as a man.

On her return voyage from India she found out that her husband had been executed for killing a man. Shortly afterward, in an unguarded moment, she told one of her mates that she was really a woman. He offered to marry her, but when she refused he (either for revenge or by accident) spread her story about. People flocked to see Gray, and she, taking advantage of her new fame, went on the stage playing male roles. When she tired of this, she applied for and received a pension for her war services and with the money opened a public house at Wapping. As proprietor she dressed like a man, although everyone knew she was a woman; indeed, the sign on her public house read "The Widow in Masquerade or the Female Warrior."[66]

Mary Ann Talbot (1778–1808) differs from most of the other woman cross dressers because she was born to a well-to-do family. Her parents died when she was quite young, and the sister who looked after her died before she was of age. Talbot's guardian shunted her off to a Captain Essex Bowen, a man she did not know. In 1792 Bowen took her to London, where he first raped her and then beat her. When Bowen was ordered to rejoin his regiment on its transfer to Santa Domingo, he insisted that Mary Anne accompany him because he worried that if left alone she might tell someone what he had done to her. Since no dependents were allowed on the ship, he had her dress as his footman and assume the name of John Taylor. The two stayed only briefly in Santa Domingo before Bowen was ordered back to Europe to reinforce the troops of the Duke of York. This time Bowen compelled Talbot to enroll in his regiment as a drummer.

Shortly after the duo arrived in Flanders, Talbot was hit by a musket ball and suffered a sword wound in a French attack. Rather than go to a hospital, she treated herself. Bowen was killed in the battle and, on searching his body, she found several letters that referred to her as well as a key to the case in which he had kept additional papers. The papers revealed that Bowen had kept the money he was supposed to have given her. Sewing the documents in the shoulders of her jacket, she decided to desert, this time disguised as a sailor looking for his ship.

Talbot ended up on a pirate ship that was captured by a British fleet under the command of Admiral Richard Howe. Recognized as being English, Talbot was taken before the admiral, whereupon she recounted many of her adventures without revealing her sex. When she indicated to Howe that she wanted to get back into battle, he had her transferred to another ship where she became a powder boy. She so impressed the captain on the new ship with her willingness to work that he made her his principal cabin boy. Wounded in battle again, this time in both the thigh and the leg, she escaped detection by the surgeon who, after making a cursory examination, sent her back to port with the other wounded. She was hospitalized for several months with no one the wiser, perhaps an indication not so much of her ability to impersonate a man but of the casualness, and even callousness, with which the wounded were treated.

No sooner had Talbot recovered than she was drafted as a midshipman on another ship that subsequently was captured by the French. Taken prisoner, she spent her time learning to make fine filigree work out of gold wire from a fellow prisoner. She was released through a prisoner exchange, and almost immediately volunteered to serve on an American merchantman leaving for New York. The captain of this ship was so impressed with her that when he arrived in New York he took her to his family home in Rhode Island and his young daughter fell in love with the youthful, swashbuckling steward.

Talbot escaped this complicated situation by going to sea again. Shortly after she arrived in London, she was seized by a press-gang that took her for a man. (Such gangs seized likely looking men and forced them to be crewmen.) She only managed to escape by revealing that she was a woman. Returning to her own ship, she told her captain what had happened, and though he offered to take her back to the United States, she decided to remain in London to track down her inheritance. She made an application for back pay for her war service but met with rebuffs from the clerks over her story; she cursed them so harshly that they had her arrested.

When Talbot appeared before the magistrate, she repeated her story and won release; other sympathizers who had heard her story raised money to help her out until she received her back pay from the naval office. Though she now clearly identified herself as a woman, she refused to wear dresses or give up her masculine habits. For a time she had a period of brief notoriety, during which she was a habitué of the theater and coffeehouses. As her money began to run out, she turned to making filigree jewelry. As she grew older, she once more tried to exploit her reputation by appearing in male roles on the stage, but this proved financially unsuccessful. Finally, she was arrested for falling behind in her rent and held in jail. Shortly after her release, she died, on 4 February 1808.[67]

Still another cross dresser was Mary East who, after her male lover was arrested for highway robbery and sent to Australia in 1732, settled down with a neighbor girl to run an inn. Since they believed the only way they could live together was as husband and wife, they drew lots to decide which one would become the husband. As a result Mary became "James How." The couple started with a small inn and eventually, as they added to their capital, purchased and ran a public house known as the White Horse. Eighteen years later, a woman patron who had known Mary East in her youth recognized her and began blackmailing her. Soon after this her female partner died, but the blackmailing continued. In desperation, Mary confessed to a male friend her true sex, and the two managed to entrap the blackmailer and her partners into confessions. The blackmailers were convicted and Mary resumed her feminine dress. She sold her public house and retired; she died a few years later, honored and respected by her friends and neighbors.[68]

The fact that some of the women cross dressers appeared on the stage emphasizes the continuation of the "breeches" parts so popular during the last part of the seventeenth century, as discussed in Chapter 4. The eighteenth-century audience was equally fascinated with these actresses. Marion Jones reports:

More than one excuse served to get actresses into breeches for the delectation of a predominantly male audience. First, of course, came revivals of old plays with parts written for boys playing women, where the plot demanded assumption of male disguises at times during the action; with the advent of actresses, titillating denouements with bared bosoms and flowing tresses became popular, and new plays were written to exploit this "disguise penetrated" motif. Next, increasingly popular after Nell Gwyn played the madcap Florimel in Dryden's Secret Love (1667), came the "roaring-girl" type of part, where the heroine adopted men's clothes as a free expression of her vivacious nature: prologues and epilogues were sometimes given by favourite actresses in men's clothes with no other apparent reason than to provide the same arbitrary thrill. Something akin to this was the practice by which an actress took the part of a male character just to amuse the audience. . . . Occasionally a whole play would be performed by women.[69]

Women even played some of the more significant male roles. In Dublin during the 1730s, a Mrs. Bellamy scored a hit in the role of Silvia in The Recruiting Officer, which involved her being disguised as a soldier. Peg Woffington, probably the most brilliant actress of her day, made her breeches debut in The Female Officer and she played it several times over, even appearing before the Prince and Princess of Wales. One verse account of her appearance emphasizes the attraction of cross dressing:

The excellent Peg
Who showed such a leg
When lately she dressed in men's clothes—
A creature uncommon
Who's both man and woman
And chief of the belles and the beaux![70]

One of the things that made the breeches role so appealing to the men in the audience was that cross dressing allowed them to better see the women's limbs and bodies, which were usually hidden by the dresses of the day. In general, the impersonation was almost instantly identified by the audience.[71]

Summary

In sum, though the eighteenth-century man was concerned about threats to his masculinity, there was great curiosity by both men and women with what the other gender was like and even some experimentation in gender-role changes. The incidence of "successful" cross dressing, if the number of recorded and semifictional accounts are any indication, remained much higher for women than for men. When males experimented, most did so as a lark or at a masquerade ball, so that the impersonation was not taken seriously. Those men who did cross dress beyond the narrow limits allowed by society, as a number of homosexuals did, were already so stigmatized by their sexual orientation that their cross dressing did not provoke the hostility that it might have. Being stigmatized, however, probably allowed homosexual cross dressers to experiment with gender roles among themselves when they came together in groups for moral and social support, even though their actual cross dressing might have been conducted more as a form of entertainment than as a serious impersonation. The notoriety attached to the Chevalier d'Éon, the accounts of various women cross dressers and hermaphrodites, and the growing popularity of masquerade balls attest to the public's continued curiosity in regard to outward manifestations of gender-role experimentation.[72]

Notes

1. John Milton, *Prolusio* VI, in *The Works of John Milton,* ed. Frank Allen Patterson (New York: Columbia University Press, 1931–38), 12: 241.

2. See Edward Le Comte, *Milton and Sex* (New York: Columbia University Press, 1978), 1–22.

3. This idea has had a long history starting in medieval Europe. See Mary Wack, *Lovesickness in the Middle Ages: The* Viaticum *and Its Commentaries* (Philadelphia: University of Pennsylvania Press, 1990), 1–24. The idea of a womanish man who loses his sense of what is proper masculine behavior by becoming enslaved to a woman is very strongly emphasized in Milton's *Samson Agonistes.*

4. See Milton, *Paradise Lost,* 4:301–3, in *Complete Poems and Major Prose,* ed. Merritt Y. Hughes (New York: Odyssey Press, 1957).

5. *Dr. Martin Luthers Tischreden oder Colloquia* (Leipzig: n.p., 1844–46), 83.

6. For greater elaboration of this thesis, see Lawrence Stone, *The Family, Sex and Marriage in England 1500–1800* (New York: Harper and Row, 1977), esp. chap. 5.

7. John Locke, *Two Treatises of Government*, ed. Peter Laslett (New York: Cambridge University Press, 1963). See also Lorenne M. G. Clark, "Women and Locke: Who Owns the Apples in the Garden of Eden?" *The Canadian Journal of Philosophy* 7 (1977): 699–724.

8. William Wollaston, "Truths Concerning Families and Relations," in *The Religion of Nature Delineated* (London: Samuel Palmer, 1726).

9. He included such discussion in his treatises "Of Polygamy and Divorce" and "Love and Marriage," but this does not mean Hume believed women were equal to men. See, for example, Steven Burns, "The Humean Female," *Dialogue* 15 (1976): 415–24, and Louise Marcil-Lacoste, "The Consistency of Hume's Position Concerning Women," *Dialogue* 15 (1976): 425–40.

10. For changes in marriage at this time, see Lawrence Stone, *The Family, Sex, and Marriage in England,* and Randolph Trumbach, *The Rise of the Egalitarian Family* (New York: Academic Press, 1978). See also Vern L. Bullough, *Sexual Variance in Society and History* (Chicago: University of Chicago Press, 1976); and Vern L. Bullough, Brenda Shelton, and Sarah Slavin, *The Subordinated Sex: A History of Attitudes Toward Women* (Athens: University of Georgia Press, 1988).

11. See Jean-Jacques Rousseau, *Émile*, trans. Barbara Foxley (London: J. M. Dent, 1911), 357; and Joel Schwartz, *The Sexual Politics of Jean-Jacques Rousseau* (Chicago: University of Chicago Press, 1984).

12. Hannah More, *Essays on Various Subjects Principally Designed for Young Ladies* (Philadelphia: Young, Stewart, and McCulloch, 1786), 145; Hannah More, *Hints Toward Forming the Character of a Young Princess,* 5th ed. (London: Cadell and Davies, 1819), esp. chap. 1.

13. Mary Wollstonecraft, *A Vindication of the Rights of Women* (London: J. M. Dent, 1929); and Eleanor Flexner, *Mary Wollstonecraft* (New York: Coward, McCann, and Geoghegan, 1972).

14. This thesis is developed at some length by Randolph Trumbach, "The Birth of the Queen: Sodomy and the Emergence of Gender Equality in Modern Culture 1660–1750," in *Hidden from History: Reclaiming the Gay and Lesbian Past,* ed. Martin Bauml Duberman, Martha Vicinus, and George Chauncey, Jr. (New York: New American Library, 1989), 129–40. For a detailed study of the character on the English stage, see Laurence Senelick, "Mollies or Men of Mode? Sodomy and the Eighteenth Century London Stage," *Journal of the History of Sexuality,* 1 (1990): 33–67; Susan Staves, "Kind Words for the Fop," *Studies in English Literature* 22 (1982): 413–28, and Susan Shapiro, "'You Plumed Dandeprat': Male 'Effeminacy' in English Satire and Criticism," *Review of English Studies,* n.s. 39 (1988): 400–12.

15. Robert Baldick, *The Duel: A History of Dueling* (London: Chapman and Hall, 1965), 55.

16. For various other definitions of the term, see *Oxford English Dictionary,* s.v. *libertine,* and Stone, *Family, Sex, and Marriage in England,* passim.

17. David Foxon, *Libertine Literature in England, 1660–1745* (New Hyde Park, NY: University Books, 1965). Though others have defined it more narrowly or more broadly, it is the Foxon periodization that is used here. See James G. Turner, "The Properties of Libertinism," in *Unauthorized Sexual Behavior During the Enlightenment,* a special issue of *Eighteenth Century Life,* IX, n.s. 3 (May 1985): 75–87.

18. *The Diary of Samuel Pepys,* ed. Henry B. Wheatley, (New York: Random

House, n.d.), 670, n3. This particular version of the diary was censored, and editor Wheatley describes the details in a footnote.

19. See John Wilmot, Earl of Rochester, *Sodom or the Quintessence of Debauchery Written for the Royal Company of Whoremasters* (Paris: Olympia Press, n.d.). For his poems with bisexual themes, see John Wilmot, Earl of Rochester, *Poems on Several Occasions,* ed. James Thorpe (Princeton, NJ: Princeton University Press, 1950), nos. 17, 20, 74.

20. For this aspect of the court of Louis XV, see Iain D. B. Pilkington, *The King's Pleasures* (London: Jarrolds, 1957); Nancy Mitford, *Madame de Pompadour* (London: Reprint Society, 1954); H. Noel Williams, *Memoirs of Madame Du Barry* (New York: Collier, 1910); and esp. Stanley Loomis, *DuBarry* (Philadelphia: J. B. Lippincott, 1959).

21. John B. Wolf, *The Emergence of the Great Powers* (New York: Harper, 1951), 76.

22. See Jacques Casanova, *The Memoirs of Jacques Casanova de Seingalt,* trans. Arthur Machen (New York: A. & C. Boni, 1932).

23. T. H. White, *The Age of Scandal* (New York: Putnam's, 1950).

24. Edward Ward, *The Secret History of Clubs* (London, 1709), 284–300, esp. 290. For a more accessible account, see Ned (Edward) Ward, *The London Spy,* ed. Arthur Hayward (New York: George H. Doran Co., 1927). For other accounts of the club, see Jonathan Wild, *Answer,* reprinted in F. J. Lyons, *Jonathan Wild* (London: M. Joseph, 1936), 278–81; *Select Trials for Murders, Robberies, Rapes, Sodomy, Coining, Frauds and Other Offences, 1720–1732, 1733–1740, 1741–1763,* 4 vols. (London: J. Wilkie, 1734–35, 1742, 1764), passim, esp. 1:328–42, 2:362–72, 3:37–38; James Dalton, *A Genuine Narrative . . . Since October Last* (London, 1728), 31–43. For popular accounts, see Daniel P. Mannix, *The Hell Fire Club* (New York: Ballantine Books, 1959); and Jack Loudan, *The Hell Rakers* (Letchworth, U.K.: Books for You, 1967).

25. Randolph Trumbach, "The Birth of the Queen: Sodomy and the Emergence of Gender Equality in Modern Culture 1670–1750," in *Hidden from History,* 135.

26. Quoted by Trumbach, "The Birth of the Queen," 139.

27. Irving Goffman, *Stigma* (Englewood Cliffs, NJ: Prentice Hall, 1963), 111.

28. See Michel Foucault, *The History of Sexuality,* trans. Robert Hurley (New York: Pantheon, 1979), 1:43.

29. David E. Greenberg, *The Construction of Homosexuality* (Chicago: University of Chicago Press, 1988).

30. Randolph Trumbach, "Modern Prostitution and Gender in *Fanny Hill:* Libertine and Domesticated Fantasy," in *Sexual Underworlds of the Enlightenment,* ed. G. S. Rousseau and Roy Porter (Chapel Hill: University of North Carolina Press, 1988), 74.

31. See Senelick, "Mollies or Men of Mode?" 36–38.

32. See, for example, A. Bray, *Homosexuality in Renaissance England* (London: Gay Men's Press, 1982); and F. Trumbach, "London Sodomites: Homosexual Behavior and Western Culture in the Eighteenth Century," *Journal of Social History* 2 (1977): 1–33, and also Trumbach, "The Birth of the Queen," 135.

33. John Addy, *Sin and Society in the Seventeenth Century* (New York: Chapman and Hall, 1989); Martin Ingram, *Church Courts, Sex and Marriage in England, 1570–1640* (Cambridge: Cambridge University Press, 1987); and Alan Macfarlane, *Marriage and Love in England: Modes of Reproduction, 1300–1800* (New York: Basil Blackwell, 1987).

34. J. Weeks, "Discourse, Desire and Sexual Deviance: Some Problems in a History of Homosexuality," in *The Making of the Modern Homosexual,* ed. K. Plummer (Totowa, NJ: Barnes and Noble, 1981), 76–111.

35. For others who support the concept of eighteenth-century changes, see John R. Gillis, *For Better or Worse: British Marriages 1600 to the Present* (New York: Oxford University Press, 1985); Roderick Phillips, *Putting Asunder: A History of Divorce in Western Society* (Cambridge: Cambridge University Press, 1988); Edward Shorter, *The Making of the Modern Family* (New York: Basic Books, 1975); Lawrence Stone, *The Family, Sex and Marriage in England;* and Randolph Trumbach, *The Rise of the Egalitarian Family: Aristocratic Kinship and Domestic Relations in Eighteenth-Century England* (New York: Academic Press, 1978). For an attempt to explain why this conflict exists, see Randolph Trumbach, "Is There a Modern Sexual Culture in the West, or Did England Never Change Between 1500 and 1900?" *Journal of the History of Sexuality* (2, 1990): 296–307.

36. It is possible that seventeenth-century Lisbon had a cross-dressing homosexual culture. This subject is being explored by Louis Mott, "Poagoda Portugués: A subcultura gay em Portugal," *Ciencia e Cultura* 40 (88):120–39. See also Mott's article in R. Vainfas, ed., *Historia e Sexualidad en Brasil* (Rio de Janeiro, 1986).

37. Michael Roche, a historian (via della Calvan, 14, 50125 Florence, Italy) who has examined some 5,000 arrest records dealing with homosexual activity in fifteenth-century Florence, reported that he had not found a single case of cross dressing.

38. E. LeRoy-Ladurie, *Montaillon: The Promised Land of Error* (New York: George Brazillier, 1978); M. E. Perry, *Crime and Society in Early Modern Seville* (Hanover, NH: University Press of New England, 1980); and G. Ruggiero, "Sexual Criminality in Early Renaissance Venice, 1338–1358," *Journal of Social History* 8 (1974): 18–37.

39. *Select Trials for Murders, Robberies, Rapes, Sodomy, Coining, Frauds and Other Offences,* 3:37–38.

40. Katharine Park and Lorraine J. Daston, "Unnatural Conceptions: The Study of Monsters in Sixteenth and Seventeenth Century France and England," *Past and Present* 92 (August 1981): 20–54.

41. Lynne Friedli, " 'Passing Women'—A Study of Gender Boundaries in the Eighteenth Century," in *Sexual Underworlds of the Enlightenment,* ed. G. S. Rousseau and Roy Porter, 246–47. For the case of Drouart see J. J. L. Hoin, *Nouvelle description de l'hermaphrodite Drouart tel qu'on le voit à Dijon en Août 1761* (Paris: 1761).

42. James Parsons, *A Mechanical and Critical Enquiry into the Nature of Hermaphrodites* (London, 1741), 9.

43. R. James, *A Medicinal Dictionary* (London, 1743–45), s.v. *tribades.*

44. G. Arnaud de Ronsil, "A Dissertation on Hermaphrodites," in *A Treatise on Venereal Maladies,* ed. Jordan de Pelerin (London: 1750), 448. See also T. Browne, *Pseudodoxia Epidemica,* 5th ed. (London, 1669), 157, for another discussion.

45. G. P. S. Binachi, *An Historical and Physical Dissertation on the Case of Catharine Vizzani, Containing the Adventures of a Young Woman Who For Eight Years Posed in the Habit of a Man . . . With Some Curios and anatomical remarks on the nature and existence of the hymen . . . to which are added certain needful remarks by the English editor,* trans. and ed. John Cleland (London: n.p., 1751), 53.

46. *Réflexions sur les Hermaphrodites, relativement à Anne Grand-Jean, qualifiée telle dans un Mémoire de M. Vermeil* (Lyons, n.p., 1765). See also Friedli, "Passing Women."

47. Terry Castle, "The Culture of Travesty: Sexuality and Masquerade in Eighteenth-Century England," in *Sexual Underworlds of the Enlightenment*, ed. G. S. Rousseau and Roy Porter, 156–80.

48. The masked balls are noted as early as the reign of Henry VIII. For overall studies of popular entertainments, see C. L. Barber, *Shakespeare's Festive Comedy: A Study of Dramatic Form and Its Relation to Social Custom* (Princeton: NJ: Princeton University Press, 1959); Michael D. Bristol, *Carnival and Theater: Plebian Culture and the Structure of Authority in Renaissance England* (London: Methuen, 1985). For the court of Charles II, see Gilbert Burnet, *History of His Own Times,* ed. Thomas Burnet (London, 1818) 1:292; William Connor Sydney, *Social Life in England from the Restoration to the Revolution* (New York: Macmillan, 1892), 367–72; and Castle, "The Culture of Travesty," 158. See also Peter Burke, *Popular Culture in Early Modern Europe* (New York: Harper and Row, 1978), 249; and Joseph Spence, *Letters from the Grand Tour,* ed. Slava Klima (Montreal: McGill-Queens University Press, 1975), 75.

49. Henry Fielding, *The Masquerade* (London, 1728), reprinted in *The Female Husband and Other Writings,* ed. Claude E. Jones, English Reprints Series (Liverpool: Liverpool University Press, 1960); Joseph Addison, *The Spectator* 14 (16 March 1711) in the collected Oxford edition of the *Spectator* by Donald F. Bond, 5 vols. (Oxford: Clarendon Press, 1965). See also Castle, "The Culture of Travesty," passim.

50. Walpole's letter to Mann, 3 March 1742, in *Horace Walpole's Correspondence,* ed. W. S. Lewis, et al. (New Haven, CT: Yale University Press, 1983), 1 (17): 359.

51. Jean Starobinski, *The Invention of Liberty,* trans. Bernard C. Swift (Geneva: Albert Skira, 1964).

52. Havelock Ellis, "Eonism and Other Supplementary Studies," in *Studies in the Psychology of Sex,* (New York: Random House, 1936), 2(2):3.

53. There is a vast literature on the chevalier. The two best books are Cynthia Cox, *The Enigma of the Age: The Strange Story of the Chevalier d'Eon* (London: Longmans, Green and Company, 1966), and Edna Nixon, *Royal Spy: The Strange Case of the Chevalier d'Eon* (New York: Reynal and Company, 1965). Both are based on primary source materials. Earlier works include Frédéric Gaillardet, *Mémoires du Chevalier d'Éon* (Paris: Ladvocat, 1836), which is highly unreliable and was corrected by Gaillardet thirty years later under the same title (Paris: E. Dentu, 1866). J. B. Telfer, *The Strange Career of the Chevalier d'Éon de Beaumont* (London: Longmans, Green and Company, 1885) is also reliable, but E. A. Vizetelly, *The True Story of the Chevalier d'Éon* (London: Tylston and Edwards, 1895) has many inaccuracies, and Telfer wrote a booklet to correct it: *Chevalier d'Éon de Beaumont: A Treatise* (1896). French works include G. Letainturier-Fradin, *La Chevelière d'Éon* (Paris: Flammarion, 1901), and Octave Homberg and Fernand Jousselin, *Le Chevalier d'Éon* (Paris: Plon-Nourrite, 1904). (This was translated into English as *D'Éon de Beaumont: His Life and Times* (London: M. Secken, 1911.) Other works in French include Pierre Pinsseau, *L'Étrange Destinée du Chevalier d'Éon* (Paris: Raymond Clavreuil, 1914), and Roger Soltau, *Le Chevalier d'Éon (Mélanges d'Histoires Offerts à Charles Bémont), Les relations diplomatiques de la France et de l'Angleterre, au lendemain du Traité de Paris* (Paris: Alcan, 1913). D'Éon himself was somewhat of a literary figure, and

several volumes of his work were published. See *Les Loisirs du Chevalier d'Éon de Beaumont,* 13 vols. (Amsterdam, 1774), and particularly his *Lettres, mémoires et négociations particulières du Chevalier d'Éon* (London: Jacques Dixwell, 1764). The chevalier is also written up in C. J. S. Thompson, *Mysteries of Sex* (London: Hutchinson, n.d.), 179–96; O. P. Gilbert, *Men in Women's Guise* (London: The Bodley Head, 1926), 103–228. A popular nonscholarly biography is by M. Coryn, *The Chevalier d'Eon* (New York: Frederick A. Stokes, 1932). What survives of the family papers, *Correspondance et papiers de famille du Chevalier d'Éon de Beaumont,* are in the Bibliothèque de Tonnerre, near his birthplace. Brotherton Library, Leeds, England, has a special d'Éon collection that includes many clippings and other information about the chevalier. The British Museum's Collection de Comte de Bastard refers to him. There are at least two novels about him: Adolf Paul's *Excellenz Unterrock* (1916) takes many liberties with his life; a more recent one by Leonard J. d'Eon, who claims the same ancestral family as d'Éon, is entitled *The Cavalier* (New York: G. P. Putnam's Sons, 1987).

54. Nixon, *Royal Spy,* 66.

55. E. Boutaric, *Correspondence secrète inédite de Louis sur polique etrangère* (Paris: Plon Nourrite, 1866), dated 4 October 1763, and trans. Edna Nixon, in *Royal Spy,* 94.

56. For a discussion of the evidence, see Telfer, *The Strange Career of the Chevalier d'Eon de Beaumont.*

57. Cox, *The Enigma of the Age,* 166.

58. *The London Times,* 25 May 1810. See also Telfer, *Strange Career,* 31–32.

59. See *Des partes des gazettes anglaises et étrangères que j'ai pu recueiller,* vol. 1, 1763–75, vol. 2, 1771–85, in the d'Éon Collection, Brotherton Library, Leeds, England.

60. Cox, *The Enigma of the Age,* 140.

61. Charlotte Charke, *The History of Henry Dumont* (London: n.p., 1756), 60, 66–67. We are indebted to Lynn Friedli for this reference.

62. For an account of his administration in New York and New Jersey, see Herbert L. Osgood, *The American Colonies in the Eighteenth Century,* 4 vols. (New York: Columbia University Press, 1924), 2:61–94. That he probably did cross dress is suggested by the fact that the charge of female impersonation was first made in 1707, long before it became such a fascinating topic of conversation in English social life. According to Philip H. Stanhope, *History of England Comprising the Reign of Queen Anne,* 5th ed. (London: J. Murray, 1889), 1:79, Cornbury's strong likeness to his cousin Anne led him to dress in elaborate and sumptuous female attire. Edward Robbins, *Romances of Early America* (Philadelphia: G. W. Jacobs and Company, 1902), stated that it was Cornbury's overindulgence in liquor that caused him to cross dress. For other accounts, see John Burns, *Controversies between Royal Governors and Their Assemblies* (Boston: privately printed, 1923); Charles Worhen Spencer, "The Cornbury Legend," *Proceedings of the New York State Historical Society,* 13 (1914), 309ff. Most scholars regard Cornbury as an extremely weak governor. Edwin Platt Turner in his *Dictionary of Modern Biography,* (22 vols. in 11 reprinted, New York: Scribner's, 1957–58) 2(2):441–43, held that New York and New Jersey never had a governor so universally detested. When Cornbury was eventually recalled, he was arrested and held in New York for his creditors. The death of his father and the subsequent inheritance he received allowed him to pay off his debts. On his return to England, his reputation improved. He was raised to the Privy Council

and served as Envoy Extraordinary on the Continent. The brief biography of him in *The National Cyclopaedia of American Biography* (New York: James T. White, 1907), 5:407, states he was such a weak governor that he sometimes dressed in the "garb of a woman and thus made his appearance publicly." More recently, Patricia U. Bonomi has risen to his defense and argues that the whole story of cross dressing is fictitious. She also feels that he was a good governor but a staunch imperialist whose ideas probably were opposed by his subjects; see her "A Portrait Questioned," *Times Literary Supplement* 4–10 May 1990, letters column. Responses to her letter challenged this interpretation. *The New York Times* ran a brief article about the controversy on 30 May 1990, B, 1.4.

63. C. J. S. Thompson, *Mysteries of Sex: Women Who Posed as Men and Men Who Impersonated Women* (London: Hutchinson and Co., n.d.), 110.

64. We are indebted to Gordon Rattray Taylor, *The Angel Makers* (London: William Heinemann, 1958), 290, for this reference.

65. Thompson, *Mysteries of Sex*, 77.

66. Ibid., 98–106.

67. *The Life and Surprising Adventures of Mary Ann Talbot in the Name of John Taylor, a Natural Daughter of the Late Earl Talbot . . . Related by Herself* (London: R. S. Kirby, 1809). This, like most other accounts of such women, is a chapbook.

68. Thompson, *Mysteries of Sex,* 78–83.

69. Marion Jones, "Actors and Repertory," in *The Revels History of Drama in English,* (1660–1750), J. Loftis et al., eds. (London: Methuen, 1976), 5:148–49.

70. Quoted by Janet Dunbar, *Peg Woffington and Her World* (Boston: Houghton-Mifflin, 1968), 39. See also J. Fitzgerald Molloy, *The Life and Adventures of Peg Woffington,* 3d ed. (New York: Dodd-Mead, 1892); and Augustin Daly, *Woffington* (Reprinted New York: Blair [1888], 1972).

71. Pat Rogers, "The Breeches Part," in *Sexuality in Eighteenth Century Britain,* ed. Paul-Gabriel Boucé (Manchester: Manchester University Press, 1982), 159–56.

72. The castrati, too, probably reached their height in the eighteenth century (see Chapter 4).

Chapter 7
Women and Cross Dressing in the Nineteenth and Early Twentieth Centuries

Male privilege in the nineteenth century continued to be deeply engrained in Western society. Accordingly, most Western institutions proceeded on the assumption that male privilege was fundamental to maintaining the existing order.[1] In legal terms, this meant that women were not regarded as autonomous subjects but were always under the control of a male—husband, father, brother, or son—and more or less treated the same way as children. A woman's social identity was defined primarily by her marital status; her status, with few exceptions, was entwined with that of her husband, bestowed upon her and not "earned." Status was also affected by a woman's reproductive potential, with that of the wife and especially the mother being higher than that of the widow or lifelong spinster. Though the birth of children could enhance a woman's status as long as it occurred within a legal marriage, children born out of wedlock were outcasts and stigmatized their mother.

There were degrees of difference, however. Since poorer families in general had little wealth to transmit to legitimate heirs, the constraints on female behavior were less severe among the lower classes than among the upper classes. In short, while biology was considered destiny, the specific destiny was also based on class and status. Perhaps the most severe restrictions were imposed on the rising middle classes rather than aristocratic women, who were often too powerful to be punished severely for breaking societal rules. Vis-à-vis the aristocratic male, however, the aristocratic female was relatively powerless.

These roles began to undergo changes, particularly in the nineteenth and twentieth centuries, which ultimately gave women more educational and professional opportunities, provided more and better jobs, established voting rights, and allowed them greater freedom to determine their own lives. As women gained power and status, however, many male commentators did not visualize this as a long overdue recasting of sex roles but as a decline in the masculine virtues. This leads one to question why, if men felt so threatened by women, they gave ground at all. Obviously, not all men felt threatened, and not all women wanted change, but the answer seems to be that women's roles were redefined during the course of the nineteenth century in such a way that it ultimately gave women a weapon to challenge some aspects of male domination, which they proceeded to do. This redefinition, when coupled with the need to meet the changes demanded by an increasingly urbanized and industrialized society, made for a growing number of successful challenges.

The Redefinition of Gender Roles

It is perhaps one of the great ironies of history that the very attempt to hold onto male dominance by emphasizing that biology was destiny—that women were immeasurably different from men because they had different sex organs, functions, and feelings—gave women the weapon to advance their cause. The traditional concept of women as men turned outside in was undermined by a new concept of difference in which sex was immutable, and biology was destiny. Nature, various nineteenth-century experts argued, had become specialized as one proceeded up the great chain of being that guided the universe. Where internal fertilization was required, where the care, protection, feeding, and rearing of the young became all-important, male and female organisms had appeared with a female designed to care for the young. The male for his part was designed to protect and was given the courage and endurance to do so. From the perspective of biology, sexual reproduction was simply the means of reproduction employed by those species in which a distinctive reproductive individual, the female, had been formed. This freed the male of the species from the burden of procreation and childbearing and allowed him the freedom to expend his energies in more noble and civilized pursuits. This implied to some that women were lower than men by the very nature and structure of the universe, and that human society had been constituted on principles of inequality with men on top and women on the bottom.[2]

Some advocates of this view took extreme positions. A few claimed that women's procreative function, something not needed in heaven, had become so specialized that there was no need for women to have an immortal soul. Others argued that men and women would occupy different places in heaven. A minority, led by Emanuel Swedenborg (1688–1722) had taught that though the soul had no sex, men and women retained different natures in the hereafter and the earthly marriages remained in force after death.[3]

Inevitably, perhaps, the first effects on women of the redefinition of gender were mostly negative. Margaret Greg summarized in 1853:

[A lady] must not work for profit, or engage in any occupation that money can command, lest she invade the rights of the working classes, who live by their labour. Men in want of employment have pressed their way into nearly all the shopping and retail businesses that in my early years were managed in whole, or in part, by women. The conventional barrier that pronounced it ungenteel to be behind a counter, or serving the public in any mercantile capacity, greatly extended. The same in household economy. Servants must be up to their offices, which is very well, but ladies, dismissed from the dairy, the confectionary, the store room, the still room, the poultry yard, the kitchen garden, and the orchard, have hardly yet found themselves in a sphere equally useful and important in the pursuit of trade and art to which they apply their too abundant leisure.[4]

Though many of the economic limitations on women's roles about which Greg complained were due to the movement of business and industry from the home to the office and factory, it also had much of the scientific and intellectual theorizing of the nineteenth century behind it. The most influential Marxist theoretician in this area was Friedrich Engels, who ignored the biological arguments by explaining that the great historical defeat of the feminine sex coincided with the development of private property. The first division of labor was that between man and woman in bearing and raising children, and the result was the development and advancement of one by the humiliation and submission of the other.[5] The male, in effect, took command in the home; the "woman was degraded and reduced to servitude" and became the "slave" of male lust and a "mere instrument for the production of children."[6] Man in his newfound sovereignty indulged himself in all kinds of sexual caprices because woman was subjugated, and her only revenge was through infidelity. Therefore, according to Engels, adultery was endemic in societies that emphasized private property.

August Bebel, a disciple of Engels, emphasized that the problems associated with being a woman could be reduced to her capacity to labor, and it was the resistance of "capitalistic" paternalism that prevented the female from fully developing her personality.[7] Men had their sphere, the world outside the home, while women were dominant at home. The woman's purpose was to bear children and be a mother, but somehow motherhood was changed from being a simple biological function to become a special calling. This change was in part initiated by males who undoubtedly viewed the redefinition initially, at least, as keeping women in their place. Still, women, by emphasizing their special calling, could also claim to be special creatures. They could accept that they lacked the physical strength of men, silently ignore their alleged mental inferiority, play upon the belief that they were less driven by sexuality than men, and reinforce the assumptions that they were more loving and made of a finer (and more delicate) material than men. Women could be upholders of the moral fabric of society and preservers of the finer things in life such as art, music, and literature.

Sexuality and Control

Almost all the false arguments used to indicate that women were inferior to men could be turned to the advantage of women. Sexuality is a good example, since some of the same voices pointing out that women were not as easily sexually aroused as men at the same time argued that the very development of civilization had been dependent upon the control of sexuality. It was widely believed that one of the differences between "civilized" and "primitive" people was that primitive tribes had greater sexual freedom than civilized communities.[8] Sigmund Freud emphasized this:

We believe that civilization has been built up under the pressure of the struggle for existence, by sacrifices in gratification of the primitive impulses, and that it is to a great extent forever being re-created, as each individual successively joining the community, repeats the sacrifice of his instinctive pleasures for the common good. The sexual are amongst the most important of the instinctive forces thus utilized; they are in this way sublimated, that is to say, their energy is turned aside from its sexual goal and diverted towards other ends, no longer sexual and socially more valuable.[9]

By implication, civilization itself depended upon strong control of the sexual instinct. The traditional hostility to sex expressed in Christian discourse, which at the same time emphasized the asexuality of women, gained a new scientific basis in the eighteenth century and particularly in the nineteenth century. The "scientific" apostle of a new justification for sexual moderation was S. A. D. Tissot (1728–87), a Swiss physician who drew upon the medical beliefs of the time to put forth his new theory. Based on clinical observations of the sequelae of what we now know to be the third stage of syphilis, Tissot concluded that "overindulgence" in sex was the cause of cardiovascular syphilis (the weakening of the heart and the blood vessels), neurosyphilis (in which the central nervous system is involved), skin eruptions, unhealing gumma, tabes dorsalis (a gradual deterioration of the spinal cord), paresis (degenerative general paralysis), and vigorous types of psychoses. Unfortunately, these sequelae were not positively identified as resulting from the same causative agent, *Treponema palladium* (a spirochete), until the beginning of the twentieth century.

Before the germ theory was developed, physicians tended to derive their treatment from a number of different theories and had developed elaborate systems based upon them. Many of the theories proceeded from the assumption that good health was a natural state and that illness developed from some kind of imbalance. Treatment involved helping the body restore the proper balance. Different systems advocated different treatments. One system defined wellness as resulting from a proper mixture of excitability and lack of excitability. Too little stimulation was bad, but excessive stimulation was believed to be worse because it could debilitate a person by exhausting the potential for excitability. Treatment depended on diagnosis: those diseases arising from excessive excitement (sthenic) and those from deficient excitement (asthenic). The natural balance was a fragile one, and too much stimulation could transform an asthenic ailment into a sthenic one.

Two lovers kissing and being in each other's presence gave an impetuosity to the nerves, but intercourse itself, while giving temporary relief, could also release too much turbulent energy and, if carried to excess, could cause illness. Another theory maintained that the lymphatic glands as well as the muscular nervous system had vital activity. Secretions of body fluids had to be controlled because they could drain the vital essences residing in every part of the body.[10]

Tissot's system differed from the others in that he put such heavy reliance on sexual activity. The basis of his theory was that physical bodies suffered a continual wasting through secretions, including urine, feces, and perspiration; unless this waste was periodically restored, death would result. Though eating restored much of the waste, even with an adequate diet the body could waste away through diarrhea, loss of blood, and more importantly for our purpose, seminal emission. Tissot was particularly impressed with the dangers of seminal emission, which, unlike diarrhea or loss of blood, the individual could control. He also observed that semen itself was important to male well-being since its appearance during adolescence was the factor that caused beards to grow and muscles to thicken. Moreover, amputation of the testicles, the producers of sperm, led to effeminization. Thus, he argued that when semen is lost, it temporarily weakened the male. He recognized that some loss was necessary for the reproduction of the human race, but frequent loss caused irreparable damage. The most dangerous loss of semen was that which occurred when the individual spilled it through masturbation. Masturbation, or onanism, was defined by him as all seminal emissions not intended for procreation. Regular loss of semen, Tissot held, would eventually result in:

1. Cloudiness of ideas and sometimes even madness.
2. Decay of bodily powers resulting in coughs, fevers, and consumption.
3. Acute pains in the head, rheumatic pains, and an aching numbness.
4. Pimples of the face, suppurating blisters on the nose, breast, and thighs, and painful itchings.
5. Eventual weakness of the power of generation, as evidenced by impotence, premature ejaculation, gonorrhea, priapism, and tumors of the bladder.
6. Disorders of the intestines, resulting in constipation, hemorrhoids, and so forth.

Though Tissot recognized that everyone addicted to onanism (which would include using contraceptives) did not always suffer the ills he described, he felt that most did even if it was not always visible. The great evil was masturbation because it was so ubiquitous, could be done in secret, and was addictive.

Onanism, Tissot held, affected females the same way as males but, in addition, caused them to be subject to hysterical fits, incurable jaundice, violent cramps in the stomach, pains in the nose, ulceration of the cervix, and uterine tremors. It deprived females of decency and reason, lowering them to the level of the most lascivious, vicious brutes. Even worse than masturbation in the female was mutual clitoral manipulation, something which caused women to love other women with as much fondness and jealousy as they did men. Onanism, in fact, was far more pernicious than excesses in simple fornication, although this too was dangerous. Onanism was particularly debilitating to those who had not yet attained puberty, because it tended to destroy mental faculties by putting too great a strain on the nervous system.[11]

Though we might now have difficulty in understanding how all the ills attributed to onanism could be taken seriously, Tissot's work was widely read and believed. Moreover, he seemingly had science on his side. Observations supporting Tissot came from the mental institutions where caretakers observed that mental patients spent much of their time manipulating their genitals. Instead of attributing this to the boredom of asylum life or to the lack of inhibitions, it was regarded as a causal factor for their insanity. Tissot as well as others had noted that after an orgasm a person feels somewhat lethargic, often taking a brief nap, thus providing further proof of the draining of bodily energy. They theorized that if this energy drain continued for very long, it would easily lead to imbalances in the body. Finally, they observed that many individuals with a long history of sexual activity with multiple partners, as many of those who contracted syphilis had, suffered from the symptoms described by Tissot (but which were actually from tertiary syphilis). In short, Tissot created a plausible explanation that could be made to fit the facts he observed.

Tissot's ideas became widespread. Disseminating them to an American audience was Benjamin Rush (1745–1813), the dominant medical figure in America at the end of the eighteenth century and a signer of the Declaration of Independence. Rush, an advocate of John Brown's (1735–88) medical ideas about the importance of nervous energy, argued that sexual intercourse was a major cause of excitement. He taught that careless indulgence in sex would lead to "seminal weakness, impotence, dysuria, tabes dorsalis, pulmonary consumptions, dyspepsia, dimness of sight, vertigo, epilepsy, hypochondriasis, loss of memory," and other potentially fatal ills. Though Rush recognized that sex was essential for procreation and that abnormal restraint in sexual matters could be dangerous, he cautioned his readers about overindulgence.[12]

Tissot's ideas, however, found their strongest support among nonphysicians, some of whom carried the ideas to ludicrous extremes. For example, Sylvester Graham (1794–1851), best remembered today for his advocacy of unbolted wheat, or Graham flour, believed that his contemporaries suffered from an increasing incidence of debility of all sorts, much of which resulted from sexual excess. He advocated a kind of dualism whereby the body contained both an animal and organic life. Animal life was represented by the organs of sensation, voluntary motion, and volition, while organic life included those organs and powers concerned with the function of nutrition, respiration, circulation, secretion, absorption, and excretion. Both the animal and organic aspects of the body were controlled by networks of nerves.[13]

Reproduction, almost alone of the body's functions, was related to both the animal and organic life systems and thus put a unique stress on both systems. Graham went further to argue that it was not only an orgasm that posed danger to the body but also lascivious thought and imagination. Too many lascivious thoughts, just like too much masturbation, could lead to insanity.[14] Desire could also be affected by eating stimulating substances such as highly seasoned food, rich dishes, excessive meat, and so forth. He was particularly worried about the loss of semen and equated the loss of an ounce of semen to the loss of several ounces of blood. With each ejaculation a man lowered his life force and thereby exposed his system to disease and premature death. He urged married individuals to limit their sexual indulgence to not more than twelve times a year. His work went through ten editions between 1834 and 1848, was translated into several languages, and obviously added to the growing anxiety about untrammeled sexuality.[15]

Another influential force in highlighting the dangers of sex was the French surgeon Claude-François Lallemand, whose book was published in an American edition in 1839. Lallemand was primarily concerned with spermatorrhea, the involuntary loss of male semen, which he felt would lead to insanity. Since spermatorrhea in adults was an inevitable consequence of youthful masturbation, parents had to be ever-vigilant. Equally dangerous was the inflammation of youthful minds through reading lascivious books; even daydreaming was dangerous, for young people either began to masturbate to gratify their "morbid" thoughts or had involuntary emissions at night. Lallemand's American translator added to the author's "evidence" by pointing out that the reports of the Massachusetts State Lunatic Hospital at Worcester indicated that fifty-five of the 407 inmates (forty-three males and twelve females) had become insane as a result of their masturbatory habits. Thus, even though a person ceased masturbating in his adult life, he might still become insane because of spermatorrhea, or he could suffer other serious consequences.[16] There were many other writers who wrote along similar lines.[17]

Certainly, some readers of this pro-chastity, antisexual material wondered why, if sexual activity was so harmful, most of humanity had not become insane in the past. But those promoting the new "scientific findings" answered that the problem was exacerbated by the growing complexities of modern civilization and a higher evolutionary development of humanity. George M. Beard, for example, argued that modern civilization had put such increased stress on men and women that larger numbers of people were suffering from nervous exhaustion. Such exhaustion, he held, was particularly great among professionals, who represented a higher evolutionary stage than the less advanced working classes; thus, as men and women advanced, it became increasingly necessary to save their nervous energy. Beard believed the human body was a reservoir of "force constantly escaping, constantly being renewed" but frequently in danger of imbalance. A major cause of nervous exhaustion was sexual intercourse; unless the energy that went into it was carefully regulated and guarded, nervous exhaustion would result.[18]

There was, however, a way in which nature had provided to save men from the dangers of sex, namely, by making the female more or less indifferent to sex. This, for example, was the argument of the English physician William Acton (1814–75). Acton, worried about the great drain on the nervous system imposed by the loss of semen, felt the only solution was to engage in sex infrequently and then without prolonging the sex act. He thought that men were able to do this because God had created women indifferent to sex in order to prevent the male's vital energy from being overly expended. Only out of fear that their husbands would desert them for courtesans or prostitutes (women whose sexual drives were somehow out of kilter) did most women waive their natural distaste for sex and submit to their husbands' ardent embraces. Because women were reluctant to perform the necessary biological functions related to impregnation, he advised husbands to perform the necessary task in as expeditious way as possible, with the least possible damage to the nervous system.[19] Few theorists went as far as Acton, but many women ultimately found his arguments useful in advancing the cause of women's rights.[20]

Victorianism and the Cult of Motherhood

Even those who recognized that women had sexual desires, however, agreed that motherhood, in essence, was a woman's destiny, and it was dangerous to try to thwart nature's purpose. Motherhood was a demanding job, for it entailed not only pregnancy but the raising of the child. Since the child was not ready for life, he or she had to be subjected to special treatment, a sort of quarantine, before being allowed to join the adults. If children were to be isolated from society, it seemed obvious that women, the natural guardians of children, should also be isolated. Motherhood in the nineteenth century increasingly became a special calling, and thus men continued to assume that women were men's intellectual and physical inferiors; they also looked upon them as more innocent and childlike, as though women had to be protected as much as children.

Collectively, these attitudes came to be termed Victorianism, although Victorianism consisted of much more than mere prudery. In a sense, Victorianism represented a compromise between the heroic and utopian aspects of the new ethics and the real life of ordinary people who strove to follow conventional Christianity. Victorianism outwardly emphasized respectability, even as, beneath the surface, a seething sexuality persisted, as indicated by the growth of prostitution, pornography, and similar "hidden" aspects of society. Victorianism originated in Great Britain, which, as the most powerful nation of the time, set the tone in many matters of morals, manners, and artistic taste. The term is also associated with the self-satisfaction engendered by the great increase of wealth that characterized the upper middle classes in the nineteenth century and led the middle class in particular to adopt conscious rectitude and an unquestioning acceptance of male authority as the norm, thereby allowing them to believe and publicly profess that their society was more moral than those of the past.

Victorianism was also partly the result of industrialization, since the Industrial Revolution of the late eighteenth and early nineteenth centuries had forced women to alter their life-styles, placing them into direct conflict with the customs and institutions that had been based more or less on economic exigencies of the past. Although the Industrial Revolution itself did not determine how the family would be organized or what social attitudes toward women would be, its widespread influence gave further emphasis to the nuclear family. As women, particularly those of the middle class, found themselves confined to a home that had lost much of its economic importance, the Victorians moved, consciously or unconsciously, to make the home the center of social life by placing new emphasis on the family. This involved paying great reverence to the woman's role in raising children and in providing a haven for the male to retreat from the problems of the outside world. A new concept of motherhood developed, enveloping the woman in a mystique that asserted her special status but at the same time kept her confined. Working-class women were hired in the factories and neglected their families, and aristocratic women remained outside the bounds of middle-class morality (as did actresses), but the "good" woman—the true middle-class woman, as befitted her new-found moral purity and spiritual genius—had to devote herself to the task of homemaking, something that in the past had not been regarded as particularly important.

Chastity was the mark of the new gentility, and though chastity or its lack might be difficult to prove, presumptions were readily made. Thus, there were many things a proper lady could not or would not do. If a girl's dress was too revealing, her ornaments too provocative, her speech and gestures too bold, some people would assume she was not a virgin. Appearances counted for more than reality. It was absolutely essential that a proper girl look and behave with a "respectable" modesty.

Such attitudes and expectations were so restrictive that many women did not want to or could not bear them; often, the only outlet for their discontent was in church work or literary pursuits. Religion, in a sense, became a justification for what they wanted to do but otherwise could not, and even women's suffrage became overlaid with the concepts of raising the standards of morality in the sense that it sought to allow the purer and finer species, the woman, to vote. Victorianism taught women to think of themselves as a special class, but once they became conscious of their uniqueness, they could no longer accept uncritically the strict role definitions drawn up for them. Finer creatures, they felt, should raise the moral level of society. Denied liberty, they sought power, and not infrequently, the way to gain power was through their children. Motherhood came to be elevated into a mystique, which Sigmund Freud later made into a pseudoscientific basis of existence.

Since women were expected to demonstrate a meticulous personal daintiness, their gestures were to be void of signs of masculinity, and their clothes and hairdress were to have a precarious fragility. Women who were not delicate by nature became so by design, since those who failed to conform were usually ostracized by other women. The world was regarded as being made up of good and bad: The bad women represented sexuality, the good stood for purity of mind and spirit, unclouded by the shadow of any gross or vulgar thought. The largest group of bad women were the prostitutes, who were thought to have inherently poor morals. Even women's creative activities were restricted to certain fields. They could paint or sketch, but not too creatively and not in oils, which were too messy; they could play a musical instrument, but not professionally; and they could only play instruments that did not require spreading their legs, pursing their lips, viscerally demonstrating their muscles, or messing their dress or coiffure (usually, this meant they played the piano). Such restrictions could be expanded indefinitely, but their common result was that "proper" women became by design and training wan, ethereal, sedentary, passive persons, symbols of chastity and delicacy.[21]

Those women who were active and energetic were compelled to conform to the standards by the increasingly restrictive clothing that came into fashion during the nineteenth century. From crinoline hoop skirts to corsets, the intent of women's fashion seemed to be to restrict activity. Corsets were especially confining, and in order to meet the demands of fashion, young girls had to be put into corset trainers as early as age eight or nine; their activities were correspondingly restricted. Ultimately, women continued wearing them for everyday occasions and not just for dress affairs. For a time in the 1880s, the dress was made to cover the body tightly from the neck to the knee so that it was impossible to take large steps. The knees were actually tied together in order to keep the walk graceful.

And yet it was by playing on their role as mothers, as specially endowed to raise children, as preservers of the finer things, that women built their political power. In one of the early issues of *Ladies' Magazine*, Sarah Hale wrote that authority over men must

never be usurped; but still, women may, if they will exert their talents, and [by] the opportunities nature has furnished, obtain an influence in society that will be paramount to authority. They may enjoy the luxuries of wealth, without enduring the labors to acquire it; and the honors of office, without feeling its cares, and the glory of victory, without suffering the dangers of the battle.[22]

Motherhood became almost a cult in mid-nineteenth-century America. Books on mothers of famous men, especially Mary Washington, mother of George Washington, poured from the presses in the 1840s and 1850s; their message was that men achieved greatness because of the instruction and inspiration they received from their mothers.[23] Correspondingly, the authority of the father in the middle-class American family declined for, unlike the nurturing mother, the urban father left the home to work, often for ten or twelve hours a day. The cult of motherhood offered women, at least those who had children, a basis of respect. Even women without children, however, could come to be looked upon as mothers by caring for others, as Clara Barton did during the Civil War.[24] Since women had special abilities with children, it was perhaps inevitable that they also moved into the classroom as teachers. Over the course of the nineteenth century, women began to constitute the overwhelming majority of grade-school teachers.[25]

After the Civil War, women's clubs served as bastions of culture and moral uplift. Women were at the forefront in organizing the campaign for temperance (and ultimately prohibition), since alcohol was perceived as a threat to the family and the home. Likewise, it was women's duty to bring their husbands to cultural events, including musical presentations, artistic exhibits, or readings by traveling poets or novelists.

The early suffragists were divided between arguing that women should have a vote because it was their inalienable right and because they could provide a moral uplift to society. It was probably the latter argument more than the former that convinced the male authorities to extend the vote to women, although motives varied. For example, one of the reasons that Wyoming, the first territory to give women the vote, did so was that very few women had settled there, and it was hoped that the right to vote would make Wyoming more appealing.[26]

Once women received the ballot, they would become empowered to eliminate many of the legal barriers against them. But even before this occurred on a national level, women, through their concern for children and the disenfranchised, were able to enter the social reform movement. Jane Addams, the founder of Hull House in Chicago in 1889, was a pioneer in the settlement house movement, and her slightly less well-known contemporary, Lillian Wald, a nurse, founded the Henry Street Settlement in New York. Florence Kelly, who worked with Addams at Hull House, lobbied for passage of the Illinois Factory Inspection Act and special protection for women and child workers.

Jeanette Rankin, a social worker, became the first woman to serve in Congress when Wyoming elected her in 1916.

Joining the Battle at Home and at War

Still, despite the gains from these changes and the growing number of women who broke through former limitations, many women still found the easiest way to escape their restrictive assigned role was to pass as a man rather than to fight what they believed to be an almost impossible battle against male prejudice. War demands not only relaxed barriers for women at home while the men were away but allowed women to do things outside the home that would not have been possible otherwise.

In the American Civil War, for example, many women followed Florence Nightingale's example in the Crimea and volunteered as nurses. Others, not content with such tasks, wanted more direct action and, disguising themselves as men, enlisted. Private Frank Fuller, alias Frances Hook, of the Ninetieth Illinois Regiment, carried a rifle and served until being wounded and captured at the Battle of Chattanooga. A private of the 125th Michigan Cavalry turned out to be Elizabeth Compton.[27]

Both sides in the Civil War had their male impersonators. Loreta Janet Velazquez wrote about her experiences in the Confederate Army and explained how she managed to pass as a man. As was the case with many other cross dressers, Velazquez claimed to have disguised herself to be with her husband, but such statements seem to be pro forma, since she continued to serve in the army long after his death. When she decided to enlist, she had a New Orleans tailor make her a half-dozen wire-net shields which she wore in order to disguise her true form, since

[a] woman's waist, as a general thing, is tapering, and her hips are very large in comparison with those of man, so that if I had undertaken to wear pantaloons without some such contrivance, they would have drawn in at the waist and revealed my true form. . . . So many men have weak and feminine voices that, provided the clothing is properly constructed and put on right, and the disguise in other respects is well arranged, a woman with even a very high-pitched voice need have very little to fear on that score.[28]

Her disguise also included a tight-fitting undershirt of silk and lisle thread over the wire-net shield, held in place by straps across the chest and shoulders. Around her waist she wore a band with eyelet holes arranged so that the pantaloons would stand out. When her true sex was eventually discovered (in part, because her wire netting became disarranged), she was sentenced to ten days in jail and fined ten dollars.[29]

On the Union side, perhaps the most famous case was Sarah Emma Edmonds Seelye, alias Franklin Thomson. As a girl in New Brunswick, Canada, Emma, as she was known, read a novel by M. M. Ballou entitled *Fanny Campbell: or, The Female Pirate Captain,* published in Boston in 1844. The novel told about a girl whose lover was captured by pirates; by cutting her curls and stepping into the "freedom and glorious independence of masculinity," the heroine managed to rescue him. How much the story influenced her is uncertain, but at the age of fifteen young Emma fled her family home in order to escape from an unwanted marriage. In order to support herself, she donned male garb and worked at first as a Bible salesman but then enlisted in the Union Army. She managed to serve for two years until illness forced her to retire, still undetected. Soon afterward, she published her well-received memoirs under the title *Nurse and Spy* (Hartford, 1864). She later married and became a mother, but still managed to be officially accepted into the George P. McClellan Post, Grand Army of the Republic (GAR), in 1897. She was the only woman member of the GAR, the forerunner of the American Legion.[30]

The ease with which a woman could impersonate a man is evidenced again by the fact that many were not detected until after their deaths.[31] An indication of their numbers is given by Mary Livermore, a nurse with the Union Army, who estimated that there were four hundred such women in the Union Army.[32]

Yet it was not only in the army that they appeared. Charles Durkee Pankhurst, a stagecoach drive in California, was discovered to be a woman after her death in 1879. Some call Pankhurst the first woman to vote in California, although she did so disguised as a man.[33] Several women were known as "Mountain Charley," including a woman who lived as a male trapper in the western territories in the 1850s, and at least two women wrote books claiming to be this legendary person.[34] How many women lived as men can never be known with certainty, but their numbers were numerous; from 1850 on, local newspapers often reported the death of men who turned out to be women. Many of the women who passed were petite. Babe Bean of San Francisco, who was five feet two inches tall and weighed about a hundred pounds, managed to live most of her adult life as a man. She first donned men's clothes in order to go to the Philippines during the Spanish-American War. She got there by serving as a cabin boy and continued to wear men's clothing. On her return to San Francisco, her sisters tried to discourage her from masquerading as a man but she persisted, adopting the name Jack Bee Garland. It was not until her death in San Francisco on 18 September 1936, that her masquerade was detected.[35]

A more recent case involves Billy Tipton, a jazz musician who died in 1989. Tipton initially decided to live as a man in order to advance her musical career, but she later married, adopted sons, and raised them as their father. Tipton's wife explained that they had agreed to abstain from intercourse because Tipton claimed to have suffered an injury that required wearing a broad surgical bandage across the abdomen for support. The drummer who played with the Billy Tipton trio for ten years remembered that some members of the audience would joke about Tipton's baby face and high-pitched voice, remarking that he looked too feminine to be a man; but he stated he would fight anyone who challenged Tipton's masculinity.[36]

What seems evident from these stories is how much clothing helped determine one's gender. Once a person dressed passably as a man and adopted the proper posture and walk, few were questioned, even in the army. The ability to pass is illustrated by the case of Maria Bochkareva, who fought in the Russian Army in World War I in male clothing. Despite the fact that, when questioned, Bochkareva did not deny being a woman, she was accepted as a man. After she had endured two unhappy marriages, Bochkareva began dressing in male clothing while working on a construction job and kept doing so afterward. She personally pleaded with the czar to allow her to enlist in the army, which he permitted. Even though her comrades-in-arms knew she was a woman, they regarded her as their comrade. During the 1917 revolution, she became a leader of an all-female group known as the Petrograd Women's Battalion of Death. The battalion suffered disastrous losses on the Western Front, and their final action came in October 1917, when they fought unsuccessfully to defend the Winter Palace against the Bolsheviks.[37] Bochkareva mentioned that, although at first she had to stay awake almost all night to protect herself from unwanted advances in the barracks, once the others found out she wanted to be a soldier and was not interested in sleeping with them, they accepted her as a colleague.

A woman cross dresser's first contact with her male colleagues often proved traumatic. Marina Yurlova, for example, was standing amid a crowd of women and children who were accompanying a group of soldiers to war when she found herself accidentally pushed onto a railway car; to protect herself she became an unofficial soldier. She reports that she had never seen a naked man before she was housed in an all-male barracks, and she was very conscious of the pungent smells around her, particularly the soldiers' damp foot wrappings (worn in lieu of socks) hung up to dry, stale tobacco smoke, and the unwashed bodies. It was only after she overcame her revulsion of living in close quarters and her fear of naked men that she believed she was becoming a true soldier.[38]

One of the most famous Russian female soldiers was Nadezha Durova (1773–1866), who served nearly ten years in the Russian Light Cavalry during the Napoleonic Wars and left the army in 1816. She saw combat in 1807 and 1812–14 and later wrote a detailed account of her life in the army. Her most recent editor claims that her depiction of a junior officer's life gives one of the more detailed accounts of everyday life in a squadron and platoon of the period. She began her army career at the age of twenty-two, when, disguised as a boy, she ran away from her home in the foothills of the Ural mountains. She later wrote that she had wanted to escape the "sphere prescribed by nature and custom to the female sex." After her retirement from the army, apparently due to her inability to advance to any higher rank, she kept to men's clothing and masculine speech habits. Aleksandr Pushkin began publishing her manuscript in 1836. When they met Pushkin attempted to kiss her hand, but she snatched it back, saying, "O, my God! I got out of that habit long ago." Pushkin had trouble persuading her to use her real name rather than, Aleksandr Andreevich Aleksandrov, the name she had used in the military. In her later memoirs she emphasizes that her rebellion was not against being female per se but against the restrictions put on her sex. She had married in 1801 and gave birth to a son in 1803, but she never discussed her marriage. According to one perhaps apocryphal story, after her retirement her son wrote a letter to her, addressing her as mother and asking for her blessing in his upcoming marriage. She refused to answer it because of this salutation.[39]

According to some estimates, hundreds of Russian women disguised as men fought in World War I. The *London Graphic* reported as early as 1915 that some fifty soldiers had been discovered to be women at their death or when they were being treated for wounds,[40] and their numbers increased as living conditions in Russia worsened. It is quite possible that some of the women soldiers' comrades had known they were women, but as Anne Eliot Griesse and Richard Stites have observed, they were largely indifferent; their fellow soldiers were mostly peasants who knew from experience that women were capable of enduring the privations of war as well as they survived other hardships.[41] Russian peasant women had long worked as hard as men in the fields and at other forms of manual labor.[42]

Motives for some of the more famous cross dressers remain obscure. One whose motives remain veiled is James Barry, who attained the rank of Inspector-General of Hospitals and served in the British Army for more than forty years without being discovered. We do not even know her female name today. Barry did not fit the standard masculine image, being described as a peppery little figure with dyed red hair, a high-pitched voice, and tiny white hands, who looked absurd in the full-dress uniform with cockaded hat and huge sword. Still, it was not until her death in 1865 that she was found to be a woman. Born in 1795, James Barry graduated from the Edinburgh Medical College in 1812 and was commissioned in the British Army a year later. There is even some evidence that early in her life she had given birth to a child, but if so, she did not allow it to impede her successful impersonation. She had a contempt for authority and strong ideas about reform that antagonized some of her coworkers, since she did not hesitate to advocate them at every opportunity. In addition to her experience in South Africa, where she was the colonial medical inspector, she worked as a medical officer in Jamaica, Saint Helena, Barbados, Antigua, Malta, Corfu, the Crimea, and Montreal, before returning to England, where she retired in 1859.[43]

The motives of Captain Flora Sanders, an Englishwoman who served in the Serbian army in World War I, on the other hand, were more straightforward. Sanders recalled that as a very small child she used to pray every night that she might wake up in the morning and find herself transformed into a boy.[44] Though most of her fellow soldiers knew she was a woman, they accepted her as one of them; they particularly valued the fact that she was English, for her involvement represented to them a hopeful sign of possible additional English aid. Her familiarity with guns, her knowledge of French and German, her nursing skills, and especially her willingness to put aside the restrictive female role of that time helped ensure her acceptance by her comrades.

Sometimes the impersonation was less successful, as in the case of the eighteen-year-old English would-be journalist Dorothy Lawrence. Denied an opportunity to go to the front during World War I, she persuaded two English soldiers she had met in a Parisian café to provide her with a uniform. She then cut her hair, bound her breasts, placed padding in her clothing, stained her skin with dilute furniture polish (to produce the requisite manly bronzed complexion), and set out for the front with a forged pass and a real identification disc.[45] After serving for some ten days and getting her story, she disclosed her true identity to the officials; after being interrogated, she was sent to a French convent, where she had to swear not to make her experiences public. Apparently, her short-term attempt to impersonate a man in order to get a story antagonized the military authorities.

Sometimes the demands of war exposed impersonations that had been going on in civilian life, as was the case in England of a woman printer known as Albert F. Albert F. was one of those drafted in World War I to meet the increasing manpower demands of a decimated army. Though "his" employer applied for a deferment for "him," Albert was ordered to report to the Medical Examining Board in August 1916. Albert asked for a private medical examination because of a cardiac condition, and he produced a National Health Insurance form as substantiation. The request was denied, and during the subsequent examination Albert was found to be a woman. Described as a slightly built, fair-haired, and smooth-faced conscript, with a soft and gentle voice, the recruiting sergeant was later questioned as to why he had not suspected Albert was a woman. He replied that he had no reason to do so since many of the young men called up "have effeminate voices, and when a great many men are being dealt with . . . individual characteristics are passed without comment."[46]

Albert had been married and had two children, both of whom died in infancy. She left her husband and moved into a lodging house, where she met the woman who later became her "wife." Fearing her former husband might find her, she assumed a male identity and began a new life in London, where she was highly regarded by her employer.

Obviously, this impersonation has a stronger lesbian connotation than many of those previously mentioned. But as we have seen, lesbianism does not in itself explain cross dressing. Some of the complicating factors are evident in the case of Colonel Barker, née Valerie Arkell-Smith. She wrote that

trousers make a wonderful difference in the outlook on life. I know that dressed as a man I did not, as I do now I am wearing skirts again, feel hopeless and helpless. Today when the whole world knows my secret I feel more a man than a woman. I want to up and do those things that men do to earn a living rather than to spend my days as a friendless woman.[47]

Arkell-Smith was born on the island of Jersey in 1895, the daughter of a gentleman farmer and a woman of independent means. The family moved to England in 1897, but Valerie spent much of her childhood attending a convent school in Brussels. After her coming-out party, Valerie took up war work, first as a nurse, then as an ambulance driver, and finally as a member of the Women's Auxiliary Air Force. In 1918, she married Lieutenant Harold Arkell-Smith, an Australian officer, but the marriage lasted only six weeks. She then became involved with another Australian, Ernest Pearce-Crouch, with whom she lived until 1923 and by whom she had two children. She then left him to assume her new identity as Victor Barker and, as such, married Elfrida Howard in 1923.

Posing as a retired military official, Barker made little attempt to keep out of the public limelight. In 1927 she joined the National Fascisti, a militant breakaway group from the British Fascist Party. She soon took over responsibility for the organization's boxing program, originally established to help members get into combat shape in order to more effectively fight the "reds and the pinks" in the community. She also actively participated in disrupting Communist Party meetings. Though the group remained small in numbers and was largely confined to London, it received considerable attention in the press. Adopting the black shirt uniform, the party used other fascist symbols as well, and it also accepted many of the myths of the German Nazi Party. Like its German counterpart, the party was virulently anticommunist and antisemitic. The party's solution to the problems facing Great Britain was to establish a government of experts with a governing executive council of real "men" who had the will and power to rule.[48]

Barker's impersonation was exposed in 1929, when, as a result of her connection to a bankruptcy case, she was held in Brixton Prison to await trial. When her biological sex was reported, she was also charged with perjury for pretending to be a man in order to marry Elfrida Howard. Found guilty, she was sentenced to nine months in Holloway Prison for Women. Perhaps because her lawyer succeeded in arguing that she posed as a man in order to earn a better living than what she could as a woman, the press, despite the sensational nature of the trial, often presented her in a sympathetic light. Elfrida Howard, like the wife of Billy Tipton, claimed not to know that her husband was anything but a man until the trial. When questioned about her sex life, she reported that the "colonel" had told her they could not have normal sexual relations because of Barker's wartime injury. That Howard was not as unaware as she claimed was later proved when it became clear that she had initially known Barker as Mrs. Pearce-Crouch; the two first met when Barker came into Howard's father's chemist shop dressed as a Land Army girl in trousers and an open shirt. Howard, however, stuck to her story that, because Barker "[courted] me as a man, . . . I believed she was a man."[49]

Howard's denial of knowledge of her partner's biological sex is almost a standard characteristic of cases in which a woman cross dresser is unmasked. By the denial, both partners could escape charges of being lesbians, since the public found it difficult to believe that intercourse could take place without the "male" partner revealing "his" true sex. This allowed the cross dresser to claim, as most did, that they had impersonated men in order to get a job, accompany a loved one, or gain freedom, and this explanation struck a responsive chord in both men and women.

Some lesbian contemporaries of Colonel Barker were upset by her impersonation and attempted to distance themselves from her. Radclyffe Hall, best known as the author of *The Well of Loneliness*, the first novel in English to describe explicitly a lesbian relationship,[50] was angered by the press's reaction to Barker's trial. She wrote to her agent, Audrey Heath, that the "colonel" was a "pervert of the most undesirable type" who ought to be "drawn and quartered." She complained that Barker had not only got all the bad publicity but then after "marrying a woman" had gone and "deserted her."[51]

Historical and Fictional Accounts of Lesbian Cross Dressers

And yet many of the cross dressers of Barker's time and earlier were lesbian. An example is the case of Murray Hall, née Mary Anderson, who died in New York City in 1901. Born in Scotland, Anderson was left an orphan at an early age; shortly after the death of her only brother, she put on his clothes and went to Edinburgh, where she began working as a man. When her biological sex was discovered after she was treated for an illness, she left for the United States, where she lived and worked as a man for thirty years, acquired considerable money, became active in Tammany Hall politics, and gained a reputation as a man-about-town. She married twice, and though the first marriage ended in separation, the second lasted for twenty years until her "wife" died. She liked to associate with pretty girls and was almost jealously protective of them. She was slight, not particularly masculine in build, and had a squeaky voice; but her mannerisms were so masculine that no one ever questioned her. She smoked, chewed tobacco, drank, and could sing a ribald song as well as any man. To disguise her figure, she always wore baggy trousers and a long coat, even in summer. She is said to have died of breast cancer, and when her sex was finally disclosed, it was a revelation, particularly to her adopted daughter.[52]

Another American lesbian who lived as a man was Carolina Hall, a Boston watercolor painter who resided for a long period in Milan, Italy. Sometime before 1801, Hall had discarded female dress and taken up residence as the husband of an Italian woman somewhat her junior. She called herself Mr. Hall and appeared to be a thoroughly normal young man, a good shot with a rifle and fond of many sports. She traveled widely with her "wife" and was a hail-fellow-well-met with everyone. Her sex was discovered after her death from advanced tuberculosis, hastened, according to the report, by excessive drinking and smoking.[53]

Still other cases abound. Ellen Glen, alias Ellis Glenn, was a Chicago swindler of the turn of the century who preferred to dress as a man and had many love affairs with women.[54] Nicholai de Raylay, the confidential secretary to the Russian consul, was found after her death in Chicago in 1906 to be a woman. The twice-married Nicholai had been divorced by her first "wife" after ten years of marriage because of misconduct with chorus girls. The second "wife," a chorus girl who had a child from a previous marriage, was devoted to her. Both wives were firmly convinced, at least so they claimed, that their husband had been a man, and they thought the idea that de Raylay could have been a woman ludicrous, although "he" was slight in build and not particularly masculine in appearance. De Raylay always wore a long-waisted coat to disguise the lines of her figure. Careful arrangements had been made in her will to avoid detection, but these plans were frustrated when she died in a hospital.[55]

Cora Anderson, of Milwaukee, de Raylay's contemporary, posed for thirteen years as a man, and during that time lived with two different women without her true sex being discovered.[56]

Lucy Ann Slater, alias the Reverend Joseph Lobdell, alias the "Female Hunter of Long Eddy," another turn-of-the-century figure, was eventually arrested when she was recognized by a former acquaintance. On petition of her "wife" she was released, although some time later she was institutionalized and eventually died of "progressive dementia."[57]

Some nineteenth-century fictional accounts also give us insight into the phenomenon of cross dressing. One classic is Théophile Gautier's 1835 novel *Mademoiselle du Maupin,* in which the sexually enigmatic Théodore de Serranes is beloved by both the narrator d'Albert and d'Albert's mistress, Rosette. Théodore dressed in male attire in order to become acquainted with a young man whose appearance pleased her and to whom she later revealed herself as a woman. But the plot becomes more complicated for, invariably, cross dressing affects the person doing the cross dressing as well as the observer.

I was imperceptibly losing the idea of my sex, and I hardly remembered, at long intervals, that I was a woman; at the beginning, I'd often let slip some phrase or other which didn't fit in with the male attire that I was wearing. . . . If ever the fancy takes me to go and find my skirts again in the drawer where I left them, which I very much doubt, unless I fall in love with some young beau, I shall find it hard to lose the habit, and instead of a woman disguised as a man, I shall look like a man disguised as a woman. In truth, neither sex, is really mine. . . . I belong to a third sex, a sex apart, which has as yet no name.[58]

A more recently discovered instance of real-life cross dressing is the case of Mary Diana Dods who, as David Lyndsay, published a number of books, poems, and short stories; as Walter Sholto Douglas, she was the husband of Isabella Robinson Douglas. Dods and Isabella Douglas were aided by Mary Shelley, wife of Percy Bysshe Shelley and author of *Frankenstein,* in their efforts to live a normal married life. Dods's recent biographer, who uncovered the deception, wrote that

> when she put those culottes on to become Mr. Walter Sholto Douglas, husband and father, she broke with the deformed, confusing reflection of Miss Mary Diana Dods, spinster. . . . As Mr. Douglas, Dods could establish a life and a career for herself on the Continent. Leaving behind the years of financial and identity struggle, she instead became a person who attracted attention, admiration, and affection.[59]

Cross Dressing as Liberation

Still, many women both of Dods's time and later cautiously justified their cross dressing as necessary to avoid the more restrictive women's clothing and therefore never attempted to pass as men. George Sand (Amandine-Aurore-Lucie-Dupin, baronne Dudevant, 1804–76), the French novelist who was a pioneer of the social or "problem" novel, was one such person. Another was the English artist Hannah Gluckstein (1895–1978), who insisted on being known as Gluck. She dressed as a man in clothes designed by Victor Steibel and Elsa Schiaparelli, had passionate love affairs with numerous society women, and insisted on exhibiting her works only in one-"man" shows. Born to wealth, she used it to live as independently as possible on her own terms; consequently, she attracted much publicity among the rich and famous who purchased her paintings during the 1920s and 1930s. Later, she faded from view, although she continued to paint; a retrospective in 1973 brought her renewed attention, which she continued to enjoy until her death.[60]

The most famous of American cross dressers was Dr. Mary Walker, who received an M.D. degree from Syracuse Medical College in 1855. When Walker married a classmate, Albert E. Miller (from whom she later was divorced), she insisted on wearing her reformed dress of long trousers, over which she wore a short dress. During the Civil War, Walker served as an assistant surgeon, and for her service she received the Congressional Medal of Honor. When the rolls were purged in 1917 over questionable cases of such awards, Walker and many others were stricken from the list. Both Walker's dress and her medical expertise came under attack, particularly after she quit advocating a reformed dress for women in the 1870s and began appearing only in masculine apparel, consisting of striped trousers, a stiff-fronted white shirt, frock coat, and a high silk hat. Her one concession to femininity was her long hair, which she claimed she wore so that everyone would know she was a woman. Her insistence on wearing male clothes made her the subject of many jokes and exposed her to numerous indignities, including arrest; her notoriety ultimately overshadowed her sincere championing of women's rights. She died at the age of eighty-seven in an army hospital in Oswego, New York, on 21 February 1919. One of her more hostile biographers, James A. Brussel, wrote:

Mary Walker's history clearly indicates a well-established diagnosis of paranoia, representing a compromise with reality unwelcomingly thrust upon a militant and determined ego that revolted against its sex, rebelling—not in a mere turn to homosexuality—but in an open and as complete as possible, switch to the opposite sex. At best, Mary Walker was a poorly adjusted and chronically unhappy wretch of a woman.[61]

Brussel's diagnosis of Walker, however, was made posthumously in the 1960s and did not reflect so much the opinion of Walker's day as it did later psychoanalytic theory. Her contemporaries regarded her simply as eccentric. One of her more notorious activities was to approach any man she saw smoking and knock the cigar or pipe from his mouth with a tightly rolled umbrella. This, she claimed, was part of her campaign to eliminate the "nicotine evil." Her contributions to society include the invention of the return receipt for registered mail and the removable collar.[62]

Interestingly, there is a second Mary Walker, an English female contemporary of the American, who as Thomas Walker served as a stoker on a Cunard boat, a porter on the Great Western Railway, and a barkeeper. When her biological sex was discovered in 1867, she lost her job as a barkeeper, whereupon she became destitute. She continued to cross dress, however, and later was picked up for begging in men's attire. She became the subject of a nineteenth-century ballad titled "She-He Barman of Southwark," which included the verses:

The ladies like the trousers,
Of that there is no doubt
Many would be a barman,
But fear they'd be found out.[63]

Indeed, the survival of over a hundred ballads that deal with women cross dressers in the period 1650 to 1850 emphasizes the ubiquity of the phenomenon and public fascination with it. The verses usually describe a young girl in love who leaves her father's house, is forced to disguise herself as a soldier or sailor, has a stormy love relationship in which she shows unusual courage, and generally ends up married.[64]

For the most part, the ballads seem to be based on real cases and emphasize the exteriority of gender markers and how socially constructed much of what we call gender really was.

One nineteenth-century observer of the American scene, impressed by the number of women who dressed and acted like men, commented that the practice was

a matter of very general observation, in large cities particularly; and I have little doubt that a fair proportion of cases reported by the newspapers, in which young girls suddenly disappear from their homes, for a longer or shorter period of time, may thus be accounted for. To show, however, that these manifestations of virginity [*sic*] are in most cases purely psychical, though we frequently find associated with them a certain masculinity of physical texture, and coarseness of feature, there is seldom any trace of the more distinct masculine appendages, such as hairy legs, beard, and mustache.[65]

A. J. Munby, the English poet and diarist, provides a mine of information on cross-dressing women, particularly in the lower classes where he, unlike other men of his education and background, had excellent opportunities for observation. One reason for this was because he was secretly and happily married to his maid. To keep his relationship secret, Munby confined most outings with his wife to working-class neighborhoods, where he would be unlikely to meet any of his peers. He recorded numerous instances of working-class women who dressed as men at masked balls and on various other occasions, noting that when cross dressed they felt free to swear and to be "slapped around" and pulled about in supposedly manly ways. One woman informant who wore a sailor's outfit and smoked a cigar told Munby that she was a bonnetmaker by trade but came to the masked balls because it was a "greater spree": "I come in a different character every time. I like smoking very well, but don't smoke when I'm in women's clothes—oh no!" To Munby female cross dressing was a harmless, even innocent, activity, and he made a careful note that the women he met who wore men's clothing were not working as prostitutes.[66]

Summary

Clearly the concept of separate male and female spheres that had so dominated the discourse on the relation between the sexes was gradually being undermined in the nineteenth and early twentieth centuries. In the nineteenth century, sexual difference was not a static phenomenon but was determined by dynamic and contextually fluid relationships between people. This state of flux resulted in considerable tension, if the incidence of cross dressing is any guide. Men were particularly troubled by the changes confronting them, since their sense of masculinity was associated with their ability to distinguish their male behavior and status from that of women. And women, by emphasizing the virtues assigned to their subordinate status, effectively increased this sense of male insecurity. Some women increasingly seized opportunities to live out the male role, while women in general gained new confidence in themselves by playing upon their special role within their own sphere. The male response in the face of these developments is the subject of the next chapter.

Notes

1. Christiane Klapisch-Zuber, *Women, Family, and Ritual in Renaissance Italy* (Chicago: University of Chicago Press, 1985). For a discussion of the arguments for what was termed patriarchy, see Vern L. Bullough, Brenda Shelton, and Sarah Slavin, *The Subordinated Sex* (Athens: University of Georgia Press, 1988), 1–15.

2. For pre-Darwinian notions, see Arthur O. Lovejoy, *The Great Chain of Being* (reprinted, New York: Harper and Row, [1936] 1960), 186–307. For later ones, see John Farley, *Gametes & Spores: Ideas About Sexual Reproduction* (Baltimore, MD: Johns Hopkins University Press, 1982), 110–13.

3. Emanuel Swedenborg, *The Delights of Wisdom Concerning Conjugal Love after Which Follow the Pleasures of Insanity Concerning Socratic Love*, translated from the Latin (Philadelphia: Francis and Robert Bailey, 1796), passim.

4. Quoted by Ivy Pinchbeck, *Women Workers and the Industrial Revolution, 1750–1850* (London: Frank Cass, 1969), 315–16.

5. Friedrich Engels, *The Origin of the Family, Private Property and the State*, 4th ed. (reprinted, New York: International Publishers, [1891] 1942), 49, 79. Humiliation is our term. Various translators have used different terms.

6. Ibid., 50.

7. August Bebel, *Woman Under Socialism*, translated from the 33d German edition by Daniel De Leon (New York: New York Labor News, 1905), 5.

8. William N. Stephens, *The Family in Cross-Cultural Perspective* (New York: Holt, Rinehart and Winston, 1953), 246.

9. Sigmund Freud, *A General Introduction to Psychoanalysis*, trans. Joan Riviere (New York: Garden City Publishing, 1941), 23–24. See also Freud, *Civilization and Its Discontents* (London: Hogarth Press, 1930).

10. John Brown, *The Elements of Medicine*, translated from the Latin by the author, new edition revised by Thomas Beddoes, 2 vols. in 1 (Portsmouth, NH: William and Daniel Treadwell, 1803). For a discussion of some of these theories, see Lester S. King, *The Medical World of the Eighteenth Century* (Chicago: University of Chicago Press, 1958), 143–57. Perhaps the originator of these ideas in eighteenth-century Europe was Hermann Boerhaave (1668–1738), but also important were Georg Ernst Stahl (1660–1734), with his concept of vitalism, and Frederick Hoffman (1660–1742), who emphasized the importance of *tonus*, the ability to contract and dilate, which he said was regulated by the nervous system.

11. See S. A. D. Tissot, *Onanism, or a Treatise upon the Disorders of Masturbation*, trans. A. Hume (London: J. Pridden, 1766).

12. Benjamin Rush, *Medical Inquiries and Observations upon the Diseases of the Mind* (Philadelphia: Kimber and Richardson, 1812), 347.

13. Sylvester Graham, *A Lecture on Epidemic Diseases Generally and Particularly the Spasmodic Cholera* (Boston: D. Cambell, 1838), 5–7.

14. Sylvester Graham, *A Lecture to Young Men, On Chastity, Intended Also for the Serious Consideration of Parents and Guardians,* 10th ed., (Boston: C. H. Pierce, 1848), 42–44, 45–47, 78–86. The book was originally published in 1834. For a discussion of Graham, see Stephen Willner Nissenbaum, "Careful Love: Sylvester Graham and the Emergence of Citorian Sexual Theory in America, 1830–1840," Ph.D. diss., University of Wisconsin, Madison, 1968.

15. For a general discussion of American sexual thinking during the period, see John S. and Robin M. Haller, *The Physician and Sexuality in Victorian America* (Urbana: University of Illinois Press, 1974); Charles E. Rosenberg, "Sexuality, Class and Role in Nineteenth-Century America, *American Quarterly* 25 (1973): 131–53; Carroll Smith-Rosenberg and Charles Rosenberg, "The Female Animal: Medical and Biological Views of Woman and Her Role in Nineteenth-Century America," *Journal of American History* 9 (1973): 332–56; and many others. For a specific contemporary example, see the note "Excessive Venery, Softening of the Brain," *New England Journal of Medicine,* 36 (1847): 41–42.

16. M. [Claude-François] Lallemand, *On Involuntary Seminal Discharge,* trans. William Wood (Philadelphia: A. Walden, 1839). The original French edition was published in 1836.

17. One of our favorites was J. H. Kellogg, *Plain Facts for Old and Young* (Burlington, IA: I. F. Sneger, 1882).

18. George M. Beard, *Sexual Neurasthenia, Its Hygiene, Causes, Symptoms, and Treatment with a Chapter on Diet for the Nervous,* ed. A. D. Rockwell (New York: E. B. Treat and Co., 1884), 58, 134–207. See also his article, "Neurasthenia or Nervous Exhaustion," *Boston Medical and Surgical Journal* 3 (1869), and the book, *American Nervousness: Its Causes and Consequences* (New York: Putnam's, 1881). For a discussion of Beard's work, see Charles E. Rosenberg, "The Place of George M. Beard in Nineteenth-Century Psychiatry," *Bulletin of the History of Medicine* 26 (1962): 245–59; and Philip P. Weiner, "G. M. Beard and Freud on 'American Nervousness,'" *Journal of the History of Ideas* 17 (1956): 269–74.

19. William Acton, *The Functions and Disorders of the Reproductive Organs in Childhood, Youth, Adult Age, and Advanced Life Considered in Their Physiological, Social, and Moral Relations,* 5th ed. (London: J. & A. Churchill, 1871), 135–40.

20. See, for example, Mrs. E. B. Duffey, *What Women Should Know: A Woman's Book About Women. Containing Practical Information for Wives and Mothers* (Philadelphia: J. M. Stoddart, 1873), 97, 99.

21. These ideas have been developed at greater length in Bullough, Shelton, and Slavin, *The Subordinated Sex.* See also Cynthia Eagle Russet, *Sexual Science: The Victorian Construction of Womanhood* (Cambridge, MA: Harvard University Press, 1989). For a slightly different view, see Karen Lystra, *Searching the Heart: Women, Men, and Romantic Love in Nineteenth Century America* (New York: Oxford University Press, 1989).

22. Sarah Hale, Editorializing in *Ladies Magazine* 1 (1828): 422–23.

23. Ann Douglas, *The Feminization of American Culture* (New York: Alfred A. Knopf, 1928), 74.

24. For biographies of some of these care-givers, see Vern L. Bullough, Olga Church, and Alice Stein, *American Nursing: A Biographical Dictionary* (New York:

Garland, 1988), vol. 1, and vol. 2, by Bullough, Lili Sentz, and Stein (New York: Garland, 1991).

25. See Willystine Goodsell, *The Education of Women: Its Social Background and Problems* (New York: Macmillan, 1923); Mabel Newcomer, *A Century of Higher Education for American Women* (New York: Harper, 1959); and Eleanor Wolf Thompson, *Education for Ladies, 1830–1860* (New York: King's Crown Press, 1947).

26. See, for example, Andrew Sinclair, *The Better Half: The Emancipation of American Woman* (New York: Harper and Row, 1965), 208–19. See also Ellen Carol DuBois, *Feminism and Suffrage* (Ithaca, NY: Cornell University Press, 1978); and Sarah Slavin, *Women and the Politics of Constitutional Principles* (Washington, DC: American Political Science Association's Task Force on Citizenship and Change, 1985).

27. Matilda Joslyn Gage, as cited in Stewart H. Holbrook, *Dreamer of the American Dream* (Garden City, NY: Doubleday, 1957).

28. Loreta Janet Velazquez, *The Woman in Battle*, ed. C. J. Worthington (Hartford, CT: T. Belknap, 1876), passim.

29. Ibid.

30. Her story is recounted by Sylvia Dannett, *She Rode with the Generals: The True and Incredible Story of Sarah Emma Seelye, alias Franklin Thomson* (New York: Nelson, 1960).

31. See for some examples Rosanne Smith, "Women Who Wanted to Be Men," *Coronet* (September 1957): 62–64; and C. J. S. Thompson, *Mysteries of Sex: Women Who Posed as Men and Men Who Impersonated Women* (London: Hutchinson, n.d.), 139–52.

32. Mary Livermore, *My Story of the War* (Hartford, CT: A. D. Worthington, 1876), 120.

33. Mary Chaney Hoffman, "Whips of the Old West," *American Mercury* 84 (April 1957): 107–10.

34. For a discussion of the various Mountain Charleys and the biographical accounts of two of them, see E. J. Guerin, *Mountain Charley or the Adventures of Mrs. E. J. Guerin, Who Was Thirteen Years in Male Attire*, introduction by Fred W. Marzulla and William Kotka (Norman: University of Oklahoma Press, 1968).

35. Louis Sullivan, *From Female to Male: The Life of Jack Bee Garland* (Boston: Alyson Publications, 1990).

36. *New York Times*, 2 February 1989, A18.

37. Maria Bochkareva, as told to Isaac Don Levin, *Yashka: My Life as Peasant Officer and Exile* (New York: Frederick A. Stokes, 1939).

38. Marina Yurlova, *Cossack Girl* (London: Cassell, 1934), 45, 53.

39. Nadezha Durova, *The Cavalry Maiden*, trans. Mary Elizabeth Zirin (London: Angel Books, 1988). This book consists of a memoir on her childhood and her own selection of excerpts from the journals of her military years. Her edited journals include *The Cavalry Maiden* (1836) and *The Notes of Aleksandrov* (1839), as well as a series of autobiographical and fictional works. For further information, see the introduction by Zirin.

40. Quoted in "Warrior Women," *Literary Digest* (19 June 1914): 1460.

41. Anne Eliot Griesse and Richard Stites, "Russia: Revolution and War," in *Female Soldiers—Combatants or Noncombatants? Historical and Contemporary Perspectives*, ed. Nancy Loring Goldman (Westport, CT: Greenwood Press, 1982), 65.

42. Julie Wheelwright, *Amazons and Military Maids: Women Who Dressed as Men in the Pursuit of Life, Liberty and Happiness* (London: Pandora, 1990), 33.

43. Isobel Ray, *The Strange Story of Dr. James Barry: Army Surgeon, Inspector-General of Hospitals, Discovered on Death to be a Woman* (London: Longmans, Green, and Co., 1958).

44. Flora Sanders, *The Autobiography of a Woman Soldier: A Brief Record of Adventure with the Serbian Army 1916–1919* (London: Witherby, 1927), 9.

45. Dorothy Lawrence, *Sapper, Dorothy Lawrence: The Only English Woman Soldier, Late Royal Engineers, 51st Division, 179th Tunneling Company, BEF* (London: John Lance, 1919), 58.

46. "Women's Attempt to Join the Army," *Hornsey Journal*, 28 August 1917, and quoted in Wheelwright, *Amazons and Military Maids*, 44–45.

47. *The Sunday Dispatch*, 31 March 1929, and quoted by Wheelwright, *Amazons and Military Maids*, 50.

48. "Woman's Strange Life as a Man," *Daily Express*, 6 March 1929, and "How the Colonel's Secret was Revealed," *The Daily Sketch*, 6 March 1929.

49. The London newspapers were full of the story. "Colonel Barker Prosecuted," *The Times*, 28 March 1929; "Perjury Charge," *The Times*, 26 April 1929; "Colonel Barker Sentence," 26 April 1929; "Woman's Strange Life as a Man," *Daily Express*, 6 March 1929; "Old Bailey Trial for Colonel Barker," *Daily Express*, 28 March 1929; "How the Colonel's Secret Was Revealed," *Daily Sketch*, 6 March 1929; "Colonel Barker Sent for Trial," *Daily Sketch*, 28 March 1929; "Colonel Barker in the Dock at the Old Bailey," *Daily Herald*, 25 April 1929.

50. Radclyffe Hall, *The Well of Loneliness* (London: Jonathan Cape, 1928; New York: Covici Friede, 1929). The novel was banned in England in November 1928, six weeks after it was published.

51. Radclyffe Hall to Audrey Heath, 29 March 1929, quoted in Michael Baker, *Our Three Selves: The Life of Radclyffe Hall* (London: Hamish Hamilton, 1985), 254.

52. Havelock Ellis, "Sexual Inversion in Women," in *Psychology of Sex; Part 4; Sexual Inversion* (reprinted, New York: Random House, [1901] 1936), 1:246–47.

53. Ibid., 247.

54. Ibid.

55. Ibid., 248.

56. Ibid., 249.

57. J. Richardson Parke, *Human Sexuality: Medico-Literary Treatise* (Philadelphia: Professional Publishing Company, 1906), 267–68.

58. Théophile Gautier, *Mademoiselle de Maupin*, trans. Joanna Richardson (Harmondsworth: Penguin Books, 1981), 329–30. See also Joanna Richardson, *Théophile Gautier: His Life and Times* (New York: Coward-McCann, 1959), 29, who wrote (erroneously, we believe) that the novel was based on a premise that cannot bear the scrutiny of reason, namely, that a woman could pass among the young and old, men and women, amorous and experienced, month after month, as a man. Hopefully, this book demonstrates that this is not so far-fetched as Richardson believes.

59. Betty T. Bennett, *Mary Diana Dods: A Gentleman and a Scholar* (New York: William Morrow, 1991), 265–66.

60. Diana Souhami, *Gluck 1895–1978: Her Biography* (London: Pandora Press, 1988).

61. James A. Brussel, "Pants, Postage, and Physic," *Psychiatric Quarterly Supplement* 35 (1961): 332–45.

62. The only full-length biography of Mary Walker is by Charles McCool Snyder, *Dr. Mary Walker* (reprinted, New York: Arno Press, 1974). Other articles about her include Lidya Poynter, "Dr. Mary Walker—Pioneer Woman Physician," *Medical Woman's Journal* 53 (October 1946): 10; and Linden F. Edwards, "Dr. Mary Edwards (1832–1919): Charlatan or Martyr?" *The Ohio State Medical Journal* 54 (1958): 1296–98. Descriptions of her activities can be found in the *New York Medical Journal* 4 (1867): 314–16 and 5 (1867): 167–70. See also "Dr. Mary Walker's Eccentric Dress Drew Attention from Her Real Achievements," *The Literary Digest* (15 March 1919).

63. Charles Hindley, *Curiosities of Street Literature* (London: Broadsheet King, 1966), 2:141. See also *Morning Star,* 31 March 1868, and Derek Hudson, *Munby: Man of Two Worlds: The Life and Diaries of Arthur J. Munby, 1828–1910* (London: Abacus, 1974), 188.

64. See Dianne Dugaw, *Warrior Women and Popular Balladry, 1650–1850,* Cambridge Studies in Eighteenth-Century English Literature and Thought, vol. 4 (Cambridge: Cambridge University Press, 1989).

65. Allen M'Lane Hamilton, "The Civil Responsibility of Sexual Perverts," *American Journal of Insanity* 52 (1895–96): 505–7.

66. Only extracts of the diaries have been published. See the A. J. Munby diaries in Trinity College Library, Cambridge, particularly entries for 27 January 1862, 12:54, and 4 June 1862, 13:109. See also Wheelwright, *Amazons and Military Maids,* 112–13.

Chapter 8
Men, Gender Concepts, and Transvestism in the Nineteenth Century

Throughout this book it has been apparent that in Western cultures masculinity has been the standard by which society defines itself. Femininity, on the other hand, has been a catchall category for all those characteristics males have not claimed as their own. Sometimes, indeed, the definitions of masculine and feminine seem to have taken their meaning as polar opposites: If men are strong, women are weak; if men are steadfast, women are fickle; if men are dominant, women are subordinate. These norms have usually been defined in terms of the ruling classes, and as one moved down the social scale, the lines by necessity became somewhat blurred. A peasant man, for example, when dealing with "his betters," had to be careful not to antagonize them. A noblewoman, though subordinate to her husband, clearly had power over any males who worked her family's land or served in her house. In the United States, a black man, whether slave or free, often had to act in ways which for a white person would have been labeled effeminate. He could not afford a confrontation with whites and had to submit to various indignities.

Throughout history these class definitions of masculinity and femininity are better known for the ruling and literate classes than for others. But even within the ruling classes, there were people who did not meet societal standards of masculinity or femininity, and often there were special classes of men who were not supposed to act quite as masculine as others—monks and priests, for example, in medieval Europe. Still, to describe a man as showing feminine weakness, however this might be defined, was to put him down, while to portray a woman as showing masculine strength or intelligence was strong praise indeed.

In the nineteenth century, definitions of masculinity and femininity began to converge across class lines, with the same standards being applied to all classes, even though politically it was not always possible for men or women in the lower classes to fully adopt these standards. The watershed for change was the French Revolution and the Napoleonic wars that followed. Fought by volunteers and conscripts instead of the traditional mercenaries, the wars in effect "democratized" the concept of manliness, and the masculine ideals of the rising middle class were validated as the societal norm.[1] Simultaneously, the role of women was being modified in order to maintain a clear division between men and women.[2] The result here was the doctrine of "separate spheres" for the two sexes. As indicated in the previous chapter, women were increasingly defined as being "little affected by sensuality," "a species of angel," and "a purer race" set apart from men in order to inspire the rest of humanity with all the noble and generous sentiments.[3] The development of the two spheres gave women dominance in their own sphere, which revolved around children and the home. This sphere grew more important as society became more urbanized and the male, who had once been ever-present in the rural family, was removed from the home to work in the factory, mine, or office.

Redefining the Appearance of Masculinity

Men demonstrated their value by action and by being economically productive, avoiding ostentation, and making their deeds speak for themselves. Seemingly, they renounced their right to lace and frills to concentrate on the practical, and men's costumes gradually grew less colorful, less varied, and less ornamental. Men's dress during the last part of the eighteenth and first part of the nineteenth century changed far more than women's, although since that time variations in men's costumes have become negligible, and trousers became the standard garb of the male. The ideal gentleman worked in an office, where he accumulated the wealth with which his wife dazzled society, while he tried to conform, at least outwardly, to the standards of solidity and sobriety.

Some fashion historians have called this the "Great Masculine Renunciation," since the peacock male finery of earlier periods was rejected as both unmanly and undemocratic. The aristocrats and pseudoaristocrats who earlier had set the fashions for men now were determined to be less obtrusive, and even Louis Philippe, the king of France (reigned 1830–48), began to wear the clothes of a bourgeois man. Many of the new fashion standards were set by the English dandies who, though they devoted considerable time and effort to their costume, tried to give the impression that they did not. The leader of the new fashion standards was George Bryan Brummell (1778–1840), or Beau Brummell, who instead of lavish display emphasized "sang-froid, polite impertinence, cold sarcasm, irony, taste and elegance."[4]

Brummell had a knack for wearing the unobtrusive and the simple with "a certain exquisite propriety," always avoiding loud colors, jewelry, and superfluous embellishments. His style owed its success to the support of the Prince of Wales, later George IV (reigned 1820–30). When the king withdrew his patronage, Brummell fell heavily into debt and died in poverty, but his style of the unobtrusive and the simple remained a basic tenet in masculine dress.[5]

An assessment of his influence appears in Edward George Bulwer-Lytton's (1803–73) novel, *Pelham or the Adventures of a Gentleman* (1828), which fictionalizes a Beau Brummell–like character named Russelton. Russelton is depicted as the

contemporary and rival of Napoleon—the autocrat of the great world of fashion and cravats—the mighty genius before whom aristocracy had been humbled and *ton* ["fashion"] abashed—at whose nod the haughtiest noblesse of Europe had quailed—who had introduced, by a single example, starch into neckcloths, and had fed the pampered appetites of his boottops on champagne—whose coat and whose friends were cut with equal grace—and whose name was connected with every triumph that the world's great virtue of audacity could achieve.[6]

The clear-cut and simple lines of the new fashions tended to emphasize the masculine form, and for a time it led to an all-out effort, particularly among the older military officers, to turn to artificial support to maintain their sagging masculine appearance. David Kunzle argues that the widespread demobilization following the end of the Napoleonic wars in 1815 left many ex-military officers without the kind of social cachet that being an officer had given them. Since many were no longer young, they tried to maintain their foothold on the edge of society by emphasizing their manly form, to be a Brummell without the physical assets of youth. "Too poor to impress otherwise, they flaunted a pinched waist and swaddled throat, which were satirized as comic substitutes for the armorial bearings they lacked in reality."[7]

The would-be dandies prepared themselves for their appearance in the ballroom or opera box by reconfiguring their silhouettes through tight lacing. So tight did they lace themselves that they often fainted, leaving their concerned friends to cut the stays and administer smelling salts. Just how widespread the practice was remains unclear, since sources are not always detailed and much of the illustrations of it are based on the caricatures of George Cruikshank and others. Still, an

English military manual of 1830 seems to imply that stays were to be worn by cavalry officers: "The coat, padded well in every direction, sits perfect, while it is rendered small at the waist by the use of stays—or a belt, as the former term should never be uttered in ears polite."[8]

Though the British military increasingly abandoned stays as the century progressed, French and Austrian officers used them for several more decades as a way of distinguishing themselves from the enlisted men. The Germans, however, did not, and it was the German military success that finally led to the abandonment of the corset among the military officers. Though officers remained more dandified than the enlisted men, their basic uniforms were similar. The military's abandonment of the corset also marked a departure from the earlier "cult of youth," but the military and other institutions continued to exalt "masculine" behavior among their members.

Building a Manly Character

Another aspect of the democratization of the concept of masculinity was a new emphasis on sports, which for the most part meant the adoption of the sports of the common people by the universities and the English public schools in the first half of the nineteenth century. One of the leaders in this movement was Thomas Arnold, the headmaster of Rugby School between 1828 and 1842. The rules of a new-style rugby had already been adopted at Rugby before Arnold became headmaster. But under Arnold, the school became not merely a place where a certain amount of classical or general learning could be obtained but also an institution concerned with the formation of character, in which athletics had a significant role. Athletics supposedly trained young men to assume their duties in life. The institutionalization of rugby was one aspect of this, but so was the concept of discipline. Arnold had established the prefect system in which the seniors (sixth form boys) were expected to exercise a moral influence over the younger students.

Closely allied with the prefect system was the practice of "fagging," which existed in English schools before Arnold but became an important part of his system of discipline. Younger boys had to carry out a variety of tasks for the older boys. These "duties" might well have involved sexual initiation, since it was from the term *fagging*, which originally meant carrying out a task that causes weariness, that we derive a slang word for homosexual. Arnold had also encouraged flogging; he believed in corporal punishment, and he expected the older boys to discipline the younger boys, as the masters disciplined their students. In this proving ground fraught with homoeroticism and sadism, sports became a way of releasing pent-up tensions and building comraderie. It became a way for individuals to show leadership, gain distinction, and become men.[9]

The manly character emphasized at Rugby, Eton, and other public schools led to such statements as those claiming that the victories of the British army began on the playing fields of Eton, which in spite of its class bias, emphasized the new cult status of sports. As working-class games were adopted into the public school and became organized, sports previously reserved for aristocrats, such as shooting and riding, were democratized (although much more so in the United States than in England). Increasingly, sports became the measuring stick for a "real" man, and it was believed that through athletics a boy learned not only sportsmanship but fortitude and manliness.

The British ideal of middle-class manliness was exported to the rest of the English-speaking world and to much of Europe as well. One journal writer in 1864 stated that since England could no longer depend on its aristocracy, it had to depend on the males of the middle class. He urged middle-class boys to cultivate their minds and bodies, to discipline themselves to endure and obey, and to practice self-restraint as well as chivalry.[10] Chivalry in this context meant being protective of women and others who lacked physical strength. The male ideal was characterized by controlled strength, decisiveness, and dominance, together with "hardness," which was defined as the absence of bodily and intellectual fat. The concern for proving one's manliness came close to being an obsession.[11]

Achieving this new vision of masculinity was not easy, since men had to be continually on the alert to forces that might subvert or weaken it. Many of these enemies were subsumed under the category of vice, those elements in society that would lead young men, often at the height of their sexuality, astray. Though we tend to think of antivice crusaders of the nineteenth century as protecting female virtue, their real concern was with protecting the "threatened" masculinity of the young male. The crusaders against prostitution, sexually transmitted diseases, homosexuality, drinking of alcoholic beverages, and pornography regarded their tasks as essential if vulnerable young boys were to develop into proper manhood.

Particularly dangerous were the rapidly growing cities, which were often seen as cesspools of evil. The cities allowed young men anonymity, freedom, and a marketplace of potential vice. No longer under the discipline of the family, the young male somehow had to be taught discipline, thus new institutions were founded to help the growing boy learn the ways of being men without being trapped in perverse byways. Among the new organizations was the Young Men's Christian Association, founded by Sir George Williams (1821–1905) in London in 1844. The YMCA and similar groups, most of which eventually joined together, were to provide meetingplaces for young men who were living in lodging houses or in apartments and working in the London business houses. Later, the Boy Scouts appeared for younger boys as an organization for teaching the correct path to manhood; emphasis was placed on the idea that "real" men were brave, loyal, and trustworthy as well as clean and reverent. As the boys developed into men, male bonding was further encouraged by the development of the club; such clubs had begun in the eighteenth-century in England but received a great impetus in the nineteenth century and spread from England to the United States and elsewhere.

In the United States, those who were not well enough off to belong to clubs joined the so-called social fraternities, such as the Benevolent and Protective Order of Elks (founded 1868), the Loyal Order of Moose (1888), and the Fraternal Order of Eagles (1898) as well as the English group that later spread into the United States, the Independent Order of Odd Fellows (which was founded in the eighteenth century). These groups served to encourage male bonding and, in the process, socialize males into their expected roles. Even Masonry, though it is usually not thought of as such, was designed to encourage male bonding based upon images of masculinity and craftsmanship.[12] All of these organizations eventually developed auxiliary organizations for women, but the women's groups did not infringe upon male prerogatives. Similarly, on American college campuses in the nineteenth and twentieth centuries, fraternities also enhanced male bonding in much the same way as the drinking, dueling, and other societies at European colleges and universities.

As the social groups declined during the course of the twentieth century, new groups such as the Rotarians, Kiwanis, and other service clubs, as well as the Junior Chamber of Commerce, emerged. Though all of the clubs increasingly tended to emphasize service as a justification for their existence, they also served to define and set standards for masculinity and, until the last decade or so, to remain all-male.

Throughout much of history, war has been judged to be the ultimate test of manliness. Often this test was confined only to certain classes, and in fact, it served to justify the very existence of the aristocracy. With the invention of gunpowder and canon, the base of the army was broadened, but it was not until the rise of mass armies in the last part of the eighteenth and first part of the nineteenth century that the definitions of masculinity came to be applied to warriors from both the upper and lower classes. When wars were as disastrous as the American Civil War, they became masculine endurance tests, since the brave and the weak were slaughtered together. The ideal war was a short one, more or less easily won through deeds of derring-do. The ideal action was something like the charge of the Light Brigade, a foolhardy effort during the Crimean War that nearly wiped out a regiment but which caught the imagination of the poets and the public as an example of masculinity at its best. As immortalized by Alfred, Lord Tennyson,

> Into the valley of Death
> Rode the six hundred.
>
> . . . .
>
> Theirs not to make reply,
> Theirs not to reason why,
> Theirs but to do and die . . .[13]

Equally foolhardy, but more successful, was Theodore Roosevelt's charge up San Juan Hill. Every boy for several years after wanted to emulate his heroism. Roosevelt personified a self-made man: a sickly Eastern mother's boy who, forsaking the ways of the city, had gone to the "wild west" to live among cowboys and made himself over in the process. As Roosevelt wrote, "America will cease to be a great nation whenever her young men cease to possess energy, daring, and endurance, as well as the wish and the power to fight the nation's foes."[14] He and coauthor Henry Cabot Lodge went so far as to write that what America needed more than anything else was a war to test its manhood. Ruggedness, forthrightness, the ability to speak softly and carry a big stick, endurance, bravery, and loyalty to one's comrades were the values Roosevelt stressed to impressionable young men. When the Spanish-American War began, Roosevelt could hardly wait to get into what he called a "bully fight." He recruited a regiment which he named the Rough Riders, a term originally applied to the Pony Express, though the men rode no horses into battle. He remembered the charge up Kettle Hill, which perhaps was poetically changed to San Juan, as the greatest day of his life. He boasted that he had killed a man with his own hands. He told the Boy Scouts who visited the White House when he was president, "Don't flinch, don't foul, hit the line hard."[15]

The most successful war in terms of image-making in the last part of the nineteenth century was the brief seven month Franco-Prussian War of 1870–71. With the French defeat, the Prussian style of manliness soon became the ideal in Europe. The eagerness with which the young men volunteered at the beginning of World War I is a carryover of this romantic image of war as quick success and instant heroism, and it was only as the war dragged on, when individual deeds of heroism seemed not to affect the outcome, that disillusionment set in.

Though Americans tended to define manliness in the same way as the British, they did so with greater urgency during the last part of the nineteenth century, because the increasing "feminization" of American schoolteaching at the elementary level led to worries that boys and society in general were becoming increasingly feminized.[16] Women, it was feared, were gaining too much control over the impressionable male youths who were now under their authority not only in preschool years but in school as well, since schoolteaching fell within the female sphere of influence and women were thus seen as better suited to teaching elementary school children than men.

One response to the perceived threat of feminization was the effort to make children's fiction much more gender-distinct. Fiction aimed at boys was increasingly marked by unrealistic adventure stories in which women played only minor roles, allowing boys to visualize a world of "real" men wherein they could emulate the hero without feminine interference.[17] With the appearance of the so-called dime novel in 1860, hero-worship became the standard fare in forming masculine ideals for American boys. The novels tended to emphasize rugged individualism while exalting the poor over the rich, the self-made over the silver spoon, the purity of the country over the vice of the city. Heroes were Revolutionary patriots; frontiersmen like Daniel Boone and Davy Crockett; and two-gun sharpshooters like Wild Bill Hickok, Jesse James, Billy the Kid, and (more sedately) Buffalo Bill. In the 1890s came the Meriwell brothers, Frank and Dick, who proved their manliness and resourcefulness in all sorts of adventures, this time with the added flavor of the prep school and varsity sports. In this setting, colleges were not so much a training ground for scholars but a place where male bonding took place and boys could demonstrate their gains in manliness. Frank was always kidnapped before the Harvard game (he was from Yale) but always escaped in time to score the winning touchdown. He roamed the world foiling plots but never smoked or drank.

Similarly, Horatio Alger wrote over 130 popular novels (which sold more than twenty million copies). Most were based on the principle that a struggle against poverty and temptation inevitably led a boy to wealth and fame, providing that he also treated the girls and women he met with chivalrous respect. Inevitably, Teddy Roosevelt also became a dime-story hero. *From Ranch to White House: The Life of Theodore Roosevelt*, written by the veteran dime-novelist Edward S. Ellis, made him a model for all red-blooded American boys. Roosevelt is portrayed as overcoming the handicaps of nearsightedness and being born into a "blue-blood" family, free from having to toil for a living. Though suffering from asthma, young Roosevelt refused to be pampered; he swung dumbbells and became a boxer—by his own efforts the weakling turned into a "real" man. In true dime-story fashion, the youthful Roosevelt is said to have been dismissed as a Sunday School teacher at the Episcopal School (he attended and taught there while a student at Harvard) because he gave one of his students a dollar for beating up on a bully who had pinched the boy's sister. In fact, Roosevelt had resigned over his unwillingness to subscribe to Episcopalian doctrines, but it is from such stories that the ideals of male chivalry spring.[18]

Even when dime novels dealt with actual individuals, they somehow manipulated their subjects' life events to convey the accepted ideas of masculinity and the chivalrous treatment that should be extended to women. The cowboy novels especially gave new life to the kind of chivalry Roosevelt emphasized. As the movies replaced the dime novel in the twentieth century, manliness continued to be socially defined in what came to be known as horse operas, with the cowboy hero portrayed as a laconic, trustworthy, brave, loyal, and chivalrous man known for his actions and deeds rather than for his learning or intellect.

Increasingly, too, in America as in England, sports became a source of image-making for manliness that crossed class and other lines of social and geographic divisions. Although for a brief time at the turn of the century the elite Ivy League was deemed by the sports-writing establishment to be the only place where All-Americans were produced, this was soon disproved by the more democratic Midwestern state universities. What had begun in England and in America as participant sports played intramurally increasingly became an extra-mural activity of the most talented, who competed for the honor of their alma mater against rival institutions. Whereas originally every boy had been encouraged to play in the spirit of sportsmanship rather than outright competition, winning became all-important.

Every aspect of society, even religion, seemingly had to define itself in more "muscular" terms or become suspect of being feminized. Though men dominated the hierarchical structure of religious organizations, many aspects of worship had been deemed more suitable for women than men, since they belonged to the "finer" sphere of femininity. Women were believed to be responsible for bringing men to church. To make religion more masculine, "muscular Christianity" developed and even spread to the evangelical revivalists. Billy Sunday, for example, upset at what he felt to be the feminized image of Jesus, hit back by describing him as "no dough-faced, lick-spittle proposition. Jesus was the greatest scrapper that ever lived."[19] Such anti-intellectualism was held to be masculine. Similarly Bruce Barton, who founded one of the major advertising firms of the time, pictured Jesus as a supersalesman, an example to be emulated in order to become more effective in the masculine world of business.[20]

Despite the democratizing of the masculine ideal, however, the realization of separate spheres for men and women was not equally possible everywhere. Economics and geography still played a part. Clear distinctions between male and female domains were more likely to exist among the more well-to-do, since the poorer women simply could not afford the leisure of upper-class women. Similarly, the lines between the sexes were far less distinct for rural women, whose work was diverse and physically demanding, than for city women, whose work and duties rarely overlapped with those of their male counterparts.

Though males could still glory in their superiority over women, there was also a feeling among men that it was much harder to be a man than to be a woman for, after all, a man had to achieve his "manhood" while a woman only had to be born female. Women, too, could cross over into male territory when it suited their interests but, when threatened, they would cross back to their own, demanding protection. John Marquis, a nineteenth-century American whose letters have been preserved, wrote that "I used to often wish I was a woman and not obliged to *fight* my way." Marquis probably would have enjoyed the passivity and dependence so associated with the woman's role and he certainly resented the need to "put on masculinity." But he was forced to work hard and fight his way; as a man he felt he had no other choice.[21]

Carried to an extreme, the demands of masculinity could turn into a kind of bullying, as it did in the English public schools with their discipline and forced conformity. In some American schools and neighborhoods, masculinity could be defined as anti-intellectualism at its worst, whereby music, literature, and all the "finer" things were feminine and those boys who were interested or excelled in those pursuits were defined by the dominant male group as feminine. Terms such as *queer, fag, fairy,* or even *girlish* were applied to boys who outwardly seemed to express an interest in anything assigned to the women's sphere. Boys developed various ways of coping with such denigrating terms, and some simply resigned themselves to being labeled feminine. Others conformed outwardly but within identified those nonconforming parts of their personality as somehow expressing femininity. In our own studies of cross dressers, discussed in Chapter 13 in this book, we found that many of the male cross dressers who identified themselves as heterosexual had adopted an almost dichotomized personality. They were well adjusted outwardly to the male world, but in order to express what they regarded as the feminine side of themselves, they felt a need to cross dress; in this way they could adopt, even temporarily, the feminine gender role but otherwise preserve their masculinity.

Fetishization of Women's Apparel

The separate-sphere concept also made women less understandable and more mysterious to men; the stricter the separation, the more defined the spheres, the more mysterious women were. And as personal privacy became increasingly possible, the opportunities for men to misunderstand women grew proportionally. As mothers, sisters, caregivers, and teachers, women had daily contact with males and, in fact, helped nurture them into becoming men. In these capacities, women spent a good deal of time offering support and trying to better understand men's needs. Men, however, tended to objectify women rather than attempt to understand them, and this objectification often eroticized the female and those objects identified with the female, such as women's underclothes. In the mind of one commentator, women's underclothes were comparable to "a tinted flower, whose innumerable petals become more and more beautiful and delicate as you reach the sweet depths of the innermost petals." Only when the mysteries of the underclothes are overcome does one find the rare orchid, (the real woman) who "surrenders the fragrance of her mysteries only in the intimacies of love."[22] Describing the lingerie on display at a department store, Émile Zola in one of his novels said that it looked "as if a group of pretty girls had undressed, piece by piece, down to the satin nudity of their skin."[23] In short, underclothes for some men seemed to replace women. Clothing has always been used to separate and probably accentuate sexual differences, but in the nineteenth and twentieth centuries women's fashion was geared to emphasize sexual attraction. Women themselves were taught to regard at least some of their lingerie as sexy to males, because it was "the veiled, secret part, the desired indiscretion conjured up; the man in love expects silky thrills, caresses of satin, charming rustles, and is disappointed by an unshapely mass of rigid lingerie."[24]

One woman commentator, Marguerite d'Aincourt, assumed that brides might initially be too modest and shy to wear seductive lingerie or to appear partly dressed, but such items should still be part of trousseaux because the bride would come to appreciate them.

[She will] understand the value of this Orient silk or batiste . . . [with] insertions of lace, all quivering with the Valenciennes which decorates it in flounces at the hem. They will get used to this transparent web, which, in front—from the start of the throat to the waist—reveals the charming grace of a young and supple bust.[25]

Women have been encouraged to be narcissistic in dressing, at least to some degree, and fashion has often dictated that the height of style cannot be achieved without some kind of self-denial, even pain. This narcissism is evident in some of the descriptions of the new style of underclothes at the end of the nineteenth century.

This paradise of fine and soft lingerie . . . this warm and luxurious temple that shakes at our least shiver; this little fortune that the elegant woman hides under her dress . . . [serves] to tranquilize [her]. . . . This consciousness of our femininity [develops only] when, in all disinterestedness, for ourselves alone . . . we have obtained from the lightly touching and delicate underclothes . . . the discreet lightness of breath and the penetrating savor of the caress.[26]

Inevitably, the new female underclothes of the last part of the nineteenth century were of interest to men. The exposure of the new style underpants, as in the cancan, attracted men in droves and made Paris the centerpiece of many a man's visit to Europe. Numerous erotic postcards from the late nineteenth and early twentieth century showed women exposing their elaborate underclothes. The novelist Colette in *My Apprenticeship* describes Willy's apartment as "strewn" with postcards "celebrating the attractions of underclothes."[27] Color was important in this eroticization, and men were said to particularly enjoy seeing white skin emerging from a black sheath. A common experience among teenage boys before fashion magazines were quite so explicit in showing various forms of undress was to peruse the mail-order catalogues. They often used the pictures of models in underclothes as an aide in their masturbatory fantasies. For some men (and even some women) female underclothes inevitably became a fetish.

The female corset, as it developed in the middle of the nineteenth century, is a good example of how undergarments came to have symbolic value. Corsets were not simply sold as waist cinchers or form makers but as preservers of feminine virtue. They were said to give protection by giving added strength to resistance, but it was also claimed that they made women better able to endure their lot. They helped rearrange the female figure, emphasizing a narrow waist and resultant hourglass figure that gave prominence to the bust and buttocks. Many items of women's apparel, in fact, have been designed to emphasize or bring attention to certain aspects of the female figure, from bras to nylon stockings to high heels. High heels, for example, are designed to force the wearer to lean backward, thereby accentuating the buttocks and the breasts, but heels also force women to walk with smaller steps, emphasizing their supposed helplessness. This combination of narcissism and masochism, which is so often present in women's fashions, has aroused a great deal of interest among men in what women wear. Perhaps their own lack of glamorous clothes as well as the lack of variation has encouraged this.

Since one of the major purposes of fashionable women's clothing has been to confine and limit action,[28] it would seem logical that women, or at least some women, wanted and enjoyed this, even if it caused pain. Evidence of what can only be called a masochistic fetishism among some women of fashion comes from the women's magazines of the last part of the nineteenth century, wherein women gave testimony, primarily through the letters' columns, to the pleasures of pain.

This tendency toward masochism appears initially in the *English-woman's Domestic Magazine*, which was established in the 1850s and soon became widely circulated and read. Initially coedited by Samuel Beeton and his wife Isabella, the magazine in 1860 introduced a correspondence section, the nature of which changed after a series of illustrated articles on the "Human Form Divine" had appeared in 1866. By that time, Beeton's wife had died, and he had complete control over the magazine. He expanded its trim size and, in the process, increased the amount of space allotted to correspondence. Much of the correspondence was devoted to tight lacing.

Writers soon developed that constant characteristic of fetishist correspondence, of conversing in the proper sense of the word, agreeing, arguing, begging to differ, building up a special sense of community. They politely express gratitude to each other, and to the editor, for having opened his columns to this "instructive and important" and "all-absorbing" discussion, for allowing them to close ranks against the enemy, and to "rally to the banner now unfurled."[29]

Although initially opposed to tight lacing, Beeton, apparently in response to the demands of his readers, changed his position. And while he never quite supported tight lacing for all women, he stated that not all women were harmed by it and even occasionally recommended "a glove-fitting corset" as ideal for tight lacing. The fetishist correspondence over tight lacing flourished for about eight years, with perhaps a third of the column's space devoted to it—this in a magazine that campaigned for women's suffrage and married women's property bills. How representative the correspondence was of readers is difficult to estimate. Probably, only a very small percentage actually wrote, but from other sources the column is known to have been a widely read feature. It is possible that some of the letters were made up by the editors, although scholars do not think this was the case.

Not so surprisingly, some men had the same fetishistic interest in the female corset, and they too responded in the letters' column of the *Englishwoman's Domestic Magazine.* It seems obvious from the correspondence that fetishistic interest in female lingerie and corsets was one of the factors involved in male cross dressing in the last part of the nineteenth century, if not before. Some of the males who confessed to wearing female corsets gave lengthy autobiographical accounts. The first letter by a male appeared in November 1867, from a person known as Walter who had had the corset first imposed on him at an Austrian school, apparently as part of disciplinary training perhaps because corsets were worn by Austrian officers. He soon began to like women's corsets and continued to wear them ever since. He was "convinced of the comfort and pleasantness of tight lacing." Second only to corsets as letter-writers' fetishes were women's shoes which, with their high heels, also served to confine women's actions. Though, again, most of the correspondents were women, some men also wrote in. For example, a "Robin Adair" in the September 1870 issue stated that, after having had a pair of women's boots made for him with 2½-inch heels, he was "astonished to find how delightfully easy they were to walk in, and how much smaller and neater my feet appeared than in my own more clumsy foot-gear."[30]

Further confessions of males appeared in the *English Mechanic* and *Knowledge,* both edited by Richard Procter. These two magazines were devoted to scientific interests and hobbies. In 1873 and again in 1876, the *English Mechanic* ran articles on women wearing corsets. The male readers overwhelmingly responded in favor of corset wearing, not only for women but in some cases for themselves; they argued that corsets improved health by curing corpulence, indigestion, tiredness, and many other occupational diseases of the sedentary life. Some even admitted they had pleasant internal sensations while wearing corsets. Interestingly, the male correspondents, in contrast to the women respondents in the women's magazines mentioned above, devoted a great deal more discussion to technical minutiae relating to construction, flexibility, strength, manner of lacing, and so forth, and very little to the psychological aspects. The respondents must have represented a sizable number of men, since the magazine later reported that there were at least forty corsetieres in London specializing in a male clientele.

In *Knowledge,* from mid-1881 through early 1882, about fifty letters on corsets were published. The correspondence was in response to an article on consumption (tuberculosis) in which it had been claimed that the disease was much rarer in Turkey than in England. One authority had explained this as being due to the fact that Turkish women did not wear tightly laced corsets. Defenders of tight lacing immediately replied that tight lacing had nothing to do with tuberculosis and actually helped patients with TB. So impressed with the correspondence was editor Procter that he tried the "tight-lacing cure" for several months before abandoning it. An American colleague, the editor of *Scientific American,* concluded after reading the letters that tight lacing was probably safer than most antifat nostrums of the time.[31]

In fact, whenever any magazine ran a feature on tight lacing, there was an outpouring of letters, many of which came from men. *The Family Doctor* in 1886 ran a series of articles with illustrations of the female waist at different periods, along with discussion of garters, high heels, and other ornaments. The series helped *The Family Doctor* attain the largest circulation of all medical magazines combined, but it also led to what can only be called a fetishistic correspondence by both men and women that lasted for nearly seven years.[32]

To help people learn about the benefits of tight lacing, several individuals set themselves up as corset trainers, promising to discipline the young in the ways of the corset. Though their primary purpose was to help girls achieve the discipline necessary to get a waist of sixteen or seventeen inches, some trainers also disciplined boys, probably in girl's corsets, as the discussion about transvestite fantasy fiction later in this book demonstrates. The schools, if they can be called schools, were publicized by word of mouth, and no known advertisement exists. The only evidence for their existence, in fact, is that the correspondents in the magazines refer to such institutions.

Once males began writing about the desirability of wearing a female corset, other correspondents were encouraged to write about other kinds of cross dressing. One male letter writer to *The Family Doctor* wrote that nothing "is more pleasant or comfortable than a tight pair of good satin corsets" with which, he reported, he could achieve a 16½-inch waist and a bust and hips of thirty-two inches. He added that sometimes he went beyond corsets:

I must say that it is very comfortable to dress up in a pretty dress, bonnet or hat, and high heeled boots, with a tiny-waist into the bargain. Having done this often, I have been struck by the number of men who admired me, and would, no doubt, have liked to put their arms around my small waist. If they had only known I was also one of their sex![33]

This kind of narcissistic masochism is very similar to that seen in letters written by some women correspondents. Another man wrote that because he had to keep his neck and chin wrapped up (he suffered from a "weak throat"), he was once lent a fur boa by a woman friend and so enjoyed it that he decided to try other articles of feminine clothing, including corsets. A woman friend helped him narrow his waist from thirty-one inches to twenty-two inches, and he had since discarded his male dress and went everywhere as a woman, which was possible because he made his living as a painter of watercolors and could support himself.[34]

Cross Dressing in the Homosexual Community

Fetishism, if it can be called that, was just one reason for cross dressing. Some male homosexuals in the last part of the nineteenth century continued to dress as women in order to live with another man as his wife; others cross dressed for a lark, or perhaps even, as can later be documented, to solicit other males. It is also possible that by dressing as a woman these men were able psychologically to rationalize their homosexual relationships as "normal," in that they were really women.

The most publicized case of cross dressing at this time had overtones of homosexuality, and it posed a perplexing phenomenon to the newspapers of the day, as evidenced by a comment in the legal and police news section of *The* [London] *Graphic* for 7 May 1870:

There has been of late years a great extension of the taste for private theatricals, while, at the same time, the burlesque at our public theaters have accustomed people to that once detestable object, a man personating a female character, and making a by-no-means bad-looking woman. Possibly these facts have induced a practice which has unquestionably become more common of late, namely, the mania among young men of girlish appearance for dressing themselves up like women. It is said that there are hair-dressing establishments at the West End where a young gentleman, although previously bearded like the bard, may emerge within an hour's time so disguised by chignon, rouge, and pearl powder that his own mother would fail to recognize him. The two young gentlemen who were arrested the other day at the Strand Theatre for thus disowning their sex, appear to have had a complete collection of the artillery both of male and female charms at their residence in Wakefield-street, Regent Square.[35]

The two who were arrested, Ernest Boulton and Frederick William Park, indicate the complex nature of late Victorian cross dressing. Both Boulton and Park enjoyed playing female roles in amateur theatricals and frequently appeared in public dressed as women. Some plays were specifically written for this purpose, such as Oscar Wilde's *The Importance of Being Earnest,* while in other cases, men simply played roles written for women.

Boulton and Park lived together with Lord Arthur Clinton. A servant claimed that she thought Boulton was Lord Arthur's wife, and in fact Boulton, who went by the name of Stella, had engraved visiting cards with "Lady Arthur Clinton" printed on them. Park used the name Fanny when cross dressed. Both men were arrested, apparently for "soliciting," in April 1870 as they left a theater which they had attended dressed as women. Since they had no other clothes with them, they also appeared in these clothes in the police court:

Boulton wore a cherry-coloured evening silk dress trimmed with white lace; his arms were bare, and he had on bracelets. He wore a wig and plaited chignon. Park's costume consisted of a dark green satin dress, low necked, trimmed with black lace, of which material he also had a shawl round his shoulders. His hair was flaxen and in curls. He had on a pair of white kid gloves.[36]

Letters found in their rooms implicated Clinton as well as others in cross dressing, and the prosecutor, rather than charge them with committing a felony (something that would have been difficult to prove), simply charged them with conspiracy to commit a felony. The lord chief justice Lord Cockburn strongly disapproved of such indictments, for, as he stated, defendants could be charged with conspiracy only when there was proof that a crime had been committed, and in this case, no such crime could be documented. Still, Cockburn's strictures were ignored by the prosecution. Clinton died before the trial, and though Boulton and Park were acquitted because there was no evidence of a crime, the charge of conspiracy was to become a favorite of prosecuting attorneys for all kinds of crimes. (It was, for example, widely used in America during the McCarthy period.)[37]

H. Montgomery Hyde, who wrote about the case, believed that Boulton and Park were transvestite homosexuals, but there is much confusion in the record because the whole phenomenon seemed to be new to the police and to the court. Neither man testified, but Boulton's mother did. There are at least two accounts of her testimony, and though they do not always agree, they do not contradict one another. She reported that her son from childhood had shown an extraordinary aptitude for playing female characters. As a child he would put on a female dress and appear as a girl. His transformation was so complete that it deceived her friends and even her own mother. She treated her son's cross dressing as a harmless pastime and allowed him to pursue it in private theatricals, where his performances were always popular and successful. She admitted that on one or two occasions she had supplied dresses for him.[38]

During the hearing at the police court (not at the formal trial), it also came out that both men had previously dressed as women to attend a ball that was given by Amos Westrupp Gibbings, another cross dresser. Gibbings had frequently dressed as a woman and, like Boulton and

Park, had acted in amateur theatricals as a woman. He said he had given the ball to gratify many of his friends who had seen him act and who wondered whether he could sustain a womanly character in a more intimate setting. He decided to prove he could by inviting a score or so people to attend a ball. Somehow this number had swollen to forty-five by the time the party was held, including eight women, thirty-one men, and six cross-dressing men besides himself.[39]

Though there was an attempt by the defense to dismiss their cross dressing as a lark, it appears to have been far more complicated. Gibbings, Boulton, Park, and others in their group enjoyed impersonating women, and Gibbings had rented special rooms with a Thomas Cummings (and apparently Boulton and Park) to store feminine disguises, since he felt he could not keep them in his own apartment. When the police examined the contents of the specially rented rooms, they found various items of women's costumes, including six stays, two of which were claimed by Gibbings.[40] Probably not all those who attended Gibbings's party were homosexual, although it might well be that Boulton and Park were homosexuals who cross dressed for the thrill of passing and risk taking. Though they were not wearing corsets when they were arrested, they had on the petticoats, bustles, and crinolines necessary for their costume. It is their tie-in with Clinton, a known homosexual, that seems to give the best evidence that they were homosexual rather than heterosexual men who enjoyed cross dressing. Gibbings, however, was indignant when the prosecution implied that he might have walked the streets hunting for male homosexuals, although, certainly, his denial was quite possibly his only recourse in the face of formal charges. The importance of this trial and the subsequent publicity not only emphasizes the existence of a cross-dressing community in London but also the widespread public curiosity over it.

Cross-dressing balls that were apparently patronized by the homosexual community are documented at several places in the nineteenth century, including the United States. They might well be a variant version of the masked balls of an earlier age. One of the earliest descriptions in the United States was that of C. H. Hughes, a St. Louis specialist in nervous and mental diseases, who published a brief description entitled "An Organization of Colored Erotopaths":

I am credibly informed that there is, in the city of Washington, D.C., an annual convocation of negro men called the drag dance, which is an orgie of lascivious debauchery beyond pen power of description. I am likewise informed that a similar organization is lately suppressed by the police of New York City. In this sable performance of sexual perversion, all of these men are lasciviously dressed in womanly attire, short sleeve, low-necked dresses, garters, frills, flowers, ruffles, etc., and deport themselves as women.[41]

This association of cross dressing with blacks reflects nineteenth-century racist beliefs that blacks were lower on the evolutionary scale and therefore more likely to engage in sexual perversions.[42] It was not until some fourteen years later that Hughes realized that what he had described as black "erotomania" was not confined to the black community, and it was with some shock that he found transvestite balls attended by whites in his own community. The ball, however, was held in the black ghetto, as were many others across the United States during much of the twentieth century, since police were more likely to give tacit permission to have them there, and the black community proved somewhat more tolerant of sexual variance than white society. Still, Hughes concentrated on the blacks who masqueraded in women's garb and who, when arrested, were all freed on bonds put up by white patrons.

The levee resort at which these black perverts were arrested is a rendezvous for scores of West End butlers, cooks, and chauffeurs. Apartments in the house are handsomely furnished and white men are met there. The names of those negro perverts, their feminine aliases and addresses appear in the press notices of their arrest, but the names of the white degenerates consorting with them are not given.[43]

Such balls were regarded by Hughes as part of the homosexual community, although this fact alone does not prove that the nonhomosexual cross dresser did not attend.

The association of blacks with such "perversions" as cross dressing is also notable in one of Mark Twain's lesser novels, *Pudd'nhead Wilson*. Pudd'nhead ran into a mystery early one morning when he happened to look out to the Driscoll house, where he saw

[a young woman] where properly no young woman belonged; for she was in Judge Driscoll's house, and in the bedroom over the Judge's private study or sitting-room. This was young Tom Driscoll's bedroom. He and the Judge, the Judge's widowed sister, Mrs. Pratt, and three Negro servants were the only people who belong in the house. Who, then, might this young lady be? . . . Wilson was able to see the girl very well, the windowshades of the room she was in being up, and the window also. The girl had on a neat and trim summer dress, patterned in broad stripes of pink and white, and her bonnet was equipped with a pink veil. She was practicing steps, gaits, and attitudes, apparently; she was doing the thing gracefully, and very much absorbed in her work. Who could she be, and how come she came to be in young Tom Driscoll's room?[44]

It turned out that the woman was no woman but Tom Driscoll, who was using his cross dressing as a disguise to rob houses. Twain paints him with other negative characteristics to imply that a person who would enjoy putting on women's clothes was a dissolute character. The story reveals that Driscoll had actually been born a slave; his mother (who was one-sixteenth black) had switched him with the master's baby shortly after he was born. Twain describes the young impersonator as immoral and uses several other hateful adjectives to further stress the association of blacks with "deviancy." Driscoll eventually murders his "uncle" before his masquerade is discovered. Quite obviously, in Twain's world, male cross dressers were immoral people.

However, Twain also seems to believe it normal for boys to wonder how the opposite sex lives, for he has Huck Finn dress as a girl more or less as a lark. When he is recognized by Mrs. Loftus, she remarks,

You do a girl tolerable poor, but you might fool men maybe. Bless you child when you throw at a rat or anything, hitch yourself up on tiptoe and fetch your hand over your head as awkward as you can, and miss your rat by six or seven feet. Throw stiff-armed from the shoulder, like there was a pivot there for it to turn on, like a girl; not from the wrist and elbow with your arms out to one side, like a boy. And, mind you, when a girl tries to catch anything in her lap she throws her knees apart, she don't clap them together.[45]

Multiple Motivations for Cross Dressing: Between the Separate Spheres

Outside of fiction, apparently, a lark might sometimes turn into serious impersonation. Havelock Ellis, for example, recorded the case of Commander James Robbins of Cooper's Mills, Maine, whose case survived in several newspaper accounts.

Mr. Robbins isn't squeamish about showing himself in petticoats. He enjoys wearing them; he has worn them when opportunity presented itself all his life long, and he wears them scientifically, too. In the first place, there's no halfway business about it. Every detail of feminine attire is there, and Mr. Robbins is rightly fussy about the details. There is no woman in Cooper's Mills who owns so many dresses of such excellent material as does the commander of the Cooper's Mills Post. He takes pride in having only the best. His lingerie is elaborately tucked and ruffled, edged with lace and fashioned according to the most approved models of any lady's wardrobe. The material is of the finest quality, and when Mr. Robinson lifts his skirts the eye gets a vision of ruffles, lace and "all such like" of dazzling whiteness and immaculate smoothness.

Though the commander wore corsets continually, he changed gowns several times during the day to meet the needs of the task he was doing. In the morning he wore print gowns in order to assist with the housework. In the afternoon he wore somewhat more elaborate garb. He did jewelry work at home, and his bench, lathe, and tools were in the front hallways of his house.[46] The reportorial attitude of these accounts is surprisingly tolerant, although Robbins's "hobby" is regarded as highly unusual. Commander Robbins, quite clearly, was a male counterpart to Dr. Mary Walker, discussed in Chapter 7.

As indicated in the next chapter, the number of male cross dressers in the nineteenth century was sufficiently large that the courts themselves became concerned about them. Aware of their ignorance, judges asked for help, and this led members of the medical community to investigate the phenomenon. The more they investigated, the more cross dressers, both male and female, they found. Though women cross dressers have been seen throughout this book, men who cross dressed on any kind of regular basis outside of the stage and the homosexual community have been rare. What seems to have happened in the nineteenth century is that the redefinition of the women's sphere, even with its limitations, made it increasingly attractive to men. Undoubtedly, some men were attracted to cross dressing by fetishistic impulses, others as a kind of play-acting within the homosexual community, and still others as an erotic experience; but it also seems that many men simply did not like the limitations put on them by the standard definitions of masculinity and found the feminine life-style more attractive.

Undoubtedly, there are many reasons for cross dressing, some of which are explored later in this book, but in this period increasing numbers of men appear who lived as women most of their lives and were only discovered to be men when they died. Such was the case of Lavinia Edwards, an "actress" who died at the age of twenty-four in London in 1833. The postmortem revealed that Edwards was a man of very feminine appearance who had removed any evidence of his beard by plucking the hairs with tweezers. His roommate, Maria Edwards, indicated that they had been traveling around the British Isles making their living on the stage, with both playing female characters. Other than the fact that Lavinia had been born in Dublin, little else was known about him.[47]

Another person whose background remains mysterious was Jenny de Savalette de Lange, who had lived as a woman in Paris for at least fifty years before his death at Versailles in May 1858. All sorts of stories were told about him, including the suggestion that he was really Louis XVII and had escaped his executioners. It is possible he took on the identity of Jenny de Savalette in order to extort money owed to a person of that name, but his real identity has never been established. As his biographer remarked, we know little about his life and absolutely nothing about the reasons for his disguise; we cannot, therefore, offer any plausible conjecture. He simply lived and acted as a woman.[48]

The chance discovery of the true sex of Edwards and de Savalette

leads one to postulate that there were probably many other impersonators who lived as women without discovery. Though Lavinia Edwards
was very feminine looking, Jenny de Savalette was described as tall,
thin, and lopsided, leaning like an umbrella in the wind. She had hard
features, her voice was shrill and cracked, and she dressed in out-of-
date fashion. Many people were said to have remarked that she resembled a man, yet no one ever challenged her, and she apparently had
several suitors.

One of the more interesting cases of cross-gender behavior during
this time involved the writer William Sharp (1855–1905), who was also
known as Fiona Macleod. His adoption of a feminine pseudonym for
some of his later work was not merely an attempt to write in a different
style but to be a woman. His wife wrote that after he became Fiona
Macleod, rarely a day passed "in which he did not try to imagine
himself living the life of a woman, to see through her eyes, and feel and
view life from her standpoint, and so vividly that 'sometimes I forget I
am not the woman I am trying to imagine.'"[49] Lillian Rea, his secretary
during his Fiona Macleod period, wrote that Sharp believed "he had a
woman's soul" living within himself that was distinct from his man's
nature.[50]

Sharp himself wrote, perhaps in justification of his growing awareness of the femininity within him:

We are brought up within such an atmosphere of conventional untruth to life
that most people never perceive the hopeless futility in the arbitrary ideals
which are imposed upon us—and the result for the deeper endless tragic
miscarriage of love, peace, and hope. But, fortunately, those of us who to our
own suffering do see only too clearly, can still strike out a nobler ideal—one
that does not shrink from the deepest responsibilities and yet can so widen and
deepen the heart and spirit with love that what else would be immedicable pain
can be transmuted into hope, into peace, and even into joy.[51]

In a sense, Sharp's adoption of a second identity corresponded to the
theory then in vogue that the prophetic artist was psychologically
hermaphroditic by nature.[52] Though there is no documentation that
Sharp ever cross dressed, the mindset he expressed was also used by
others who cross dressed in order to put themselves even more into the
minds and thinking of the opposite sex.

One example of such cross dressing was reported by W. L. Howard, a
Baltimore physician, at the end of the nineteenth century. In a case he
entitled "Psychical Hermaphroditism" he recounted the words of a boy
who claimed he wanted to be a girl: "I played with dolls; girls were my
companions; their tastes were my tastes; music, flowers, millinery interested me and do to this day."[53]

Still another motivation for male cross dressing that appears in the late nineteenth and first part of the twentieth century was the basic feeling that sex was somehow evil and that women (and girls) were somehow purer and more moral than men. Cross dressing was a way to achieve sexual satisfaction without engaging in intercourse, or even touching the penis, and many continued to achieve orgasm through cross dressing even when alternatives were available. Others, however, did masturbate while cross dressed. One early twentieth-century transvestite, for example, indicated that while he usually only cross dressed when he was with his girlfriend, the "urge is so strong" that he also masturbated while in costume.[54] The correlation between masturbation and cross dressing will be explored later in this book, as will cross dressing onstage and professional female impersonation.[55]

Summary

Though not all women accepted the separate-sphere argument, it proved an important weapon in their fight to demand change and greater freedom. This concept also put forth a definition of masculinity that many men felt unable or unwilling to accept; instead, they wanted to claim some of the positive aspects of the female role for themselves. Though women continued to cross over into male roles for freedom and opportunity, some males saw the feminine role as ultimately more expressive of their inner nature. Though many elements went into this belief, including eroticism, excitement, and fetishism, it also had emotional connotations that gender-merging seemed to satisfy.

In short, the separate-sphere argument had limitations for men as well as women, and the feminine ideal proved attractive to some men who thought they could achieve it only by dressing and acting like women. Many men resented being classed as uncaring, unloving, stoic providers and did not want to compete in the marketplace or on the athletic field to prove their masculinity. As the extent of this dissatisfaction came to the attention of nineteenth century medical professionals, they were led to ask new types of questions regarding the nature of sex and gender—questions with which we are still wrestling today.

Notes

1. Dorinda Outram, *The Body and the French Revolution* (New Haven, CT: Yale University Press, 1989), 156.

2. See the Marquis de Condorcet, "On the Admission of Women to the Rights of Citizenship," in *Selected Writings,* ed. Karen Offen, *Women: The Family and Freedom* (Stanford, CA: Stanford University Press, 1983), 106.

3. These are statements by Necker de Saussure, *L'Éducation progressive,* quoted in *Victorian Women,* ed. Erna Hellerstein, Leslie Hume, and Karen Offen (Stanford, CA: Stanford University Press, 1981), 184–85.

4. See Ludmilla Kybalova, Olga Herbenova, and Milena Lamarova, *The Pictorial Encyclopedia of Fashion,* trans. Claudia Rosoux (London: Paul Hamlyn, 1966), 255.

5. Captain William Jesse, *Life of Brummel* (London, 1844).

6. Edward George Bulwer-Lytton, *Pelham or the Adventures of a Gentleman,* as quoted in Kybalova et al., *Pictorial Encyclopedia of Fashion,* 255.

7. David Kunzle, *Fashion and Fetishism: The Social History of the Corset, Tight-Lacing and Other Forms of Body Sculpture in the West* (Totowa, NJ: Rowman and Littlefield, 1982), 115.

8. A Cavalry Officer, *Whole Arts of Dress or the Road to Elegance and Fashion* (London: n.p. 1830), 83, quoted by Kunzle, *Fashion and Fetishism,* 117.

9. See Vern L. Bullough and Bonnie Bullough, "Homosexuality in the Nineteenth Century English Public School," in *Homosexuality in International Perspective,* ed. Joseph Harry and Man Singh Das (New Delhi: Vikas Publishing House, 1980), 123–33.

10. Bruce Haley, *The Healthy Body and Victorian Culture* (Cambridge, MA: Harvard University Press, 1978), 206.

11. Some of the ideas in this section are based on an unpublished paper by George L. Mosse, "Masculinity and Decadence," presented at the Gay and Lesbian Caucus at the American Historical Association, December 1990, in New York City. See also David D. Gilmore, *Manhood in the Making: Cultural Concepts of Masculinity* (New Haven, CT: Yale University Press, 1990); Leonard Kriegel, *The Myths of American Manhood* (New York: Dell, 1978).

12. For a development of this theme see Mark C. Carnes, *Secret Ritual and Manhood in Victorian America* (New Haven, CT: Yale University Press, 1989), and Mary Ann Clawson, *Constructing Brotherhood: Class, Gender, and Fraternities* (Princeton, NJ: Princeton University Press, 1989).

13. Alfred, Lord Tennyson, "The Charge of the Light Brigade." There are many editions of the poem.

14. This appears in *Hero Tales from American History,* which he coauthored with Henry Cabot Lodge. Quoted in Dixon Wecter, *The Hero in America: A Chronicle of Hero-Worship* (reprinted, New York: Charles Scribner's Sons, [1941] 1972), 377. Wecter's book has become a classic.

15. Ibid., 374–91.

16. For discussions of the entrance of women into the teaching ranks, see Redding S. Sugg, *Motherteacher: The Feminization of American Education* (Charlottesville: University of Virginia, 1978), and Polly Welts Kaufman, *Woman Teachers on the Frontier* (New Haven, CT: Yale University Press, 1984). For the increasing "feminization" of American culture, see Ann Douglas, *The Feminization of American Culture* (New York: Knopf, 1977).

17. A beginning exploration of this was made by Claudia Nelson, *Boys Will Be Girls: The Feminine Ethic and British Children's Fiction, 1857–1917)* (New Brunswick, NJ: Rutgers University Press, 1991). See also Richard Hofstadter, *Anti-Intellectualism in American Life* (New York: Knopf, 1963), 341–64.

18. Ibid., 375.

19. Quoted by Hofstadter, *Anti-Intellectualism in American Life,* (New York: Knopf, 1963), 116.

20. Bruce Barton, *The Man Nobody Knows: A Discovery of the Real Jesus* (Indianapolis, IN: Bobbs-Merrill, 1925).

21. Karen Lystra, *Searching the Heart: Women, Men, and Romantic Love in Nineteenth-Century America* (New York: Oxford University Press, 1989), 150.

22. This quote by Octave Uzanne is from Valerie Steele, *Fashion and Eroticism: Ideals of Feminine Beauty from the Victorian Era to the Jazz Age* (New York: Oxford University Press, 1985), 205.

23. Ibid.

24. Ibid., 207.

25. Ibid., 206.

26. Ibid., 207.

27. Ibid., 199.

28. This is emphasized by Lawrence Langner, *The Importance of Wearing Clothes* (New York, 1959).

29. Kunzle, *Fashion and Fetishism*, 225. Some of this correspondence was collected by William Barry Lord, *The Corset and the Crinoline* (London: W. B. L., 1868), and by E. D. M., *Figure Training: Or, Art the Handmaid of Nature* (London: Ward, Lock and Tyler, 1871).

30. We quote these from *Men in Petticoats: A Selection of Letters from Victorian Newspapers,* ed. Peter Farrer (Liverpool: Karn Publications, Garston, 1987), 4.

31. Kunzle, *Fashion and Fetishism*, 229. For the American reference, see "Causes and Remedies for Corpulence," *Scientific American,* (4 November 1882): 289.

32. During the first six-month period, corsets elicited about forty printed letters, more than the total number of letters on all other subjects put together. The level settled down at around twenty to thirty letters per six-month period, when other fetishistic subjects such as earrings, gloves, spurs, and tattooing appeared. The magazine summed up its controversy over tight lacing in the issue of 6 July 1889; it reported that there had been 165 letters on tight lacing with a total of ninety-four in favor (forty-five women and forty-nine men), and fifty-seven against (thirty-two women and twenty-five men). Fourteen had remained neutral (five women and nine men). Of those who had experienced tight lacing themselves, sixty-five reported favorable results (forty-five women and twenty men), and eight reported unfavorable results (seven women and one man).

33. *The Family Doctor,* 16 June 1886, p. 263, cited in Farrer, *Men in Petticoats,* 11.

34. *The Family Doctor,* 7 July 1881, p. 295, cited in Farrer, *Men in Petticoats,* 14.

35. *The Graphic,* 7 May 1870, legal and police news section.

36. [London] *Times,* 30 April 1870, p. 11.

37. See William Roughhead, *Bad Companions* (Edinburgh: W. Green and Son, 1930), 149–83; see also H. Montgomery Hyde, *The Love That Dared Not Speak Its Name* (Boston: Little Brown, 1970), 93–98, 123–24.

38. [London] *Times,* 13 May 1871, p. 12; *Annual Register,* 1871, p. 112; and Farrer, *Men in Petticoats,* 6.

39. [London] *Times,* 30 May 1870, p. 13.

40. [London] *Times,* 16 May 1870, p. 13. The value of the clothing was set at over two hundred pounds, a sizable amount for the time.

41. C. H. Hughes, "Postscript to a Paper on 'Erotopathia,'" in *The Alienist and Neurologist* 14 (October 1893): 731–32.

42. See Sander L. Gilman, *Sexuality: An Illustrated History* (New York: John Wiley and Sons, 1990), 290–95.

43. C. H. Hughes, "Homo-Sexual Complexion Perverts in St. Louis," *Alienist and Neurologist* 28 (1907): 487–88.

44. Mark Twain, *Pudd'nhead Wilson* (New York: Mark Twain, 1899), 53–54.

45. Mark Twain, *Adventures of Huckleberry Finn* [1884]. Annotated by Michael Patrick Hearn (New York: Clarkson N. Potter, 1981), 127.

46. Havelock Ellis, *"Eonism and Other Supplementary Studies,"* in *Psychology of Sex* (reprinted, New York: Random House, [1928] 1936), vol. 2, part 2, 30–32.

47. C. J. S. Thompson, *Mysteries of Sex,* (London: Hutchinson & Co., n.d.), 197–200.

48. O. P. Gilbert, *Men in Women's Guise: Some Historical Instances of Female Impersonation* (London: John Lane the Bodley Head, 1926), 231–66.

49. Elizabeth A. Sharp, *William Sharp (Fiona Macleod): A Memoir* 2d ed., 2 vols. (London: Heinemann, 1912), *Memoir*, 1:82.

50. Lillian Rea, "Fiona Macleod," *The Critic* 48 (May 1906): 460.

51. Sharp, *William Sharp*, 2:123–24.

52. See Flavia Alaya, *William Sharp—"Fiona Macleod" 1855–1905* (Cambridge: Harvard University Press, 1970), 135. We are indebted to Alaya for guiding us to many of the references. She also includes a bibliography of the works by Sharp and Macleod.

53. W. L. Howard, "Psychical Hermaphroditism: A Few Notes on Sexual Perversion, with Two Clinical Cases of Sexual Inversion," *Alienist and Neurologist* (April 1897): 1–8. See also Vern L. Bullough, "A Nineteenth Century Transsexual," *Archives of Sexual Behavior* 16, no. 1 (1987): 81–84.

54. See Magnus Hirschfeld, *Transvestite: The Erotic Urge to Cross Dress*, trans. Michael A. Lombardi (Buffalo, NY: Prometheus Books, 1991). This particular reference is from case 9, p. 63.

55. See also Julia Epstein and Kristina Straub, *Body Guards: The Cultural Politics of Gender Ambiguity* (New York: Routledge, 1991), and Marjorie Garber, *Vested Interests: Cross-Dressing and Cultural Anxiety* (New York: Routledge, 1992), for other examples of cross dressing.

Part II
Modern Perspectives

Chapter 9
The Development of the Medical Model

In the eighteenth and nineteenth centuries a shift in the paradigm governing the control of sexual behavior occurred as the various Christian churches lost enforcement power and as other aspects of human conduct increasingly fell under the purview of the state and the medical establishment. The state had been gradually moving into the business of controlling sex since the medieval period, but by the eighteenth and nineteenth centuries, that interest broadened to include attempts to control marriage, contraceptives, homosexuality, and general public "lewdness," including cross dressing. People whose public activities departed from societal norms were likely to be adjudged criminals instead of sinners. Judges, serving as the decision-makers regarding sexuality, found that traditional descriptions of sexuality were inadequate. Venerable phrases such as *the crime against nature* included a variety of sexual behaviors, as did the term *paederastia.* Johan Ludwig Casper, a widely read nineteenth-century German expert on medical forensics, commented that paederastia was not an accurate term for intercourse between an adult male and a young boy because such proclivities could also occur between two adults of the same age and sex. Similarly, he wrote, sodomy was defined to include bestiality. What was needed was more specificity in terminology.[1]

Forensic scholars encouraged medical professionals to consider sexuality, particularly stigmatized sexuality, as a part of their domain. Members of the stigmatized groups were also anxious for better definitions and more sympathetic treatment for themselves. Unfortunately, the past history of medical intervention had not been particularly positive. The pioneer medical researcher in the field of sexuality, S. A. D. Tissot (1728–97), was convinced that masturbation was a chief cause of insanity.[2] Though medical treatises on sexual topics multiplied thereafter, these were not particularly sophisticated. Masturbation, or onanism, remained a catchall category that often included homosexuality and cross dressing. Even when homosexuality was separated from masturbation, cross dressing was not recognized as a separate activity.

The first researcher to focus entirely on homosexuality was Karl Heinrich Ulrichs (1825–95), who was also probably the modern world's first self-proclaimed homosexual.[3] Ulrichs had gathered his courage and announced to his family in 1862 that he was what today would be called homosexual. He also indicated that he felt compelled to publish on the topic in order to explain his condition to others. He coined the term *urning* to describe what we now call homosexuality and argued that urnings were a third sex.

His first work, a booklet entitled *Vindex*, was published in 1864. Using the pseudonym Numa Numantius, Ulrichs described his theory of Uranian (lesbian and gay) love. Other booklets soon followed, and by 1879 he had produced twelve publications ranging in length from twenty pages to over one hundred pages. The later works appeared under his own name.[4] One of the values of Ulrichs's work is that he alerted the medical community to the existence on a wide scale of incidence of what came to be called homosexuality.

Carl Westphal (1833–90) is the physician usually given credit for putting the study of stigmatized sexual behavior on a scientific basis. In an 1869 article in the *Archiv für Psychiatrie und Nervenkrankheiten,* he described two cases of persons who cross dressed. The first was a young woman who from her earliest years enjoyed dressing like a boy and engaging in boy's games. She was sexually attracted only to women. The second case involved a man who wanted to wear women's clothing and live as a woman all the time. His sexual orientation is not clear from the case study. Westphal categorized both cases as "contrary sexual feeling" (*konträre Sexuellempfindung*). Although he was aware of Ulrichs's work and, in fact, became interested in stigmatized sexual behavior because of it, he preferred his own term.[5]

Delving further into the subject was Richard von Krafft-Ebing (1840–1902), who invented or popularized many of the diagnostic categories now applied to differing expressions of sexuality. His major work, *Psychopathia Sexualis,* was first published in 1887.[6] It went through many editions, revisions, and translations and was probably the most widely read and influential medical work on sex before the Kinsey reports. Krafft-Ebing, although influenced by Ulrichs, believed that the purpose of sex was reproduction and that all sexual activities undertaken without that ultimate purpose were "unnatural practices" or "perversions of the sexual instinct." These activities were the focus of his book, and with each succeeding edition of the book new "perversions" and new case studies were added. He did not address the subject of cross dressing in any detailed way, but he did collect and analyze at least four case histories of persons who were involved in some form of cross dressing. Two such histories were included in his series of cases illustrating fetishism, which he defined as "the association of lust with the idea of certain portions of the female person, or with certain articles of female attire."[7] All of the cases of fetishism involved men. For most, the erotic focus was on a single body part, such as hair, hands, or breasts, or on articles of clothing such as shoes or handkerchiefs. Sometimes these articles were erotically charged only when they were worn by a woman; other objects assumed erotic attributes even when they were not worn.

A subclassification in the section of his book dealing with fetishism was labeled dress fetishism. He explains that the dress fetishist does not focus on a woman as a sex stimulus. Rather, the sexual interest is concentrated on the article of female attire. It was under this classification of dress fetishism that Krafft-Ebing reviewed two cases of men who were caught wearing women's underwear. The first was a forty-five-year-old shoemaker who had stolen more than three hundred articles of women's clothing, including chemises, drawers, night caps, and garters, as well as a female doll. He had been stealing these articles since he was thirteen. At the time of his arrest he was wearing a chemise. The other case tells of a young butcher who was arrested while wearing a bodice, corset, vest, jacket, collar, jersey, chemise, fine stockings, and garters under his overcoat. Since age eleven he had been troubled by a desire to wear a chemise belonging to his elder sister. He did this whenever possible, and the activity was accompanied by an ejaculation. When he left the family home, he purchased chemises and other articles of women's toilette for himself. Complete outfits were found in his room. Krafft-Ebing indicated that putting on these garments was the aim of the young man's sexual instinct and that the practice had ruined him financially. He had come to the attention of the doctor after his arrest.

A third case history, less related to transvestism, involved a young man who was sexually aroused by stolen aprons. At age fifteen his attention had been attracted by an apron that had been hung out to dry. He put it on and masturbated behind the fence. From that time on he could not see aprons without repeating the act. If he met anyone wearing an apron, he felt compelled to steal it. He was sent to sea at age sixteen so that he would not be confronted with aprons; he performed well as a sailor, but back on land he again was confronted with his fetishism. He sought to free himself of his weakness by a sojourn with the Trappists, but when he left them he returned to his old ways. As a result of his thefts he was committed to an asylum.[8]

A fourth case is presented in the section of the work devoted to homosexuality, and Krafft-Ebing describes this history as representing a stage in the transition to paranoia, which he defined as a form of insanity. The man was a physician and wrote his own case history. At times during his childhood he had felt quite feminine, but he went through periods of compensating for these feelings and became adept at sports and other boyish activities, although he considered such activities a mask of his true self. When he began masturbating at age fifteen, he felt (as argued by the medical theory of his day) that this was very harmful to his psyche and that it was the reason he felt more like a woman. Despite these anxieties, he functioned well enough to complete medical school, serve in the army, and marry. He indicated that he would have preferred not to marry but was forced to do so by family and social expectations. He described his wife as an "amiable and energetic lady, of a family in which female government was rampant."[9] His sex life was apparently heterosexual, but he always fantasized that he was a woman. He fathered five children and continued his work as a physician.

As he grew older he suffered from gout, and in an attempt to treat himself, he took an overdose of hashish. He hallucinated that he had been changed into a woman, and when he recovered he retained this feeling even to the point of believing that he experienced menses. He described what he called his "complete effemination" as including the feeling that he was actually a woman who was attracted to men, although his desire was not focused on any one man. He thought of himself as a woman during coitus, and even imagined himself to be pregnant.[10] Krafft-Ebing concluded the case history with the following remarks:

The badly tainted patient was originally psycho-sexually abnormal, in that, in character and in the sexual act he felt as a female. The abnormal feeling remained purely a psychical anomaly until three years ago, when, owing to severe neurasthenia, it received overmastering support in imperative bodily sensations of a *transmutatio sexus* which now dominate consciousness. Then to the patient's horror, he felt bodily like a woman; and, under the impulse of his imperative feminine sensations, he experienced a complete transformation of his former masculine feeling, thought and will. . . . At the same time his "ego" was able to control these abnormal psycho-physical manifestations, and prevent descent into paranoia.[11]

Krafft-Ebing tried to establish causes for all the sexual behaviors he considered abnormal, searching for hereditary defects in the patient's family history, including relatives who were in mental institutions, who had been in trouble with the law, or who were thought to have low intelligence. These "taints" were thought to cause deviant sexual practices, which he termed *degeneracy* or *perversions*. Thus, his case studies often began with a statement as to whether or not the family was "tainted" or "defective." Although he considered the constitutional problem to be related to the nervous system, it is not at all clear from his writing or those of his contemporaries what the pathology within the nervous system was. Sometimes he focused on an event or situation in childhood that seemed to fit into a causal sequence, but he did not discuss these possible social-psychological antecedents of sexual behavior. In addition, he seemed to view life as a never-ending duel between animal instincts and morality, with the animal instincts often winning. Only willpower and strong character could emancipate a person from the meanness of his or her corrupt nature.[12]

Magnus Hirschfeld

Taking a radically different tack in the study of sexuality was another German, Magnus Hirschfeld (1868–1935). A physician, Hirschfeld was a self-avowed homosexual and reformer of sex laws, as well as a pioneer in the study of sexuality. In 1897 he founded, with the help of three of his friends, the Scientific Humanitarian Committee, an organization aimed at helping homosexuals and other persons whose sexuality was considered deviant.[13] Possibly because he had experienced the discrimination associated with being a member of a sexual minority group himself, he was always personally concerned about the well being of his patients and research subjects; the contrast between the tone of his writing and that of Krafft-Ebing is remarkable. Hirschfeld coined the term *transvestism* to differentiate the phenomenon from other sexual behaviors. The literal meaning of this term comes from *trans* ("across") and *vestis* ("dress"). He felt the term described the key behavior in a simple and straightforward way, although Hirschfeld conceded that this was only the most obvious characteristic of the condition he described. In 1910 Hirschfeld published what may well be the key work on cross dressing, even to this day. Its title in English was *The Transvestites: An Investigation of the Erotic Drive to Cross Dress.*[14]

Hirschfeld reviewed the cases of sixteen men and one woman, most of whom were his patients. The others he located using a variety of leads, including a newspaper account he followed up on, correspondence with people he heard about, and referrals from colleagues, including at least one person who came to his attention through the sexologist Iwan Bloch. These cases provided a data base for his observations, but he also drew on a study of female impersonators and the psychiatric literature of the time. He found that cross dressing usually started early.

> In most of the cases we can trace the urge back into their early childhood, that it increases during puberty, comes clearer into their awareness at this time and then remains almost unchanged for their entire lives. This tendency is connected with a peculiar sense of shame even in the early years, so that we can assume that it is rooted in the sexual life.[15]

Although most of the persons he studied were heterosexual in their orientation, Hirschfeld also characterized some of them as "monosexual" or "auto-erotic," and a few were homosexual. He argued that their dominant sexual urge was focused on themselves dressed in women's finery rather than on other persons of either sex. The one woman in the group indicated some attraction to women, but eventually, she married and had children. In her history she focused on the freedom and life-style that a man's identity provided her more than on erotic pleasure.

As Hirschfeld examined his data, he commented on the fact that the dominant view in psychiatry at the time was that female impersonators were all homosexual. He was convinced that this was an erroneous assumption and cited an empirical study by an unnamed author that had been published in the 1901 volume of the *Annual for Sexual Intermediaries,* which he edited. Fourteen female impersonators were included in the study; seven were heterosexual, four homosexual, and three bisexual.[16]

In the tradition of Ulrichs and Westphal, Hirschfeld suggested a theory of intermediaries. He pointed out that although the two sexes were thought of as dimorphic, there were many people who were not entirely manly or womanly. They could depart from the norm in one of four ways: (1) sex organs, (2) other sex characteristics, (3) sex drive, or (4) other emotional characteristics. Persons who were intermediaries because of their sex organs were hermaphrodites; they were well defined in the medical literature. However, there were also some people whose secondary sex characteristics were not true to their sex; these include women with small breasts or a narrow pelvis and men who lacked facial hair. The third group of intermediaries included those who were attracted sexually to their own sex, as well as men who wanted to be passive and women who were aggressive in lovemaking. The fourth group included transvestites as well as people who thought, felt, or acted like the opposite sex in any aspect of their lives. Hirschfeld worked out the many permutations of these differences and concluded that the variety of intermediaries was almost infinite because there were so many secondary sex characteristics, so many variations in what a person considered sexually attractive, and so many behaviors and emotions that could not be classified as being predominantly manly or womanly.[17]

This led to a problem of differentiating transvestism from other sexual intermediaries. Hirschfeld speculated:

How in fact are we to understand this peculiar urge to cross dress. . . . Is it perhaps only a matter of a form of homosexuality? . . . However, more accurate testing revealed that this was not the case because the main marker of homosexuality . . . is the sex drive towards persons of the same sex. We saw in most of our cases there was not a trace of it. . . . To be sure some of them had homosexual episodes, which is not unusual for heterosexuals, but they were so transient and superficial that truly inborn homosexuality—and only congenital homosexuality can be true—is not a question here.[18]

Hirschfeld also rejected fetishism as a diagnostic label because fetishists focus on one article of clothing or one part of a woman's body. In his words:

The fetishist at times also takes the woman's shoe or slip to bed for purpose of sexual stimulation. To bring himself as close to "the beloved" as possible, he in fact also wears woman's underwear under his suit. He prefers to wear the latter's, while transvestites like to wear new underwear.[19]

Masochism was also considered in the section on the differential diagnosis:

Masochism is pleasure of pain, regardless whether it is more of a suffering of physical pain, the tolerating of emotional torment or more of a physical or emotional constraint. The essence of masochism is pleasure-emphasized dependence, as the sexual domination of sadism. Unimportant are the extraordinarily great number of ways and means by which the willingness to suffer and the willingness to allow suffering, the slavery and the tyranny of love, symbolically are brought to expression. As in the case of all sexual anomalies, masochism, too, already makes itself visible in early childhood by giving slight indications of the character of the drive to come later. Among our cases too, there are a few whose clearly masochistic characteristics were evident long before puberty. . . . In many of our adult transvestites, too, there are many kinds of things that make a masochistic impression. So we find that they mention the penetration of earrings or the tight lacing of corsets as especially pleasurable. Also, the wish of some of them to take a position with the greatest service possible as chambermaids and housemaids. They preferred very "energetic" and manly women. They said as Number 13 did, "I expect the woman to take the initiative." Particularly the universal urge to be the supine partner during intercourse points to sexual passivity. To some of them, however, the woman's role itself was felt to be, in the main sexually humiliating.[20]

TABLE 9.1. Secondary Analysis of Hirschfeld's Original Seventeen Cases.

No.	Age	Sexual Orientation*	Married	Occupation	Age at first cross-dressing episode	Cross dresses for erotic pleasure	Desires role of opposite sex	Experiences homosexual fantasy
1	30+	a		Merchant	Young man	X		
2	30+	a	X		Pre-school	X		X
3	40+	a	X	Artist	Pre-school	X	X	X
4	30+	a	X	Merchant	8	X		
5	40+	a	X	Applied art	4	X		
6	40+	b	X	Artist	10	X		X
7	40+	d		Civil servant	12	X		
8	20+	a	X	Physician		X		
9	30+	a	X	Military		X		X
10	50+	a		Teacher	School age	X		X
11	40+	a	X	Technician	16	X		
12	20+	d		Lawyer	School age	X		
13	40+	c		Embroiderer	School age		X	
14	30+	a	X	Journalist	School age		X	
15**	20+	b	X	Sailor	15		X	
16	20+	a	X	Locksmith	School age	X		
17	20+	a	X	Lawyer	Young man	X		X

*Sexual Orientation: a = heterosexual, b = bisexual, c = homosexual, d = auto-erotic.
**Number 15 is a woman. All others are men.

As an example of the link between masochism and transvestism, Hirschfeld reviewed the novel *Gynecocracy: A Narrative of the Adventures and Psychological Experiences of Julian Robinson.*[21] This nineteenth-century work describes erotic bondage and punishment scenes as well as cross dressing. Hirschfeld commented:

His anonymous work certainly is in part erotic, but so dominated by psychological insight, that it almost stands alone in British erotica, and also captures a first row in the world literature of this sort of self-confession next to the works by Rousseau, Restif and de Sade.[22]

Hirschfeld's observations about the anthropological literature led him to conclude that most cultures differentiate the dress of males and females and many forbid cross dressing. He quoted biblical passages to this effect and remarked that the Jewish tradition was similar to other Asian and Near Eastern cultures in this regard, partly because women were considered so inferior to men.

The law, he said, was also negative. It was illegal to cross dress in Germany and France during Hirschfeld's time. He cites many newspaper accounts of both men and women who were arrested for cross dressing. Sometimes the cross dressing was a function of disguise for criminal activity, but often the individual was picked up because he or she looked suspiciously like the opposite sex. Hirschfeld's newspaper files even included several arrests of women who apparently looked like cross dressers when they were dressed as women. He was interested in reforming these punitive statutes, and on occasion, he wrote letters to the police or accompanied patients to the police station to vouch for them.

Table 9.1 summarizes the seventeen cases that constituted Hirschfeld's core study. All but one of the group were men. The woman in the study wanted the full-time life and work role of a man, even though she later married and had children. Three of the men also wanted the full-time work role of the opposite sex. These latter four might have become transsexuals had they lived at a later time. Case No. 7 might be called a fetishist instead of a transvestite because, although he cross dressed, his greatest joy came from contemplating breasts. At age ten he became excited when he went to the pantry and dripped milk over his nipples. Thereafter, anything to do with breasts and milk were highly erotic for him, to the extent that he considered *cow* and *udder* to be erotic words.

There are some missing data in Table 9.1 because the case study method allows variation in the data presented from one case to the next. For example, Case No. 8, the physician, and No. 9, the army officer, did not reveal the age at which they started cross dressing. Nevertheless, there are generalizations about transvestism that can be made from the table and the original data. The group was primarily heterosexual, with a scattering of homosexuality. Autoeroticism in the form of cross dressing may well have been the major sexual outlet among the group; for three people it was the only outlet. Although most people were married, six mentioned homosexual fantasies. Some of the marriages were purely conventional without much of a sexual element.[23]

Hirschfeld tried to look at every facet of the question in his search for understanding. He argued that transvestism, particularly among men, was different from homosexuality because the focus of the male transvestite was on the clothing rather than the sex partner. The homosexual man who cross dressed did so as part of attracting and enjoying sex with his same-sex mate. The transvestite man who was incidentally homosexual was more focused on the clothing. Thus, the difference in the homosexual man and the transvestite man was not in behavior but in their focus of pleasure. He argued that transvestites differed from fetishists because fetishists tended to attach the object of the fetish to a beloved person; transvestites focused on themselves and their clothing. Masochism was often linked to the transvestite phenomenon, and the pain of earrings and girdles seemed to enhance the pleasure of cross dressing for many. They also tended to seek out masculine women and liked to be passive in the sex act with them.

Although Hirschfeld reported many instances of women cross dressing, he commented less on their motivation. From the data presented, it often seemed to be a desire for the role of the man rather than for the clothing of the man. He clearly identified a group of women cross dressers who were not lesbians, but their interest was in the work roles and life-style of men rather than their clothing. Some of the male transvestites were also interested in the female role rather than the dress, and they usually lived full- or part-time as women.

For the most part, Havelock Ellis, another major twentieth-century sex researcher, agreed with the Hirschfeld's findings. Ellis, however, was concerned about the term *transvestism,* which he argued narrowed the focus to garments. The cases he reviewed often focused as much on the role of the opposite sex as on the clothing. In his first paper on the topic, published in 1913, Ellis used the term *sexo-aesthetic inversion* in place of *transvestism* and described four cases of the anomaly.[24] He was particularly interested in the case history of a sixty-six-year-old man of letters who felt very close to women. He occasionally changed clothes with his wife. At about age fifty-seven he noted a thickening and enlargement of his breasts, which he greatly enjoyed; he thought often about the joy that must come to women from suckling a healthy child. Ellis commented about this case history:

The condition presented by R.M. seems to me to be sexo-aesthetic inversion in its most complete form. In that form it brings home to us the unsatisfactory nature of the term "transvestism." The element of cross-dressing was, indeed, present, but in [such a] slight and unessential a degree to be almost negligible. . . . The inversion here is in the affective and emotional sphere and in this large sphere the impulse of cross-dressing is insignificant.[25]

However, as Ellis talked with colleagues about his paper, he decided that the use of the word *inversion* was misleading, since it suggested homosexuality and most of the cases he had studied were either heterosexual or not particularly interested in sex. He therefore decided that the best term would be *eonism,* using the name of the eighteenth-century cross dresser, the Chevalier d'Éon. He argued that the term avoided the problems inherent in the other terms and followed the precedent used for sadism and masochism which invoked the names of well-known models of the behaviors.[26]

Ellis did not consider eonism to be a particularly troublesome problem, since most of the people he studied were able to lead lives they found satisfactory and did not harm others. His focus was scientific; like Hirschfeld, he was trying to understand the phenomenon, and he made no proposals to change the individuals he studied.

Psychoanalytic Explanations

After Ellis and Hirschfeld, most of the studies on cross dressers were by psychoanalysts whose views were fundamentally different, probably because their goal was therapeutic rather than research oriented. Most followed Krafft-Ebing's lead in depicting transvestism as a perversion, and like Krafft-Ebing, many associated it with fetishism[27] as well as with borderline or psychotic functioning.[28] Pared down to its essentials, the psychoanalytic model holds that adjustment problems are primarily caused by childhood experiences that stunt or divert the psychosocial development of the child. The role of the psychotherapist is to help the client remember, understand, and defuse the explosive negative feelings that surround the causal experiences. The treatment method was popularized by Sigmund Freud and his contemporaries.[29]

Although Freud had no direct interest in transvestism, he developed a psychoanalytical model to explain stigmatized sexual behavior in general. He emphasized that childhood experiences included many experiences that are sexual in nature and that mental illness is not necessarily hereditary.[30] In a 1928 paper on fetishism, Freud reported what he had observed in several cases wherein the patient's sexual object choice was ruled by a fetish. In one case the man was erotically aroused by the shine on a nose. Freud pointed out that the nose was clearly a substitute for a phallus. In other cases the fetish was not so easily linked, but it always had the same phallic meaning. However, the phallus was not just any penis; it was the mother's missing penis. Freud speculated:

Probably no male human being is spared the shock of threatened castration at the sight of the female genitals. We cannot explain why it is that some of them become homosexual in consequence of this experience, others ward it off by creating a fetish, and the great majority overcome it. It is possible that we do not yet know, among the many factors operating, those which determine the more rare pathological results; we must be satisfied that we can explain what has happened.[31]

Since Freud did not write a paper or review cases of transvestism, this more general explanation of the psychopathology of fetishism was adopted by the psychoanalysts who used his work as the basis of their approach to treatment for cross dressing. They would explain that the male transvestite as a boy or young man somehow had seen his mother's genitals and realized she lacked a penis. The realization created horrible anxiety for him because he feared losing his own penis. This event could cause other sexual pathology as well as transvestism. The process was similar for young girls, but Freud hypothesized that it was envy of the penis they lacked that was the root cause of their psychopathology.

One of the psychoanalysts who developed these ideas further was Wilhelm Stekel, who treated a variety of sexual problems including transvestism. Stekel also added to the specialized language of psychoanalysis. In the preface to his book *Sexual Aberrations: The Phenomenon of Fetishism in Relation to Sex,* he explains three important terms: "For those readers who are unacquainted with my new terminology as it is uniformly carried out in these volumes, I may say that parapathia stands for neurosis; paralogia for psychosis, and paraphilia for perversion."[32]

Stekel and his colleague Emil Gutheil classified fetishism as one of the paraphilias and included one case history dealing with transvestism (written by Gutheil) in their book on fetishism. They did, however, differentiate between fetishism and transvestism.

Despite its striking inner resemblance with fetishism, we cannot consider transvestism as a form of genuine fetishism. It is a special form of a compulsion neurosis in which the patient's desire for the genitals of the other sex is displaced to the clothing.

The transvestite satisfies himself with the appearance of belonging to the opposite sex; he makes use of the clothing in order to possess some rudiment of reality in the fictitious transformation which he has accomplished. Whereas the fetishist reconstructs an infantile scene and becomes a child again in order to experience something definite, the transvestite projects his wish into the future and anticipates the great miracle, the miracle of his sexual metamorphosis. Fetishism is thus retrospective and transvestism prospective in purpose.[33]

Interestingly, the case used to illustrate transvestism was that of a woman, Elsa B., who had come in for a medical investigation as a result of her application to the police to be allowed to wear men's clothing. She reported that she had been rejected by her mother and raised by grandparents; she cross dressed at an early age and looked masculine. She wore her hair short, like a man's, and urinated standing up. Her erotic thoughts were directed toward women, but she had scruples about engaging in homosexual activities. Her erotic pleasure came from putting on men's clothing; this act was pleasurable even to the point of orgasm.

Gutheil interpreted Elsa B.'s problem as an Electra complex, which was expressed in her identification with her father and brother, her penis envy, and her incestuous love for her mother. Her cross dressing and pleasurable orgasms in men's clothing were thus tied into this incestuous love. Religion also played a part in her paraphilia, since her religious fantasies, mentioned in the psychoanalytic sessions, blocked her from expressing her true homosexual desires in a more direct manner; instead, she focused on clothing.[34]

Gutheil and Stekel critiqued the work of Hirschfeld; whereas they credited him for his identification of the phenomenon, they faulted him for overlooking the importance of latent homosexuality as an important causal factor in transvestism. They identified homosexual tendencies in most of Hirschfeld's case histories and explained his failure to do so as due to his inability to utilize deep psychoanalytical analyses. They also argued that Hirschfeld ignored the importance of psychological factors in the genesis of sexual aberrations, relying too heavily on his belief in constitutional factors.

The reason why such a capable scientist as Hirschfeld could have overlooked this important trait of transvestism in his voluminous and exhaustive studies is to be found in the fact that he dispensed with the technique of deep psychological analysis. Some of his patients affectedly denied homosexuality (cases I, III, and VIII); or they dream (nearly all) of sexual embraces with individuals of their own sex, e.g. cases II, III, IV, VII, and others; or (nearly all of them) claimed that they could cohabit only in 22 *succumbentes* [women on top or in otherwise passive role] (I, III, V, XIII, and others); or finally they were manifest homosexuals such as cases VII, XII, and XV. We know that the so-called heterosexual transvestites have only masked their homosexuality.[35]

Gutheil's explanation makes it clear that there were many ways by which the analyst could identify homosexuality, whether it was admitted, denied, dreamed about, or manifest. Even if the client claimed he was heterosexual, the psychoanalyst could still label him as a latent homosexual. This passage helps explain some of the anger expressed by contemporary transvestites who report that their psychoanalysts did not listen to them when they tried to explain their problem as cross dressing rather than homosexuality. Any analyst who adhered to Stekel and Gutheil's findings would take every denial of homosexuality as an admission. The client could not help but feel that he was not heard.

Karl Abraham, another early psychoanalyst, also published a case history of a man who desired to be a woman and in his daydreams imagined himself changed into a woman. He had no apparent desire to cross dress. He identified with his mother and had a headache every month, which he called his period. Abraham, following Gutheil and Stekel, explained this as a homosexual impulse component.[36]

As the psychoanalytic tradition grew in the first half of the twentieth century, the focus on psychological factors (instead of inherited, constitutional factors) became more accepted. Analysts tended to explain transvestism either as a type of homosexuality or a flight from homosexuality caused by some event in childhood that created castration anxiety. Cross dressing was explained as an attempt to overcome the fear of castration by creating an imaginary phallic woman and then identifying with her.[37] Psychoanalyst Otto Fenichel argued that the fantasy of the phallic girl reassured the transvestite that he would not lose his penis because both men and women would thus have phalluses.[38] Imagining that girls have penises allayed the castration anxiety of the transvestite.[39] In addition, some psychoanalytic writers argued that the goal of the male transvestite was to replace his mother and arouse sexual feelings in the father and possibly supplant her in his affections.[40]

A case was reviewed by George Peabody and colleagues wherein a twenty-one-year-old male patient told of a dream in which he looked under a girl's skirt and saw male genitalia. He indicated to his therapist that he had no clear idea of the anatomy of the female genitalia and did not want to accept the idea that women did not have a penis.[41] As a child this client had accidentally seen his mother undressed; he saw her genitalia and realized she did not have a penis. According to the psychoanalysts, this fear of castration and its denial through the creation of a phallic woman is often precipitated by an incident wherein a boy accidentally sees his mother or sister undressed and notes the absence of a penis. The child then constructs an imaginary woman with a penis and dresses to become that woman. In some of the explanations, the clothes represent the phallus.[42]

Despite the dominant psychological focus, vestiges of a concern for hereditary factors continued to appear in the psychiatric literature, which led therapists to scrutinize the relatives of clients. In addition, even those scholarly papers that explained the cause of transvestism as castration anxiety also searched for other likely influences in the histories of their clients. N. Lukianowicz, writing in 1959, listed four such likely pivotal events in the lives of children that showed up in the case studies of transvestism conducted by psychiatrists and other medical researchers: the parent rejects the child, the parent dresses the child in the garb of the opposite sex, the parent favors a child of the opposite sex in the family, or the parents reverse roles.[43]

Real or imagined parental rejection is often mentioned in the case studies. This is particularly devastating if another child of the opposite sex is treated better than the subject. The rejected child then adopts the dress of the favored sex in an attempt to obtain parental approval. If the rejected male child perceives his sex organs as the cause of his rejection, he may want to remove the offending parts. Lukianowicz cites several instances of attempted self-mutilation.[44]

Many histories of transvestites recount incidents when they were cross dressed by their parents. This was particularly true in an earlier period, when boys were kept in baby dresses until they were toilet-trained. It is reasonable to think that some families may have delayed the switch to boys' clothing beyond normative time for this event. (Transvestite fantasy literature emphasizes this factor even more than do actual case studies.) The histories also frequently mention aggressive mothers and weak or submissive fathers, which later became a favorite explanation for homosexuality in the psychiatric literature. Mothers or sisters who exposed themselves to the children are also mentioned as the stimulus for transvestism.[45]

Using insights from the psychiatric literature, "Janet" Thompson in 1956 analyzed the transvestite phenomenon, drawing on his own experiences and association with more than fifty transvestites. He indicated that his condition originated before age five and was due to a faulty identity formation, which he attributed to the family environment, including an overprotective mother. He also argued that the strictures placed on male children against crying or showing the softer side of their personality was part of the causal sequence. Cross dressing was done in secret, and he reported finding it enjoyable from the first instance. Thompson married twice. The first time his wife did not know about the cross dressing, and it became a source of unhappiness. After her death, a second wife was informed before the marriage, but that wife went through a "nervous breakdown" and then sought a divorce. At the time the article was published, Thompson was living full-time as a woman, working as an artist and remodeling apartments.[46]

John Randall, a British physician-psychologist published a 1958 study of fifty cases of transvestism and transsexualism drawn from his practice. The group included thirty-seven males and thirteen females. Many of these people had requested sex reassignment surgery, but he felt most of them should not have it. All of the thirteen women in the group had cross dressed since childhood; they had played with boys' toys, preferred boys' games, and often wore shorts or jeans instead of girls' clothes. All but one of the women were lesbian. One heterosexual woman had lived with a male transvestite with whom she was orgasmic. Later on, she married a different man and tried to talk him into cross dressing, but he refused. She became depressed and had attempted suicide three times before coming in for treatment.[47]

Randall decided that he could best describe the total sample by dividing it into two groups: a homosexual group and an obsessive-compulsive group. Generally, the transsexual patients were in the homosexual group, while the obsessive-compulsive patients were in the transvestite group. It was an interesting distinction, and the idea of transvestism being characterized by an obsessive-compulsive disorder continues to appear in the later literature.[48]

In 1960, Vernon W. Grant, an American psychologist, published a detailed case study of a cross dresser but did not offer any interpretation of the psychodynamics of the case. He explained that he believed there had been too much theorizing with too little data. The subject was an only child, raised by his mother and grandmother. He remembered wearing high-heeled shoes belonging to his nursemaid at age four, but his mother told him he had started doing it at age two. Shoes remained his passion throughout his life. At age thirteen he started masturbating while looking at pictures of shoes in fashion magazines. As he grew older he bought women's shoes; sometimes he wore the shoes with men's clothing and sometimes he cross dressed. He dreaded being caught, and he wore women's clothes partly so he could wear the shoes out in public, but he also realized that the risk of being caught was very exciting to him. He was not attracted to men but fantasized sex with men when he cross dressed. He also had masochistic fantasies that involved bondage. He married, but found sex dull except when his wife allowed him to wear women's shoes to bed.[49]

An overview of transvestism by David Cauldwell in 1964 combined several scholarly articles about transvestism with case studies. Particularly important was an article by Harry Benjamin, who reflected on the phenomenon in light of its differentiation from transsexualism. He believed the two phenomena were related on a continuum, with the transvestite showing milder symptoms and the transsexual being the most troubled.[50] Winfield Scott Pugh classified the sexual orientation of transvestism using five categories: heterosexual, bisexual, homosexual, narcissistic, and asexual. These categories are consistent with those outlined by Hirschfeld and the case histories presented in the Cauldwell volume.[51]

In 1971 Robert Stoller described what he had learned from the literature and from studying his own patients. He indicated that transvestite men were primarily heterosexual, but that most of their phallic-centered erotic activity focused on women's clothing. The knowledge that they have a penis under their women's garments is part of the pleasure experienced by male transvestites. Stoller had strong views about the etiology of transvestism in men. He argued that it was caused by mothers or other females who wanted revenge on their boys for being masculine. They did not cross dress the child as an infant (as is the case for mothers of transsexuals); rather, they waited until he had a chance to develop some masculine attributes and then moved against him by forcing him to cross dress. The child may also have had an emotionally distant, passive father. Stoller made a passing reference to the fact that questionnaire studies or interviews usually did not identify a cross-dressing mother figure but he held that it could be found with deeper probing. Sometimes even a picture in the old family album would show the child cross dressed. In short, he was determined to find a controlling mother figure.[52]

One of the best papers found in the psychoanalytic literature was authored by Ethel Person and Lionel Ovesey in 1978. They indicated that there had been a gradual shift in psychoanalytic theory away from a heavy focus on the sexual instinct and the oedipal constellation and toward a concern with the development of the ego. They suggest that "perversions" are, in fact, sexual neuroses that develop as compromise solutions to unconscious conflict. They classified the sexual neuroses into two types: (1) those that inhibit pleasure, such as erectile failure, premature ejaculation, and sexual avoidance; and (2) those that facilitate pleasure, such as fetishism, sadism, masochism, exhibitionism, and voyeurism.

Person and Ovesey's clinical description of transvestites is similar to that found in the cross-sectional studies we discuss in Chapter 12, although they described more psychopathology than is found in the nonpatient samples. They argued that male transvestites are never overtly effeminate in boyhood. Cross dressing usually begins in childhood or adolescence, and it is usually initiated by the child himself. Sometimes it starts as nonsexual activity then becomes sexualized at puberty. Cross dressing in some men is intermittent in the beginning, then follows an increasing pattern, until the point that it may become continuous. Sometimes the sexual component drops away but the cross dressing continues as an antidote to anxiety. Transvestites are preferentially heterosexual, but they may have a history of occasional homosexual encounters. They frequently express preference for a subordinate role in sexual intercourse; sometimes they are masochistic in practice or fantasy. Their fetishistic arousal can be intense, but their interpersonal sexuality is almost always attenuated. Relationships with children are dutiful and distantly loving. They tend to be aggressive and competitive in their relations with men, and they often suffer from bouts of depression.

Person and Ovesey see transvestism as closely related to transsexualism and effeminate homosexuality. They trace these disorders to an unresolved separation anxiety. Transsexuals unconsciously resort to the fantasy of symbiotic fusion with their mothers, while effeminate homosexuals and transvestites adopt less drastic measures, including the incorporation of transitional objects (such as dresses) into their lives. In the course of their practice, Person and Ovesey have seen adolescents who went through a transvestic phase without behavioral sequelae in later life, suggesting that this phase may appear during the course of developmental conflicts in sexual development but that such conflicts can be resolved unless a more significant deficit in ego development prevents resolution.[53]

The codification of the psychiatric community's thinking on transvestism is reflected in the definition of the term in the *Diagnostic and Statistical Manual*, revised third edition (DSM-III-R), of the American Psychiatric Association. Though homosexuality was omitted from the list of mental disorders in 1973,[54] the continued listing of transvestism can be partly explained by the fact that transvestites have neither been studied as much as homosexuals and lesbians nor are they as well organized as the gay power movement, which developed sufficient strength to demand that homosexuality be removed from the *Manual*. No such movement has been seen in the transvestite community.

The DSM-III-R definition of transvestism has been narrowed to focus on men who have recurrent, intense urges to cross dress and sexually arousing fantasies that disturb them. Since most transvestites live ordinary lives and never come in contact with the psychotherapeutic community,[55] a significant portion of the cross-dressing population is not covered by the DSM-III-R. This definition excludes people who cross dress for relief of tension or gender discomfort but who have no sexual excitement, and it points out that care must be taken in the differential diagnosis to exclude transsexualism and male homosexuality. The diagnostic criteria for "Transvestic Fetishism" (disorder No. 302.30) reads as follows:

A. Over a period of at least six months, in a heterosexual male recurrent intense sexual urges and sexually arousing fantasies involving cross dressing.
B. The person has acted on these urges or is markedly distressed by them.
C. Does not meet the criteria for Gender Identity Disorder of Adolescence or Adulthood, Nontranssexual Type or Transsexualism.[56]

Three aspects of this definition can be questioned. Cross dressing by women is not included, although there is good evidence that it exists albeit in different forms. The separation of heterosexual and homosexual cross dressing cannot be defended on any rational grounds, for the data suggest that the transvestite focuses on clothing rather than the sex act, so the sex of the partner is not a crucial element in the pattern. In practical terms the separation on the basis of sexual orientation casts the heterosexual transvestite as being ill (with a DSM-III-R listing), while the homosexual transvestite is considered well adjusted.

The third questionable aspect of the definition is the linkage with sexual arousal as a necessary component of transvestism. Evidence suggests that some older transvestites do not experience erotic arousal, although this may have occurred at a younger age. Even among those who have a sexual arousal, fetishism may not be the best term. Hirschfeld differentiated between the fetishist and the transvestite, explaining that the fetishist is excited by the idea that an item of clothing was associated with a beloved person while the transvestite is excited by *wearing* the clothing and would prefer a new dress, for example, rather than one that belonged to someone else: "In short, fetishists lack the expressed urge to put on the form of the beloved object, to identify with it, as it were, to change themselves into it."[57]

Even among those transvestites who experience erotic arousal when they cross dress, the focus is as much on themselves as on their clothing. They are excited by a cross-gender game that includes the way they move their bodies and think about issues, so a definition that categorizes their activities as a subtype of fetishism is probably an oversimplification. Present efforts to reverse the DSM do not include any plans to change the definition of transvestite fetishism in any substantive way.[58]

Summary

This chapter has briefly summarized the development of medical interest in stigmatized sexual activity, including transvestism. Originally motivated by medical forensics, the medical community gradually changed the paradigm for explaining and controlling sexuality. At first, the classification system adopted was simple: sexual behavior was divided into normal and abnormal, and homosexuality was the "abnormality" that received the most attention. This broad classification system was supported by Ulrichs, who argued for the existence of a third sex (called *urnings*) that included bisexual and homosexual people. Westphal called non-normative sexual activities *contrary sexual feelings*. Using the same model with variation, Hirschfeld used the term *sexual intermediaries* and differentiated transvestites from other intermediaries. Causality for non-normative sexual behavior was attributed to vaguely defined hereditary or constitutional factors.

Krafft-Ebing focused on the details of differential diagnosis, although he lumped transvestism with fetishism. He was the most negative and judgmental of all the early sexual scientists, and perhaps because of this, he was the most popular with both the medical and lay communities of his day. Ellis was as passionate about data gathering as Krafft-Ebing but much more compassionate about the people he studied. He disagreed with Hirschfeld's terminology for transvestism but supported his findings with additional case histories.

The early twentieth-century psychiatrists moved away from an exclusive belief in hereditary factors and focused instead on trying to find key elements in the case histories that would help them understand and treat their clients. Castration anxiety and homosexual panic were the major explanations for transvestism. The major focus of nineteenth- and twentieth-century research was on male cross dressers, but many of the researchers who collected a series of cases identified an occasional woman.

Modern psychotherapists still focus on childhood experiences as the cause of cross dressing but have significantly broadened their view beyond castration anxiety to look at other experiences, including early forced cross dressing, parental neglect, parental or sibling exhibitionism, and domination by mothers. The definition of transvestism in the DSM-III-R reflects the medical model, but its usefulness is compromised by the fact that it includes only a small portion of the people who cross dress.

Notes

1. John Ludwig Casper, *A Handbook of the Practice of Forensic Medicine*, translated from the third German edition by George William Balfour (London: New Sydenham Society, 1864), vol. 3.

2. Samuel A. Tissot *L'Onanisme, Dissertation sur les maladies produites par la masturbation,* 4th ed. (Lausanne, 1769).

3. Hubert Kennedy, *Ulrichs: The Life and Work of Karl Heinrich Ulrichs, Pioneer of the Modern Gay Movement* (Boston: Alyson Publishers, 1988).

4. Numa Numantius [Karl Heinrich Ulrichs] *Forshungen über das Rätsel der Mannmännlichen Liebe* 12 booklets (Leipzig: Heinrich Matthes Publishers, 1864–1879). (City and sometimes publisher differ.) It was republished and edited by Magnus Hirschfeld, 12 vols. (Leipzig: Spohr, 1898), and this edition was reprinted by Arno Press in 1975. The complete works have been translated into English by Michael A. Lombardi-Nash under the title *Research on the Riddle of Man-Manly Love*, 4 vols., mimeographed (Jacksonville, FL: Urania Manuscripts, 1988–89), and this is scheduled for publication commercially in 1993 (Buffalo, NY: Prometheus Books).

5. Carl Westphal, "Die konträre Sexuellempfindung," *Archiv für Psychiatrie und Nervenkrankheiten* 2 (1869): 73–108; see also Vern L. Bullough, "The Physician and Research into Human Sexual Behavior in Nineteenth Century Germany," *Bulletin of the History of Medicine* 63 (1989): 247–67.

6. Richard von Krafft-Ebing, *Psychopathia Sexualis: With Especial Reference to the Antipathic Sexual Instinct: A Medico-Forensic Study*, translated and adapted from the twelfth German edition by F. J. Rebman (New York: Physicians and Surgeons Book Co., [1906] 1933).

7. Ibid., 218.

8. Ibid., 253.

9. Ibid., 310.

10. Ibid., 322.

11. Ibid., 323–24.

12. Ibid., 5.

13. Charlotte Wolff, *Magnus Hirschfeld: Portrait of a Pioneer in Sexology* (London: Quartet Books, 1986).

14. Magnus Hirschfeld, *The Transvestites: An Investigation of the Erotic Drive to Cross Dress*, [Die Transvestiten] trans. Michael Lombardi-Nash (Buffalo, NY: Prometheus Books, 1991 [originally Leipzig: Spohr, 1910]).

15. Hirschfeld, *The Transvestites*, 125.

16. No author, "Woman-Man Onstage," [Vom Weibmann auf der Bühne] *Jahrbuch für sexuelle Zwischenstufen*, 3, 1901. Cited in Hirschfeld, *The Transvestites*, 142. The journal was edited and published by Hirschfeld; he was probably also the author of the article, since it was his custom to write articles without attribution for the journal.

17. Hirschfeld, *The Transvestites*, 215–36.

18. Ibid., 147–48.

19. Ibid., 159.

20. Ibid., 171–72.

21. Viscount Ladywood, *Gynecocracy: A Narrative of the Adventures and Psychological Experiences of Julian Robinson (Afterwards Viscount Ladywood Under Petticoat Rule)* (Paris, 1893, reprinted New York: Grove Press, 1971). Hirschfeld used the 1893 edition, but he places the origin of the work in the 1880s.

22. Ibid., 173.

23. Hirschfeld, *The Transvestites*, 121–24.

24. Havelock Ellis, "Sexo-Aesthetic Inversion," *Alienist and Neurologist* 34, part 1 (May 1913): 3–14; part 2 (August 1913): 1–31.

25. Ibid., part 2, 25.

26. Havelock Ellis, "Eonism," in *Studies in the Psychology of Sex*, vol. 2, part 2 (New York: Random House, [1906] 1936), 1–120.

27. R. C. Bak, "Fetishism," *Journal of the American Psychanalytic Association* 1 (1953): 285–98; Emil Gutheil, "An Analysis of a Case of Transvestism," in *Sexual Aberrations: The Phenomenon of Fetishism in Relation to Sex,* ed. Wilhelm Stekel (New York: Liveright Publishing Co., 1930), 345–51.

28. T. Hora, "The Structural Analysis of Transvestism," *Psychoanalytic Review* 40 (1953): 268–74; M. D. Lewis, "A Case of Transvestism Associated with Multiple Body Phallus Identification," *International Journal of Psychoanalysis* 11 (1930): 345–51.

29. Sandor Ferenczi and Otto Rank, *The Development of Psycho-Analysis,* Caroline Newton (New York: Dover Publications, [1924] 1956).

30. Sigmund Freud, *Three Essays on the Theory of Sexuality,* translated and newly edited by James Strachey (New York: Basic Books, [1910] 1962), and his "Heredity and Aetiology of the Neuroses," in *Collected Papers,* vol. 1: *Early Papers on the History of the Psychoanalytic Movement,* trans. Joan Riviere (New York: Basic Books, 1959). The paper was first published in 1896.

31. Sigmund Freud, "Fetishism," *The International Journal of Psycho-Analysis* 9 (April 1928): 161–66.

32. Wilhelm Stekel, *Sexual Aberrations: The Phenomenon of Fetishism in Relation to Sex,* authorized English version from the first German edition by S. Parker (New York: Liveright Publishing Co., [1922] 1930).

33. Emil Gutheil, "An Analysis of a Case of Transvestism," in Stekel, *Sexual Aberrations,* 2:281–318.

34. Ibid., 2:281–318.

35. Ibid., 2:312–13.

36. Karl Abraham, "Über hysterische Traumzustande," *Jahrbuch für Psychoanal. Forsch.* 2 (1910), cited by Ellis, "Eonism," 16.

37. N. Lukianowicz, "Survey of Various Aspects of Transvestism in Light of our Present Knowledge," *Journal of Nervous and Mental Disease* 128 (1959): 36–64.

38. Otto Fenichel, *The Psychoanalytic Theory of Neuroses* (New York: Norton, 1945).

39. Otto Fenichel, "The Psychology of Transvestism," *International Journal of Psychoanalysis* 11 (1930): 212–37; George A. Peabody, Arthur T. Rowe, and James H. Wall, "Fetishism and Transvestism," *Journal of Nervous and Mental Disease* 119 (1953): 339–50.

40. Lukianowicz, "Survey of Transvestism."

41. G. A. Peabody, A. T. Rowe, and J. M. Wall, "Fetishism and Transvestism," *Journal of Nervous and Mental Disease* 119 (1953): 339–50.

42. Lukianowicz, "Survey of Transvestism," 36–64.

43. Ibid.

44. Ibid.

45. Ibid.

46. "Janet" Thompson, "Transvestism: An Empirical Study," *The Mattachine Review* (December 1956), reprinted from *The International Journal of Sexology* (Bombay, India). Reprinted with permission of the author.

47. John B. Randall, "Transvestism and Trans-Sexualism: A Study of 50 Cases," *British Medical Journal* 2 (25 December 1959): 1448–52.

48. Ibid.

49. Vernon W. Grant, "The Cross-Dresser: A Case Study," *Journal of Nervous and Mental Disease* 131 (1960): 149–59.

50. Harry Benjamin, "Trans-sexualism and Transvestism," in *Transvestism:*

Men in Female Dress, ed. David Cauldwell (New York: Sexology Corporation, 1964), 23.

51. Winfield Scott Pugh, "Transvestism and Homosexuality," in *Transvestism,* David Cauldwell, 23–32.

52. Robert J. Stoller, "The Term 'Transvestism,'" *Archives of General Psychiatry* 24 (March 1971): 230–37.

53. Ethel Person and Lionel Ovesey, "Transvestism: New Perspectives," *Journal of the American Academy of Psychoanalysis* 6 (1978): 304–22.

54. See Ronald Bayer, *Homosexuality and American Psychiatry: The Politics of Diagnosis* (New York: Basic Books, 1981).

55. Virginia Prince and P. M. Bentler, "Survey of 504 Cases of Transvestism," *Psychological Reports* 31 (1972): 903–17; Vern L. Bullough, Bonnie Bullough, and Richard Smith, "A Comparative Study of Male Transvestites, Male to Female Transsexuals and Male Homosexuals," *The Journal of Sex Research* 19 (August 1983): 238–57.

56. American Psychiatric Association, *Diagnostic and Statistical Manual of Mental Disorders,* revised 3d ed. (Washington, DC: American Psychiatric Association, 1987).

57. Magnus Hirschfeld, *The Transvestites,* 161.

58. Allen Frances, Michael B. First, Harold Alan Pincus, and Thomas A. Widiger (Task Force on DSM-IV), *DSM-IV Options Book,* Washington DC: American Psychiatric Association, 1991.

Chapter 10
Drag Queens and Cross Dressing on the Stage

One of the more fascinating aspects about the medicalization of cross dressing, as discussed in the last chapter, is what was ignored in setting definitions and presenting examples. It was not only in everyday life that an increase in cross dressing, particularly among men, occurred but on the stage as well. As the gender divisions became more formalized over the course of the nineteenth century, gender impersonation became a staple of the stage. During the first part of the nineteenth century, more women than men played cross-dressing roles, but increasingly toward the end of the century, female impersonation dominated the scene.

Male Impersonation on the Stage

The revival seemed to occur with the onset of the Revolutionary and Napoleonic wars in France, where a major theme in several plays featured women who went to war as men, usually to aid their husbands or lovers. Setting the pattern for such plots was Guilbert de Pixeré-court (1773–1844), who wrote parodies of classical theater, burlesques, and spectacular melodramas. In England, however, the breeches role reached its height in the extravaganza, a genre which most effectively theatricalized the growing Victorian taste for fantasy and in which, despite growing official prudery, it was safe to challenge gender stereotypes.[1] The nineteenth-century extravaganza was a combination of burlesque, ballad opera, French revue, and fairy tale. Particularly important in its development was the actress-producer Madame Vestris (Lucia Elizabeth Mathews, née Bartolozzi, 1797–1856). She took over the management of the Olympic Theatre, and proved to be a barrier-breaker in her management skills as well as in breeches parts, many of which were specially written for her. Her productions achieved great popularity with the middle classes and reflected their standards, mores, and concerns. Vestris proved particularly intriguing, since she could run a theater successfully, play the coquette on stage, and at the same time do a passing imitation of a male. One critic wrote that in "a word, we never remember an instance of an actress who contrived to be at once so very much of a gentleman and yet so entire and unaltered a woman."[2]

In fact, unlike male impersonators on the popular stage later in the century, nothing in the available evidence suggests a "sustained, realistic attempt on the part of the extravaganza actress to recreate or mimic adult male behavior."[3] This meant that the actress playing the male role had to act boyishly but still retain feminine attributes, and it was this sexual ambiguity that seemed most to please the audience. Indeed, such actresses came to be known as the "principal boys," a term that remained in the pantomime vocabulary into the twentieth century. Many women who played the role made no effort to hide their "swelling busts" or "tapered limbs" and even those whom nature had given a more androgynous figure emphasized the small feet and hands of idealized femininity. The best "boy" actress was expected to reveal a substantial amount of leg yet somehow maintain enough feminine characteristics to fend off the most criticism of inappropriateness.

One feminist critic has remarked that the portrayal of male characters by women in the extravaganzas

illustrates the obsessive concern with sexual imagination. . . . [These] "epicene princes" who become heroes within the fictional construct of the play win the love of beautiful women, kill dragons and monsters, brave demons, outwit enemies, and rescue maidens. Without violating the sexual decorum of character, the actress could imaginatively cross quite safely sexual boundaries related to romantic love and behavior considered gender specific.[4]

Cross-gender casting, in other words, provided an opportunity for women vicariously to have the sort of mythic adventures many desired to have but which were denied by the gender conventions of the day. It allowed those greatly concerned with respectability to explore sexual boundaries at least on a subliminal level, but it was never so realistic that it threatened the males in the audience.

Though the popularity of the extravaganzas declined over the course of the century, the impersonation it popularized was continued in the English pantomime, which by the nineteenth century had become a uniquely English comic drama form. One of the keys to its uniqueness was the replacement of the earlier harlequin or clown roles by various cross-dressing characters. Presiding over this change was Augustus

Harris (also known as "Druriolanus," because of his dominance of the Drury Lane theater district), who took over the Theatre Royal in 1880. He managed to attract star performers from the music halls and classical stage to his Drury Lane theater to play the comic roles in his pantomimes, and under his direction the "dame" or "drag" roles (female impersonators) grew in importance while those for the principal boys declined.[5]

Among the actresses who became known for their principal boy parts was Marie Wilton, who later, as Mrs. Sydney Bancroft, became a noted actress in straight comedy. Sometimes audiences watching the best of the impersonators could question their own adherence to gender restrictions. Charles Dickens, for example, described one of Wilton's performances:

There is the strangest thing in it that even I have seen on the stage. The boy, Pippo, by Miss Wilton. While it is astonishingly impudent (must be, or it couldn't be done at all), it is so stupendously like a boy, and unlike a woman, that it is perfectly free from offence. I have never seen such a thing. . . . She does an imitation of the dancing of the Christy Minstrels—wonderfully clever—which in audacity of its thorough going is surprising. A thing that you *cannot* imagine a woman doing at all; and yet the manner, the appearance, the levity, the impulse and spirits of it, are so exactly like a boy that you cannot think of anything like her sex in association with it.[6]

Another woman who became quite famous for her breeches parts was Vesta Tilley (Matilda Alice Powles, 1864–1952). She specialized in portraying the young man-about-town, even though her clear soprano voice always made it obvious to her audience that she was a woman. Still, the daring of her male impersonation caused the prudish Queen Mary to turn her back on Tilly's act at a royal command performance in 1912.[7] Some of the male impersonators went beyond the stage and played a more masculine role offstage as well. In Vienna, for example, the folksinger Josefine Schmeer took to wearing men's clothes in her everyday life.

In the United States, male impersonation was introduced onto the variety stage by Anne Hindle (born c. 1847) and Ella Wesner (1841–1917), both of whom portrayed swaggering, cigar-smoking, swearing young men. Both were also veterans of the English music hall, where the male impersonators were allowed much more vulgarity than had been the case for those playing the masculine roles in the extravaganzas or pantomimes. This more boisterous male impersonation role probably reflected social class influences, since the music hall and the burlesque had a strong working-class appeal.

Still, there continued to be male impersonators in the tradition of Madame Vestris, such as Bessie Bonehill (d. 1902) who, with her mezzosoprano voice, played the role of the male with much less vulgarity and more realism than Hindle and Wesner. Although Schmeer, Hindle, and Wesner have been identified as lesbians, most of the male impersonators of the time emphasized their femininity in their offstage activities, thereby making their onstage cross dressing much less threatening to their audiences. Even Hindle and Wesner were discreet enough in their offstage life that their sexual preferences remained unknown and unsuspected to most. Undoubtedly, however, their stage personae served as models for the more masculine lesbians in the audience.

Male impersonations were not confined to the pantomime or burlesque, since several actresses also attempted male roles on the legitimate stage. Sometimes such roles were simply those of adolescent boys. For example, from the very first performance of Peter Pan (1903 in London; 1904 in New York), a woman played the title role of the boy who never grew up. Several actresses achieved fame in the role, from Nina Boucicault, the first Peter, to Paula Chase, to Maude Adams, to Mary Martin. Other times, the male impersonation roles were less obvious, such as the various male roles in Shakespearean drama. Kitty Clive (1711–85) is alleged to have been the first woman to play Hamlet, but the most famous and acclaimed actress to do so was Sarah Bernhardt (1845–1923). In the nineteenth century alone some fifty actresses played the Danish prince. The tradition continued in the twentieth with Dame Judith Anderson (1898–1992) perhaps being the most notable. Such roles demonstrate another important aspect of cross dressing for women on the stage, namely, the opportunity it presented for demonstrating their versatility as actresses. Generally, women's roles were less varied than those written for men, and there were few major roles for older women. This meant that the aging actress faced the prospect of playing secondary or subordinate roles or trying to play someone much younger than she actually was. It was almost as if she had to play a breeches part to demonstrate that she had greater potential than society was willing to attribute to an older woman. Both young and older actresses, however, took roles as men. The American actress Charlotte Cushman (1816–76), for example, played Romeo to her sister's Juliet and was complimented for her "living, breathing, animated, ardent" portrayal of the young man.

Some plays seemed to be particularly attractive to actresses. Among them was John Gay's eighteenth-century *Beggar's Opera,* which often had a woman taking the role of Macheath, the light-hearted highwayman who proved so attractive to women. One of the first to play this role was Madame Vestris, who delighted in impersonating the swaggering womanizer.[8]

The nineteenth century also saw women playing trousers roles in opera, particularly in the roles of male adolescents, for which the actress's voice was no impediment to her disguise. Among such roles were Hansel in Humperdinck's opera, *Hansel and Gretel,* Cherubino in Mozart's *The Marriage of Figaro,* and Oscar in Verdi's *Un Ballo in Maschera.* There were also specific cross-dressing roles, such as Leonora in Beethoven's *Fidelio,* wherein Leonora disguises herself as a man to rescue her husband from prison. In dramatic contrast is the role of Octavian in Richard Strauss's twentieth-century opera *Der Rosenkavalier.* This role is a major one and demands much of the actress, since she not only has to play a boy but flirt with other men as a boy and later act the role of a man happy with his mistress.

Probably it was only by publicly casting a woman in the role that such flirting with males, and hints of homosexuality, would have been tolerated by opera audiences of the time. There were, however, limits to how far a woman could go on stage. Archibald Gunter's play, *A Florida Enchantment,* premiered in 1896 and received disastrous reviews by critics who were upset at the sex changes taking place onstage. The play portrayed the transformation of a woman into a man (acted by a woman), as a result of eating a magic seed, and her ensuing misadventures in love with other women. Her black maid was also transformed into a man by eating the same magic seed, and some men were transformed into women. Once transformed into a man the main character swears, swaggers, and sets out on the conquest of a number of other women. One critic went so far as to call it the worst play ever to be produced in New York and was particularly upset that such animal feelings were depicted on the stage by a woman. The world, he wrote, "recognizes lots of things," but does not speak about them, and they certainly should not appear onstage.[9]

On the American stage black women as well as white women played the cross-dressing role, and among the leading black male impersonators in the first part of the twentieth century were Gladys Bentley (Gladys Ferguson) and Bobbie Minto (1907–60). But although many women performers in the English music halls and American burlesque (including Ella Shields, Hettie King, and even Gracie Fields) continued to have male roles in their repertoires, it was not until the rise of the second wave of feminism in the late 1960s and early 1970s that male impersonation achieved the level it had in the nineteenth century. This new wave of impersonation was a more direct kind of male impersonation than had appeared in the Victorian era. It was much more openly political, since it was often used to make statements about the traditional limitations of women's roles or the possibilities of new opportunities for women, as in Eve Merriam's revue, *The Club* (1976), Timberlake Wertenbaker's, *New Anatomies* (ICA Theatre, 1981). In Simone Benmussa's *The Singular Life of Albert Nobbs* (1977), the heroine must live as a male waiter in order to survive, while in Manfred Karge's *Man to Man* (1987), a widow adopts her husband's identity to keep his well-paying job as a crane operator. In Caryl Churchill's *Cloud Nine* (1979), sexual cross-casting is an important aspect of the play's inquiry into gender roles. Women comediennes also took the opportunity to add a cross-dressing role to their repertoire. Among the most interesting was Lily Tomlin, who in her one woman show, created a male lounge singer, Tommy Velour, who is plausible even to the hair on his chest.[10]

One of the difficulties with women impersonating men throughout much of the twentieth century was that until the new wave of male impersonators, there had been no real training ground, as there had been for female impersonators, for learning and experimenting in the opposite role. Each woman who attempted to do so had to do so on her own. Male impersonators lacked the opportunities for training offered by the Shakespearean theater or by the cabaret female impersonator shows. Certainly, the nineteenth-century stage offered the opportunity for light-hearted impersonation, but at the same time it discouraged serious impersonation. In a sense, this tended to make women amateurs in a realm that allowed for male professionals.

One exception to this trend has been in Japan, where there is a tradition of male impersonation on the stage, although it only dates from 1914, the year the all-female Takarazuka Revue Company was founded outside Osaka. This revue company might well have been influenced by the tradition of Shaoxing opera in China, wherein all the roles were played by women (a conscious reversal of the Beijing Opera, whose roles were performed by men). Shaoxing opera, named after the city of Shaoxing, a city in Zhejiang province, was popular in Shanghai, Nanjing, and other cities. In the Japanese version, performers are chosen through an annual competition among suitable unmarried girls who are judged on their diction, singing, and Japanese and Western dancing. Successful candidates then undergo rigorous training in several disciplines, including the art of male impersonation. The star of the review is the *otokoyaku*, or male impersonator, who is often featured in fan magazines and who traditionally has had strong appeal to schoolgirls. In fact, the appeal of the Takarazuka is mostly to women, and over 70 percent of the audiences are female (although the performers are also much sought after as wives by Japanese men, and this is an important factor in the quick turnover of personnel). Growing out of the Takarazuka was the all-female Shochiku Revue, which resembles a lavish Las Vegas show. Although the companies make considerable efforts to control the sex lives of the performers in all the Japanese male impersonator shows, some do form lesbian attachments, and in 1988 two of the graduates of the Takarazuka were involved in a failed love-suicide pact.[11]

Female Impersonation on the Stage

Female impersonation, which had been declining since women had been allowed to appear as themselves on the legitimate stage in the seventeenth century, made a comeback in the nineteenth century. It became an entrenched part of the British pantomime, particularly during the Christmas season. Major actors often took a woman's role, but it was always clear that the person playing the *dame* (the pantomime term for female roles played by men) was a man; he dressed as an absurd and ugly woman, and much of the comedy was derived from the fact that he was burlesquing himself as a male actor. Even in this form, however, the stage impersonator made an effective challenge to traditional ideas of gender. Peter Ackroyd has written that the comic female impersonators evoked fears of female aggression and overt sexuality as well as fears about homosexuality. By subtly and humorously representing such fears, the "dame" could defuse them through laughter.[12]

The major home of female impersonation in England during much of the last part of the nineteenth century was not so much the pantomime but the music hall, which grew out of the Song and Supper Clubs at all-male taverns. The host, acting as chairman, persuaded some of his customers to get up and do a "bit," which many did as an impersonation of women. From the tavern music hall came the more proper music hall, the first of which was the Canterbury, opened in Lambeth in 1852. Originally, the Canterbury included excerpts from ballet and opera, but from the first it also included such female impersonators as E. W. Marshall, who regularly assumed skirts for his songs. Soon, most male performers had a drag number that involved at least wearing a bonnet or a shawl and for some much more. It was from these opportunities that female impersonators could perfect their acts.

Gradually, the costume of the female impersonators became more elaborate as there was cross-fertilization between the pantomime and the music hall. Female impersonators who worked the halls during much of the year took on the role of the dame in the Christmas pantomime, the costume of which became ever-more glamorous and costly. One of the most famous female impersonators was Dan Leno, who played his first pantomime date in 1888 and did so regularly almost up to his death at the age of forty-three in 1904. One theater critic, Clement Scott, described him:

When we see Dan Leno as a woman and hear his delightful patter it never strikes us that he is a man imitating a woman. It is a woman who stands before us, the veritable Mrs. Kelly, not a burlesque of the sex, but the actual thing. He catches every expression, every trick, every attitude, every inflexion of voice, and all is done without suspicion of vulgarity. In his grim earnestness consists his humour. The comedian who laughs at his own jokes soon becomes wearisome, but it is Dan Leno's astonished face when he looks at the laughing audience that gives him his power. In brief, a most admirable, versatile, persuasive, volatile and intense comedian and artiste. Whenever he is on the stage, be it theatre or music hall, he literally holds his audience tight in his power.[13]

In the United States female impersonation was a feature of comic travesty early in the nineteenth century. George Holland, for example, who played Ophelia in travesty of Hamlet in 1828, has been called the forerunner of "legitimate burlesque" in the United States. In 1839 William Mitchell played a female part in a burlesque ballet:

First time in this or any other country, a new comic burlesque ballet, entitled "La Mosquito," in which Monsieur Mitchell will make his appearance as *une première danseuse*, and show his ability in a variety terpsichorean efforts of all sorts in the genuine Blerochahahucoacavonienne style. . . . The ballet is founded on the well known properties of the mosquito, whose bites render the patient exceedingly impatient, and throw him into a fit of slapping and scratching and swearing delirium commonly called "Cacoethes Scratchende," causing the unfortunate being to cut capers enough for a considerable number of legs of mutton. The scene lies in Hoboken.[14]

Mitchell performed his dance in an exaggerated makeup as Miss Fanny Elssler and burlesqued a graceful ballerina with comic humor, at least according to contemporary writers.

The training ground for the new generation of female impersonators was the minstrel shows and vaudeville. The association with minstrel shows is almost symbolic of the ambiguous nature of female impersonation as it was perceived by the audience. Robert Toll points out that "women, like Negroes, provided one of the few stable 'inferiors' that assured white men of their status."[15] These all-white male actors not only played in blackface but also were featured in almost every show as what were called "plantation yellow girls" (that is, mulattoes) and as the white daughters of plantation owners. The female impersonators quickly became the stars of the show, and in the immediate post–Civil War period they were the highest paid of the minstrel performers. The man who dominated the role in this period was Francis Leon, who was so convincing an "actress" that a Rochester, New York, critic wrote that many men refused to believe he was a man. During an appearance in New York in 1870, he told a reporter that he wore only "genuine" women's clothing, not costumes, and that his wardrobe included some three hundred dresses.[16]

As a network of railroads developed, much of the comedic routine of the minstrels separated out into vaudeville and burlesque, an American version of the British music hall, and traveling performers, many of them female impersonators, perfected their acts across the nation. Bert Savoy (born Everett Mackenzie, 1888–1923) introduced an outrageous red-haired caricature, garish and brassy, who gossiped about her absent girlfriend Margie. Savoy began his stage career touring the mining camps of Montana and Alaska and the barrooms up and down the Yukon. He later joined up with Jay Brennan (who also occasionally cross dressed) to form a celebrated double act that appeared in such shows as *Miss 1917, Hitchy-Koo,* and even the Ziegfeld Follies of 1918. When Savoy died in 1923, Edmund Wilson wrote for *The Dial:*

One instrument in the great jazz band of New York has suddenly silenced: Bert Savoy is dead. But the comic character he created will never be forgotten by those who saw it. When he used to come reeling on the stage, a gigantic red-haired harlot, swaying her enormous hat, reeking with corrosive cocktails of the West Fifties, one felt oneself in the presence of the vast vulgarity of New York incarnate and made heroic.[17]

Savoy obviously was able to project something that was clearly feminine, even in a tough and vulgar way. After he died his partner Brennan joined forces with another female impersonator, Stanley Rogers, and the two continued working together on the stage and later in some of the early talking pictures.

Many of the vaudeville performers included an impersonation act. One of the most popular duos was Edward Harrigan and Tony Hart who, in their nationality skits, played stereotypical Germans and Irishmen, but also included skits involving a married couple with Hart playing the female role. The tradition continued into the twentieth century, and among those who played drag roles were Charlie Chaplin, Stan Laurel, and Groucho Marx. (Marx's first job in vaudeville was as a female impersonator.) Occasional impersonations remained an important part of comedy routines when vaudeville moved into television. Milton Berle and Flip Wilson included female impersonations in their television acts, and almost every major comedian at one time or another appeared in drag, from Jack Benny to Bob Hope to Jerry Lewis.

Cross-dressing roles were also seized upon by some men as occasions to play out their fantasies of being women. This was particularly true in amateur theatrical performances where plays involving cross dressing not only proved extremely popular to the audience but gave opportunities for the secret cross dresser to go public. Particularly popular were such classic drag plays as *Charley's Aunt*, written by Brandon Thomas in 1892. Men in amateur theatricals also often played women's parts not intended for men, and although we often only learn of such impersonations incidentally, they were widespread. The Lambs Club, a private group founded in 1874 by and for theater people, often featured plays involving prominent female impersonation. Most of the all-male colleges put on reviews (a tradition still observed by the Harvard Hasty Pudding Club) and, for a time, so did many coeducational colleges, such as the University of Chicago and its Black Friar Club. Would-be cross dressers sought such groups out, as had the Englishmen Ernest Boulton and Frederick William Park (discussed in Chapter 8) who came to public attention when they were charged with soliciting in drag.

The most famous impersonator in the first half of the twentieth century was Julian Eltinge (born William Dalton, 1882–1941), who moved from George M. Cohan's touring minstrel show to the center of the legitimate stage. He raised female impersonation from the drab female of the music hall or the brassy vaudevillian to beautiful creatures who emphasized charm and delicacy. He made his Broadway debut in 1903 and came to London in 1906, where he gave a command performance for Edward VII. His success led to a number of shows conceived especially for him, all of which used the same theme of a man who for some reason or other was forced to disguise himself as a woman. Though Eltinge was a large-boned baritone, when cross dressed he wore costumes that were the height of fashion, and his impersonations of elegant women, which were free of parody, made him internationally famous. Among his plays were *The Fascinating Widow, The Crinoline Girl, His Night at the Club, Countess Charming,* and *Her Grace, the Vampire.*[18]

Interestingly, Eltinge seemed to have been better liked by the female audience than the male, perhaps because he was so realistic that his "obvious femininity" threatened many males' own concept of masculinity. Eltinge managed a deconstruction of the gender stereotypes of the time and, in the process, emphasized the inherent instability of what was assumed to be natural.[19] So great was Eltinge's popularity with women that a popular magazine hired him to write a regular column on beauty hints for female readers. At the same time, Eltinge's official publicity emphasized his real masculinity as well as his devotion to his mother. He retired in 1928 but remained active in the Lambs and Friars clubs. As testament to his popularity, a New York theater was named after him. In 1938 the impresario Billy Rose brought him back from retirement for a show at the Diamond Horseshoe on Broadway, but this was his last public appearance in drag, and he died of a cerebral hemorrhage in 1941.[20]

Though there was a growing concern about drag shows as possible covers for homosexuality, if anything, they grew more popular in the aftermath of both World War I and World War II. Since women were only on the fringes of the military in World War I and more or less segregated in World War II, drag shows were very much part of the military experience, as they were on all-male college campuses. Only a few performers from college drag shows went on to the professional stage, but numerous stars of army shows did succeed in stage careers, emphasizing the social class differences of the professional versus the amateur. In March 1923, *Variety* announced there were more female impersonators than ever before in vaudeville that season, noting that one house had three impersonators on one bill.[21] One of the best known female impersonators of the post–World War I period was Karyl Norman, who was billed as the "Creole Fashion Plate." Norman, whose real name was George Podezzi (1897–1947), switched from baritone to soprano voice and alternated sexes in his act. He was a fixture on the vaudeville circuits, which he traveled with his mother (who also acted as his dresser). His clothes were a major part of his act, and he placed great emphasis on appearing realistically as a woman. His decline in popularity coincided with the death of his mother, shortly after which he went into retirement.[22]

A quite different type of female impersonation was found at the circus, in a tradition that dates at least from the Napoleonic era, when the Franconis presented an equestrian version of *Madame Angot* with males disguised as women playing the female equestriennes. Here the justification for men playing the parts was their greater strength, although the best impersonators also tried to appear as graceful women. Some became almost full-time impersonators. For example, the American equestrienne Ella Zoyara was really Omar Kingsley (1840–79), and the English trapezist Lulu was El Niño Farini (b. 1855). Though there is some question about the true sex of Kingsley, there is no question about Emil Mario Vacano (1840–92), who appeared as an equestrienne under the names Miss Corinna and Signora Sanguineta. Probably the most famous circus female impersonator was Barbette (born Vander Clyde Broodway, 1904–73), who performed on the trapeze as a girl. He had begun his career as a trapeze and tight-rope performer in the Ringling Brothers Circus and from there moved into vaudeville on the Orpheum circuit. According to his story, at one performance, one of the female members of a triple trapeze act was unable to appear, and Broodway disguised himself in her clothes to fill in. He continued to develop the act, using other male trapeze artists disguised as girls to add more interest. Barbette would appear at the opening of his vaudeville act at the top of a staircase in a tight, shimmering dress with a huge train of white feathers. He would gracefully move down to a couch with cushions at the side of the stage and do a partial strip act, removing his headdress and skirts before mounting the trapeze. To soften the lines of his well-developed muscles, he wore silk tights over woolen tights. His career ended with a high-wire accident that left him temporarily paralyzed. After he recovered, he moved to Los Angeles, where he earned his living choreographing and arranging trapeze acts for the movies.[23]

Both Eltinge and Norman, and perhaps Barbette, marked the rise of a different kind of female impersonator, one who no longer burlesqued women but who acted or appeared to act as a woman. This is sometimes referred to as "glamour drag," and it demands much more realistic impersonation than had been done in the burlesque or music hall. Such impersonation required almost full-time dedication. With the development and growth of movies and the gradual decline of vaudeville, the new training ground for the impersonator changed from the music hall and burlesque to the cabaret or nightclub. Such a club in pre-Hitler Germany was featured in some of the Christopher Isherwood stories collected in *Goodbye to Berlin* (1939), from which the musical *Cabaret* was developed. In the musical Joel Gray played a role that required female impersonation (film version, 1972).

The Drag Queen and Female Impersonation

Female impersonation acts also appeared in American nightclubs, probably originally in gay bars or pubs, which usually had a token kind of stage. Increasingly, the female impersonator began to be associated with the gay community, although not all who included impersonation routines in their acts were gay. Though occasional female impersonation was acceptable, usually as a comic interlude, a full-time professional, such as Julian Eltinge had been, was increasingly linked with homosexuality, and instead of the curiosity that had greeted an earlier generation, impersonation was often denounced as a perversion; to be successful, the impersonators had to emphasize their maleness offstage. In fact, for a time cities such as Los Angeles prohibited cross dressing onstage because the police saw it as signifying homosexuality.

This linkage emphasizes that the growth of the gay female impersonator coincided with the growth of collectivities of persons who recognized themselves as being homosexual and who sought each other out. Exaggerated femininity was often a means of communication, as in the case of the Molly clubs. It was not until the last part of the nineteenth century that there are references to such associations in the United States. One of the early references to the existence of wide-spread cross dressing in male circles in the United States dates from 1871; it describes restaurants in Philadelphia that were frequented by men dressed in women's attire.[24] In 1884, an anonymous letter writer to *The Alienist and Neurologist* referred to the large number of persons who dressed like the opposite sex in all the large cities. Increasingly, he complained, men cross dressing as women were being described as perverts because the medical establishment found it difficult to under-stand how any sane man would submit "voluntarily to the tortures of tight corsets and high-heeled boots and false hair, hoops, pull-backs and frizzes." The writer, however, wondered why a person could not dress as he or she pleased and advocated the establishment of resorts or retreats where individuals could cross dress freely.[25]

Failing the existence of such retreats, the bars in metropolitan areas offered an alternative. Dr. Charles Torrence Nesbitt wrote of the exis-tence of several beer gardens in New York City in the late 1880s and early 1890s where males dressed in "elaborate feminine evening cos-tumes, 'sat for company' and received a commission on all the drinks served by the house." He added that there were not only beer halls but dance halls where many male couples, many of them dressed as women, could appear together.[26]

One such New York club was described by Earl Lind, alias Jennie June and Ralph Werther. Lind reported going as early as 1895 to what he called "Paresis Hall," dressed up in his feminine finery. He was at pains to proclaim that the hall was as innocuous as any other club.

Its existence really brought not the least detriment to any one or to the social body as a whole. More than that: It was a necessary safety-valve to the social body. It is not in the power of every adult to settle down for life in the monogamous and monandrous love-nest ordained for all by our leaders of thought.[27]

Such clubs not only served as refuges for the female impersonator but also as contact places for gay partners, both short-term and long-term.

Like the music halls, clubs relied upon their members for entertain-ment; they often performed in drag, and many of them became quite professional in their acts in the process. From the gay clubs, the female impersonators moved into clubs that catered to wider audiences. One of the first clubs to offer regular revues of female impersonators was the Jewel Box in Miami, which opened its doors to the public in 1938. Probably equally famous was Finnochio's in San Francisco, which still exists today. The Club 83 in New York, My-Oh-My in New Orleans, and others served as a circuit and gave regular employment to impersonators. As female impersonator shows developed that appealed to tourists and to the general public rather than a gay clientele, a distinction emerged between such shows and the small, intimate bar where a lone female impersonator might be featured. In the days before gay or lesbian bars could publicly advertise, one way of announcing that gays would be welcome would be to feature a female impersonator of one sort or another.

This meant that most drag shows came to be aimed at a gay audience. One woman, who reported attending drag shows in gay bars from London to Provincetown, stated that the shows often demonstrated not only a virulent misogyny and a cruel travesty of the feminine but were a humiliating experience as well. She added, however, that all drag need not be degrading for women and held that performances could be reframed into a ritual of inversion to actually speak for women. Many of the drag shows aimed at tourists did just this, and she found that some of these shows effectively deconstructed the illusion of female pulchritude prescribed by society:

Drag artists in South London nightclubs now play for all-female audiences, "hen parties." Dressed in an orange feather boa, Tommy Osborne commented that the "audience sees drag artists as surrogate women, voicing their hidden feelings." Cross-dressing makes it possible for him to function as a shamanistic figure of release: "Mind, if a man told the jokes I do, they would think it rude. But with a man dressed up as a woman, they scream back."[28]

Drag has had another function in the gay community, namely, its association with prostitution. The word *queen* applied to such prostitutes is believed to have a double derivation, coming from both the standard English word, that is, the wife of a king, and the obsolete term *quean,* or "prostitute." The carryover of this usage into the gay community would imply that cross-dressing prostitutes are not a new phenomenon. *Queen* is also a term used to describe the very effeminized male, and in many correctional institutions such individuals are segregated and placed in special units known as queens' tanks, supposedly to protect them from other men.

In trying to understand the association of cross dressing with male homosexuality, it is important to emphasize, as we have in earlier chapters, that public identification as a homosexual stigmatized the individual, particularly in the case of the passive, or receptive, homosexual. The individual could either openly conform to the heterosexual mores, as most homosexuals in the past have, or flagrantly embody the socially imposed stigma of the effeminate male by becoming drag queens. Often the difference between the nonconforming and the conforming person is based on social class (a topic discussed in Chapter 13), but even when it is not, assuming the role of drag queen puts limits upon job opportunities and tends to channel one into being either a professional performer or prostitute or both.[29] The drag queen who goes on stage flaunts his homosexuality in an economically successful and somewhat respectable way; the drag queen prostitute might be equally economically successful but much less respectable.

But not all drag queens are prostitutes, and not all male prostitutes are drag queens. Within the category of drag queens are both professionals and amateurs. The professionals are those who, according to Esther Newton, earn their living as female impersonators:

> Professional drag queens are, therefore, professional homosexuals; they represent the stigma of the gay world. Not surprisingly, as professional homosexuals, drag queens find their occupation to be a source of dishonor, especially in relation to the straight world. Their situation in the gay world is more complex. The clever drag queen possesses skills that are widely distributed and prized in the gay world; verbal facility and wit, a sense of "camp" (homosexual humor and taste), and the ability to do both "glamorous" and comic drag. In exclusively gay settings such as bars and parties, drag queens may be almost lionized. But in public—that is, any domain belonging to the straight world—the situation is far different. Female impersonators say that in public, they never "recognize" a homosexual whom they know unless they are recognized first.[30]

The female impersonator has to sell his skill to live, and even though society at present is relatively more tolerant of homosexuality than in earlier times, the gay bar still provides a key meeting place for gays to get away from the fear of hostile pressure from the straight world.

Newton distinguished two different patterns for professional female impersonators, one of which she called the street impersonator and the other the stage impersonator. Street impersonators tended to do "record acts," that is, singing or dancing to a taped recording, while stage impersonators tended to work live, singing their own songs. The street impersonator was often a jobless young homosexual man who publicly epitomized the homosexual stereotype of a feminized male. These men form the underclass both of the gay world and the world of the professional female impersonator. Their way of life is present-oriented, to survive, and is closely associated with prostitution. Street cross dressers specialize in public, confrontational deviance.

Many of the street impersonators act as B-girls as part of a female impersonation act, that is, they push drinks to the customer. This usually means they are served a colored mixture of iced tea while the customer pays for supposedly hard liquor. They get a percentage of what they make.[31] Though technically they are not supposed to solicit sexual partners as they push the drinks, there are ways of getting around such prohibitions. Thus there is a thin line between the street female impersonator and the prostitute, and the difference probably is whether the street impersonator has a paying job and can survive without additional income from prostitution.

The line is much wider for the stage impersonator. Many gay cross dressers are really street prostitutes who have no pretense of going on stage, although this does not mean that they are uninterested in their appearance as women. They simply act as prostitutes who specialize in oral sex with male customers (both homosexuals and heterosexuals). Transvestite prostitutes or would-be transsexuals (many call themselves preoperative transsexuals) are a standard part of the prostitute scene in the major cities.[32] The stage cross dressers, however, do not allow the stigma to become attached to their personal lives, limiting it instead to the stage context. Stage impersonators are usually located in the larger cities where there are jobs, and some belong to the American Guild of Variety Artists (AFL-CIO). Many of them achieve a reputation that goes beyond the gay community and play in tourist cities and entertainment spots, including Finnochio's or Queen Mary in Los Angeles and elsewhere. T. C. Jones (1920–71), a veteran of the Jewel Box, was introduced to the general public in the Broadway *New Faces of 1956* and continued to tour in his own revue until his death. Craig Russell (b. 1948) is widely known and extremely versatile,[33] while Charles Pierce is more known for his vitriol than his verisimilitude.[34] Probably the best known of all these cross dressers in the last half of the twentieth century was the English impersonator known as Danny LaRue (Daniel Patrick Carroll, b. 1927), who in the 1970s was the highest paid entertainer on the English stage. After working as a window dresser and sales clerk, he went into the army, where he appeared in some drag shows. Bitten by the acting bug, he played in amateur theatricals and was hired by an all-male show that toured England and in which he played several women's roles. He then moved into nightclub acts, and as he built up his reputation, he went back on the London stage, only this time in plays built around him. In 1969 he played in *Charley's Aunt* on television, and thereafter he continued to appear in television. His first film, released in 1972, was entitled *Our Miss Fred.*[35] LaRue was not an impersonator in the tradition of Julian Eltinge, since he played more of a burlesque comedy role. The key to his success was not to pass himself off as a woman but to dress up as a larger-than-life model of a female.[36] This is also the route taken by Barry Humphries, who has created the persona of Dame Edna Everage on television and has carried the impersonation further by writing a comic "autobiographical" novel about "herself" that recounts her climb from the kitchen sink to the corridors of power.[37]

A different type of female impersonation has been traditional in Japan and China. As indicated earlier, Japan has two traditional forms of theater in which female impersonation is a major factor: the classic Noh drama, which began in the fourteenth century, and the Kabuki theater, which evolved as a reaction to the aristocratic austerities of the Noh. Known as *onnagata*, the Kabuki actors who portrayed women were expected to play them offstage as well, living the self-effacing roles expected of Japanese women. For generations a small number of men spent their lives playing and acting as women, and it was not until after World War II that the same actor could play the female role in one play and the male in another. One of those who continued to specialize in female roles is Nakamura Utaemon VI (b. 1917). (The "VI" after his name emphasizes that the tradition of the *onnagata* was passed down in families from father to son or other immediate family members; and he is the sixth in his family.) One of those best known in the early 1990s for his ability to portray women is Bando Tamasuburo (b. 1950), who is also a well-known homosexual. He extended his roles to include Western drama, and his repertory includes the roles of Lady Macbeth and Desdemona. Homosexuality has always been associated with the Kabuki theater, and one critic has described it as a "peculiar eroticism" with "homosexual overtones."

In Kabuki the women most often portrayed are courtesans, although other characters are young girls, princesses (or daughters of high-born or wealthy persons), and the victims of cruel circumstances. Since the Kabuki is highly stylized, the actor playing the woman's role has to follow rules of dress, deportment, gesture, and even make-up that have been relatively unchanged for centuries. This method of acting emphasizes that if a woman attempted to play a female part in the Kabuki, she in effect would have to imitate the gestures and style perfected by the female impersonator. So intense has been the effort of the *onnagata* to perfect the stylized female gestures that it has been traditional in Japan for the would-be Geisha to study them in order to learn how a woman should act.[38] Leonard C. Pronko described the *onnagata* as

> a profound symbol of the mystery of metamorphosis, which is the mystery of the theatre. He seems to join two totally different worlds, not only in his double identity as actor and character, but in his dual role of man-woman. The *onnagata* is a dynamic and gigantic archetypal figure possessing, beyond his theatrical dimension, a metaphysical dimension. Whether the spectator is aware of it or not, the *onnagata* stirs in his unconscious a dim memory of some perfection partaking of both feminine and masculine, the great Earth Mother who is creator and sustainer, the divine androgyn in whose bisexuality both dark and light are harmonised.[39]

It is not only Japan that has a long tradition of female impersonators on the stage, but many of the countries of Southeast Asia and China as well. By the eighteenth century the Chinese impersonator, known as a *tan* actor, had to undergo seven to ten years of training and be exceptionally adept as a dancer and in the gestures associated with women in order to perform onstage. As in Japan, the female impersonators lived as women offstage as well as on, and many were well-known homosexuals. Some, known as *shiahng gung* or *shiahng gu*, acted as hustlers on the side. Much of this aspect of the theater disappeared during the twentieth century, and during this time the most famous of Chinese impersonators, Mei Lan-fang (born He Ming, 1894–1961), became world famous. In 1924 he was voted the most popular actor in China. Though he eventually married and had a family, Mei in his youth, like many of his predecessors, had a reputation as the lover of several powerful warlords. Internationally famous, he made stage appearances in the United States, Japan, and the Soviet Union, among other places; he also appeared in numerous films. During part of World War II he retired from the stage, even growing a moustache to emphasize his divorce from his previous role, but immediately after the war he made a sensational comeback. His death coincided with an effort to end such roles in China, and for a time the *tan* actor was forbidden. As the restrictions of the Cultural Revolution lessened, the *tan* again appeared on stage, but the training school, which had been so much a part of the tradition, was no more.[40]

Perhaps the greatest Chinese spy of the twentieth century was also a female impersonator: the opera dancer Shi Pei Pu, who became the mistress of a French diplomat, Bernard Boursicot, in 1964. So effective was Shi Pei Pu's impersonation that he managed to appear pregnant and to have a child, which Boursicot thought was his own. In 1983 it was discovered that the dancer was a male spy, much to the shock of the diplomat who claimed never to have suspected that Shi Pei was a man or a spy. The incident was made into a Broadway play by David Henry Hwang in 1988 under the title *M. Butterfly*.[41]

Roger Baker, who examined the life histories of several major American impersonators, argued that the nature of professional female impersonation has changed and that where once heterosexuals dominated, homosexuals now hold sway. He argues that this occurred because the full-time impersonators in the years between 1930 and 1950 had begun as youngsters in some other branch of show business, such as dancing or acrobatics, and then drifted into impersonation. After 1950, however, he found that most had gone directly into female impersonation.[42] We are not so certain about his generalizations and feel that he was overly concerned to separate female impersonators of the past from homosexuality. Unfortunately, we know little about the sexual orientation of many of the impersonators of the past, but several, like Barbette, are known to have been homosexual. Moreover, it is not clear that all professional impersonators active now are homosexual. Professional impersonation is simply one aspect of the gender-blending that takes place in society; society today is more tolerant of overtones of homosexuality and lesbianism than in the past, and more tolerant of openly gay performers in impersonation roles. Certainly, it is easier to speak about homosexuality, and the movie *Outrageous* (1977), starring Craig Russell, and the movie and later Broadway play *La Cage aux folles* (1979), featuring Michel Serrault, emphasized homosexual female impersonation.[43] The 1982 movie, *Victor/Victoria* made it even more obvious by having Julie Andrews pretend to be a gay Polish count who was a female impersonator.

Though there is a widespread belief that the gay professional female impersonator is not really a transvestite—that is, not interested in the clothes or the role reversal cross dressing allows—but is simply camping it up, the matter is much more complicated. A good example is that of a person who, under the name Carol Ann Masters (b. 1921), described how female impersonation allowed him to fulfill his lifetime desire to dress and act as a woman. Writing in 1949, he attributed his desire to the fact that his mother dressed and treated him like a girl until he was in the sixth grade. After a tour in the military during World War II, where among other things he had played the female role in some army shows, he ended up in California, where his cross-dressing ability at gay parties led to a modeling career and women's roles in five films. Eventually, he left the Hollywood scene and returned to his home, where he decided to become a professional female impersonator. He went to modeling school, studied music, had a skin analysis, and was advised on makeup. When he wrote he claimed to be the leading female impersonator in the country. He added that though he often appeared in public as a man when he was not performing, at home he preferred to dress and act like a woman.[44]

Professional female impersonation, however, is not a static thing, and if there was a growing shift to professional impersonators who were homosexual, as Baker seemed to imply in the post–World War II period, a second change took place in the late 1960s when preoperative transsexuals entered the field in the shows aimed at tourists. Preoperative transsexuals can be defined as those individuals who no longer depend upon makeup and waist cinchers to create an illusion of femininity but have turned to female hormones to develop their breasts and give them more feminine curves and have undergone electrolysis treatment to remove hair and beards. One of the first and most famous of such impersonators was the French cabaret artiste, Coccinelle (Jacques Charles Dufresnoy), who eventually underwent sex change surgery.[45] In her biography she noted that the impersonators in her show were divided into impersonators who were simply men in drag and those who were acquiring real feminine characteristics through hormones, surgery, and other means. This trend was accentuated in the 1980s, and probably the majority of the tourist shows feature preoperative transsexuals who have natural breasts and feminine curves, even though technically to perform as a female impersonator they retain their male genitalia. Roger Baker reported that the traditional English impersonators felt this no longer created illusion or impersonation, and they resented the competition. In Paris, where the Chez Madame Arthur and Le Carrousel represented the financial heights for would-be impersonators, most performers in the 1980s admitted to using hormones or other means to become more natural in their feminine appearance. Preoperative transsexuals appear in Germany as well, and they are increasingly part of the American scene, at least among what Esther Newton called the professional stage impersonators. This trend only emphasizes that it is much too simplistic to dismiss the impersonators of the past as only homosexual queens who loved to swish around and to claim that cross dressing and role reversal were not important to them.

One reason the would-be transsexual appears in the role of female impersonator is because it provides a way for the more talented to earn money for the surgery, since the transsexual in transition often has difficulty in securing a job. The existence of the preoperative transsexual as female impersonator, however, changes the nature of impersonation somewhat. Still, the gay female impersonator acts remain ubiquitous and very much a part of the gay life-style, as is the drag ball, but even here, the nature of the act has changed. In fact, the role of the drag queen has undergone some reevaluation in the gay community, as gay liberation has encouraged further examination of gender stereotypes.

After Stonewall

Helping to force such reexamination within the gay community is the fact that the street drag queens were the leaders in the Stonewall Rebellion in June 1969, an extensively covered event that marked the public emergence of homosexuality in the pages of the family newspaper. Stonewall Inn was a dimly lit dance bar in Greenwich Village which served as a haven for cross-dressing prostitutes ("street queens") as well as for lesbian cross dressers who were usually denied entrance to most other bars. Stonewall and similar bars at the lower end of the social scale in the gay community served as a strong magnet for police raids since the customers were both among the least powerful in the gay world and the most visible and were often engaged in soliciting. During one of the police raids (shortly after midnight on June 27), one of the lesbian cross dressers struggled with the police, and her struggle galvanized not only the drag queens but the watchful crowd that had assembled outside on the street. The crowd, if only because the bar was in a predominantly gay neighborhood, also included a large number of gays and lesbians. Roused by the struggles that ensued, the crowd began to taunt the police. Soon the arresting officers found themselves threatened by a hailstorm of cobblestones and bottles. The result was three days and nights of confrontation between the police and the street queens and their allies. The battle became immortalized in gay legend as the Stonewall Rebellion, and the media, too, sensationalized its significance. Because the raid raised the political consciousness of the street queens, it marked also a collective change in their and other gays' attitudes as well; it has come to be celebrated as a watershed in gay liberation. One result, at least among some gay cross dressers, was the politicization of cross dressing through what has been called gender-bending, or "gender fuck."

Gender-bending emphasizes not so much traditional kinds of cross dressing but a confusion of costume whereby the illusion of assuming the opposite sex is not intended to convince the viewer of authenticity but to suggest ambiguity. Since it also involves women as well as men, the viewer could not be certain whether the person was a man or woman. Gender-bending not only represents a challenge to traditional gender concepts but also to cross dressing as it previously existed in the gay community.

Giving popular expression to this changing picture of gender expression was the extension of gender-bending into rock music, particularly the growth of glitter rock, in which the stars took on glitter costumes and used campy pastiches of popular culture for radical effects. The Cycle Sluts and, later, the street theater group, the Sisters of Perpetual Indulgence, parodied traditional drag by mixing macho beards, leather, and hairy chests with spangles, false eyelashes, net stockings, and nuns' habits. In *The Rocky Horror Picture Show,* which had a continuous run off-Broadway and across the country, the hero played by Tim Curry, though dressed in drag, was clearly recognizable as a male. When the musical was made into a movie in 1975, it quickly established itself as a cult favorite; even as of this writing, special showings continue to be given, and many audience members attend in gender-bending costumes.

Despite the possibilities of being labeled homosexual, or perhaps because of it, the public outrageousness of the Cycle Sluts and others was seen even by heterosexual rock musicians as a new means for challenging their audience. Extreme makeup and outfits were adopted by Alice Cooper, the New York Dolls, and Kiss, among others. In England Mick Jagger and the Rolling Stones turned to cross dressing as part of their act, and David Bowie presented an androgynous allure. The logical terminus of this approach was reached with Boy George, who dressed onstage and off as a girl. His early publicity touted him as asexual or perhaps bisexual. (Interestingly, the gender-bending practiced by male rock stars was not so evident among woman rockers, but it did reach country and western music through k. d. lang who, in spite of her androgynous appearance in male cowboy outfits complete with ten-gallon hat, became extremely popular and won a Grammy award in 1990.) From rock music, the movement spread to other forms. Even ballet had its Les Ballets Trocadero de Monte Carlo, founded in 1974, which though it purported to be a "weapon of sexual politics," was described differently by one male dancer in the transvestite company: "We are not imitating women . . . we are ballerinas."[46]

There was cross-fertilization between the new generation of rock stars and gender-bending in the gay community. One result is evident in the movie *Paris Is Burning* (1991), which features black and Hispanic drag queens and the drag balls of Harlem. One reviewer emphasized that the movie was not about men attempting to look like women but about the efforts of a despised double minority—both ethnic and sexual—to can live out their dreams in a world of their own creation. Jennie Livingston, who directed and photographed the film, stated that making it forced her to examine her own hangups about class, and the more she delved into the topic, the more she realized how insightful the drag queens were. Having bought into the American dream, they successfully imitate the power structure that excludes them; at the balls, they are given the opportunity to achieve their dreams of fame, success, and beauty.[47]

Earlier public imitation followed some of the gender-blending popularized among the new generation of drag queens, from a new generation of males wearing the long hair popularized by the Beatles to the more androgynous costumes of their successors. One of the more obvious results was unisex clothing, which essentially came to mean jeans and a shirt for both sexes. Masculine clothing, even Jockey shorts, were adopted for women, while men adopted some of the jewelry, ruffles, and frills associated with traditional female costumes as well as new-styled shorts without a fly.

Summary

During this period of change, cross dressing itself underwent changes. The first step was the separation of heterosexual transvestism from the gay queen, a development that is examined in the next chapter. One result of this separation was the implication that heterosexuals who cross dressed did so for reasons different from those of homosexuals, an often repeated assumption that was even incorporated in the medical and professional literature. But we argue that this does not bear up under analysis, particularly as male cross dressers find a wider variety of opportunities open to them. Some drag queens have come to emphasize that femininity is a natural part of their character. One gay cross dresser explained that he was not interested in passing as a woman but in wearing women's clothes since they make him feel glamorous and pampered. For him men were powerful and butch, not glamorous, and one of his fantasies was to be escorted by a "young, handsome man" while he was cross dressed. Others have said that sex is the furthest thing from their minds when they are dressed up.

One gay wrote that, to some degree, male gays have to act out traditional gender roles but added that he enjoyed cross dressing.

It's not just the clothes, it's the whole role. Men are willing to try on a lot of different roles, But they're terrified of being feminine. Whether they're gay or straight, putting on a dress will compromise their masculinity. They lose the symbols of their power over women—and the power they want to have over one another. They become the kind of sex object they've made women into: helpless—at least on the surface of it—the pursued. But I don't mind that. I want to feel everything I'm capable of feeling.

Besides, Sherry [the female name he uses] releases me from Arnold. She's relaxed, sensuous, flirtatious. She likes to be courted and pampered. And in bed she wants to be made love to like a lady—she's *lazy*. Sherry's feminine in a way that Arnold can't be—and doesn't want to be. Arnold, after all, was raised from the time he was born—to be a man, and that has its limitations. He's a leader—guarded, aggressive, dominant. . . . He's got a prominent position in the business world. Sherry wants her own identity, soft and sexual. And Arnold doesn't want to compromise.[48]

Another gay cross dresser wondered whether men—"protected and imprisoned in their roles" in a world that separates the masculine and the feminine and which pretends that they are naturally distinct—can explore the range of expression or emotion without sometimes perhaps borrowing from women their props.[49] This concern appears to have reached large numbers of gays, since in this age of gay liberation, cross dressing still forms a significant part of the gay scene. Drag balls have moved into high society; for example, one ball sponsored in 1991 by the Designers Industry Foundation for AIDS raised a million dollars.[50] The female impersonator contests, which long have existed in the gay community, have gone national, with the winning queens from each area competing against each other just like candidates for Miss America or Miss Universe.[51] The admission by at least some gay queens that they regard cross dressing as a way of expressing their feminine selves is similar to the statements of some heterosexual cross dressers and shows that the gay cross dresser is not necessarily different from the heterosexual one, even though for a time there was a great effort to emphasize a difference. Perhaps such a distinction was necessary in the cases of cross dressers who were married and had families and did not want to be associated with homosexuals, but the phenomenon is much more complex than this simple dichotomy; gender-blending, in fact, is deeply embedded in the human psyche.

Notes

1. See Stephen Prickett, *Victorian Fantasy* (Bloomington: Indiana University Press, 1979), 95ff.

2. Review by Leigh Hunt in *The Examiner* 30 July 1820, and quoted in William Appleton, *Madame Vestris and the London Stage* (New York: Columbia University Press, 1974), 21–22.

3. Kathy Fletcher, "Planché, Vestris, and the Transvestite Role: Sexuality and Gender in Victorian Popular Theatre," *Nineteenth Century Theater* 15, no. 1 1987: 25. See also Roger Baker, *Drag: A History of Female Impersonation on the Stage* (London: Triton, 1968), 137–38; Peter Ackroyd, *Dressing Up: Transvestism and Drag: The History of an Obsession* (New York: Simon and Schuster, 1979), 102; Laurence Senelick, "The Evolution of the Male Impersonator on the Nineteenth Century Popular Stage," *Essays in Theatre*, 1, no. 1 (1982): 31–44.

4. Fletcher, "Planché, Vestris, and the Transvestite Role," 31.

5. The term *drag* did not come into popular usage until after 1870 and was taken over from homosexual slang. It is believed to derive from comparing the train of a gown to the drag or brake on a coach or train. The term was also used to describe a man who wore women's clothes with criminal intent, i.e., to commit a crime or to solicit others as a prostitute; Eric Partridge, *A Dictionary of Slang and Unconventional English*, 7th ed. (New York: Macmillan, 1970), 239.

6. This is quoted in Baker, *Drag*, 138. We were unable to trace Dickens's correspondence, but the play in which she appeared and which brought on Dickens's comment was H. J. Byrone's *The Maid and the Magpie*.

7. Baker, *Drag*, 209.

8. See Laurence Senelick, "The Evolution of the Male Impersonator on the Popular Stage," *Essays in Theatre* 1 (1982): 31–44.

9. Various pieces of information about the reaction to the play were collected by Jonathan Ned Katz, *Gay/Lesbian Almanac: A New Documentary* (New York: Harper and Row, 1983), 291–92.

10. In addition to the books and articles cited above, see A. Holtmont, *Die Hosenrolle* (Munich: Meyer and Jessen, 1925); Gisela Bleibtreu-Ehrenberg, *Der Weibmann* (Frankfurt: Fischer, 1984); and Laurence Senelick, "Transvestism, Theatrical," in the *Encyclopedia of Homosexuality*, ed. Wayne R. Dynes, Warren

Johansson, and William A. Percey, 2 vols. (New York: Garland Publishing, 1990), 2:1314–23. See also Marjorie Garber, *Vested Interests: Cross Dressing and Cultural Anxiety* (New York: Routledge, 1992), who deals with the theater and movies in greater detail than does this chapter.

11. Senelick, "Transvestism, Theatrical," 1316.

12. Peter Ackroyd, *Dressing Up*, 104.

13. Quote from Scott appeared in *Dan Leno Hys Book, Written by Himself* (London: Greening and Co., 1903), quoted by Baker, *Drag*, 165–66.

14. Quoted from C. J. Bulliet, *Venus Castina: Famous Female Impersonators Celestial and Human* (reprinted, New York: Bonanza Books, [1928] 1956), 274–75.

15. Robert C. Toll, *Blacking Up: The Minstrel Show in Nineteenth-Century America* (New York: Oxford University Press, 1974), 163. See also Hans Nathan, *Dan Emmett and the Rise of Early Negro Minstrelsy* (Norman: University of Oklahoma Press, 1962); Dailey Paskman and Sigmund Spaeth, *Gentlemen, Be Seated! A Parade of the Old-Time Minstrels* (New York: Doubleday, Doran, 1928). Let us use this occasion to personally thank Bob Davis for bringing much of the material on American female impersonation to our attention. He sent us Xerox copies of sources and guided our research into this area previously unknown to us. Much of this section is based on clippings and extracts whose source is not always identified.

16. Toll, *Blacking Up*, 142–44.

17. Edmund Wilson, *The Dial*, August 1923, quoted in Baker, *Drag*, 214.

18. Baker, *Drag*, 210–13.

19. For a more sophisticated discussion than is possible in this brief mention of such challenges to gender, see Eve Kosofsky Sedgwick, *Epistemology of the Closet* (Berkeley: University of California Press, 1990). She does not deal with cross dressing specifically, but we would hold that it is in cross dressing that stereotypes are most easily challenged.

20. Baker, *Drag*, 213.

21. Quoted by Baker, *Drag*, 213.

22. Ibid., 213.

23. Much of the information in this section is derived from undated and unprovenanced clippings as well as from Baker, *Drag* (passim), and Ackroyd, *Dressing Up* (passim).

24. See George H. Napheys, *The Transmission of Life, Counsel on the Nature and Hygiene of the Masculine Function*, 9th ed. (Philadelphia: Fergus, 1871), 29. See also Milton Rugoff, *Prudery and Passion* (New York: Putnam's, 1971), 269, 331.

25. E. J. H., "Correspondence," *Alienist and Neurologist* 5 (2, 1884): 351–52.

26. These descriptions can be found in his papers, which are deposited in the Duke University Library. Extracts can be found in Katz, *Gay/Lesbian Almanac*, 218–22. There are also references to such bars in Lincoln Steffens's discussion of Jacob Riis in *The Autobiography of Lincoln Steffens* (New York: Literary Guild, 1931), 223–34. For other references, see Allan McLane Hamilton, "Insanity in Its Medico-Legal Bearings," in *A System of Legal Medicine*, ed. A. H. Hamilton and Lawrence Godkin, 2 vols. (New York: E. B. Treat, 1894), 2:49–50.

27. Earl Lind, *Female Impersonators*, edited with an introduction by Alfred W. Herzog (New York: Medico-Legal Journal, 1922), 146–48.

28. Elaine Showalter, *Sexual Anarchy: Gender and Culture at the Fin-de-Siècle* (New York: Viking, 1990), 166–67. The quotations of Tommy Osborne come from Joy Melville, "The Ladies Let It All Hang Out," *The Guardian*, 19 July 1988.

29. Irving Goffman, *Stigma* (Englewood Cliffs, NJ: Prentice-Hall, 1963), 111.

30. Esther Newton, *Mother Camp: Female Impersonators in America* (Englewood Cliffs, NJ: Prentice-Hall, 1972), 3–4.

31. A description of such practices can be found in Kenneth Marlowe, *Mr. Madam: Confessions of a Male Madam* (Los Angeles: Sherbourne Press, 1964), 80–81.

32. Some of the best accounts of the hustling life appears in novels. See, for example, John Rechy, *City of Night* (New York: Grove Press, 1963). This is an account of a hustler's life in New York City, New Orleans, Los Angeles, and other places in California. In the introduction to the 1985 reissue of the book, Rechy explained how he came to write it and details the degree of the novel's correspondence to his own life. Another account is by Michael Kearns [Grant Tracy Saxon], *The Happy Hustler: My Own Story* (New York: Warner Paperbacks, 1975), a takeoff on Xaviera Hollander's *The Happy Hooker* that recounts the adventures of a bisexual male prostitute who cross dresses.

33. See *Craig Russell and His Ladies,* photos by David Street (Toronto: Gage Publishing, 1979).

34. A good overview of the area is E. Carlton Winford, *Femme Mimics* (Dallas: Winford Company, 1954).

35. See Peter Underwood, *Life's a Drag: Danny LaRue and the Drag Scene* (London: Leslie Frewin, 1974).

36. Ibid., 103.

37. Dame Edna Everage [Barry Humphries], *My Gorgeous Life: The Life, the Loves, the Legend* (New York: Simon and Schuster, 1992).

38. See Aubrey S. and Giovanna M. Halford, *The Kabuki Handbook* (Rutland, VT: Charles S. Tuttle, 1956), passim, but especially pp. 391–92. See also Earle Earnest, *The Kabuki Theatre* (New York: Grove Press, 1956); A. C. Scott, *The Kabuki Theater of Japan* (London: George Allen and Unwin, 1955), and Leonard C. Pronko, *Theater East and West* (Berkeley: University of California, 1967).

39. Pronko, *Theater East and West,* quoted in Baker, *Drag,* 153.

40. See A. C. Scott, *The Classical Theatre of China* (London: George Allen and Unwin, 1957); Baker, *Drag,* 155–56. His first and only American visit to the United States was sponsored by the China Institute of America, and an impressive who's who of the American social and intellectual elite (including John Dewey, Mrs. Woodrow Wilson, Rabbi J. B. Wise, Mabel Boardman, and Otto H. Kahn) greeted him. We have in our collection a copy of the program of the first tour in the 1920s.

41. See *The New York Times,* 11 May 1986; *The Times* (London), 6 May 1986; *Daily Mail,* 6 and 7 May 1986; Joyce Wadler, "For the First Time, The Real-Life Models for Broadway's *M. Butterfly* Tell of Their Strange Romance," *People* 30 (8 August 1988): 91. For the play, see David Henry Hwang, *M. Butterfly* (New York: New American Library, 1989). The play uses the incident but also considerable artistic license for the plot, including having the French diplomat end up in drag at the end.

42. Baker, *Drag,* 224–25.

43. There were second and third versions produced several years later, featuring the same players.

44. His brief autobiography was printed by D. O. Cauldwell, *Transvestism: Men in Female Dress* (New York: Sexology Corp., 1956), 85–92.

45. Mario A. Costa, *Reverse Sex: The Life of Jacqueline Charlotte Dufresnoy* (London: Challenge Publications, 1962).

46. Ackroyd, *Dressing Up*, 118.

47. The film was reviewed in *Newsweek* (12 August 1991): 62; the para-phrases from Livingston come from this article.

48. Darrel Yates Rist, "Decorating the Wounded Butch: The Politics and Passion of Men Who Cross-Dress," *The Advocate* (19 February 1985): 29.

49. Ibid.

50. *Newsweek* (3 June 1991): 71.

51. For example, the Buffalo queen was chosen in August 1991, and she was even featured in the local daily newspaper (something that would not have occurred in earlier years). See *The Buffalo News,* (8 September 1991): E2.

Chapter 11
Transsexualism

Despite the efforts of Hirschfeld, Ellis, and others to establish transvestism as a separate diagnostic category, it did not immediately become one and, in fact, remained a comparatively unexplored subject for several decades. It was not until after World War II that interest in the subject reappeared in the professional literature, and as research progressed, it became clear that cross-gender behavior included not only a desire to dress and impersonate the opposite sex but also, for some individuals, a desire to change one's sex. The latter group came to be called transsexuals and were thus distinguished from other transvestites.

The appearance of the new diagnostic category was not the result of a theoretical breakthrough. Rather it appeared on the scene as the result of the development of a surgical treatment for the extreme form of transvestism. In a sense, transsexualism was a socially constructed phenomenon. Ordinarily, a diagnosis is made independent of the planned treatment, but in the case of transsexuals, the treatment became the diagnosis. In this chapter the events surrounding this development and its theoretical implications for our understanding of gender will be explored.

Early Cases

In 1950 a young man approached Christian Hamburger, a Copenhagen surgeon, complaining of severe depression and a conviction that he could not continue his life as a man.[1] He felt that he was a woman and could not escape the idea that nature had made a mistake in giving him a male body. He told Hamburger that he had acquired a set of female clothes, secretly put them on, and shaved his pubic hair to shape it like a woman's. His work as a laboratory technician had given him access to estrogen, which he had for a time administered to himself. After conducting a thorough physical and psychiatric evaluation of the young man, Dr. Hamburger and his associates decided to treat him with additional female hormones (parenteral estrogen). The dose was larger than he had given himself, and it changed the shape of his body to a more feminine contour while his behavior, gait, and voice became feminine. His beard became sparse, and electrolysis was used to remove the remaining facial hair. Hamburger and his colleagues, using the theories of the time, diagnosed the case as one of genuine transvestism and differentiated it from two other types of transvestism: the fetishist who, as a consequence of a neurotic obsession, concentrates on one or more articles of dress, thereby developing an interest in cross dressing, and the homosexual man of the passive type who desires to dress in women's clothing.

The patient, who later took on the name Christine Jorgensen, was then castrated under provisions of the Danish Sterilization and Castration Act of 1935, which allowed castration when the patient's sexuality made him likely to commit crimes or when it involved mental disturbances to a considerable degree.[2] In 1952, he expressed a further ardent wish to have the last visible remains of his detested male sex organs removed, so his penis was amputated one year after his orchiectomy. Technically, however, as a castrated man whose penis had been removed, the patient had not undergone a sex change, and no attempt was made at that time to construct a vagina or other female sex organ for him. Hamburger and his colleagues reported the case of Christine Jorgensen, as she later became known, in the *Journal of the American Medical Association* the following year. They pointed out that they had not actually changed the sex of their patient, because his chromosomal sex remained the same, but that they had relieved his distress by creating the external appearance of a sex change. They also noted that they had discovered an analogous case done in 1943 in Germany, which indicated this was not the first case in which transvestism was treated surgically.[3]

In fact, there were several other earlier cases of sex change surgery. The most well known was that of Lili Elbe, described in a 1933 book by Niels Hoyer.[4] Lili had started life as the well-known Danish painter Einar Wegener, who became convinced that a sort of twin being, a female, shared his body. He visited several doctors, some of whom thought he was homosexual. Another treated him with x-ray therapy, while still another told him he probably had a set of rudimentary female organs inside his body. He went to Berlin, where he had his penis and testicles removed and ovarian tissue from a healthy twenty-six-year-old woman transplanted into his abdomen. A new passport in the name of Lili Elbe was secured, and the king of Denmark declared her earlier marriage null and void. She then returned to Berlin to have a vagina constructed preparatory to marrying a French painter; she died in Berlin in the immediate postoperative period.

The earliest known case of modern surgical intervention was that of Sophia Hedwig, who in 1882 had been masculinized by a surgical attempt to make her external genitalia appear more like a male's. Whether this could be called a change of sex, or an attempt to treat pseudohermaphroditism is unclear. Nevertheless, Herman Karl, as Sophia Hedwig came to be known, did officially change his sex.[5] Another case that is sometimes cited as an early instance of sex reassignment surgery (SRS) for a transsexual is that of Robert/Roberta Cowell. The son of an English surgeon, Robert grew up as an active boy. He later learned to fly, served in the Royal Air Force during World War II, and later became a race car driver and engineer. Subsequently, he became depressed and found that in many ways he was feminine and identified with women. He went to both a psychiatrist and a physician and was diagnosed as a genetic female. As explained in Cowell's autobiography, she probably had an adrenal genital syndrome at birth that caused the clitoris to enlarge sufficiently for her to be assigned to the male sex. After the diagnosis Cowell decided to become a woman. Hormone treatment and plastic surgery was done and she officially changed her sex.[6] This case differs from that of Jorgensen, who was a chromosomal male. There were also a number of other early attempts to change the sexual designation of individuals.[7]

A friend of Cowell's, Michael (Laura) Dillon, may have been the first female-to-male transsexual. Laura and her brother Robert were raised by their unmarried aunts in an aristocratic British home. Dillon is described as having had no genital abnormalities, only a consuming desire to be a man. Her sex reassignment surgery took several years and was completed in 1949. It included a mastectomy and the construction of an artificial phallus but no hysterectomy or oophorectomy (removal of the ovaries). To counteract the continued output of estrogen, she was put on large doses of testosterone. Her surgery was done by Sir Harold Gilles, who had gained experience in sexual surgery by working with men wounded in the war and in doing surgical modifications on children with ambiguous genitalia. After the surgery, Dillon attended medical school, worked as a ship's doctor, and eventually died as a buddhist monk in India.[8]

Another physician, Alberta Lucille/Alan Hart, might also be considered among the first female-to-male transsexuals. She had consulted a psychiatrist because of her fear of loud noises and eventually ended her analysis in 1917 by obtaining a hysterectomy, changing her identity to that of a man, and marrying a woman. The case was written up by the psychiatrist. As a man, Hart worked as a radiologist and wrote a popular account of radiology and four novels. Not much is known about Hart, but at least one of his novels, *The Undaunted,* deals with a homosexual theme.[9]

The case that became a media event, however, involved Christine Jorgensen. After the news of her case reached the press in December 1952, she became world-famous. Seizing the opportunity, Jorgensen sold her story to journalists from the Hearst newspapers and went on the stage. Much later, she also wrote her own autobiography.[10] Reading about the Jorgensen case led other people, primarily men who felt themselves to be similarly afflicted, to consider surgery. Hamburger reported that he and his colleagues received a total of 465 letters from interested individuals.[11]

There were also two very critical letters prompted by the Hamburger article in *Journal of the American Medical Association.* A New York psychiatrist, G. H. Wiedeman, criticized Hamburger for not doing a more thorough psychological workup or treating the patient with psychotherapy instead of surgery. He remarked:

It is true that reports on the treatment of transvestites are scarce in the psychoanalytic and psychiatric literature. This is due to the extreme reluctance of transvestites as well as of other sexual deviates to undergo any treatment that would remove the perversion and deprive them of their perverse gratifications. The difficulty of getting the patient into psychiatric treatment should not lead us to compliance with the patient's demands, which are based on his sexual perversion.[12]

The second letter criticized both Hamburger and his patient, arguing that the only thing that would have helped Jorgensen was "intensive, prolonged, classic psychotherapy."[13]

Changing Definitions and Terminology

Although Hamburger had called the condition "genuine transvestism" to distinguish it from other types of cross dressing, the label *transsexualism* was soon applied, and the operation came to be called sex reassignment surgery (SRS). Obviously, plastic surgery on the genital organs does not change the chromosomal sex, even though it gives the appearance of a sex change. In a paper read before the Society for the Scientific Study of Sex in 1963, Harry Benjamin indicated that for the past ten years he had been using the term *transsexualism* in his lectures to describe the phenomenon.[14] Benjamin attributed the first use of the term to David O. Cauldwell, who in 1949 had written an article for *Sexology* describing a case of "psychopathia transsexualis" in which a girl wanted to be a man.[15] Daniel G. Brown had also used the term,[16] and Hirschfeld in 1910 called one of his patients a psychic transsexual.

In explaining the term *transsexualism,* Benjamin divided male transvestites into three major types. The first groups included transvestites who led reasonably normal lives. Most of them were heterosexual men who could appease their feelings of gender role disharmony by cross dressing. They derived erotic satisfaction from cross dressing, but this might decrease over time. Though these patients might display neurotic symptoms, they were seldom seen by doctors. Their clash was with society and the law. Transvestites in the second group were more emotionally disturbed. They required psychological guidance and endocrine therapy. The third type of transvestism was identical to transsexualism. This type represented a disturbance of the normal sex and gender role orientation. The individual wanted to be a full-fledged woman and have a male sex partner, or vice versa. The condition could present as fully developed transsexualism from the beginning, or it might gradually appear after short or long periods of transvestism. However, the male transsexual was much less interested in the symbol of female attire. He wanted to be a woman and function as a woman. Transsexuals, he noted, were very often unhappy people.[17]

Benjamin had by this time seen 200 transvestites, 125 of whom he diagnosed as being transsexuals, including 108 men and seventeen women. In most patients the onset was described as being "as early as I can remember." Benjamin remained puzzled by the etiology. A moderate sexual underdevelopment was present in 30 percent of the patients, as had been the case with Christine Jorgensen, but the chromatin tests all conformed to the anatomic sex. Since the etiology of transsexualism remained puzzling, it was usually attributed to unfavorable conditioning. Benjamin found evidence of this in 21 percent of the cases, but he could identify no causal sequence for at least half of the cases. This led him to speculate about such factors as imprinting. This type of early learning is documented in young birds, whereby some baby birds bond to the first animal they see, even if it does not belong to their species. He wondered if imprinting somehow took place among humans, and that transsexual patients were imprinted with the wrong gender. Finally, he speculated about prenatal exposure to hormones. What led to this suggestion was the fact that twenty-eight out of the first ninety-one patients he had examined exhibited hypogonadism, even though he could detect no current hormonal abnormalities.[18]

Benjamin held that the administration of hormones was an important part of the management of transsexuals, with estrogen prescribed for men and androgen for women. Motivations for surgery for men included:

1. For men who love heterosexual men, the desire to be normal sex partners to them.
2. Unhappiness with their gender.
3. A marked feminine appearance.
4. Legal problems related to cross dressing.

The operation for males consisted of either castration or drawing the testicles into the abdomen, the amputation of the penis, and plastic surgery to create a vagina-like opening. Benjamin did a follow-up study of forty men, and most of the time the outcomes of the operations were satisfactory.

He reported a somewhat different pattern for the few females he had seen (the ratio at that time was six males to every female). Most of the females had been tomboys from earliest childhood. Conditioning could be identified as an etiological factor in two of the seventeen. Physical examination usually revealed a more or less distinct hypogonadism. Absence of menstruation or a very scanty menses and a late menarche were reported by nine patients. Quite consistently, the female-to-male transsexuals wanted the male role in order to marry and become husbands.

Treatment for women was with androgens (testosterone), which created male hair growth, deepening of the voice, growth of the clitoris, and sometimes acne. In addition, seven had hysterectomies, mastectomies, or both. Benjamin concluded that in the case of transsexualism, since the mind cannot be adjusted to the body, the adaptation of the body to the mind seems not only indicated but recommended.[19]

As the public became aware through the Jorgensen case and others, an increasing number of individuals sought sex reassignment surgery. One case receiving particularly wide publicity in the 1970s was Jan Morris (formerly James Morris), a British journalist who, before seeking transsexual surgery, covered Sir Edmund Hillary's successful climb of Mount Everest. Her autobiography became a best seller and further familiarized the public with the concept of transsexual surgery. In a second autobiography, published in 1991, she offers no theories for her "tangled" life, although she claims to be introspective by nature. Interestingly, her four children and her wife supported her decision to undergo sex reassignment surgery.[20]

Many of those who, like Jorgensen and Morris, wanted surgery, were referred to Harry Benjamin, who provided hormonal treatment and support while he searched for surgeons to do the sex reassignment. With support from the Erickson Foundation, a fund established by an early female-to-male transsexual, the Johns Hopkins Gender Identity Clinic was established in 1965, and the clinics' first sex reassignment surgery was performed in 1966. Soon afterward, gender identity programs were established at the University of Minnesota, Stanford University, the University of Oregon, and Case Western Reserve. Interdisciplinary teams including psychiatrists, psychologists, and surgeons were formed to diagnose and treat transsexuals.[21] These centers were very influential in the development of the scientific understanding of the concept of gender.[22] The funds from the Erickson Foundation and other grants not only provided for a psychiatrist or psychologist on the team but also furnished support for research related to transsexualism. In this same era the federal government increased its support of basic research in medical schools, and though no federal money was given for transsexual surgery, the additional funds proved important in changing the nature of research into issues related to transsexualism. For most of the twentieth century, research into gender-related issues had been only a sideline for busy psychiatrists who collected case histories and, as time provided, tried to analyze them and search for meaning. However, the new generation of researchers, financed by private or public grants, had a much better understanding of modern research methods than the earlier generations of physicians and could specialize on particular questions, such as the influence of hormones on behavior. Those scientists who became part of the new wave of gender identity teams helped bring about a better understanding not only of transsexualism but of a variety of related conditions. Several of them became important for their theoretical and empirical work in the field of gender identity.

Diagnostic Criteria

As experience with the condition accumulated, a consensus developed about the diagnosis of transsexualism focused on a long-standing preference for the role (not just the appearance) of the opposite sex. The term *gender dysphoria* was often used to indicate the extreme position held by the transsexual patients, who were found to be much more distressed by their gender identity than transvestites. In addition, the transsexuals who presented for surgery were often anxious and depressed, had attempted suicide, and reported a generally unhappy childhood.[23] Many of them believed that they already belonged to the opposite sex. Many, but not all, were homosexual in orientation when they presented for treatment, which meant that they might have seen sex reassignment surgery as a means for them to become heterosexual.[24] In some centers, in fact, a homosexual orientation was an early requirement for the surgery, but as evidence accumulated, it became clear that some changed their sexual preference after the operation and that not all transsexuals, regardless of background, became heterosexual. This requirement has since been dropped as a necessary condition.[25] The early transsexual population was made up primarily of men who wanted to become women, but the ratio has changed over time to about four men to one woman, with the Swedish data showing a ratio of one to one.[26]

In 1980 the term *transsexualism* was recognized as an illness in the third edition of the *Diagnostic and Statistical Manual of Mental Disorders.* The definition was revised and simplified in the revised third edition in 1987. The essential criteria are as follows:

A. Persistent discomfort and sense of inappropriateness about one's assigned sex.
B. Persistent preoccupation for at least two years with getting rid of one's primary and secondary sex characteristics and acquiring the sex characteristics of the other sex.
C. The person has reached puberty (before that the diagnosis of Gender Identity Disorder of Childhood is used).[27]

A subcommittee is now working on a revised definition of gender disorders, including transsexualism, for the next edition of the manual. The proposed changes are not radical, but there seems to be a movement for trying to make the definition less dependent on surgical intervention. In addition, more careful attention is being paid to appropriately defining gender dysphoria in both males and females.[28]

Because the transsexual is so often distressed with his or her current body, Lindgren and Pauly developed a thirty-item body image scale, which they found helpful in differentiating transsexuals from transvestites and homosexuals.[29] The scale measures the level of dissatisfaction with various body parts including genital organs, breasts, facial hair, and so on. After surgery there is a significant decrease in the level of dissatisfaction among transsexuals but not among homosexuals.

As the definitions have become more formalized, screening out homosexual men who want to escape the stigma of their same-sex erotic orientation has been regarded as an increasing problem for the gender identity clinics. It is a sad commentary on our society that some people feel less of a stigma about being transsexual than they do about being homosexual.[30] One reason for the exclusion, however, is that many of those trying to escape homosexual labeling were so often disappointed by the outcome of the surgery.[31] Diagnosis of transsexualism, however, is complex, and many differences remain about who is or is not transsexual. One of the major diagnostic problems stems from the active grapevine for transsexuals which coaches sex reassignment candidates on the correct responses to the questions of psychiatrists and other health care providers.[32]

Dissatisfaction among some of those who had undergone the surgery led a group of professionals in the field to establish the Harry Benjamin International Gender Dysphoria Association. The members drew up a 1979 document entitled *Standards of Care* for the hormonal and surgical reassignment of gender dysphoric persons. The standards and the principles explaining the standards are twelve pages long in mimeographed form. Excerpts (with editing to conserve space) are presented here:

1. Hormonal and/or surgical sex reassignment (SRS) on demand is contraindicated.
2. Hormonal and SRS (genital and nongenital) must be preceded by a firm recommendation for such procedures made by a psychiatrist or psychologist.
3. The psychiatrist or psychologist who makes the recommendation for SRS shall have known the patient in a psychotherapeutic relationship for at least three months.
4. A period of three months during which the patient lives full-time in the social role of the other sex shall precede hormonal therapy.
5. Six months in the other sex role should elapse before nongenital SRS (surgery to the face, hips, etc.).
6. Genital SRS shall be preceded by at least twelve months in the social role of the genetically other sex.
7. If a good case can be made for an improvement in functioning, a diagnosis of schizophrenia does not necessarily preclude SRS.
8. The recommending psychiatrist or psychologist will seek peer review for the recommendation for SRS.
9. The surgeon performing the SRS is guilty of professional misconduct if he or she does not receive written recommendations of the procedure from two behavioral scientists, at least one of whom is a psychiatrist.
10. The physician prescribing hormonal treatment must warn the patient of the potential side effects and monitor the patient with appropriate blood chemistry studies.
11. A urological examination will be done prior to SRS.
12. Fees will be reasonable.[33]

The standards at many clinics are more difficult to meet than those outlined above. The Clarke Institute in Toronto also requires the patient be physically healthy, gainfully employed, not psychotic, not mentally retarded, not married, and able to document a minimum of two years living in the opposite gender role, including one year without even hormonal treatment.[34] Some clients find the standards too strict, or they resent the long psychological workup when they want only the surgery. They argue that the gender identity clinics are paternalistic and research-minded and that the standards can be very expensive, since SRS is often not covered by insurance. Consequently, despite the efforts of the Harry Benjamin Association and other groups to set official standards, much of the SRS is done by individual surgeons rather than the university clinics.

For many years in the 1960s and 1970s the largest volume of SRS in any one place was done by Georges Burou of Casablanca in Morocco. Burou was a skilled surgeon who is credited with the development of the surgical technique for SRS on male-to-female (M–F) clients that is now used almost universally. This technique involved using penile tissue to create a functional vaginal wall. Before his innovation, attempts to create a vagina using intestines or other tissue had not been particularly successful, and many of the early male-to-female subjects went without this aspect of the surgery.[35] As of this writing the major specialist in M–F surgery is Stanley Biber, a Colorado surgeon who has done SRS for more than 2,000 clients. He does a much less elaborate workup than the gender identity centers and struggles to keep his fees reasonable. He receives many queries from potential female-to-male (F–M) patients but does SRS for them only rarely, because the technology is not yet well developed.[36] If the past is any indication, as Biber's skills develop he will do more. His reputation in the transsexual community is good, and his large volume has allowed him to develop his surgical skill.

This raises the question about who should make the decision as to whether an individual should have SRS. Is it the highly trained medical and psychological team or is it the individual? A few years ago the question would not have been asked, but the consumer movement puts a new light on the question. SRS is plastic surgery, yet in the major centers, the requirements make it seem to be much more. Is it the mystical power of the sex organs, with all of their magical and religious connotations, that make the decision so fraught with meaning that plastic surgery for a face does not have? In addition, the elaborate rules of the treatment centers are always based on the knowledge and assumptions of the time; for example, the early rule that patients must present as homosexuals was based on an assumption that the same sexual orientation would remain after surgery (and thus the individual would magically become heterosexual). This assumption was false. There are male-to-female transsexuals who originally presented as homosexuals and are now lesbians; and there are lesbian female-to-male transsexuals who are now homosexual men.

Treatment

The comprehensive workup done at the gender identity clinics begins with careful observations, interviews, and psychological testing. If the diagnosis is transsexualism, the testing phase is followed by a period of living in the opposite gender. There is widespread agreement that this trial period may be the most important evaluative process, since it allows the clients to see the real advantages and disadvantages of the role they seek.[37] They can see that changing sex roles does not solve many of life's problems, and sometimes the new role has disadvantages that may not have been obvious. For example, some M–F transsexuals are unaware of the wage discrimination they will encounter if they become women. A test of living in the opposite gender role for at least one year is considered crucial, and two years is better. Testosterone is given to F–M patients, and estrogen and progesterone are given to M–F patients.[38]

The surgery for M–F transsexuals includes a bilateral orchiectomy (excision of the testicles) and, following the Burou technique, an inversion of the penis to form a vagina. Breast augmentation is usually performed. Sometimes other surgery is done to change the size of the nose, shave the larynx, or otherwise change the body contour. SRS for F–M clients is more complex and involves a series of operations by which the ovaries, Fallopian tubes, uterus, and breast tissue are removed. Some F–M patients stop at this point and do not have a penis constructed because the techniques for phalloplasty have not yet been perfected. However, a recent improvement involves augmentation of the clitoris. Sometimes skin is grafted from the arm or some other part of the body to form a penis that can be permanently stiffened by using bone tissue. It is not yet possible to construct a penis with which the F–M can both urinate and engage in sexual activities. Many F–M clients are content to use a prosthesis that can be fitted into the vagina much like a tampon.[39]

Evaluation of Outcomes

In 1979 the Johns Hopkins hospital announced that it was discontinuing SRS, and although there were probably a variety of reasons for this decision, a study done by the head of the clinic, Jon Meyer, was given as the official reason.[40] He reported that in 1971 a follow-up study had been begun on one hundred transsexual patients: thirty-four who had been operated on and sixty-six who had not. All had applied to the Gender Identity Clinic and been evaluated. Twenty-four had SRS at Johns Hopkins, and ten went elsewhere. The sixty-six remaining patients were initially evaluated but either changed their minds or were turned down for surgery. Some had gone through trial periods living in the role before surgery, and some had not. Only 50 percent of the sample could be located for the follow-up study, mostly those who had the surgery. The fact that so many could not be located, however, does not mean that they did not have the surgery. They might have had it done elsewhere and intentionally cut their ties with Johns Hopkins. One M–F patient who had difficulty with a poorly constructed phallus asked to have it removed but did not ask for any other changes. No other operative patient indicated they wanted to have their surgery undone. However, a scale of adjustment was constructed that measured frequency of address change, job and educational level, marriage adjustment, and frequency of psychiatric contact. The operative patients did not score significantly better on the scale than the unoperated patients who had gone through a variety of experiences including psychotherapy, hormonal treatment, cross-living, or none of the above. On the strength of these findings, the author concluded that SRS offered no advantages.[41]

Though it is clear that Meyer's research was fraught with so many methodological flaws (including self-selected samples, no real measure of adjustment, and poor response rates), that many peer review journals would have rejected it, it did receive publication in part because there had been so few long-term follow-up studies.[42] One rare exception to flawed studies such as Meyer's was the work of Ira Pauly, who in 1968 reported a generally favorable outcome from SRS according to available data.[43] In 1981, after the Meyer report, Pauly again reviewed the literature covering follow-up studies on transsexualism and still found generally favorable results. Of the 283 male-to-female patients reported, he found that the results were reported as satisfactory for 71 percent of the sample, uncertain for 18 percent, and unsatisfactory for 8 percent; 2 percent had committed suicide. Among the eighty-three female-to-male patients, the satisfactory rate was 81 percent, while 13 percent were uncertain, and 5 percent reported dissatisfaction (percentages are rounded off). There were no suicides among the F–M group.[44]

In 1981, B. Lundström and his colleagues reviewed Pauly's work, added cases located by Lundström, and concluded that an unsatisfactory result occurs in 10 to 15 percent of the SRS patients. Increasing age and social instability were correlated with unsatisfactory results. Secondary transsexuals (patients who wanted surgery because they were homosexual) had a higher frequency of unsatisfactory results.[45] Lundström and his group commented:

We conclude that sex reassignment surgery is the treatment of choice for carefully evaluated, genuine, primary transsexuals. SRS should not be offered [to] patients with secondary gender dysphoria, those with unstable past histories, and patients over the age of 35. It is clear that the decision to offer SRS does not negate the clear indication for supportive psychotherapy before and after SRS.[46]

In 1986 Gunnar Lindemalm presented data on a smaller number of M–F clients (thirteen) but the study covered long years of follow-up— six to twenty-five years (median of twelve years). Clients were followed by the staff of the psychiatric clinic at the Karolinski Hospital in Stockholm. Surgical outcomes were generally disappointing, with only one-third of the patients reporting a functioning vagina. (Apparently, the technique developed by Burou was not used until later in Sweden). The overall sexual adjustment was about the same after surgery as before. Despite surgery and hormonal treatment, most retained their libido. Psychosocial adjustment showed a slight improvement after surgery. One patient requested a reversal and went back to living as a man before any attempt had been made to construct a vagina. Another three people were judged as showing varying degrees of repentance by the researchers. The study team emphasized the fact that they did not allow the doctor who had endorsed the study in the first place to do the follow-up or judge the level of repentance. They considered the practice of using the same behavioral scientist a biasing factor in some studies. However, it is interesting to note that the repentant people were considered reasonably well adjusted.[47]

An evaluation of SRS was requested by the Netherlands Gender Center Foundation to see whether the surgery that had been done in the Netherlands was effective in terms of alleviating or removing the gender dysphoria that had motivated patients to seek the procedure. A study of thirty-six female-to-male transsexuals and 105 male-to-female transsexuals was done by Bram Kuiper and Peggy Cohen-Kettenis using detailed interviews. The majority of the persons interviewed reported being happy or very happy, and if they did report feelings of dysphoria, it was not related to their gender identity. This contrasted significantly with their sense of unhappiness before the surgery. Detailed data about suicide attempts were gathered from twenty-one F–Ms and seventy-two M–Fs, with 19 percent of the F–Ms and 24 percent of the M–Fs reporting suicide attempts before treatment started and only two suicide attempts in each group after treatment started. Given the depth of unhappiness suggested by the suicide data, the authors found the current level of happiness impressive. However, the authors offered a note of caution; they pointed out that it is possible that when SRS is initiated, the level of commitment it demands is very significant, thus people would tend to try to reduce the level of cognitive dissonance rather than admit that their efforts were all in vain.[48]

In 1990 Richard Green and Davis Fleming reviewed eleven follow-up studies published between 1979 and 1989; included were 130 reassignments from female to male and 220 reassignments from male to female. The findings were consistent with the earlier composite reviews. Reassignment from female to male was reported as satisfactory 97 percent of the time, with 3 percent reported as unsatisfactory. More problems emerged with the M–F reassignments, with 87 percent having a satisfactory outcome and 13 percent unsatisfactory. The criteria for a satisfactory outcome varied widely, but not regretting the decision to have surgery seemed to be a criterion shared by the various researchers.[49]

These various studies emphasize that the authorities within the gender identity and gender dysphoria field evaluate SRS favorably but cautiously. Criticism from the outside, however, has been more strident and has come from a variety of vantage points. The first group to mount an attack were psychoanalysts who remained with the Freudian tradition. The two letters to the editors of the *Journal of the American Medical Association* published in 1953 were from traditional analysts. One of those letters was from Mortimer Ostrow, who in 1974 published a report on the research activities of a group of eight analysts who met every month over the years to share their experiences working with clients. They did not recognize transsexualism, but defined transvestism as a perversion caused by early childhood experiences that resulted in anxiety—primarily castration anxiety—and which could be treated only by psychoanalysis.[50] Other psychoanalysts who attacked the idea of SRS included Joost A. M. Meerloo, who thought that the patients were usually transvestites who, for some neurotic or psychotic reason, wanted a change of sex status and that the physicians who participated in the SRS process were collaborating with the patients' psychoses.[51] Similarly, Charles Socarides, in a report based on one "transsexual" patient, held that transsexuals were homosexuals who recast their identity in order to alleviate their guilt and to ward off their paranoiac psychosis.

While these criticisms may well have been at least partly valid, they are tainted with self-interest. SRS was a much-publicized alternate treatment modality that caused the psychiatrists to lose their monopoly over a segment of the client population. More troublesome is the anger expressed by the traditional psychiatrists toward the clients, which was even greater than what they vented at the surgeons. Since they put the would-be transsexual clients down with words such as *perversion* and called them "deviants" or "psychotics," it is not surprising that clients sought the new alternative. As time passed, the criticism from the psychiatric community decreased. This may be because the field of psychiatry broadened to include other approaches to therapy or the die-hard Freudians either died or rethought their earlier opposition. Recent criticism of SRS is from a different perspective.

An article by Dwight Billings and Thomas Urban in *Social Forces* argued that transsexualism was not a diagnosis that exists for an objective illness; rather, it was a socially constructed problem created by the medical establishment. They accused physicians of inventing the idea and the Erickson Foundation of selling it:

Transsexual therapy, legitimated by the terminology of disease, pushes patients toward an alluring world of artificial vaginas and penises rather than toward self-understanding and sexual politics. Sexual fulfillment and gender-role comfort are portrayed as commodities available through medicine.[53]

Many feminists support this same line of thinking. Using the work of Michel Foucault as starting point, they argue that even the more established definition of persons in terms of sexual orientation (homosexual or heterosexual) was an eighteenth- and nineteenth-century development.[54] Transsexualism is clearly a more recent, twentieth-century development, and its origins as a social construct seems even more obvious. Janice G. Raymond pointed out that SRS was an invention of the medical-psychiatric complex, which developed a surgical approach to a moral and political issue. This avoidance of the real issues helped reinforce the current sex stereotypes. She believes that, instead of operating on people who want to live a less stereotyped sex role, we should support their right to broaden their horizons.[55] Holly Devor argues that gender roles are themselves social constructs. She located and interviewed fifteen women who had lived at least part of their lives as men, yet only three had considered SRS and none of them had gone through with it. She calls this process of living a partial male role "gender-blending." Devor perceives the current norms of gender as paternalistic and discriminatory and argues that gender-blending is a strategy women can use to get some of the advantages ordinarily reserved for men.[56] Other feminists have noted that since M–F transsexuals seem to use the most conservative females as models, SRS does not create allies to the women's movement.[57] The ethnographic study by Anne Bolin carefully documents the difficult paths trod by her subjects as they went through the SRS process. Her definition of SRS as a rite of passage is thought-provoking, suggesting that society should be able to devise a less traumatic ritual to allow the change.[58]

There is also criticism of SRS from clients or would-be clients who would like to see more thoughtful treatment from health care providers rather than abolishment of treatment. In an unpublished paper, Dallas Denny criticized the university-affiliated gender clinics for failing to be patient-oriented, pointing out that since none of them could handle the large numbers of patients who came to them after 1965, they tended to choose the people they wanted for research. This was distressing to potential patients, and it probably distorted the research. Denny summarizes this problem as follows:

The clinics viewed sex reassignment as a last-ditch effort to save those with whom other therapies and interventions had failed. Those who were accepted for treatment were usually prostitutes, those with substance abuse problems, sociopaths, those who were schizophrenic, those who were profoundly depressed or suicidal, and others who were considered "hopeless"—i.e., likely to die anyway. It was a classic misapplication of the triage method, with those most likely to benefit from the intervention being turned away, and the terminal cases receiving treatment.[59]

Denny has now established a support group that is independent of the medical establishment: The Atlanta Educational Gender Information Service (AEGIS). In a recent document published by AEGIS, Denny reviews the transsexual process with all its attendant difficulties, so people who think they want the surgery realize the many problems involved in changing sex. Denny points out that another reasonable alternative to sex change surgery for the transgendered individual is to simply cross dress and live permanently in the opposite sex role. Others have advocated this in the past, but generally the law and the courts were more hostile to men cross dressing than women. Still the idea may gain followers and grow more influential if it becomes legally possible for men to do what women so often have done.[60]

Causes of Transsexualism

The struggle of the professional therapeutic community to find causality for a cross-gendered identity has been a long and difficult one, but progress has been made in the twentieth century. An early focus of research was to try to decide whether the cause was physiological or psychological—nature or nurture. Albert Ellis addressed this issue in 1945. He searched through the literature and found 84 persons who were either true hermaphrodites (persons with the sex organs of both sexes) or pseudohermaphrodites (persons with partial sets of one or both sex organs). Thirty-nine had been assigned as babies to the male sex and forty-five to the female sex. When the group raised as boys grew up, 87 percent were attracted to females; 73 percent of the group raised as girls were erotically attracted to males. However, even more interesting was the fact that all but two of the eighty-four stayed in the sex roles they had been assigned. These findings, he held, supported the proposition that erotic orientation depends more on sex assignment and rearing than on the gonads.[61]

Later, John Money and his colleagues were able to do a similar study with patients instead of just their records. Money, Joan Hampson, and John Hampson studied 105 hermaphrodites. They dropped the distinction between pseudohermaphrodites and hermaphrodites because the errors in sexual differentiation were considered too complex to fit these two categories. They used five biological determinants of sex: (1) chromosomal sex, (2) gonadal sex, (3) hormonal sex, (4) internal accessory reproductive structures, and (5) external genitalia. There were thirty individuals with a sex assignment that differed from one of the five biological determinants. Only five members of the sample had a gender role identity or an erotic orientation that was different from their assigned sex.[62] They concluded that psychosexuality was neutral at birth and determined almost entirely by socialization. They identified the critical period for the development of gender identity as before twenty-seven months of age.

Money's work on gender identity continued for more than four decades. He saw patients who had presented themselves for possible SRS, but he concentrated much of his research on children who had been born with ambiguous genitalia. He argued that it was important to differentiate between gender identity—which is the individual's subjective awareness of an identity as male, female, or ambivalent— and sexual orientation—which determines whether one is erotically aroused by persons of one's own sex, the opposite sex, or both. This conceptual differentiation had certainly been lacking in many earlier works by writers who focused on transvestism, often clustering or confusing transvestism with homosexuality. Using Money's format, a transvestite can be either heterosexual, homosexual, bisexual, or asexual. A heterosexual man or woman can be masculine, feminine, or ambivalent about gender identity.[63]

Data were gathered from further longitudinal studies of clients seen in the psychohormonal research unit at Johns Hopkins for the 1972 book *Man & Woman, Boy & Girl,* which Money wrote with Anke A. Ehrhardt. The authors explain that the dimorphic separation of males and females into just two sexes is an oversimplification, as we have pointed out throughout this book. Biological gender is sometimes ambiguous, and the systems controlling gender differentiation can break down in a variety of ways. For example, instead of the normal configuration of either XX chromosomes (producing a female) or XY (producing a male), other patterns may occur: An XXY or XXXY pattern, results in Klinefelter's syndrome, in which the reproductive system looks male but the testes are infertile. In Turner's syndrome, there is an abnormality of one of the X chromosomes, and other abnormal chromosomal patterns result in hermaphroditism.

After conception, ambiguous genitalia can also be produced by abnormal hormonal stimulation of the growing embryo. The sex organs start their development from common tissue, and if no further differentiation takes place, the infant will be female. However, male infants are further influenced by the hormones produced by the developing testes, which produce two hormones: the müllerian-inhibiting substance (which suppresses the development of a uterus, fallopian tubes, and upper vagina) and testosterone (which stimulates the development of the male genitalia). Failure of either of these hormones results in female or ambiguous genitalia. A female fetus can develop ambiguous genitalia if there is overstimulation of the adrenal gland during prenatal life. Interacting with the hormones are neural pathways that influence gender and role identity.

After birth, the physiological factors interact with the environment, further shaping gender identity. The authors believe that learning itself has a physiological component, because what is learned is stored in the brain. Socialization of the child into a girl or a boy starts at birth and continues to influence her or him throughout life. Money and Ehrhardt cite cases in which children with ambiguous genitalia were assigned the wrong sex, yet their socialization turned them into functioning men or women. Matched pairs of chromosomal females with adrenal genital syndrome, which causes masculinization, were followed. In each of these pairs one of the two had surgical reassignment to a boy, and one was treated with cortisone to suppress the androgen produced by the adrenal glands so that the child became a normal girl. The children who looked like boys had enlarged clitorises that resembled penises, and they functioned as boys. Money and Ehrhardt argued that if the decision was made early enough, and providing it was unambiguous enough, socialization rather than chromosomal sex would be the key variable in determining gender identity. This implied that nurture was stronger than nature in determining gender identity. The authors explained that many problems with the adjustment of children with ambiguous genitalia stemmed from the unclear message parents received from the health professionals; such parents did not clearly socialize the child as girl or boy.[64]

As Money continued his research, he found that gender identity and gender roles were even more complex than had originally been conceptualized—and even more so than he earlier had believed. His 1991 work, which compares the biographies of paired persons with various types of hermaphroditism reared in different sex roles, clearly illustrates the fact that there are no simple answers; gender dysphoria is undoubtedly related to a complex causal sequence involving multiple physiological and psychological variables.[65]

Another researcher interested in transsexualism, Robert Stoller, started studying the phenomenon at the University of California at Los Angeles in 1962. He indicated that he could find no evidence that there was any genetic, constitutional, or biochemical abnormality in transvestites or in most transsexuals. During the first ten years of these studies, he saw three young boys whom he diagnosed as childhood transsexuals. All were brought for psychiatric evaluation between the ages of four and five because they insisted that they were, in fact, girls. They followed their mothers around, played with girls, cross dressed, and had feminine gestures. Stoller described the mothers as "neuter" in their appearance and demeanor. They had been boyish young women, and all were unhappy with their marriages. The fathers were busy with their own lives and not attentive to the children, so the boys lacked male role models. Stoller argued that:

In each case the essential psychodynamic process seems to be excessive identification with their mothers, caused by the inability of these mothers to permit their sons to separate from their mothers' bodies. . . . In many essential ways, they treat the infant as if he were a part of their own body and therefore part of their own identity. The most fundamental way these mothers produce this blurring of identity is by literally keeping the child up against their bodies for far more hours of the day and night than occurs in normal mother-infant relationships.[66]

Stoller differentiated the causal sequence for transsexual and transvestite boys, claiming that transsexualism was the result of a mother-infant symbiosis wherein the father was either psychologically or physically absent. Transvestism, he claimed, was caused by a hateful mother who blackmailed her son and did not allow him to develop a separate identity. The mother's actions caused a castration anxiety, which in turn led to transvestism and effeminate homosexuality.[67]

This psychiatric approach was countered by research supporting a physiological causality for gender dysphoria.[68] Milton Diamond made a comprehensive review of the literature on the topic of gender identity and sexual orientation and argued that there was less malleability than the nurture theorists had indicated. The animal research studies he reviewed clearly pointed to a primacy of physiological forces governing both gender and sexual orientation, thus Diamond questioned whether we were so far removed from animals that we were born without any sexual programming.[69] He was fascinated by the twin studies of homosexual men done by Franz Kallman which suggested a somatic influence on sexual orientation.

Kallman's study involved eighty-five sets of twins wherein one subject was homosexual; forty-five of the twins were dizygotic (derived from two eggs) and forty pairs of twins were monozygotic (derived from one egg) twins. Among the dizygotic twins the concordance for homosexuality was 11.5 percent to 42 percent, depending on whether they were completely homosexual or had experienced only one homosexual encounter. However, among the monozygotic twins, the forty pairs did not include a single co-twin of an overtly homosexual man who did not score at least midway on the Kinsey scale of sexual orientation. There was total concordance.[70]

The idea that socialization can produce a permanent gender identity was also challenged by later findings. In 1974 Julianne Imperato-McGinley and her colleagues reported a previously unrecognized type of pseudohermaphroditism caused by a deficiency of the enzyme 5-alpha reductase. This enzyme is needed in the prenatal period to convert testosterone into a stronger androgen, dihydrotestosterone, the hormone responsible for differentiation of the urogenital sinus and the urogenital tubercle. Consequently, the male child who lacks this enzyme has testes but does not have normal external genitalia.[71] The researchers located thirty-three persons with this type of pseudohermaphroditism in the village of Salinas in the Dominican Republic. Before the disorder became obvious in the community, these children were labeled girls at birth, but as the townspeople came to understand the phenomenon, they labeled them "penis at 12" children. At birth, the testes looked like an inguinal or labial mass and the penis looked like a clitoris. At puberty their voices deepened and their phalluses enlarged and became sexually functional. A study of the original thirty-three persons indicated that nineteen had been raised as girls, and data could be located for eighteen of them. They were described as living as girls until puberty, at which point their bodies began to change in the masculine direction. A male gender identity developed for all but two of the eighteen. One changed his gender identity and thought of himself as a man but remained in a female work role. Erotically, he behaved and felt like a man. Another retained both the gender identity and role of a woman.[72] The fact that so many of these individuals were able to set aside their sex of rearing made for uncertainty over any firm belief in sex neutrality at birth.

Another important researcher of the transsexual phenomenon was Richard Green, who did a longitudinal study of boys who acted feminine. Early in his career as a psychiatrist, Green spent time both at the Harry Benjamin Clinic in New York and at the University of California at Los Angeles Gender Identity Research and Treatment Clinic, where he interviewed people who requested transsexual surgery. These histories clearly indicated that the cross-gender identity had developed at a very young age (in the preschool years). It was marked by cross dressing and other feminine behavior among boys or a tomboy life-style among girls. Many of the people he saw indicated that they had always known they belonged to the opposite sex.

Although Green found this to be a useful experience, he criticized the reliability of the case histories, because people sometimes forgot or even wholly reconstructed their histories. In addition, the relationship of the psychiatrist to the patient seeking transsexual surgery was compromised for research purposes, since the psychiatrist also served as "gatekeeper" to sexual reassignment surgery. The clients knew the psychiatrist was the gatekeeper, and the grapevine in the transsexual community alerted people to the types of scenarios that were approved for surgery and those that resulted in the surgery being denied.

Green thus decided that he would do a longitudinal study of a population of children who appeared to be at risk for a transsexual adult life.[73] *The Sissy Boy Syndrome and the Development of Homosexuality* reported a fifteen-year follow-up of a sample of fifty "feminine" boys who exhibited a high degree of cross-gender behavior, as illustrated by cross dressing, playing with dolls, using cosmetics, female role playing, feminine gestures, and assertions of wanting to be a girl. These boys were matched with a control group of fifty boys of comparable age, ethnicity, and parental education. Both groups were studied using parental questionnaires and interviews, interviews with the boys, psychological testing, and observations of playroom activity.

Some stereotypically female behavior was found in the control group, but in none of the control subjects was it the dominant mode of play and relationship. Control group boys occasionally played with dolls or even cross dressed, but none of them did it frequently. Some of the control group boys did not like sports or rough-and-tumble play. The follow-up studies included interviews, questionnaires, and psychological tests, usually at yearly intervals.[74]

The major finding of the study to date is that "feminine boys" are more likely to mature into homosexual or bisexual men than are most boys. Green was able to locate two-thirds of the two samples to interview them as adolescents or young adults. Three-fourths of the feminine boys were homosexual or bisexual, as measured by their sexual fantasies and/or behavior. One of the control group men was homosexual. Only one member of the feminine group was considering transsexual surgery, but from the interview data reported in the book, he sounded somewhat ambivalent about the idea. He would clearly like to be a woman but was not at all sure he would want to go through the difficulties related to sex reassignment surgery.[75]

A set of identical twins was included in the study. The firstborn, named Frank after his father, grew up very masculine; he played ball with his father and used his father as a model. The other child, Paul, underwent a serious childhood illness and spent more time with his mother because of hospital and doctor visits; he tended to follow her around and to play with dolls and girls. The twins were studied because Paul, the feminine child, was considered problematic. As adults neither of them cross dressed but both were bisexual. Paul married a woman and visited a male lover from time to time. The more masculine man had sex with both men and women but was ashamed of his homosexual liaisons; he was a hustler and once was arrested for prostitution. Green sees these twins as the microcosm of his study. Their socialization made them different, with Paul being ultrafeminine and Frank being macho, but heredity entered the picture and both became bisexual.[76]

Green reported that no members of the sample became transvestites. These findings certainly suggest that not every feminine boy grows up to cross dress, but they do not tell us much about the genesis of either transvestism or transsexualism. The fact that so many of them became homosexual is fascinating, since the sample was supposedly chosen to include boys who were at risk for transsexual behavior. Green does not speculate very much about this aspect of his findings. The book is written as if he had been trying to find the genesis of homosexual behavior. Green carefully tested Stoller's assertions that mothers who spent too much time holding their boys may have made them feminine, but Green's data did not support this hypothesis. He was able to show that the feminine boys spent less time with their fathers, but it is not clear whether this was a cause or a consequence of their feminine behavior.

Summary

Sex reassignment surgery was popularized after Christine Jorgensen made her surgery public in 1952. The availability of surgery as a treatment possibility caused the medical and scientific communities to rethink the diagnosis of transvestism and distinguish people who wanted both to live in the role of the opposite sex and to have different genitalia. In the early days of the transsexual movement, most of those persons wishing to do so sought SRS, even though the technical problems related to the surgery had not yet been solved. The technique for male-to-female surgery has now been perfected, although the surgery for female-to-male is less well developed. Still, there are a growing number of people who can be called transsexuals (because they want to change their gender role) who have decided to cross dress and live their preferred role full-time with the help of hormonal therapy but without surgery.

An important consequence of the transsexual movement was the interest it sparked in studies of gender identity and sexual orientation. That research has not yet given us definite answers about the source of gender identity or sexual orientation, but our understanding is growing. We can now safely say that both gender identity and sexual orientation are the result of a combination of nature and nurture.

Notes

1. Christian Hamburger, George K. Sturup, and E. Dahl-Iversen, "Transvestism: Hormonal, Psychiatric, and Surgical Treatment," *Journal of the American Medical Association* 152 (30 May 1953): 391–96.

2. Danish Sterilization and Castration Act No. 176, 11 May 1935, and the earlier Danish Sterilization Act No. 130, 1 June 1929. There were similar laws in Norway, Sweden, Holland, and certain parts of Switzerland. Citation is from Hamburger et al., "Transvestism," 393.

3. Ibid.

4. Niels Hoyer, *Man into Woman* (New York: E. P. Dutton and Co., 1933).

5. Hans Houstein, "Transvestism and the State at the End of the Eighteenth and Nineteenth Centuries," *Zeitschrift für sexual Wissenschaft* 15 (1928–29): 353.

6. Roberta Cowell, *Roberta Cowell's Story* (Melbourne: William Heinemann, 1954).

7. For example, the *Zeitschrift für sexual Wissenschaft* 16 (1929–30): 145, reports the case of Toni Claus Hans F. den Antrag, who attempted to change his birth record from male to female. His application was denied, although he wore female clothing, looked completely feminine, and thought of himself as a female even though he had male genitalia.

8. Liz Hodgkinson, *Michael, née Laura* (London: Columbus Books, 1989).

9. Jonathan Ned Katz, *Gay/Lesbian Almanac* (New York: Harper and Row, 1983), 516–22.

10. Christine Jorgensen, *A Personal Autobiography* (New York: Paul S. Eriksson, 1967).

11. C. Hamburger, "Desire for Change of Sex as Shown by Personal Letters from 465 Men and Women," *Acta Endocrinolica* 14 (1953): 361–75.

12. George Wiedeman, [Letters], "Transvestism," *Journal of the American Medical Association* 152 (16, 1953): 1553.

13. Mortimer Ostow, [Letters], "Transvestism," *Journal of the American Medical Association* 152 (16, 1953): 1167.

14. Harry Benjamin, "Clinical Aspects of Transsexualism in the Male and Female," *American Journal of Psychotherapy* 18 (July 1964): 458–69.

15. David O. Cauldwell, "Psychopathia Transsexualis," *Sexology* 16 (December 1949): 274–80; Cauldwell developed the term further in two booklets: *Questions and Answers on the Sex Life and Sexual Problems of Trans-Sexuals* (Girard, KS: Haldeman-Julius Publications, 1950), 3, and *Sex Transmutation—Can One's Sex be Changed?* (Girard, KS: Haldeman-Julius Publications, 1961).

16. Daniel G. Brown, "Inversion and Homosexuality," *American Journal of Orthopsychiatry* 28 (April 1958): 424–29.

17. Harry Benjamin, *The Transsexual Phenomenon* (New York: The Julian Press, 1966).

18. Harry Benjamin, "Nature and Management of Transsexualism," *Western Journal of Obstetrics and Gynecology* 72 (March–April 1964), 105–11.

19. Ibid.

20. Jan Morris, *Conundrum* (New York: Harcourt Brace Jovanovich, 1974). Morris reexamined her decision in a second autobiography, *Pleasures of a Tangled Life* (New York, 1991).

21. Ira B. Pauly, "Gender Identity Disorders," in *Human Sexuality; Psychosexual Effects of Disease,* ed. Martin Farber (New York: Macmillan, 1985), 295–316.

22. Ira B. Pauly and Milton T. Edgerton, "The Gender Identity Movement: A Growing Surgical-Psychiatric Liaison," *Archives of Sexual Behavior* 15 (1986): 315–26.

23. Leonard Derogatis, Jon K. Meyer, and Noella Vazquez, "A Psychological Profile of the Transsexual" *Journal of Nervous and Mental Disease* 166 (1978): 234–54; Donald S. Strassberg, Howard Roback, Jean Cunningham, Embry McKee, and Paul Larson, "Psychopathology in Self-Identified Female-to-Male Transsexuals, Homosexuals, and Heterosexuals," *Archives of Sexual Behavior* 8 (1979): 491–96; Byron Stinson, "A Study of Twelve Applicants for Transsexual Surgery," *The Ohio State Medical Journal* 68 (1972): 245–49; N. Uddenberg, J. Wålinder, and T. Höjerback, "Parental Contact in Male and Female Transsexuals," *Psychiatrica Scandavia* 60 (1979): 113–20.

24. Kurt Freund, Betty W. Steiner, and Samuel Chan, "Two Types of Cross-Gender Identity," *Archives of Sexual Behavior* 11 (1982): 49–63.

25. Ibid.; see also Betty W. Steiner, "The Management of Patients with Gender Disorders," in *Gender Dysphoria: Development, Research, and Management,* ed. Betty W. Steiner (New York: Plenum Press, 1985), 325–50; Peter M. Bentler, "A Typology of Transsexualism: Gender Identity Theory and Data," *Archives of Sexual Behavior* 5 (1976): 567–84.

26. Elizabeth A. McCauley and Anke A. Ehrhardt, "Role Expectations and Definitions: A Comparison of Female Transsexuals and Lesbians," *Journal of Homosexuality* 3 (Winter 1977–78): 137–46; Ira B. Pauly, "Gender Identity Disorders," in *Human Sexuality: Psychosexual Effects of Disease,* ed. Martin Farber, 295–316; J. Wålinder, B. Lundstrom, M. Ross, and I. Thuwe, "Transsexualism, Incidence, Prevalence and Sex Ratio: Comments on Three Different Studies," *Proceedings of the Sixth International Gender Dysphoria Association* (Coronado, CA: 1979), cited by Pauly and Edgerton, "Gender Identity Movement."

27. American Psychiatric Association, "Diagnostic Criteria for 302.50, Transsexualism" in *Diagnostic and Statistical Manual of Mental Disorders,* revised 3d ed. (Washington DC: American Psychiatric Association, 1987), 76.

28. Susan J. Bradley, Ray Blanchard, Susan Coates, Richard Green, Stephen B. Levine, Heino F. L. Meyer-Bahlburg, Ira B. Pauly, and Kenneth J. Zucker, "Interim Report of the DSM-IV Subcommittee on Gender Identity Disorders," *Archives of Sexual Behavior* 20 (1991): 333–43.

29. T. Lindgren and I. Pauly, "A Body Image Scale for Evaluating Transsexuals," *Archives of Sexual Behavior* 4 (1975): 639–56; Ira B. Pauly and Thomas W. Lindgren "Body Image and Gender Identity," *Journal of Homosexuality* 2 (Winter 1976–77): 133–42.

30. Michael W. Ross, Lesley J. Rogers, and Helen McCulloch, "Stigma, Sex and Society: A New Look at Gender Differentiation and Sexual Variation," *Journal of Homosexuality* 3 (Summer 1978): 315–30.

31. Ray Blanchard, "Gender Dysphoria and Gender Reorientation," in *Gender Dysphoria: Development, Research, and Management*, 365–92.

32. Dwight Billings and Thomas Urban, "The Socio-Medical Construction of Transsexualism: An Interpretation and Critique," *Social Problems* 29, no. 3 (1982): 266–82; Ray Blanchard, "Gender Dysphoria and Gender Reorientation," 365–92.

33. Paul A. Walker (Chairperson), Jack C. Berger, Richard Green, Donald R. Laub, Charles L. Reynolds, Jr., Leo Wollman, *Standards of Care: The Hormonal and Surgical Sex Reassignment of Gender Dysphoric Persons* (Galveston TX: The Janus Information Facility, The University of Texas Medical Branch, 1979).

34. Betty W. Steiner, "The Management of Patients with Gender Disorders," *Gender Dysphoria: Development, Research, and Management*, 325–50; Ray Blanchard and Betty Steiner, eds., *Clinical Management of Gender Identity Disorders in Children and Adults* (Washington, DC: American Psychiatric Association Press, 1990).

35. Betty W. Steiner, "The Management of Patients with Gender Disorders," 336.

36. Wendi Pierce, "Interview with Dr. Biber," *Rites of Passage: A Magazine for Female-to-Male Transsexuals and Cross Dressers* 1 (December 1989): 7.

37. John Money, "Sex Reassignment as Related to Hermaphroditism and Transsexualism," in *Transsexualism and Sex Reassignment*, ed. John Money and Richard Green (Baltimore: Johns Hopkins Press, 1969).

38. Ibid.

39. Dallas Denny, "Female-to-Male Reassignment Surgery in the 90's," *Our Sorority* (June 1991): 42–44.

40. Bill Stall, "Sex Change Surgery Value Questioned," *Los Angeles Times* (16 August 1979), 20.

41. Jon Meyer, "Sex Reassignment," *Archives of General Psychiatry* 36 (August 1979), 1010–15.

42. M. Fleming, C. Steinman, and G. Bocknek, "Methodological Problems in Assessing Sex Reassignment Surgery: A Reply to Meyer and Reter," *Archives of Sexual Behavior* 9 (1980): 451–56; Richard F. Docter, *Transvestites and Transsexuals* (New York: Plenum Press, 1988), 69; John Money, *Biographies of Gender and Hermaphroditism in Paired Comparisons: Clinical Supplement to the Handbook of Sexology* (New York: Elsevier, 1991), 10.

43. Ira Pauly, "The Current Status of the Change of Sex Operation," *Journal of Nervous and Mental Disease* 147 (1968): 460–71.

44. Ira Pauly, "Outcome of Sex Reassignment Surgery for Transsexuals," *Australian and New Zealand Journal of Psychiatry* 15 (1981): 5–51. The data were

based upon eleven studies involving male-to-female patients and eight studies for female-to-male.

45. B. Lundström, I. Pauly, and J. Wålinder, "Outcome of Sex Reassignment Surgery," *Acta Psychiatrica Scandinavia* 70 (1984): 289–94.

46. Ibid.

47. Gunnar Lindemalm, Dag Korlin, and Nils Uddenberg, "Long-Term Follow-Up of 'Sex-Change' in Thirteen Male-to-Female Transsexuals," *Archives of Sexual Behavior* 15 (1986): 187–210.

48. Bram Kuiper and Peggy Cohen-Kettenis, "Sex Reassignment Surgery: A Study of 141 Dutch Transsexuals," *Archives of Sexual Behavior* 17 (1988): 439–57.

49. Richard Green and Davis T. Fleming, "Transsexual Surgery Follow-Up; Status in the 1990s," *Annual Review of Sex Research* 1 (1990): 163–74.

50. Mortimer Ostrow, *Sexual Deviation: Psychoanalytic Insights* (New York: Quadrangle, 1974).

51. Joost A. M. Meerloo, "Change of Sex and Collaboration with the Psychosis," *American Journal of Psychiatry* 124 (August 1976): 263–64.

52. Charles Socarides, "A Psychoanalytic Study of the Desire for the Sexual Transformation ('Transsexualism'): The Plaster-of-Paris Man," *International Journal of Psycho-Analysis* 51 (1970): 341–49.

53. Billings and Urban, "The Social-Medical Construction of Transsexualism," 276.

54. Michel Foucault, *The History of Sexuality*, trans. Robert Hurley (New York: Pantheon Books, 1978).

55. Janice G. Raymond, *The Transsexual Empire: The Making of the She-Male* (Boston: Beacon Press, 1979).

56. Holly Devor, *Gender Blending: Confronting the Limits of Duality* (Bloomington, IN: Indiana University Press, 1989).

57. Nora Ephron, "Conundrum" in *Crazy Salad: Some Things About Women* (New York: Bantam, 1976), 203.

58. Anne Bolin, *In Search of Eve* (South Hadley, MA: Bergin and Garvey, 1988).

59. Dallas Denny, "The Politics of Diagnosis and a Diagnosis of Politics: The University-Affiliated Gender Clinics, and How They Failed to Meet the Needs of Transsexual People," unpublished paper, 1991.

60. Dallas Denny, *Deciding What To Do About Your Gender Dysphoria: Some Considerations For Those Who Are Thinking About Sex Reassignment* (Decatur, GA: The Atlanta Educational Gender Information Service, 1990). The address for AEGIS is P.O. Box 33724, Decatur, GA 30033.

61. Albert Ellis, "The Sexual Psychology of Human Hermaphrodites," *Psychosomatic Medicine* 7 (1945): 108–25; John Hoenig, "The Origin of Gender Identity," in *Gender Dysphoria: Development, Research, and Management*, ed. B. Steiner, 11–32.

62. John Money, Joan Hampson, and John Hampson, "Imprinting and the Establishment of Gender Role," *Archives for Neurology and Psychiatry* 77 (1957): 333–36.

63. John Money, *Love and Love Sickness: The Science of Sex, Gender Difference and Pair-Bonding,* (Baltimore: Johns Hopkins University Press, 1980).

64. John Money and Anke A. Ehrhardt, *Man & Woman, Boy & Girl* (Baltimore, MD: Johns Hopkins University Press, 1972).

65. John Money, "Biographies of Gender and Hermaphroditism in Paired

Comparisons." *Clinical Supplement to The Handbook of Sexology,* ed. (New York: Elsevier, 1991).

66. Robert J. Stoller, *Sex and Gender,* vol. 2: *The Transsexual Experiment* (New York: Jason Aronson, 1976), 89–107. Quote from pp. 97–98.

67. Robert J. Stoller, "Boyhood Gender Aberrations: Treatment Issues," *Journal of the American Psychoanalytic Association* 26 (1978): 541–48.

68. John Hoenig, "The Origin of Gender Identity," 11–32.

69. Milton Diamond, "A Critical Evaluation of the Ontogeny of Human Sexual Behavior," *Quarterly Review of Biology* 40 (1965): 147–75.

70. Franz J. Kallman, "Comparative Twin Study on the Genetic Aspects of Male Homosexuality," *Journal of Nervous and Mental Disease* 115 (April 1952): 283–98; Franz J. Kallman, "Twin and Sibship Study of Overt Male Homosexuality," *American Journal of Human Genetics* 4 (1952): 136–46.

71. Julianne Imperato-McGinley, Luis Gerrera, Teofilo Gautier, and Ralph E. Peterson, "Steroid 5-alpha Reductase Deficiency in Man: An Inherited Form of Male Pseudohermaphroditism," *Science* 186 (1974): 1213–15.

72. Julianne Imperato-McGinley, Ralph E. Peterson, Teofilo Gautier, and Erasmo Sturla, "Androgens and the Evolution of Male-Gender Identity Among Male Pseudohermaphrodites with 5-alpha Reductase Deficiency," *New England Journal of Medicine* 300 (31 May 1979), 1233–37.

73. Richard Green, *Sexual Identity Conflict in Children and Adults,* (Baltimore, MD: Penguin Books, 1974), xv.

74. Richard Green, *The Sissy Boy Syndrome and the Development of Homosexuality* (New Haven, CT: Yale University Press, 1987).

75. Ibid., 114–32.

76. Ibid., 320–53.

Chapter 12
The Emergence of Organized Transvestism and Its Implications

Most of the cross dressers described in the preceding chapters dealt with their need to cross dress as individuals. Only a few organized groups of cross dressers appeared in the historical accounts, including the Hijras in India, the Kabuki actors in Japan, and the Mollies of eighteenth-century England. Despite these occasional homosexual cross-dressing groups, there is no evidence in Western culture of what might be called a transvestite consciousness before the last part of the twentieth century.

Virginia Prince: The Beginnings of Organization

The situation for transsexuals changed in 1952 with the publicity that surrounded the sex reassignment surgery of Christine Jorgensen. Following this incident, the media coverage helped transsexuals to develop a self-identity that was supported by the professionals who staffed gender identity clinics. In terms of transvestism, however, the work of one individual was significant in organizing transvestites and establishing their group identity. That individual was Virginia Prince, who was also known by the pseudonyms Virginia Bruce and Charles Prince. Though born a male and still a biological male, Prince has lived the life of a woman for over twenty-five years and before that cross dressed frequently. (This raises the question of which pronoun to use: we decided that for events of the last twenty-five years "she" will be used; for earlier periods "he" will be used unless the logic of the statement demands the female pronoun.)

Prince was able not only to define herself, but also to organize, publicize, and indoctrinate others about her parameters of transvestism. She established groups that allowed people to identify themselves and to learn how to express, in her terms, "the girl or woman within."[1] She also established a publishing house that disseminated information around the world; she traveled and made public appearances and has served as a role model for many transvestites. For twenty years or more she was the dominant voice of transvestism, and it was only in the 1980s, when she was well past the age of retirement, that others effectively challenged her leadership. Eventually, however, even those who disagreed with her came to recognize her contribution as the pioneer of late twentieth-century transvestism.

Prince also provided transvestites with a sexual script. (The concept of the sexual script was originated by sociologists John Gangon and William Simon, who emphasized that sexual activities are social activities guided by scripts.[2]) Prince argued that most transvestites were normal heterosexual men who sought only to express the beautiful "woman within." When pressed, however, she would admit that some homosexual transvestites existed, but she excluded them from her definition of transvestism and, whenever possible, from her groups. She did not approve of masochism, bondage, sadism, fetishism, or even references to sex. She also argued that only men should be considered transvestites because their roles were so restricted they needed to cross dress; women, on the other hand, could not only wear any kind of clothes they wanted but could also express a wider range of emotions, so they had no need to become transvestites. She also disapproved of sex reassignment surgery. As the club movement spread, Prince's definition of the transvestite experience was accepted, and the sexual scripts she outlined became the scripts accepted by most organized transvestites.[3] Moreover, her definition became the definition adopted by the *Diagnostic and Statistical Manual* of the American Psychiatric Association.

Prince's autobiography is a fascinating one. Born in 1913 in Los Angeles to an upper-middle-class family, his father was an eminent surgeon, while his mother was a career woman who sold real estate and handled investments.[4] He was the eldest of two children, some four years older than his sister. Virginia later wrote that she was not conscious of any predisposing factors to transvestism in what she calls Charles's early childhood (Charles was Prince's pseudonymous masculine name). In 1929 when he was sixteen, Charles accompanied his parents to Europe, where his father attended a medical convention. On the final evening of the eight-day crossing, the wife of another physician tried to persuade him to attend a fancy dress party as a girl. He refused but later admitted that he very much wanted to get fixed up as a beautiful young woman and go to the party, but there was no way he could give himself permission to do so.

Though he was unwilling to cross dress publicly on the boat, on return to Los Angeles he began accumulating a small wardrobe of feminine clothes, which was supplemented by raiding his mother's wardrobe. His covert cross dressing soon expanded into public cross dressing, and by the age of eighteen he was sneaking out of the house in women's clothes, riding the streetcar, and being tremendously excited by the adventures. He reported that on such occasions he often achieved orgasm without masturbating. Both the fear and excitement about being caught and the actual cross dressing were important to the sexual high.

The first appearance of his feminine persona in a situation where others knew he was a man in women's clothing took place at a Halloween party in 1930 where he won a prize for the best costume. He managed to keep the clothes for a couple of days in order to be photographed dressed as a woman. He continued to dress until the time of his marriage, whereupon he went through an event that is standard in transvestite literature: a purge of everything associated with his "feminine self" and a resolution never to cross dress again.

Marriage meant moving from Los Angeles to Oakland, California, to take a new job. His pledge not to cross dress held fast for some three months, although he had a strong desire to do so. It might even be said that the reason he lasted so long is that he did not have the opportunity. His opportunity came when his wife took a brief trip to visit her family in Los Angeles. He tried to dress in her clothes, but when he found that most of them did not fit, he bought others from a second-hand store. Charles, though by now feeling very guilty and worried about his sexual identity, managed to cross dress occasionally after his wife's return, and without her knowledge, by hiding his women's clothes from her.

The reason for their move north had been for Charles, who held a Ph.D. in biochemistry, to take a staff position in the University of California medical school at San Francisco. While there, he spent much of his spare time studying mental disease and neurotic behavior. When a particular patient's treatment interested him, he also attended grand rounds. One day, the grand rounds featured a discussion of a young man who had recently changed his name to Barbara Wilcox and begun living as a woman. Barbara turned out to have been in the same freshman class at the college Charles had attended in southern California and had much the same background and experiences as Charles.[5]

Subsequent grand rounds featured other transvestites or as they came to be known among his followers "TVs." Charles heard all the cases, participated in the discussions, and usually requested a photograph of the patient dressed as a woman. When he later examined one of the photographs, he found the name "Louise Lawrence" and an address written on the back. He set out to visit Louise one evening when his wife was attending a night class. This contact with Louise led to others, and it marked the first time that Charles felt he could share experiences with other transvestites, a mind-boggling notion at the time.

Shortly afterward, Charles managed to get an appointment as a patient at the Langley Porter Clinic in San Francisco with the well-known psychiatrist Karl Bowman, to talk about his cross dressing. Though Charles had seen other psychiatrists about his transvestism, they had not been particularly helpful. Bowman was different, and Charles found his advice useful. After listening to Charles's story Bowman reportedly said something to the effect of "So what else is new? What's so unusual about that? There are tens of thousands more just like you, you're not so special. What you need is to learn to accept yourself as you are and enjoy it."[6]

Soon after Charles's talk with Bowman, the grant he had been working on at the University of California in San Francisco ran out, and he returned to southern California to take a job as a research chemist with a pharmaceutical manufacturer. And it was soon after the couple's return that Charles told his wife about his compulsive cross dressing. She was upset but eventually agreed that at the times he got to the point where he felt compelled to cross dress, he would tell her; she would then have the opportunity to isolate herself at the back of the house, since she did not want to see him that way. During the next couple of years he cross dressed about every two weeks. In 1944 he became the father of a son, but this did not end his urge to cross dress. In fact, on a business trip to San Francisco he contacted one of his professional acquaintances who had presented cross-dressing patients at the psychiatric conferences and visited him dressed as a woman. Also at his colleague's house was a woman who, fascinated by Charles, encouraged him to go out publicly with her; he remembered this public cross-dressing experience for a long time as an emotional high. On his return to Los Angeles, he told his father about his cross dressing and even dressed for him. His father's only comment was to suggest that Charles visit an endocrinologist, implying that additional male hormones might help him; after that he refused to talk with his son about cross dressing and was never reconciled to his son's behavior.

In the meantime his wife, who had seen a psychiatrist about her husband's cross dressing, became convinced her husband was homosexual. She felt her only option was to get a divorce. She proceeded with filing, and the divorce became public with lurid newspaper stories about his cross dressing. Unable to escape the publicity and notoriety, Charles was forced to come to terms with the fact that he was a transvestite. Still, somehow, he survived the "shame" of exposure and continued to cross dress.

When the story of Christine Jorgensen hit the papers, Charles wrote that his first impulse was to go to Denmark for surgery. Initially, the major deterrent to such a step was the fact that his divorce had been so costly he could not afford it. The Jorgensen case, however, also forced him to sit down and try to decide whether he fit the category of transsexual or not, and he eventually decided he did not. Perhaps the fact that everyone knew he was a transvestite, including his family, helped him come to this conclusion, since he felt free to cross dress more frequently, going to parties and other events as a woman. On one of these occasions he returned to his parents house and met their new housekeeper, an older woman who had recently arrived from England; after some initial reticence, she offered him tremendous emotional support. She listened to him, talked to him about cross dressing, and helped him better conceptualize the role of a woman. Ultimately, they married.

Charles's notoriety brought him in contact with other transvestites, since many sought him out. Out of this came a small support group in the Los Angeles area which began to meet regularly. The group started to put out a newsletter called *Transvestia* and contacted other people to invite membership and readership. The newsletter ran out of money with the second issue, but Charles persisted and in 1960 began publishing a magazine with the same title, with himself as editor under the name of Virginia Prince. Originally, there were only twenty-five subscribers, but as information about the magazine spread (especially as a result of an article in *Sexology* and through its distribution in adult bookstores) the number of subscribers grew. Other publications were added by Prince, including *Femme Mirror,* which alternated monthly with *Transvestia,* and *Clipsheet,* which featured clippings from the world press about transvestism. Apparently, many transvestites had saved clippings which they shared with Prince, although *Clipsheet* soon fell by the wayside. Prince called the enterprise "Chevalier Publications" (named for the Chevalier d'Éon), and in addition to the periodicals, it also began to publish transvestite fantasy fiction.

Under the name of Virginia Prince, "he" (henceforth "she") became the spokesperson and representative of transvestism not only in Los Angeles but across the country.

A group of Los Angeles subscribers began to meet, and they formed the Hose and Heels Club. This group met informally at first, but more frequently as the meetings became an occasion for the transvestites to dress up. Out of this came the idea of a sorority, Phi Pi Epsilon (or FPE, for "full personality expression"), which soon grew from its Los Angeles base (which became the alpha chapter) to a national organization.

As the movement grew, other transvestites developed innovative enterprises, often initially with the cooperation of Virginia. A New York transvestite known as Susanna Valenti, who owned a ranch-resort in the Catskills, decided to have a national get-together; there, some sixty TVs (as they called themselves) dressed for a week, exchanging hints and even being instructed by what were called "genetic women" (i.e., biological females). Still other groups appeared, such as DREAM, a West Coast enterprise presided over by "Marilyn" from Oregon. DREAM was designed to give instruction in the art of female impersonation as well as to give social assistance. Fantasia Fair, which began meeting in Provincetown, Massachusetts, in far more public meetings, brought the growing transvestite movement out of the closet, as transvestites mingled with townspeople and tourists.

For a brief time in the early sixties, the Postmaster General's Office attempted to prevent circulation of the various transvestite publications on the grounds that they were obscene and that Prince was using the magazine to solicit sexual partners. The charges grew out of some personal correspondence of Virginia with an individual whom she thought was a woman sympathetic to cross dressing and in which she let her fantasies go wild. The person later turned out to be a man who himself was under investigation by postal officials for illicit activities of which Virginia was believed to be a part. Though admitting she wrote the letter, she tried to separate this activity from her publishing activity, and ultimately did so successfully in the courts. Still, she pleaded guilty to writing the letter and was sentenced to three years in a federal penitentiary, which was suspended providing she served five years of probation. If she was arrested for any reason, she would automatically go to prison. Since cross dressing in public was prohibited by the Los Angeles criminal code of the time, this meant she would be subject to arrest if she cross dressed. To get around this danger, her attorney persuaded the court to allow part of her probation to be served in educating the public about cross dressing. The court agreed and the result was a number of public appearances before service clubs and other groups where she talked about gender differences and in which she ultimately revealed herself as a man.

Prince's second marriage broke up in 1964, again with considerable publicity in the Los Angeles papers, and after this divorce she started living full-time as a woman. Earlier, she had made her first overseas contacts with transvestites while visiting her wife's family, and after the divorce she continued to travel in Europe and elsewhere as a woman. She had managed to build a successful business using her biochemistry background after her first divorce; after her decision to live as a woman, she sold the business but continued to receive some income as a consultant. She now had the leisure to travel, and since the U.S. passport office allowed her to list both her masculine and feminine names with a gender neutral photograph, she traveled almost everywhere with little difficulty. Wherever she went she appeared on radio or television, establishing the contacts from which grew a loosely knit international information network.

As organized transvestism grew, other groups appeared, and they often had different views of transvestism; other publishers appeared as well. Some of these groups and publications welcomed both homosexual and heterosexual transvestites; others appealed to people who fantasized about sex change but did not want to undergo surgery; and some even included transsexuals in their membership. Factions that associated transvestism with bondage and domination and leather appeared in the 1970s and 1980s, and this provoked some hostile feelings among the other groups, although at the present time the various organizations seem to have learned to tolerate each other. There is now a calendar of transvestite activities published by one of the groups with a list of events long enough to keep a dedicated transvestite traveling and busy almost every day of the year. Conventions were originally held in cities known for tolerance, such as Provincetown and San Francisco, but increasingly they are held in more mainstream cities, such as Chicago and Syracuse. Hotels and convention bureaus sign up transvestite groups just as they do other associations.

Transvestite Fantasy Literature

An interesting feature of the Chevalier publications were the fictionalized stories of men who cross dressed. There had been an underground handwritten and hand-circulated corpus of fiction that preceded Prince's efforts, and a few short novels were sold in out-of-the-way places; but Prince increased the availability of this fiction significantly, and contemporary publishers of transvestite literature have continued in this tradition. In addition, there are now several independent publishing houses that publish magazines and books that present fictionalized accounts of cross dressing. This fantasy literature is written for men who cross dress rather than for the general public.

In 1963 Hugo Beigel and Robert Feldman analyzed seventy-three of these novels and short stories and twenty unpublished manuscripts. The innocence of the protagonist was the major theme that ran through the stories. In only thirteen of the works did the male hero realize a desire to cross dress before the experience was thrust upon him by a dominant woman, a secret mission, kidnappers, or economic necessity. Beigel and Feldman argued that the theme of external compulsion presented in the fantasy literature does not at all resemble the transvestite's true etiology. In fact, they wondered if the early scientific attribution of transvestism to external forces, particularly the theme of being cross dressed as a child (the so-called petticoat punishment), was a case in which the researchers had been fooled by their clients, who had given them fantasy versions of their real lives.[7]

Neil Buhrich and Neil McConaghy published a review in 1976 that covered twenty stories written for transvestites. Eight were short stories published by the Australian journal *Feminique,* with the others coming from the British *Beaumont Bulletin,* the American *Transvestia,* and five novelettes written for the Transvestia Club in United States. In all but one the heroes were male. In the single story with a heroine, Norma, a cross dresser, is involved in a double switch. As "Norman," Norma fell in love with a girl named Nancy, who turned out to be a man. The two were married, and only in bed, after the lights were out, did they return to their true sex roles; at all other times, they lived as Norman and Nancy.

In all of the other stories, the hero was a male who was required to cross dress because of some circumstance beyond his control. In ten stories a woman helped the hero, and in four stories the hero married the woman who helped him cross dress, and they lived happily ever after. The female clothing was usually meticulously described, and in eight stories the hero publicly cross dressed and successfully fooled everyone; women admired him, men competed for his attention, and close friends failed to recognize him. Buhrich and McConaghy also commented on a different theme they found in five stories which expressed the loneliness of the transvestite. Early in the story, the hero believed himself to be alone in the world. He was discovered by or himself discovered another transvestite, and they became friends. The hero rejoiced in the fact that he was no longer alone.[8]

Robert Stoller also used the transvestite fiction to learn more about his patients. In his view, the fiction was "pornography." Arguing that pornography excites lust, he thought analysis of the fiction would provide insight into the transvestite's psychosexual development. He summarized a story to illustrate this point. The story featured a young fraternity member who went to a sorority house in order to raid the clothesline. The girls caught him, tied him up, and dressed him in their clothes. Stoller believed that the fiction depicted a psychological truth. He attributed transvestism to cruel mother figures who emasculate their young boys as revenge, thus the transvestite fiction features women forcing men to cross dress. Transvestites turn the tables on their cruel mothers by enjoying the punishment inflicted on them.[9]

To add more data to this analysis of the fantasy literature of transves-

TABLE 12.1. Summary of the Stories (N=96).

	Percentages
Age at which hero first cross dressed	
Before 13	14
Adolescent	24
Adult	48
Not mentioned	14
How was the decision made to cross dress?	
Hero decided to try it	15
Suggested by another person	26
Forced by another person	35
Forced by circumstances	16
Not mentioned	8
If forced to cross dress, who was the agent?	
Mother	12
Other female relative	10
Girlfriend or wife	20
A male	9
A group or other forces	22
Not applicable or agent not identified	27
Mentor who taught the hero the female role	
Sympathetic woman	51
Woman who was unkind or dominating	13
Both a man and a woman	9
Man	4
No mentor	20
Other mentor	3
Sexual orientation of the hero	
Heterosexual	53
Homosexual	2
Starts heterosexual; becomes homosexual	16
Masturbates only	2
Sexual orientation not indicated	27
Domination of the hero	
Domination without pain to the hero	26
Domination with pain to the hero	22
Other painful stimuli	10
Not mentioned	42
Attitude of wife or significant other to cross dressing	
Very pleased; a sexual turn-on	26
Pleased, but sexual turn-on not mentioned	27
Neutral attitude or not shown	47

TABLE 12.1. *Continued*

	Percentages
Family acceptance of cross dressing	
Not accepting	3
Slowly accepting	10
Rapidly accepting	41
Not mentioned	46
Occupation of the hero	
Professional	13
Business, sales, clerical	13
Skilled, technical	6
Servant, laborer	5
Student	26
Other	13
Not mentioned	24
Transsexual surgery	
Discussed but does not occur	4
Surgery done	16
Not mentioned	80
Other elements mentioned in the story	
The process of dressing	96
Details about clothing and makeup	86
Passing as a woman	72
Cleavage (between the breasts)	62
Lessons in female mannerisms	54
Flirting with a male	33
Shopping for clothing	26
Magical cures, feminizing potions, hormones	24
Flirting with a female	10

tism, we selected a random sample of the materials available after 1950, including a collection of handwritten and hand-circulated stories written before 1960. Among the ninety-six works of fiction were fifty-five short stories, twenty-four novelettes, twelve novels, four fictionalized case histories, and one play. A content analysis of the ninety-six works was then done to identify the common themes in the stories. Table 12.1 summarizes these themes and shows the overall percentage of each item in relation to the entire sample.

We found a historical dimension in the stories. The stereotypical story told in the Chevalier publications of the 1960s and 1970s pictured the transvestite as a very nice person—actually, more of a Barbie doll than a person. As the story opened the hero, who was an upper-middle-class business man, an actor, or a student, was forced by circumstances to cross dress. A friendly woman served as his mentor, teaching him about clothing and manners. The two of them participated in a delightful shopping spree, which never seemed to involve any concern for money. Each article of clothing was described in detail. The clothes tended to be frothy pink or slinky black, but never leather. The two of them returned home to carry out the task of cross dressing the hero. Particular attention was paid to padding so that he would end up with well-shaped breasts. His chest was taped to give an illusion of cleavage between the two breasts. Very little attention was paid to his pelvic area, except to sometimes indicate that a device is worn to hide "it" (the word *penis* was never mentioned). He might also pad his hips and buttocks to make them larger.

The nice lady mentor and the nice cross-dressed man then went out in public, and everyone was successfully fooled. He flirted with unsuspecting men, but never, ever thought of having sex with them (that would not be normal). The couple returned home, and if the mentor was the hero's legally married wife, she told him what a wonderful turn-on his cross dressing is for her, and they went to bed. If they were not married, the two usually sipped pink champagne as they watched the sun set.

With the sexual revolution, which made all kinds of expressions of sexuality more respectable, and the diversification of the club movement, the stories have changed over time. An analysis of seventeen items from Empathy Press and fourteen items from Sandy Thomas [Press] (currently publishers of TV fiction) suggests that the scenarios in the 1980s and 1990s were less "nice." The story lines continued to feature clothing, makeup, shopping, and breasts. The fictional wives were still delighted with their husbands' new clothing. However, the clothing was sometimes made of leather (especially in Empathy stories), and more of the heroes were homosexual. The line between transvestism and transsexualism was blurred, as some heroes talked about sex reassignment surgery and a few actually had it performed. In 32 percent of the items we analyzed, pain was inflicted on the hero, usually by a dominating woman. Sometimes this pain was not severe (for example, it might be the pain caused by corsets or shoes that are too tight), but other times it was the more severe pain of whipping. Pain was an important element in nineteenth-century English pornography, and it has again appeared as an element in the transvestite fantasy literature of the late twentieth century.

The results of our analysis of the literature were congruent with some of the observations made by the earlier researchers. As indicated by Beigel and Feldman, a key element was the innocence of the hero. In 76 percent of the stories we analyzed, the hero was forced or talked into cross dressing by another person or due to circumstances. We did not, however, see as strong a role for the mother; she appeared in only 12 percent of the stories. We found most of the space in the stories taken up with the details of cross dressing, a finding that was also noted in the Buhrich and McConaghy analysis.

The fantasy element in this literature is apparent. The stories depart significantly from what is known about the lives of transvestites.[10] In their study, Buhrich and McConaghy present a table that contrasts fact and fiction, drawing on facts from their own research as well as from the literature. They indicate, for example, that the first cross-dressing experience is usually carried out in secret and alone; in fiction, it is assisted by a woman who is enthusiastic about seeing men cross dressed. At first, the transvestite rarely appears in public and avoids seeing friends, but in the fictional world he goes out in public, passes successfully, and his friends do not recognize him.[11]

Our findings as summarized in Table 12.1 are congruent with this analysis. In the fictionalized versions, only 15 percent of the heroes make the decision themselves; 76 percent of the stories tell of a situation in which the hero was forced to cross dress by a mother, sister, other woman, or circumstances beyond his control. The research literature indicates that when the first cross-dressing episode occurs the young boy or man knows that he is violating the norms of the family or society and he fears punishment. His fears are usually well founded: If he is discovered, his family becomes distressed. In the past they might have disowned him; today, they might send him for psychotherapy. If he is married, his wife might divorce him; if she stays with him, she does so for reasons other than his cross dressing.[12] None of this psychological pain and anguish appears in the fantasy literature. These sharp differences between fact and fiction support Beigel and Feldman's argument that a major goal of this literature is to create a world in which the hero is innocent, so that he can escape the guilt and punishment that accompany cross dressing.

The role of the male cross dresser who is portrayed in transvestite literature is also not congruent to that of real women. Seldom does the fantasy hero do the less glamorous work often associated with women: teaching, social work, child care, dish-washing, or clerical work. Occasionally, he poses as a cleaning woman in the sadomasochistic stories, or as a nurse because of its stereotypical image. (As a nurse, however, he will more likely be depicted wiping a fevered brow than holding an emesis basin.) The role models of the fantasy literature appear to be actresses, models, or rich heiresses, whose lives have no focus other than clothing. This also gives the transvestite literature an out-of-date character. The women the hero emulates were described by Thorstein Veblen at the turn of the century as the wives and mistresses of rich men who kept them as articles of conspicuous consumption.[13]

In a broader context transvestite stories are a part of the fantasies that have been found to be common to all sexual activity.[14] Moreover, transvestism itself is a make-believe activity that involves switching roles and identities, not only from masculine to feminine but from reality to fantasy. As indicated by Annie Woodhouse, a British sociologist, when the transvestite cross dresses he pretends to be a woman, but he chooses what type of woman he will be. He often changes his voice, adopts another name, and even changes his manners and attitudes. Consequently, he is not just a man wearing women's clothing, he has another persona.

Woodhouse notes that many transvestites will claim that they understand women better than other men because of their cross-dressing experiences. In fact, however, the cross-dressing episodes probably set up barriers to understanding, because the transvestite does not actually enter into the real world of women; rather, his is an unreal world shaped partly by the transvestite fantasy literature, so he never really sees the role of women.[15] When transvestites cross dress they are not ordinary women; they are beautiful sex objects who are desired by every man and every woman. If they are married or have a lover, the role of that partner during the cross-dressing episode is to play the supporting role. The cross-dressing episode, then, has nothing to do with reality; rather, it shields the transvestite from reality.

Cross-Sectional Studies of the Transvestite Population

An important incidental result of Prince's early efforts and of the club movement that ensued was that it gave researchers opportunities to study populations of transvestites who were not necessarily clients of a psychiatrist or psychologist. This significantly broadened the focus of the research from the psychiatric patient population, but it also narrowed the focus to club members and their contacts. Because of Prince's ideology, homosexual cross dressers, who are probably the largest group of cross dressers, were excluded from the club movement.

Prince herself was among the first to take advantage of possibilities for research. In 1964 and 1966, questionnaires were sent to readers of *Transvestia*. Data were gathered from 504 subjects who described their current cross-dressing activities, marital status, and childhoods. Seventy-six percent of the group indicated they had never seen a psychiatrist. Since the earlier scholarly writing about transvestites was done by psychiatrists who studied their patients, this was a radically different view of the transvestite phenomenon than had been presented earlier.[16]

Other researchers also took advantage of the existence of the clubs to gather sociological and psychological data, including Neil Buhrich and Neil McConaghy, a team of Australian psychiatrists; Richard Docter, a California psychologist; as well as the authors of this book, who worked with the psychologist Richard W. Smith. When these studies are examined together, a description of the male transvestites who either read transvestite literature or belonged to one of the clubs emerges. Table 12.2 summarizes the data from six samples: Prince and Bentler (504 readers); Buhrich and McConaghy (35 members of an Australian club); Buhrich and Beaumont (86 members of the Australian Seahorse Club and 126 members of the American Society for the Second Self);[17] Bullough and colleagues (65 members or friends of members of three Los Angeles clubs)[18]; and Richard Docter, who passed out questionnaires at two southern California club meetings, along with members of these clubs who passed out questionnaires at national transvestite meetings.[19]

The cross-sectional studies indicated that most of these men were married at some time in their lives (78 to 88 percent), with two-thirds or more married at the time they were studied. Subjects tended to be in their thirties or forties with a few older and younger. Educational levels were high, usually with some college education, and occupational levels tended to be middle class.[20] In a detailed study of occupations that used the scale of occupational prestige developed by Hodge, Siegel, and Rossi,[21] Bullough and colleagues found that the occupational level of the transvestite group was above average for the American population and the comparison samples used in the study. Clusters of certain occupations were partly related to the southern California locale but may also be related to the psychodynamics of the transvestite clubs. These were successful men; for example, 15 percent of the study sample were engineers, 9 percent salesmen, 8 percent administrators, and 8 percent writers. Also included were technicians, stockbrokers, a contractor, an electrician, a pilot, a physician, a lawyer, and a college professor. There were some predominantly feminine-oriented jobs represented, with 3 percent of the group being hairdressers and 6 percent artists, but these stereotypical female jobs were more often noted in a comparison group of male-to-female transsexuals.[22]

Table 12.2 indicates that the majority of these men considered themselves heterosexual (72 to 89 percent). Only a very small percentage of each group are exclusively homosexual. Docter excluded the respon-

TABLE 12.2. Summary Data From Cross-Sectional Studies of Male Transvestites.

	Prince and Bentler	Buhrich and McConaghy	Buhrich and Beaumont	Buhrich and Beaumont	Bullough et al.	Docter
Heterosexual (%)	89	83	72	87	97	—
Exclusively homosexual (%)	9	3	5	6	—	—
Some homosexual (%)	28	17	44	48	18	28
Ever married (%)	78	80	88	83	—	82
Median age	30s	39	39	47	43	—
Median occupational level	high	—	—	—	upper-middle	upper-middle
Ever on hormones (%)	5	17	12	10	25	—
Considered sex change (%)	—	25	69	60	—	—
Any psychotherapy (%)	26	—	—	—	54	—
Median age at first cross dress	10	—	11	11	8	9
Two-parent homes (%)	82	—	—	—	85	80
Cross dressed by parents (%)	4–6	4	—	—	—	—
Date published	1972	1977	1981	1981	1983	1988
Sample size	504	35	86	126	65	110
Place	U.S.	Aust.	Aust.	U.S.	U.S.	U.S.

Sources: Virginia Prince and P. M. Bentler, "Survery of 504 Cases of Transvestism," *Psychological Reports* 31 (1972): 904–17; Neil Buhrich and Neil McConaghy, "The Discrete Syndromes of Transvestism and Transsexualism," *Archives of Sexual Behavior* 6 (1977): 483–495; Neil Buhrich and Trina Beaumont, "Comparison of Transvestism in Australia and America," *Archives of Sexual Behavior* 10 (1981): 269–79; Vern Bullough, Bonnie Bullough, and Richard Smith, "A Comparative Study of Male Transvestites, Male-to-Female Transsexuals and Male Homosexuals, *Journal of Sex Research* 19 (August 1983): 238–57.

dents who indicated they were exclusively homosexual because the DSM-III-R definition of transvestism excludes them, but he included people with some homosexual experience and found this cohort to be 28 percent. For many transvestites homosexual fantasies or experiences are a part of the sexual script for cross-dressing episodes. In the cross-cultural study of American and Australian club members, Buhrich and Beaumont asked subjects to indicate their sexual orientation when they were dressed as males and when they were dressed as females; 87 percent of the American sample said they were exclusively heterosexual when they were dressed as men but only 52 percent were exclusively heterosexual when they were cross dressed. Similarly, the Australian sample went from a 72 percent heterosexual orientation in men's clothing to a 56 percent heterosexual orientation in women's clothing.[23] Homosexual fantasies or homoerotic activities are clearly a part of the cross-dressing scene. This also suggests that at least some transvestites exhibit two different personas, with different attitudes and sexual activities when they are cross dressed and when they are in their male clothing.

Cross dressing is usually done at periodic intervals, and those men who are anxious or ashamed of themselves will periodically purge their wardrobes and resolve never to cross dress again. Masturbation may take place during the cross-dressing episode, but often the cross dressing itself results in ejaculation. Sometimes there are fantasies of masochism and bondage, but the transvestite does not picture himself in the sadistic role. Rather he is the victim who is tied up or beaten by a strong woman or occasionally by a strong man.[24]

As indicated earlier, there has been some controversy related to the descriptive term *fetishistic,* which is used by the DSM-III-R in connection with transvestism. The discussion focuses on two issues: (1) is *fetishistic* the best term for an erotic arousal related to cross dressing, and (2) do all transvestites experience an erotic arousal? We have indicated our concern regarding the term *fetishistic,* arguing that it is simply too narrowly focused on the dress rather than the person in the dress; we prefer the term *erotic arousal.*[25] Erotic arousal was studied by Ray Blanchard and colleagues using measurements of penile blood flow when erotic fantasy literature was presented to samples of heterosexual cross dressers and heterosexual controls. All of the cross-dressing sample experienced increased penile blood volume in response to these stories, including those cross dressers who had reported no erotic arousal when they had cross dressed in the preceding year. The authors were fascinated by this discrepancy and speculated that the subjects were unaware of the arousal, or that they denied it because it was discordant with their image of women (or ladies), or that their cross-dressing activities had become such a habit that they were unaware of arousal.[26]

In Docter's as well as the Buhrich and McConaghy studies, subjects had to report erotic response to cross dressing or "fetishism" at some time in their lives to be included in the study sample. Since these researchers adhered to the DSM-III-R definition of fetishistic transvestism, club members who did not admit erotic arousal and who reported that they cross dressed for relief from the masculine gender norms and obligations, for relaxation, or for social rewards were excluded. Such exclusions result in about a 10 percent loss of the population. For example, in the study done by Buhrich and Beaumont comparing American and Australian transvestites, the authors excluded 9 percent of their American respondents and 11 percent of their Australian respondents.[27] The distortion in the study sample probably leaves out many of the older transvestites. Harry Brierly, an English physician and psychologist who worked with transvestite patients and with a study sample of 134 members of the British Beaumont Society, argued that as transvestites age their fetishism wanes; additionally, many older transvestites cross dress in order to temporarily escape the pressures of being masculine rather than for any erotic experience.[28]

Personality Attributes of Male Transvestites: Club Members Versus Psychiatric Patients

In 1970 Bentler, Sherman, and Prince published a study of the personality characteristics of twenty-five transvestites who were not in psychotherapy. They used the Holtzman ink blot test, a projective technique similar to that of the Rorschach test, to assess twenty-two personality traits. The findings were scored against the test manual, which provides general norms for the population. They found that the transvestite members of the sample groups scored at high levels of intellect; they were "form bound," which was interpreted as rigid and compulsive, and preoccupied with pathological thought processes related to their bodies. The authors commented that this pattern was consistent with their own clinical impressions of the group.[29]

Harry Brierly used the Cattell sixteen-item personality profile to test a group of transvestites in his patient population. He compared them with control groups of homosexual patients and hospital personnel. The transvestites were characterized by depression, anxiety, feelings of guilt, and obsessional traits. When they were compared with the control groups they were found to be less assertive and more serious-minded, conscientious, and inhibited than the controls.[30] Brierly made an interesting comment comparing the transvestite patients with the homosexual patients:

These groups are different in that it may be fairly said that most homosexuals seeking treatment feel under greater pressure socially than transvestites are. The homosexual group feels less able to disguise its problems and often feels there is a social or vocational threat. The transvestite group is usually seeking help over a more personal problem which is covert and less likely to be a threat beyond the level of personal relations. The transvestite group rarely feels that others know its secrets as homosexuals frequently suspect. Such differences may well underlie personality profiles in patient groups which suggest that homosexuals have more serious problems and are more sharply differentiated from non-patient groups.[31]

Members of the Sexual Behaviors Consultation Group at Johns Hopkins School of Medicine (chaired by Peter Fagan) tested a population of twenty-one transvestites who had sought psychiatric help using as a control group forty-five heterosexual men who were tested because their wives were seeking in vitro fertilization. Two tests were used: the Derogotis Sexual Functioning Inventory (DSFI) and the Brief Symptom Inventory (BSI). The transvestites' scores on the DSFI indicated that the individuals had a feminine gender identity, a negative body image particularly in relation to sexual body parts, and less sexual experience than the control group (this finding is suspect since the DSFI does not count cross dressing as a sexual experience). The BSI scores placed the transvestite group in the top 5 percent of the population in terms of psychological distress, while the control group was much closer to the normal range of scores. The transvestite patients' scores peaked on depression, interpersonal sensitivity, anxiety, and social alienation.[32] This study is particularly valuable when it is compared with the studies of transvestite club members because the results, while congruent on the feminine attributes, are otherwise quite different. These patients are the transvestites who are distressed with themselves. Their interpersonal sensitivity may have helped to alert them to the stigma attached to their cross dressing; they feel alienated, anxious, and depressed.

The Minnesota Multiphasic Personality Inventory (MMPI), which is aimed at measuring psychological adjustment, was often used in the past to identify the feminine orientation of transvestites.[33] James Beatrice reported testing four samples: ten preoperative and ten postoperative transsexuals, ten transvestites and ten volunteer male heterosexuals. The volunteer control group scored significantly lower on the femininity scale than the other three groups, who were all at about the same level. The transvestite sample did not demonstrate any clinically significant dysfunction on the MMPI (except on femininity), but the transsexuals, particularly the postoperative cohort, scored significantly higher on the scales of paranoia and schizophrenia. Beatrice interpreted his findings as suggesting that sex reassignment surgery failed to improve the personality functioning of transsexuals.[34]

Masculinity and Femininity

In 1975 Brierly studied a group of transvestite patients using the Attitude Interest Test, designed by Terman and Miles, which measures masculinity versus femininity as a bipolar concept. Although Brierly reported that the test had been criticized for being superficial, he nevertheless used it to test a patient population made up of 117 cases including homosexual, transvestite, and other patients with psychological problems. He compared the patients with control groups of unspecified sizes from the hospital staff. Transvestites were the most feminine, with women from the hospital staff scoring as less feminine than the transvestites. The homosexual control group was on the masculine side but low in comparison to hospital workers.[35]

The criticism voiced by Brierly about the scales used for measuring masculinity was echoed by others, particularly those in the women's movement. Scales such as the Terman and Miles and the MMPI used a continuum, with masculinity at one end and femininity at the other; individuals who possessed one set of characteristics were assumed to be deficient in the other. This meant that one could not be both assertive and gentle. The feminist challenge to these assumptions led to a rethinking of the instruments and the development of new scales that measured the dimensions of masculinity and femininity as independent dimensions. This approach allowed subjects to score high in both masculinity and femininity, a situation Sandra Bem called *androgyny*, or to score low on both scales, which she termed *undifferentiated*.[36]

Docter used the Bem inventory to measure these concepts, and the transvestite cohort he studied scored higher on the femininity scale and lower on the masculinity scale. They were more likely to be classified as androgynous than the published norms for the scale. He then asked his subjects to take the test a second time while cross dressed; forty-eight subjects were willing to participate, and their femininity scores were higher, thus lending support to the idea that at least some transvestites take on different attitudes when they are cross dressed. However, when the group that took the test a second time was compared with the nonparticipants, it was found that they were already the most feminine-oriented group.[37]

A similar instrument developed by Spence and Helmreich was used by Bullough and colleagues. It measures masculinity and femininity as separate attributes then combines them on a continuum to allow comparisons with the older bipolar approach.[38] The findings of this study are congruent with those of Docter. Transvestites were compared with three different control groups: homosexual men, male-to-female transsexuals, and area residents whose sexual and gender orientation was unknown. The three sexual minorities scored lower on the masculinity scale and higher on the femininity scale than the control group, yet there were some interesting differences between them. The transsexuals were the most feminine, but the group that was lowest in masculinity was the gay control group. The transvestites fell between the external control group and the transsexuals on both attributes. The findings on the bipolar scale were the same, with transvestites closer to the external norms than the gay or transsexual men. These findings are congruent with clinical observations. The transvestite life-style protects the masculine persona by isolating the feminine attributes and allowing them expression when the subject is cross dressed.[39]

Childhood Patterns

Table 12.2 summarizes the behavior patterns and experiences of the male transvestites included in the cross-sectional studies. Most started cross dressing before puberty, and some started in their preschool years. Only rarely was the activity forced or sponsored by a parent, which is contrary to the conventional wisdom about the phenomenon. The other often-told tale is that the parents probably actually wanted a girl instead of a boy, but that does not often prove to be true. Most transvestites are raised in two-parent homes, which at least partially denies the conventional psychiatric wisdom about absent fathers. The evidence for believing a strong, protective mother is the problem is more consistent, with 45 percent of the men in the Prince and Bentler sample indicating that they considered their mothers to be the stronger parents,[40] and 66 percent of the Buhrich and McConaghy group indicating that they considered their mothers to be the stronger parents.[41] In a comparison of a student population (which included male and female heterosexual and homosexual persons) with a transvestite population, Newcomb found that the transvestite and lesbian samples were the most likely to picture their mothers as the stronger or more aggressive parents.[42] Bullough and colleagues found that the mothers of the transvestite sample members were the most likely to be housewives (81 percent), as compared with 56 percent of the gay sample, 63 percent of the transsexual sample, and 53 percent of the control group. The higher level of housewives among the transvestite group may reflect the higher social class of the sample, since in the era that the sample grew up a high percentage of working mothers tended to correlate with economic deprivation.[43]

Cross dressing started early; 73 percent of the men in the Bullough et al. study had begun cross dressing by the time they were ten; 50 percent of the Prince and Bentler sample started before ten, and the median age of the Buhrich and Beaumont samples was about eleven. Only rarely in any of the studies does the behavior first appear in adult life; however, it is ordinarily not as early or as persistent as the cross dressing of the children who become transsexuals. The young boys who later become transvestites are not necessarily feminine in other regards. Our data indicated that they were much more likely to be interested in sports as adolescents than any of the control groups (transsexual, homosexual, and undifferentiated samples); 57 percent of the transvestite group were active participants, and 20 percent were observers (attending ballgames, etc.) during their adolescent years. Only 23 percent indicated that they were not interested in sports, compared with 64 percent of the transsexual group, 51 percent of the homosexual group, and 26 percent of the undifferentiated control group.[44]

Subgroups of Transvestites

As more data about transvestite club members accumulate, it has become clear that there are variations among this population. Michael Persinger and Lawrence Stettner found that there are significant variations in public behavior which are correlated with personality variables: self-esteem and perceived control. Transvestites who score high on these attributes are more likely to go out in public.[45] Some researchers have divided transvestites into subgroups to reflect variations in the group. Buhrich and McConaghy first noted they could divide club members they were studying into two groups: those who were satisfied with cross dressing and those who desired at least partial feminization with hormones or surgery. Some of these people wanted sex reassignment surgery but refrained from seeking it for family reasons. The first group, which fits the traditional definition of transvestism, was called "nuclear"; the other group, which seemed closer to the model of transsexualism, was called "marginal." Members of the marginal group shared many characteristics with transsexuals; they often did not experience erotic arousal with cross dressing and they showed more homosexual interest.[46]

Having differentiated these two subgroups of transvestites, Buhrich and McConaghy in 1982 added a third category, "fetishistic transsexualism." They identified a group of five men who had requested sex reassignment surgery, had lived full-time as women for at least six months, considered themselves to be women even when they were nude, but reported erotic arousal to cross dressing. Two of the group had ejaculated spontaneously while cross dressed during adolescence, and all reported fetishistic arousal at some time.[47]

Richard Docter divided the group into five stages; he showed that over time and with more experience there were marked increases in the frequency of cross dressing and that more items of clothing were added. Those individuals who coped reasonably well with their habit and remained in good mental health experienced four stages in the process. However, sometimes the cross dressing escalated to the point that it was full-time, and a fifth transsexual phase followed. Docter's five stages are as follows:

Stage 1. Antecedent developmental factors prior to fetishism (ages 4 to 11).
Stage 2. Partial cross dressing with erotic arousal (ages 8 to 18).
Stage 3: Complete cross dressing and the construction of a cross-gender identity including a feminine name (ages 18 and above).
Stage 4A: Integration of the cross-gender identity into the self system (ages 18 and above).
Stage 4B: An alternate pathway with the splitting off of the cross-gender identity and a disintegration of the self system. These people are disturbed by their part-time cross-gender identity and desire to pass as a women all of the time. They may lose their erotic pleasure with cross dressing and some of them seek sex reassignment surgery.
Stage 5: Secondary transsexualism.[48]

Ray Blanchard has suggested a classification scheme that includes only one transvestite category and three types of transsexuals: borderline, heterosexual fetishistic transsexual, and homosexual nonfetishistic transsexual.[49] Most of the classifications try to account for three variables: (1) the extent of the cross gender orientation, (2) the degree to which there is erotic arousal with cross dressing, and (3) the sexual orientation toward the same sex or the opposite sex.

Cross-Cultural Transvestism

Although Hirschfeld's early definition of transvestism included all of the cross dressers he could locate, the official medical model narrowed the definition to persons who sought psychotherapy. The work of Virginia Prince and the club movement broadened the definition to include transvestite club members, but this was perhaps even more idiosyncratic than that of the original medical model. Prince's quest for respectability led her to exclude cross dressers who were homosexuals, sadomasochists, women, prostitutes, or even partial cross dressers. Because the psychiatrists accepted Prince's definition of transvestism and incorporated it into the DSM-III-R, behavioral scientists, including the authors, blindly followed the accepted definition by studying club members as if they were the universe of cross dressers. The cross-sectional studies of transvestism all originated in the United States, Great Britain, and Australia. The patterns of transvestite life we pictured was based on the official social and sexual scripts facilitated by the club movement: Cross dressing started at about age ten; it was intermittent, male, erotic, heterosexual, and middle class.

Contemporary transvestites in other parts of the world and nonclub members in the United States have different life-styles. Frederick L. Whitam has studied the transvestite communities in Java, Thailand, Guatemala, Peru, Brazil, and the Philippines as well as certain urban areas in the United States. In these areas the men who cross dress are primarily homosexual. Some of them consider themselves to be pre-operative transsexuals, and a few actually have had sex reassignment surgery. One of the terms used to refer to Javanese transsexuals and transvestites is *waria,* which is coined from the word for woman, *wanita,* and man, *pria.* Although they live side by side with the more masculine homosexuals, the life-style of the *waria* is different. They tend to work as prostitutes, hairdressers, or entertainers. As prostitutes they serve young men who use them as substitutes for women but who will eventually marry, men who try them for occasional fun, and homosexual men. *Waria* singers and dancers are very popular, particularly with the gay and lesbian community.[50] Although the details are different, Whitam has described similar male cross-dressing communities in each of the other places he has studied.[51] The social and sexual script in these communities is very different from that of the middle-class members of the Anglo-American club movement. The differences are in fact so great that the club members say these cross dressers are not transvestites but "gay queens."

Cross Dressing among Women

Although cross dressing as a historical phenomenon was much more common in women than in men, and women continue to cross dress, they are not called transvestites because the male club movement and, consequently, the DSM-III-R does not include them.[52] Prince's argument was that women cannot cross dress because they can wear anything they want without stigma, while some scholars have said that women cannot be called transvestites because they do not find cross dressing erotic. There are, however, some well-documented cases, including that of the woman described by Randall (see Chapter 9) and the woman who was the subject of the early Gutheil description ("An Analysis of a Case of Transvestism"). In 1982 Stoller published a paper on the subject which reviewed three cases in detail.[53] In order for an individual to fit his definition of transvestism, there had to be a "fetishistic" arousal to male clothing and no desire for sex reassignment surgery. As he pointed out, there are many women who cross dress, but most of them were either transsexuals or lesbians who, he said, were not aroused by clothing. The three cases he described fit his stringent criteria of not wanting sex reassignment surgery and experiencing erotic enjoyment from cross dressing.

The first case was taken from Emil Gutheil's case presentation of Elsa, who came to see Gutheil to obtain an endorsement for a police permit to wear men's clothing.[54] She did not want him to tamper with her sexual patterns. She was a thirty-four-year-old government clerk who played the violin, walked like a man, urinated standing up, and was often stopped on the street during the war (World War I) because she was taken for a man. She described her erotic response to men's clothing as follows:

As regards clothing, I may say that simply putting on men's clothing gives me pleasure. The whole procedure is comparable to that tense anticipation of pleasure which subsides in relief and gratification as soon as the transvestiture is complete. I even experience lustful satisfaction in dreams of this act. It affords me downright sexual pleasure. Simply putting on my suit can provide an orgasm.[55] . . . The transvestiture has a far greater pleasure-value in my eyes than any intercourse, and I could easily forgo the latter in favor of the former.[56] The beginning of my transvestism also occurred at this time (between 14 and 15) and I experienced my first orgasm in a suite belonging to my brother Edward. We all put on costumes for the ball, and when I looked at myself in the mirror, I found that I resembled my father remarkably.[57]

Stoller notes that she was markedly masculine in her dress and walk. She even masturbated lying prone on her abdomen and making the movements of a male in coitus. Her masculine behaviors started in childhood; she played with boys' toys and destroyed a doll she received for Christmas. Sometimes when she and her friends played "father and mother," she played the role of the mother, so she was not a completely masculine-oriented child. When she was thirteen or fourteen, she had her first affair with a girl, and later she had other female lovers.[58]

The second case was that of an unmarried woman in her thirties with whom Stoller corresponded. So far as he knew she had no biological abnormalities. She had read that some authorities in the field argued that there were no female transvestites, yet she believed herself to be one and was interested in his opinion on the matter. He quoted extensively from her letters:

I believe that perhaps there are female transvestites and I feel myself to be one. My discovery of this proclivity occurred almost accidentally. A couple of years ago, I purchased a moustache, feeling my intent to be merely a lark. However, I became fairly obsessed with the idea of wearing this accoutrement in the street. This compulsion, while short of orgiastic, was definitely erotic.[59]

She then describes how she bought male clothing and went out in public. Without the moustache, however, her face was so feminine that she was never taken for a man. She described her enjoyment in these clothes as fetishistic. She indicated that she did not want to live full-time as a man; her sexual orientation was bisexual, and she was not a transsexual: "I do not desire a penis, but I do wish that my anatomy was a bit less curvy so I could more successfully practice TV. . . . One perversity perhaps is that I like the idea of looking like a rather feminine male."[60]

Stoller's third case was well known to him, and he had reported her history in other articles. She was anatomically normal. In response to his request, she wrote about her history of fetishism:

I've experienced special feelings while dressed in levis since I was very young—possibly prior to attending school. I do remember feeling definitely sexually excited around eleven years old, and being fully aware that my Levis were a contributing factor. . . . I also discovered that wearing boots intensified those feelings. . . . When putting on the Levis, I feel very excited immediately, I feel the texture, the roughness of the material, as I pull them over my feet, over the calves of my legs, into my thighs, and somewhere inside as well as in my clitoris. It's a marvelous sensation but becomes close to painful if I'm unable to relieve the sexual tension. My sexual fantasies, when wearing the Levis, always involve a female.[61]

She explained that a key experience in her life had been a Halloween carnival in which her gang of girlfriends planned to wear Levis and white shirts. Her mother refused to buy genuine Levis because she had some other jeans. The mother justified this on financial grounds, explaining that there was a new baby in the family, her father was gone, and the money from the mother's night job was meager. She therefore stole a pair of Levis, hid in the bushes near school, and put them on before the carnival. However, when she took off her old jeans and her panties, she experienced intense sexual excitement. She stayed in the bushes, slowly pulling up her Levis, and experienced an intense orgasm. She fantasized being with a girl, but she also fantasized about her mother's approval of her. Her mother was smiling and she was happy in her fantasy.[62]

Now she feels strong and confident when she is cross dressed but is not sexually aroused. When she wears Levis, she feels superior to men. Although she reported masculine impulses since childhood, she does not look completely masculine and does not want to. She wants to be a woman and remain one. She thinks a change of sex would be absurd.

Stoller argued that the three women he described are transvestites because they were erotically aroused by male clothing; they did not believe themselves to be men and did not want to have sex reassignment surgery. They had childhoods that included intense masculine identification, but they also experienced some elements of femininity.[63]

Holly Devor studied fifteen women who dressed as men and were often mistaken for men, yet all were known as women to their close associates.[64] She calls these women gender-blenders. Devor located them through a variety of approaches, including advertisements in feminist newspapers, trade associations, and memos in gay bars, health clubs, and gymnasiums. The subjects all participated in one or two extensive interviews. Devor was able to make some generalizations about the group. They tended to come from large families and conventional backgrounds in which women were subordinate. While their families allowed them to be tomboys when they were young, they later made efforts to socialize them into traditional women's roles. However, most of the women did not admire their mothers or accept them as their role models. All but two admired their fathers.

A common theme that was reported in all of the case histories was the fact that they were all mistaken for boys or men when they were out in public. Most had had experiences that were somewhat traumatic in this regard, including being hassled by police or thrown out of women's restrooms. Despite these incidents they all continued to dress in men's or ambiguous clothing; they all had short hair and only one wore makeup. All of them hated to wear dresses or other items of women's apparel. Eleven were lesbians, although some of them had gone through heterosexual phases. Two were attracted to hypermasculine men who could share their interests in macho activities. Three women had considered sex reassignment surgery, but none had seriously moved to obtain it. Devor's interpretation of her findings is from a feminist perspective:

The gender blending females in this study learned well the tenants of the patriarchal gender schema which dominates North American society. They learned that their female sex was supposed to be the irrefutable fact which made them into women and that, as women, they were supposed to behave in a feminine fashion. They also learned, early in their lives, that femininity was the patriarchy's way of marking a portion of the population for a secondary status in the service of men.[65]

Devor sees the gender-blending pattern as a rebellion against the patriarchy. Her subjects enjoyed their masculinity and the power it gave them. She believes gender-blending could be a transitional step between the present patriarchal society and some future, better society.

She may be overinterpreting her data. The women she interviewed did not sound particularly militant, nor did they seem to be participating in a social protest movement. Rather, they seemed to be people who were making the best of the cards life had dealt them. They had been tomboys from their early years, and for some unknown reason, they did not become more feminine at puberty. When cross dressed, they looked and acted like men, and although they were sometimes unhappy at being mistaken for males, they learned to cope with and even enjoy their situation. None of them were quoted as finding their male clothing erotic; rather, they spoke about the freedom it gave them and they considered it appropriate for their life-styles. Devor, however, does not seem to have asked them if they found their male clothing erotic. These women seem to be quite similar to the many women who cross dressed throughout history.

There are however, some women cross dressers who find men's clothing erotic. They write for and subscribe to the newsletter *FTM* (taken from the acronym for female-to-male cross dressers and transsexuals), which was started in 1986 by the late Lou Sullivan, a female to male cross dresser, and is published on a quarterly basis in San Francisco. Most of the news items in *FTM* feature people who are interested in surgical sex reassignment, but Sullivan contended that some in the newsletter's audience were simply female to male cross dressers, an assertion that is supported by some of the personal advertisements and the occasional article on the topic. Sullivan argued that the literature of transvestism was biased in not including more about women.[66]

In a 1991 issue of *FTM*, a copyrighted letter by Sandy Bernstein describes her experiences as a cross dresser. She is a lesbian, but her interest in cross dressing is focused on her inherent enjoyment of the activity rather than on using it as a device to attract women. Her first memory of cross dressing was when she wore her brother's shorts to school at age five. She wore dresses or skirts to school most of the time, but looked forward to playtime when she could wear pants and a cap. She is now a successful businesswoman who dresses in men's suits, complete with ties, wing-tipped shoes, and even boxer shorts. She feels she is attractive and derives emotional satisfaction from her clothing, yet she has no desire to be a man. Her plans include collecting additional data in order to write a book about women who wear men's clothing.[67]

Although the historical record in the first part of this book includes many examples of women who cross dressed, contemporary literature on female cross dressing remains scarce. The women's pattern of cross dressing is clearly different from that of the men. Despite Prince's assertion, the claim that women are not stigmatized for cross dressing is not true. Certainly, contemporary women are allowed to wear some items of men's clothing without punishment, whereas for men this is more difficult; however, once women cross over the imaginary line that separates those who toy with men's clothing and those who violate gender norms by impersonating men, the punishments for this violation are similar to those meted out to men. These cross dressers are socially stigmatized just as men are. The major difference seems to be that only a few women focus on the erotic element in the clothing. Their sexual orientation is usually lesbian, but a small minority are sexually attracted to men. Some of the women who cross dress have sought sex reassignment surgery, and if the technical problems related to the surgery were solved, probably more would. There is, however, a significant group of women who, like others in the past, cross dress all or part of the way and live masculine lives but do not want surgery, nor are they particularly distressed by the contours of their bodies. Because the women who cross dress seem less unhappy with themselves than male transvestites, they have been slower to organize support groups and have remained virtually invisible not only to the general public but even to sexologists and other scholars. This quieter approach seems traditionally feminine. Perhaps women are more "feminine" in their approach to violating gender norms than men are.

Summary

After Hirschfeld's study of transvestism, most studies of the phenomenon were done by psychiatrists who were simultaneously treating and studying their patients. This limited the research to the more distressed transvestites who sought therapy. The situation changed in 1960, when Prince started publishing a magazine and books for transvestites and established clubs where cross dressers met. As other organizations for transvestites grew and supportive reading material became available, the social and sexual scripts for transvestites were influenced by the club norms and common beliefs. A population of transvestites who were less plagued by psychopathology emerged. This was partly because the club movement provided a less idiosyncratic sexual script, and thus made transvestism less peculiar; but the club movement also allowed to emerge a healthier group of transvestites who earlier had been closeted and thus not studied by psychiatrists. The official definition of transvestism promulgated by the clubs was that of a respectable, middle-class, male heterosexual who cross dressed intermittently and thought about or actually went out in public to "pass" as a woman for adventure.

Most of these men started to cross dress secretly at about the age of ten; the practice was reinforced at puberty with orgasmic experiences and continued throughout their lives. As they grew older (and had more autonomy), they tended to cross dress more, but they also cherished their male role and their male sex organs. They were often emphatic about being heterosexual, except when they were cross dressed. While cross dressed they had homosexual fantasies or experiences. A few actually lived full-time as women. Some transvestites sought psychotherapy when they faced crises in their lives or if their wives and families were distressed, but many never saw a therapist.

The definition of transvestism that emerges from the club movement leaves out most cross dressers; it excludes women, homosexual cross dressers, streetwalkers, hustlers, and female impersonators. Clearly, however, these groups must also be considered if the phenomenon of cross dressing as it relates to gender is to be understood.

Notes

1. In addition to written source materials the authors have known and communicated with Virginia Prince over a period of thirty years.

2. John H. Gagnon and William Simon, *Sexual Conduct: The Social Sources of Human Sexuality* (Chicago: Aldine Publishing Company, 1973).

3. Virginia Prince, *An Introduction to the Subject of Transvestism or Femiphilia* (Los Angeles: Chevalier Publications [undated, c. 1970]); Virginia Prince, *Sexual and Genderal Identity: Transsexualism vs. Transvestism* (Los Angeles: Chevalier Publications, 1971); see also her editorials and comments in the various issues of *Transvestia*, of which she was editor and publisher from 1960 to 1977.

4. Much of this account is based upon her own autobiography, which appeared in *Transvestia* 18, no. 100 (1977). *Transvestia* was a magazine founded by Prince and published by Chevalier Publications, Box 36091, Los Angeles, CA, 90036. We have made efforts to verify the story. Originally, we planned to publish Virginia/Charles's original name, but she regards this part of her past a closed book she would rather not reopen. We respect her wishes.

5. The story of "Barbara Wilcox" was written up in a magazine called *Secrets* early in the 1940s, and she received some newspaper publicity.

6. This quotation is Bowman's words as remembered by Prince in her autobiography, 11–12.

7. Hugo B. Beigel and Robert Feldman, "The Male Transvestite's Motivation in Fiction, Research and Reality," *Advances in Sex Research* (New York: Harper and Row, 1963), 198–212.

8. Neil Buhrich and Neil McConaghy, "Transvestite Fiction," *The Journal of Nervous and Mental Disease* 163 (1976): 420–27.

9. Robert Stoller, "Pornography and Perversion," *Archives of General Psychiatry* 22 (1970): 490–99.

10. Virginia Prince and P. M. Bentler, "A Survey of 504 Cases of Transvestism," *Psychological Reports* 31 (1972): 903–17; Neil Buhrich and Neil McConaghy, "Parental Relationships During Childhood in Homosexuality, Transvestism and Transsexualism," *Australian and New Zealand Journal of Psychiatry* 12 (1978): 103–8; Vern Bullough, Bonnie Bullough, and Richard Smith, "Childhood and Family of Male Sexual Minority Groups," *Health Values: Achieving High Level Wellness* 7 (July–August 1983): 238–57; Vern L. Bullough, Bonnie Bullough, and Richard Smith, "A Comparative Study of Male Transvestites, Male to Female Transsexuals and Male Homosexuals," *The Journal of Sex Research* 19 (August 1983): 238–57; Bonnie Bullough, Vern Bullough, and Richard R. Smith, "Masculinity and Femininity in Transvestite, Transsexual and Gay Males," *Western Journal of Nursing Research* 7 (1985): 317–32.

11. Buhrich and McConaghy, "Transvestite Fiction," 423.

12. Thomas S. Weinberg and Vern L. Bullough, "Alienation, Self-Image, and the Importance of Support Groups for Wives of TV's," *Journal of Sex Research* 24 (1988): 262–68; Vern L. Bullough and Thomas S. Weinberg, "Women Married to Transvestites: Problems and Adjustments," *Journal of Psychology and Human Sexuality* 1 (1988): 83–104.

13. Thorstein B. Veblen, *The Theory of the Leisure Class* (New York: Macmillan, 1899).

14. James Keating and Ray Over, "Sexual Fantasies of Heterosexual and Homosexual Men," *Archives of Sexual Behavior* 19 (October 1990): 461–75; David Smith and Ray Over, "Enhancement of Fantasy-Induced Sexual Arousal in Men through Training in Sexual Imagery," *Archives of Sexual Behavior* 19 (October 1990): 477–89.

15. Annie Woodhouse, *Fantastic Women* (New Brunswick, NJ: Rutgers University Press, 1989), pp. 134–44.

16. Virginia Prince and P. M. Bentler, "A Survey of 504 Cases of Transvestism."

17. Neil Buhrich and Neil McConaghy, "Parental Relationships During Childhood in Homosexuality, Transvestism and Transsexualism"; Neil Buhrich and Trina Beaumont, "Comparison of Transvestism in Australia and America," *Archives of Sexual Behavior* 10 (1981): 269–79.

18. Vern L. Bullough, Bonnie Bullough, and Richard Smith, "A Comparative Study of Male Transvestites, Male-to-Female Transsexuals and Male Homosexuals."

19. Richard F. Docter, *Transvestites and Transsexuals: Towards a Theory of Gender Behavior* (New York: Plenum Press, 1988), 121–65.

20. John T. Talamani, *Boys Will Be Girls: The Hidden World of the Heterosexual Male Transvestite* (Washington, DC: University Press of America, 1982), 22.

21. R. W. Hodge, P. M. Siegel, and P. H. Rossi, "Occupational Prestige in the United States," *American Journal of Sociology* 70 (1964): 296–302.

22. Bullough et al., "A Comparative Study of Male Transvestites."

23. Buhrich and McConaghy, "Comparison of Transvestism in Australia and America."

24. Neil Buhrich and Neil McConaghy, "The Discrete Syndromes of Transvestism and Transsexualism," *Archives of Sexual Behavior* 6 (1977): 483–95.

25. Docter, *Transvestites and Transsexuals*, 130–39.

26. Ray Blanchard, I. G. Racansky, and Betty W. Steiner, "Phallometric Detection of Fetishistic Arousal in Heterosexual Male Cross-Dressers," *The Journal of Sex Research* 22 (November 1986): 452–62.

27. Buhrich and Beaumont, "Transvestism in Australia and America."

28. Harry Brierly, *Transvestism: A Handbook with Case Studies, for Psychologists, Psychiatrists and Counsellors* (Oxford: Pergamon Press, 1979), 43.

29. P. M. Bentler, Richard W. Sherman, and Charles Prince, "Personality Characteristics of Male Transvestites," *Journal of Clinical Psychology* 26 (1970): 287–91.

30. Harry Brierly, "The Heterosexual Transvestite: A Gender Anomaly," *The Bulletin of the British Psychological Society* 27, no. 95 (1974): 156–57; Brierly, *Transvestism: A Handbook with Case Studies*, 43.

31. Ibid., 22–23.

32. Peter J. Fagan, Thomas N. Wise, Leonard R. Derogotis, and Chester W. Schmidt, "Distressed Transvestites: Psychometric Characteristics," *The Journal of Nervous and Mental Disease* 176 (March 1988): 214–17.

33. A. J. Taylor D. G. McLachlan, "MMPI Profiles of Six Transvestites," *Journal of Clinical Psychology* 19 (1963): 330–32.

34. James Beatrice, "A Psychological Comparison of Heterosexuals, Transvestites, Preoperative Transsexuals and Postoperative Transsexuals," *Journal of Nervous and Mental Disease* 173 (1985): 358–65.

35. Harry Brierly, *Transvestism: A Handbook with Case Studies*, 39–40; Harry Brierly, "Gender as a Component of Sexual Disorders," *Bulletin of the British Psychological Society* 28 (1975): 224–25.

36. Sandra L. Bem, "The Measurement of Psychological Androgyny," *Journal of Consulting and Clinical Psychology* 42 (1974): 155–62. For a discussion of the implications of the dimorphic system, see Marianne van den Wijngaard, "The Acceptance of Scientific Theories and Images of Masculinity and Femininity: 1959–±1985," *Journal of the History of Biology* 24 (Spring 1991): 19–44.

37. Docter, *Transvestites and Transsexuals*, 154–58.

38. Janet T. Spence and Robert L. Helmreich, *Masculinity and Femininity: Their Psychological Dimensions, Correlates and Antecedents* (Austin: University of Texas Press, 1979).

39. Bonnie Bullough, Vern Bullough, and Richard W. Smith, "Masculinity and Femininity in Transvestite, Transsexual and Gay Males."

40. Prince and Bentler, "Survey of 504 Cases."

41. Buhrich and McConaghy, "Parental Relationships During Childhood."

42. Michael D. Newcomb, "The Role of Perceived Relative Parent Personality in the Development of Heterosexuals, Homosexuals and Transvestites," *Archives of Sexual Behavior* 14 (1985): 147–64.

43. Vern Bullough, Bonnie Bullough, and Richard Smith, "Childhood and Family of Male Sexual Minority Groups," *Health Values: Achieving High Level Wellness* 7 (July–August 1983): 19–26.

44. Ibid.

45. Michael E. Persinger and Laurence J. Stettner, "The Relation of Trans-

vestite Behavior to Self-Rated Personality Characteristics," *Journal of Psychology and Human Sexuality* 43 (1991): 83–96.

46. Neil Buhrich and Neil McConaghy, "The Clinical Syndromes of Femmiphilic Transvestism," *Archives of Sexual Behavior* 6 (1977): 397–412; Buhrich and McConaghy, "The Discrete Syndromes of Transvestism and Transsexualism"; Neil Buhrich and Neil McConaghy, "Preadult Feminine Behaviors of Male Transvestites," *Archives of Sexual Behavior* 14 (1985): 413–19.

47. Neil Buhrich and Neil McConaghy, "Three Clinically Discrete Categories of Fetishistic Transvestism," *Archives of Sexual Behavior* 8 (1979): 151–57.

48. Richard Docter, *Transvestites and Transsexuals,* 195–227.

49. Ray Blanchard, "Research Methods for the Typological Study of Gender Disorders in Males," in *Gender Dysphoria: Development, Research, and Management,* ed. Betty W. Steiner (New York: Plenum Press, 1985), 227–57.

50. Frederick L. Whitam, "Transvestites and Transsexuals in Javanese Entertainment," paper presented at the Eighth Annual Berkeley Conference on Southeast Asia Studies, 1991. Berkeley, CA.

51. Frederick L. Whitam and Robin M. Mathy, *Male Homosexuality in Four Societies: Brazil, Guatemala, the Philippines and the United States* (New York: Praeger Publishers, 1986).

52. Docter, *Transvestites and Transsexuals,* 9; Prince, *An Introduction to the Subject of Transvestism.*

53. Robert J. Stoller, "Transvestism in Women," *Archives of Sexual Behavior* 11 (1982): 99–115.

54. Emil Gutheil, "An Analysis of a Case of Transvestism," in *Disorders of the Instincts and the Emotions: The Parapathiac Disorders,* vol. 2: *Sexual Aberrations: The Phenomenon of Fetishism in Relation to Sex,* ed. Wilhelm Stekel, 281–318. (New York: Liveright Publishing, 1930).

55. Gutheil, "An Analysis of a Case of Transvestism," 284, quoted by Stoller, "Transvestism in Women," 101.

56. Gutheil, "An Analysis of a Case of Transvestism," 289, quoted by Stoller, "Transvestism in Women," 101.

57. Gutheil, "An Analysis of a Case of Transvestism," 305–6, quoted by Stoller, "Transvestism in Women," 101.

58. Gutheil, "Analysis of a Case of Transvestism," discussed by Stoller, "Transvestism in Women," 101–2.

59. Stoller, "Transvestism in Women," 103.

60. Ibid., 103–4.

61. Ibid., 106.

62. Ibid., 108.

63. Ibid., 99–115.

64. Holly Devor, *Gender Blending: Confronting the Limits of Duality* (Bloomington: Indiana University Press, 1989).

65. Ibid., 145.

66. Lou Sullivan, "A Review of *Transvestites and Transsexuals: Toward a Theory of Cross-Gender Behavior,* by Richard F. Docter," *FTM* 14 (1990): 7.

67. Sandy Bernstein, "A Crossdresser's Closet: A Different Kind of 'Coming Out'" *FTM* 16 (July 1991): 3.

Chapter 13
Current Explanations of Cross Dressing

Though cross dressing has occurred throughout history, some people are more likely to cross dress than others. Why? We believe that the causal sequence in the development of gender and sexual orientation is becoming more clear, although no one study can be cited as suddenly clarifying the process. Rather, the research related to all types of gender behavior has gradually pointed to the causal sequence by which cross-gender behaviors, including cross dressing, occur. This means that an understanding of other types of gender-related behavior is basic to an understanding of cross dressing.

Gender identity is the total perception of the individual about his or her own gender. It includes a basic personal identity as a boy or girl, man or woman, as well as personal judgments about the individual's level of conformity to the societal norms of masculinity and femininity. Gender as it is perceived by others is called gender role. The two concepts are tied together, since most people show their perceptions of themselves in their dress, manners, and activities. Clothing is the major symbol of gender that allows other persons to immediately identify the individual's gender role, but there are other symbols as well, including mannerisms, gait, occupational choice, and sexual orientation. For most people their gender identity, gender role, and all the symbolic manifestations of gender will be congruent, and they will be sexually attracted to the opposite sex. However, the minority who fail to conform in some way may well be as large as 10 percent of the population. Moreover, the patterns of nonconformity vary widely, so the diagnostic categories favored by the medical community simply do not work very well.

Calling these people who do not fit neatly into the gender boxes labeled "male" and "female" nonconformists sounds as if they violated the norms of society on purpose. Since this may not be the case, most sexologists use the term *cross-gendered* to avoid this judgment. Cross-gendered means they either feel they do not fit neatly into either the male or female box or their behavior is not totally congruent with the rules and expectations of the society they live in.

The major area in which people depart from societal expectations is in sexual orientation, which is defined as the individual's view about the sexual attractiveness of other persons, including the most basic question as to whether one is sexually attracted to persons of the opposite sex, the same sex, or both, as well the details of the individual's sexual turn-on. The second most common area of cross-gender behavior is in the area of the symbolic expression of gender through clothing (including jewelry, tattoos, and other adornments). A smaller group of cross-gendered people seek a complete and permanent identity as a member of the opposite sex.

Gender identity is apparently the product of a complex interaction among three factors: (1) a genetic predisposition, (2) physiological factors, and (3) the socialization process.[1] It is no longer possible to argue that either nature or nurture alone is the answer; it is clear that both are involved in producing the complex person we call a man or a woman. It is also evident that many if not most people are not clearly and unequivocally masculine or feminine; they have elements of the opposite gender identity in their makeup. Only a minority (10 percent or so, depending on how rigid the societal rules are interpreted), however, are sufficiently cross-gendered to cause comment or punishment by the society. These are the people who are labeled and stigmatized as homosexuals, lesbians, transvestites, transsexuals, or even with more pejorative terms.

The level of societal stigma for cross-gender behaviors varies widely; behavior that is acceptable in one culture is punished in others. Europe and the United States have a rather strict dimorphic gender pattern, so, as we have seen, cross-gender behaviors in the West have been stigmatized and punished in various ways. Since the nineteenth century, when Western countries began using a medical model, significant departures from a dimorphic model of masculinity and femininity have been labeled as illness. Similarly, sexual orientations other than exclusive heterosexuality were considered an illness until 1973, when the American Psychiatric Association dropped ordinary homosexuality from the list of diagnoses it recognizes. However, "ego-dystonic homosexuality" was retained. This means that persons who are distressed by their homosexuality are still considered mentally ill, but that homosexuality per se does not imply illness.[2]

The two major clothing-related gender disorders, transsexualism and transvestism, are still listed in the DSM-III-R and are still considered illnesses. However, transvestism refers only to men, and women who cross dress are not considered sick. The illness rubric has its advantages. It allows money, sometimes even public money, to be spent for treatment, and an illness label is more benign than some alternatives, including those of "crime" or "sin." The mental illness label, however, stigmatizes and lessens human freedom. Since many transsexuals are also very depressed and want sex reassignment surgery, the illness label, with all of its disadvantages, may be reasonable; but in the case of transvestites, who seldom want or need treatment, the label probably only effectively stigmatizes their behavior.

Transsexualism, a gender identity that is completely at variance with the apparent sexual identity of the individual, has an incidence of approximately 1 : 50,000 in both men and women, although in societies where male homosexuality is severely stigmatized, some male homosexuals seek reassignment surgery and increase the apparent incidence of male transsexualism.[3] Most authorities estimate that approximately 5 percent of adult males are primarily or exclusively homosexual with approximately 3 percent of adult females preferring same-sex partners. Using data from five sample surveys done between 1970 and 1990, Roberts and Turner estimated that a minimum of 5 to 7 percent of U.S. men have had some same-sex contact as adults, although only a quarter of that group had male–male sexual contact during the previous year. In addition, the majority of men who report some homosexual contacts also report having some heterosexual contacts, suggesting that bisexuality is more common than it was previously thought to be.[4]

The incidence of transvestism among adult males is probably lower than the incidence of homosexuality and higher than the incidence of transsexualism. There are approximately 10,000 American readers of the transvestite periodicals, and a significant proportion of this group are active in one of the clubs. However, since cross dressing can be practiced in secret, the number is probably far larger than magazine subscriptions and club rolls indicate. Adding to the numbers is the large group of men who find erotic enjoyment in putting on one or more items of women's underwear and who are entirely ignored by the groups and magazines, although many are occasional purchasers of books and magazines dealing with cross dressing. While we were writing this book a local newspaper reporter did a feature story on the topic of transvestism, and a local television talk show host asked us to appear and discuss the topic. In response to this exposure, approximately thirty-five persons called our offices or home to ask questions, express an interest in locating a transvestite club, seek a referral to a psychotherapist, or just to reach out in some way. Since most people do not call the subjects of newspaper features, and some do not even read the newspaper or watch the talk shows, we figured the people who called represent the tip of an iceberg of some unknown size. The figure of 1 percent of the adult male population is often mentioned, and it conforms with our own tentative conclusions; we will use it until better statistics are available. No Buffalo area resident who called us was concerned about female cross dressers, but women cross dressers and gender-benders are often quieter about their behavior, so the numbers for women remain even more elusive.

Genetic Factors in Gender Identity

The basic dimorphic sex pattern is determined by the combinations of chromosomes, with two X chromosomes producing a female and the combination of X and Y chromosomes producing a male. In addition to carrying this basic identity, these chromosomes carry genes that cause or prevent many sex-linked diseases and a variety of other information, most of which has not been identified yet. Major genetic errors that influence gender identity, such as Klinefelter's or Turner's syndrome, have long been known, but the details of the genetic process as it relates to masculinity and femininity is still being researched. It is not possible at the present time to point to a specific gene related to a cross-gender identity, but it is possible to infer a genetic influence from secondary research data.

Clearly, every major society produces people who are cross-gendered. There are variations in the roles and functions they perform in the society and as to whether they are stigmatized or honored. In some societies cross-gendered persons are closeted, but if sufficient data are available to adequately study the society, a few of its cross-gendered persons can be identified. These data are presented in this book as well as in another book by one of us (V.L.B.) entitled *Sexual Variance in Society and History*.[5] The historical data furnishes a powerful argument in support of a genetic influence on cross-gender identities.

Frederick L. Whitam has arrived at a similar conclusion using cross-cultural data. After investigating homosexuality and cross dressing in a wide variety of contemporary cultures, including the countries of the Pacific rim, Latin America, and the United States, he noted that:

although all people in all societies with rare exceptions are socialized to be heterosexual, the predictable, universal appearance of homosexual persons, despite socialization into heterosexual patterns of behavior, suggests not only that homosexual orientation is biologically based but that sexual orientation itself is also biologically derived.[6]

Whitam also reported that, in most societies other than Germanic and Anglo-American ones, both the male and female homosexual cultures include a cross-dressing subculture. These persons regard themselves as homosexual or friends of homosexuals, and the more masculine segments of the gay world regard them as a natural part of the scene. Similarly, the lesbian subculture accepts those who cross dress as welcome members. The pronounced separation of male homosexual and heterosexual transvestites occurs primarily in Northwestern Europe and the United States. Whitam explains that this is due to the club movement started by Prince, the psychiatric community, and the burden of the stigma attached to a homosexual identity in Western countries. Conversely, it could also be argued that many cross-gendered people in the societies he studied who are primarily interested in cross dressing consider themselves homosexual because there is no alternative in their societies. Certainly, the large body of anthropological studies collected in the Human Relations Area Files (originally by a group at Yale University but now available through a computerized network) supports the observation that both homosexuality and cross dressing are widely dispersed phenomena in primitive societies, and that these patterns are accommodated by a wide variety of arrangements.[7]

If there is a genetic basis for men and women to be cross-gendered, why did it develop? What survival value would such a gene have for our prehistorical ancestors? Edward O. Wilson hypothesized a possible genetic predisposition for homosexuality in certain humans by using a theory he calls "inclusive fitness," which is defined as the sum of the individual's reproductive successes plus the reproductive success of others who carry that person's genes. He explained that there are homosexual genes that exist not only in the individual who is homosexual but in their relatives. Homosexual persons contributed to the survival of the family, since by not having children they were available to altruistically support and help the family, to serve in such roles as aunt, uncle, shaman, or medicine man, and thus aid in the survival of the family. Thus, genes for a homosexual orientation increased in frequency, not because they aided the homosexual person in his or her own survival but because they aided his relatives who shared his gene pool. This broader spread of the genes helps explain how persons with the homosexual genes could be reproduced, since they themselves often did not produce offspring. However, their availability as support persons who were themselves not tied down by children, and their practice of bonding with and supporting others of their own sex, helped their struggling tribe survive. Wilson calls this the kin selection hypothesis of the origin of homosexuality, and he argues that the studies that suggest the inheritability of a tendency toward homosexuality support his hypothesis.[8]

Wilson and his followers call this approach sociobiology. When his first book on the topic was published in 1975 it was widely criticized by a wide variety of critics. People who were hostile to gays felt that it took away some blame that homosexuals somehow deserved, while friends of gays argued that it took away freedom.[9] Careful analysis suggests that sociobiology, if it is not pushed too far, is a reasonable approach that fits well with what is already known about such conditions as sickle-cell anemia, and that genetic factors play a role in the genesis of gender identity and sexual orientation.[10]

This generalization about sociobiological influences is further supported by family studies. In a comprehensive review of these studies, Richard C. Pillard found substantial evidence that sexual orientation is familial. Among the better of these studies was one done by George Henry, who studied forty male and forty female "sex variants" and drew up elaborate family trees for the subjects. The subjects themselves provided most of the data about the sexual orientation of their relatives. His data support the existence of a family factor, since there were more bisexual or homosexual relatives than would be expected by chance. However, since the family members were not themselves interviewed, his study has been criticized.[11]

M. Sydney Margolese and Oscar Janiger asked about homosexuality in the families of two groups of men who had been recruited for an endocrine study. Among the heterosexual men, two out of twenty-four reported a homosexual relative; among the homosexual men, seventeen out of twenty-eight reported homosexual relatives.[12] Pillard and his group interviewed thirty-six homosexual men (5 to 6 on the Kinsey scale) concerning the sexual orientations of their relatives. There was a total of eighty siblings in the group. Among the thirty-five sisters only one was homosexual, but among the forty-five brothers, most were homosexual. The authors concluded that homosexuality is probably genetic, but indicated that a study that actually interviews the family members is needed, since estimates by other people are subject to bias.[13]

The Kallman twin study was discussed in Chapter 11. Kallman found that in forty sets of monozygotic twins, all were concordant for sexual orientation while most of the dizygotic twins were discordant.[14] An ongoing study by Diamond and associates was first reported in 1987. At that time there were ten sets of monozygotic twin brothers in the sample, and they found an 80 percent concordance for homosexuality. There are now thirty pairs of twins in the sample (eighteen monozygotic and twelve dizygotic), and the findings are similar. There is a 72 percent concordance for homosexuality among the monozygotic twins and a 33 to 50 percent concordance for homosexuality among the dizygotic pairs.[15] These high percentages of concordance, particularly among the monozygotic twins, is a powerful argument for a genetic factor in the causal sequence for homosexuality.[16]

Physiological Influences on Gender Identity

The physiological mechanism by which the genetic influences on sex are translated into actual cross-gender behavior is probably neurohormonal. This assumption is based on the vast and growing literature documenting the hormonal influence on gender behavior and the impact of prenatal hormones on the brain. Sex hormones are the messengers that cause bodily reactions which are interpreted as masculine and feminine. Their influence is not limited to the postnatal development of a person but may be equally or even more important in the prenatal period.[17] Human embryos of both sexes develop in an identical fashion for the first two months of gestation. Chromosomal sex, established at the time of conception, guides the process and directs the development of either ovaries or testes. If testes develop and produce sufficient androgens, male secondary sex characteristics develop. Without these hormones, the embryo remains female. However, given the appropriate genetic message, slightly more than half of the embryos will secrete androgens that trigger and support differentiation into a male.[18]

According to Anke A. Ehrhardt and Heino F. L. Meyer-Bahlburg, the neurohormonal theory became more complex as the role of additional hormones was identified. Progesterone has been shown to counteract androgens and thereby protect the brain of female fetuses from the masculinizing influence of the androgens. Recent research has also suggested that androgens are converted to an estrogen compound in order to exert their decisive masculinizing effects on the target cells. The gonadal and adrenal hormonal responses are controlled by the pituitary gland, which is in turn controlled by the hypothalamus.

The brain can itself be altered by hormonal influences, particularly during the early months of gestation when the neural tissues are developing. The research that is particularly relevant here are the studies of children with congenital adrenal hyperplasia, a genetic defect that prevents the adrenal cortex from synthesizing cortisone; instead, the cortex is stimulated to release excess adrenal androgens both before and after birth. If the child is a genetic female, her clitoris becomes enlarged and her external genitalia appear masculinized. If the child is a genetic male, his external genitalia are normal. Treatment is with cortisone, which suppresses the excess androgens. Studies of the girls who started treatment when they were born (so they were no longer exposed to excess androgen) are of particular interest because they provide a natural experiment to assess the effect of prenatal male hormones on a female fetus. Ehrhardt and Meyer-Bahlburg report that these girls differ significantly from their siblings and other controls. They enjoy rough-and-tumble play, associate with male peers and are identified by themselves and others as tomboys. They show low interest in role rehearsals as wives and mothers. The boys who had extra male hormones before birth exhibited higher energy expenditure in sports and were somewhat more likely to initiate fights than their peers. The fact that the masculinizing influence remains after the hormonal stimulation has ceased suggests that the neural pathways controlling masculinity and femininity have been affected.[19]

These same researchers, along with other colleagues, also studied a group of thirty women, aged seventeen to thirty years, who had been exposed to synthetic estrogen, diethylstilbestrol (DES) during their prenatal lives. They were compared with a control group of women from the same clinic who had abnormal Papanicolaou smears as well as with a group of their own siblings who had not been exposed to DES. The DES women demonstrated more bisexuality and homosexuality than the control groups. However, since 75 percent of the group was nearly or exclusively heterosexual, the authors suggest caution in interpreting the findings; obviously, prenatal influences are not the only factors determining sexual orientation.[20] Recent research by Simon LeVay has identified differences between homosexual and heterosexual men in a portion of the anterior hypothalamus. This region of the brain has been identified as governing sexual behavior. What these differences mean is yet to be identified.[21]

Animal studies using rats and hamsters, particularly those of Dorner and his colleagues from West Germany, have identified two different mating centers in the hypothalamus: one for male behavior and one for female behavior. Sex hormones injected into the appropriate areas stimulate the sexual behaviors, and destructive lesions inhibit the behaviors. Genetic males that experienced a temporary androgen deficiency during the hypothalamic developmental period but had normal androgen levels in adulthood were sexually aroused by same-sex animals. The higher the androgen level during the hypothalamic differentiation period, the stronger the male behavior and the weaker the female behavior, irrespective of genetic sex. For humans Dorner believes that the critical hypothalamic differentiation phase may occur between the fourth and seventh months of gestation. Dorner's experiments on humans have demonstrated different responses to injections of conjugated estrogens (Premarin) in homosexual and heterosexual men.[22]

Milton Diamond finds the physiological data impressive. He argues that prenatal hormones exert influences on neural pathways and the neuroendocrine axis (the link between the hypothalamus, the pituitary gland, and other endocrine glands). These neural pathways control future hormonal production and consequently influence sexual behavior. The scientific evidence for this assertion is just beginning to accumulate,[23] but Diamond anticipates that future research will further clarify this process. Diamond outlines four levels of behavioral sexuality that can be influenced by neural patterns:

1. Sexual patterns for maleness (aggressiveness, large muscle activity) or femaleness (passivity, nurturance).
2. Sexual identity as a male or female.
3. Sexual object choice; the sex of the individual chosen as an erotic partner.
4. Sexual mechanisms involved in erection, lubrication, and so on.[24]

Thus, Diamond argues that there are separate neural pathways for each of these facets of sexuality and that sexual behavior varies on all of these parameters.

The importance of male-patterned aggression should not be overlooked. A meta-analysis of 143 studies of the genetic differences in males and females showed consistent results. As indicated by Janet Hyde:

Out of the massive research literature on psychological gender differences, a few behaviors have emerged as showing reliable gender differences. One of those is aggression. The greater aggressiveness of males, compared with females, is generally regarded as a consistent and large phenomenon.[25]

The reason this attribute is so important to the understanding of gender is that it has given power to men, and particularly to the more aggressive men, to establish other gender characteristics, including the relative servitude that has marked the history of women as the subordinated sex.[26] This physiological component of the male makeup has led many feminists to argue erroneously that the whole concept of gender is a social construction because so many norms are seen to be self-serving for men. However, they forget that it is this underlying physiological factor of aggressiveness that has allowed males to call the shots. If the male proclivity for aggressiveness is included in the consideration of the physiological factors that make up gender behavior, the importance of the body in the determination of gender attributes is more obvious. Aggression provides power, and the importance of this power to men helps to explain the threat some men feel when they see cross-gendered males who are gentle and nurturing; such men are a threat to continued male dominance.

Richard Pillard and James Weinrich suggest that there should be further differentiation of the neural influences on gender behavior because separate components of the nervous system control masculinization and defeminization. Masculinizing and defeminizing of the hypothalamus probably occur at four to five months of gestation.[27] The masculinizing androgens are known, but the defeminizing agent or agents are not yet identified, although it may be müllerian inhibiting substance (MIS). Some people argue that the masculinizing and defeminizing agents are the same, but operate at different critical periods. By differentiating between these two processes, Pillard and Weinrich argue that they can place all gender transpositions on a periodic table. Male-to-female transsexuals and certain passive lesbians are both defeminized and not masculinized. Most homosexual men are unmasculinized and defeminized. Transvestites are masculinized but not defeminized.[28]

There is other scattered but accumulating evidence that physiological factors are involved in cross-gender identities. In a study of 241 lesbian women, Muriel Wilson Perkins found that the members of her sample had narrower hips, increased arm and leg girths, less subcutaneous fat, and more muscle than a sample of 1,260 adult women measured between 1960 and 1968. She also divided the sample into groupings according to their dominance in the sex act, and the dominant group was significantly taller than other lesbian women.[29]

A study published in 1984 by Brian Gladue and colleagues found an estrogen feedback mechanism related to sexual orientation. Men and women with lifelong heterosexual orientations and men with lifelong homosexual orientations were administered an estrogen preparation that is known to enhance the luteinizing hormone blood levels in women but not in men. The pattern shown by homosexual men was intermediate to that shown by the heterosexual women and men. Furthermore, testosterone was depressed for a significantly longer period in the homosexual than in the heterosexual men. These findings support the idea that biological markers for sexual orientation may exist.[30]

As the evidence for a biological explanation of homosexuality and other cross-gendered behavior accumulates, there has been no shortage of critics who have questioned various aspects of the work. In 1980 Garfield Tourney reviewed sixteen studies linking hormones and homosexuality and suggested that more carefully controlled studies are needed before definitive conclusions are drawn.[31] Other critics have argued that this research is overemphasizing the role of biology in predicting complex behavior and that it supports a medical or illness model.[32] A comprehensive review of all the literature suggesting biological determinants of sexual orientation was done by Louis Gooren, Eric Fliers, and Keith Courtney in 1990. While they were unable to discount arguments that certain prenatal biological factors could facilitate a homosexual orientation later in life, they point out that irrefutable evidence is presently lacking.[33]

Culture and the Socialization Process

In our society boys in the nursery are often covered with blue blankets and girls with pink ones. Although we know these culturally determined colors have only been used since the beginning of the century, the "right" color allows nursery personnel and the babies' families to begin sex role socialization from the day of birth. Studies of parental behaviors indicate that they treat girl and boy babies differently, playing more roughly with the boys and allowing them to be more aggressive. Boys are given trucks and other toys that encourage large muscle movement, while girls are started on the task of anticipatory socialization for motherhood with dolls and relatively passive toys.[34] This happens despite the fact that these nurturing skills will probably not help the young woman of today succeed in the competitive business world or achieve eminence in her chosen profession. Unfortunately, contemporary American gender identity norms have fallen victim to a cultural lag. They are pronatal at a time when the world is overpopulated, and they undervalue women. Yet the norms are sustained as long as society continues to socialize boys to be more aggressive, thus allowing them to continue to control women.

Although strong physiological influences on gender behavior have been shown in many studies, such as those reviewed above, the malleability of human beings also has been documented; such findings have been recorded by John Money, Joan Hampson and John Hampson, in their study of seventy-six children identified as hermaphrodites. Each of these children had one or more of the biological markers for sex that were not congruent with their sex assignment at birth. Nineteen members of the sample had been assigned a sex that was not congruent with their chromosomal sex; these people all developed a gender role and sexual orientation consistent with their sex of rearing. Twenty persons exhibited some sort of contradiction between their gonadal sex and their sex assignment, but all of them conformed to their sex of rearing. Twenty-seven persons had hormonal stimulation that was not synchronized with their sex assignment. Four of these people (three women and one man) changed their sex to conform to their hormonal patterns. Twenty-three members of the group developed external genitalia that were at odds with their sex assignment; they were treated with plastic surgery to make their genitals appear more congruent with their sex assignment; they did not change their sex of rearing. In summary, the authors noted that only four of the seventy-six patients changed their sex from their assignment at birth. The authors concluded that the sex of assignment and rearing was a better predictor of gender role than any of the biological tendencies. They argued that gender imprinting starts before the child's first birthday and reaches a critical period by about eighteen months. By the age of two and one half years gender role is established, and change after that time is difficult for the individual.[35]

It would be a mistake to consider the path taken by people whose bodies are different from their mind-set as an easy one. Unexpected growth of external genitalia or hormonal messages that are contradictory to socialization patterns can be particularly disturbing, and although the majority of these children did not take the path of sex change, other people feel compelled to do so. Julianne Imperato-McGinley's study of children who have a prenatal deficiency in an enzyme needed to produce dihydrotestosterone was reviewed in Chapter 11. The findings from this study are quite different from the findings of Money and the Hampsons. These boys, who live in one village in the Dominican Republic, lacked penises at birth, but later developed penises at puberty. Seventeen out of the nineteen who had been wrongly assigned to the female sex changed their gender identity at puberty.[36] Some people have argued that since the village is aware of the phenomenon, the trauma of the sex change is eased. While this may be true today, the early cases did not have village support when they went against the gender identity pattern to which they had been socialized.

The biological processes are not, however, the final word. They are further influenced by the socialization process, which includes the teaching and learning situations that shape people into their assigned gender roles. Socialization takes place primarily in small-group settings, such as the family and the peer group, but the patterns for socialization tend to be provided by the broader culture. Sometimes the cultural patterns are outdated (cultural lag) but they remain powerful forces even when they may be dysfunctional according to the goals of the society.

Socialization is also influenced by groups outside the home. One of the major functions of an organization for stigmatized individuals is to furnish a subculture for people with common problems to meet and share experiences.[37] An organization of cross dressers, for example, not only allows but defines a kind of group behavior for cross dressing. Such groups not only help give solace and end the isolation individuals face but, in the process, set new definitions of appropriate behavior. A social constructionist would describe this as "the process by which people come to describe, explain, or otherwise account for the world (including themselves) in which they live. In short, such a view attempts to articulate common forms of understanding."[38]

The organizations Prince and her followers established furnished a social script for transvestites and gave them a group identity that shaped their own self-concepts. They needed the support of the group because, as male cross dressers, they lost status by dressing as women, even though the women's role was improving in the twentieth century. These changes, in fact, made the feminine role more attractive; and when coupled with the eroticism of doing the forbidden (which gives the cross dresser a high), the greater accessibility of clothes of the opposite sex (they could be, e.g., purchased through the mail) tended to encourage experiments in cross dressing.

In the social constructionist perspective, human sexuality is viewed not as a biological given but as an ever-changing psychosocial construct. The roots of this perception are derived from symbolic interactionism, a theory that describes the development of symbolic social worlds that allow people to interact with each other.[39] In examining any aspect of human sexual behavior, interactionists see their primary task as describing the process by which sexual meanings are constructed.[40] In terms of cross dressing, the act itself is not nearly so significant as the social meanings that the participants attribute to the act and the resulting interactions. This significance is created through public discourse that not only imparts meaning but establishes categories the individuals use to organize and classify their world and themselves.[41]

Not all individuals take the same sexual categories from public discourse. One of the foundations of cognitive psychology is the belief that each individual has a different set of experiences and cognitive structures that will determine how any new information, such as that about human sexuality, is internally processed and ultimately used. If this is the case, then the mind of each individual gives meaning to sexual and identity concepts through the complex interaction of external discourse and social relations with the existing power structure.[42]

Self-concept involves both a social identity acquisition and a personal one. Both terms need definition. A social identity, in this case, is defined as the individual's knowledge that he or she belongs to certain social groups and that membership in such groups has emotional significance for him or her. Social groups can be based on sex, nationality, religion, or any number of other categories. On the other hand, a personal identity refers to specific attributes of the individual, such as feelings of competence, bodily attributes, ways of relating to others, psychological characteristics, personal tastes, and so on. Although personal and social identities usually function side by side as a self-concept, it is also possible that the social identity can on occasion function nearly to the exclusion of personal identity, particularly among groups that experience discrimination.[43]

Not all analysts of cross dressing have come from the behavioral or biological sciences. In recent years scholars in the humanities have expressed a growing interest in ambivalence and ambiguity, influenced strongly by the writings of Jacques Lacan.[44] Marjorie Garber's work is the best example of this trend. She wants to escape the bipolar notions of male and female in order to advocate a third category—not a third sex as conceptualized by Ulrich but rather a new mode of articulation, a way of describing a space of possibilities. She regards transsexualism as a distinctly twentieth-century manifestation of cross dressing and the bipolar thinking of which cross dressing itself is a tradition. Bipolar approaches create what she calls a "category crisis," because it leads to a failure of definitional distinction, when a border becomes permeable and permits border crossing. Thus category crises threaten the established class, race, and gender norms. Cross dressing is a disruptive element that involves not just a category crisis of male and female, but the crisis of category itself. In this sense, cross dressing is a commentary on our own stereotypes.[45]

Contemporary research has also challenged the belief by some psychoanalysts that cross-gender identities and homosexuality stem from a family constellation characterized by strong mothers and weak fathers.[46] Using a path analysis, A. P. Bell and associates did a detailed analysis of the lives of a sizable sample of homosexual and heterosexual men and women from the San Francisco Bay area. Homosexual men and women were more likely to report poor relationships with their fathers than heterosexual members of the study group, but it is not clear whether the poor relationships were due to their gender nonconformity or whether parental rejection was itself part of the causal sequence for homosexuality. The most common element in the childhoods of both lesbians and homosexual men was gender nonconformity. Many of the boys had developed a homosexual pattern in their teen years, although there was no evidence that this was due to a lack of opportunity for heterosexual interaction.[47]

Our own study of M–F transsexuals, transvestites and homosexual men contradicted the assumption of an absent father, as did the study by Bell of homosexual men and lesbians. However, several studies have suggested that a strong mother may be a part of the picture for some transvestites.[48] They are less obviously cross-gendered as children than transsexuals and are more interested in sports and other masculine activities.[49] Transvestites conform to masculine societal norms and use cross dressing as a secret outlet for relief. Since they do not cross dress as early as transsexuals, they are better able to keep it secret or at least less of an issue in the family. As adults they score high on femininity scales, but they are not necessarily low in masculinity, except when they cross dress. The key element in their socialization pattern is that they somehow learn to develop a double persona.

It is likely that most cross dressers are also cross-gendered in other regards: in their sexual orientation, selection of occupations, or other attributes. However, a special group of heterosexual cross dressers has emerged, primarily due to the influence of Virginia Prince and the club movement. The social influence forming the behavior patterns of this group of respectable, middle-class men is very clear since heterosexual identity is highly valued by many members of the group.[50] This high valuation of heterosexual identity, to the point of homophobia for some, may be another key factor in the socialization process that helps some young boys who feel cross-gendered to choose to cross dress but consciously to avoid homosexual experiences.

The Theory of Multivariant Causality for Transvestism, Transsexualism, and Homosexuality

The current theory suggested by the research literature for the formation of gender identities and sexual preferences that diverge from the norms includes three steps.

1. A genetic predisposition for a cross-gender identity is present, including high or low levels of activity and aggression.
2. Prenatal hormonal stimulation supports that genetic predisposition.
   a. During the prenatal period, the hormonal stimulation indelibly marks the neural pathways so the pattern that produced the cross-gender identity is continued after birth.
3. A socialization pattern shapes the specific manifestation of the predisposition.

This theory posits that certain children are born with a gender identity that leans to the other side of the gender continuum to varying degrees. These children are not born with a specific identity as a homosexual, a transvestite, or a transsexual; these patterns are shaped by the socialization process, but the socialization process has a different impact on children who have a cross-gender tendency than it does on children whose gender identity conforms with their biological sex.

Feminine Boys

The research literature about feminine boys provides examples of this theory by showing how the socialization process specifies the paths that can be taken by children who are born with the tendency to develop a cross-gender identity. Although the folk wisdom has long linked feminine behavior among boys with later homosexuality, Irving Bieber was the first researcher to emphasize the point. He studied 106 male homosexual patients who were being treated by Bieber or other psychiatrists and found that early cross-gender behavior was the most common element in their backgrounds. He attributed this early behavior to parental patterns that emphasized a strong, binding relationship with mothers and weak or absent fathers.[51] Frederick Whitam and Michael Zent note that other researchers have also found the link between early effeminate behavior and later homosexuality, although more is now known about the socialization process.[52] They interpret the family dynamics differently. In their cross-cultural studies, they found that in areas where homosexuality is less stigmatized, such as the Philippines and Latin America, the relationships between homosexual children and their fathers are good. In the United States, where the cultural patterns attach more stigma to homosexuality, parents tend to be more disturbed when they note that their son is feminine or find out he is homosexual, and a rift develops between fathers and their homosexual sons. Whitam and Zent perceive the hostility as a parental reaction and a withdrawal rather than as the cause of the homosexuality.

Using a structured questionnaire, Michael Newcomb asked samples of male and female homosexuals, male and female heterosexuals, and male transvestites to describe and evaluate their parents. There were no differences between the male homosexual and heterosexual samples, but there were differences among the transvestite and lesbian samples. These two groups perceived their parents as less sex typed; their mothers were more dominant and independent than their fathers.[53]

The longitudinal studies of children who are severely cross-gendered from early childhood are important in evaluating the social and psychological influences on their later gender identity and sexual orientation. The study done by Richard Green was described in detail in Chapter

11. Fifty feminine boys were studied over a fifteen-year time span. They had been referred to the gender center of the University of California at Los Angeles because they were feminine; they cross dressed very early (94 percent by age 6), played with dolls, preferred girl playmates, and indicated they wished they had been born girls.[54] Three-fourths of the feminine boys became homosexual. There was only one homosexual man in the fifty-member control group. One member of the feminine group was considering sex change surgery, but there were no adult transvestites in either group.[55]

In addition to the Green study, there have been several other smaller-scale longitudinal studies of feminine boys. Bernard Zuger, a psychiatrist, followed sixteen boys who were referred to him; their effeminate behavior included cross dressing, wearing lipstick, feminine gesturing, a desire to be a girl or a woman, and a lack of interest in or dislike of sports and boys' games. In all cases, these behaviors appeared before age six. When he first reported on the group in 1966, he had followed them for ten years but only half of them were old enough to have settled on a sexual orientation. He indicated that four were confirmed homosexuals, three were probably homosexual, two were heterosexual, and one could not yet be classified.[56] Twelve years later, Zuger reported that ten of the sixteen men were homosexual, one was a transvestite, one was transsexual, two were heterosexually oriented, and no decision could be made for the remaining two. Zuger indicated he could not have predicted the differential paths from the early behaviors. The child who became the transsexual had cross dressed as early as age one or two, but the same symptoms appeared in some of the other cases with different outcomes.[57]

Phil S. Lebovitz studied sixteen young men who had been seen as children for effeminate behavior at the University of Minnesota Hospital. At the time of the follow-up study, the subjects were between sixteen and twenty-seven years of age. The group included three transsexuals, one married transvestite, two homosexuals, three married, and seven unmarried men. Lebovitz argued that different patterns were observed in the early and late cross dressers. Those who started cross dressing before age six were much more likely to have a "deviant" sexual identity as an adult.[58]

Money and Russo reinterviewed a group of feminine boys that Green had originally worked with and reported that all five were homosexual.[59] Charles Davenport reported an eight- to ten-year follow-up study of ten subjects who were referred to him for feminine behavior including cross dressing. Four were heterosexual, two homosexual, one transsexual, and the outcome in three cases was uncertain.[60]

Table 13.1 summarizes the data from these longitudinal studies.

TABLE 13.1. Summary of the Longitudinal Studies of Feminine Boys.

Author	Date	Number	Homo- sexual	Hetero- sexual	Trans- vestite	Trans- sexual	Uncertain
Green	1976 1987	33	25	8			
Zuger	1966 1978	16	10	2	1	1	2
Lebovitz	1972	16	2	3	1	3	7
Money and Russo	1979	5	5				
Davenport	1986	10	2	4	—	1	3
	Totals:	80	44	17	2	5	12
	Percent:	100	55	21	2.5	6	15

Sources: Richard Green, "One-Hundred Ten Feminine and Masculine Boys: Behavioral Contrasts and Demographic Similarities," *Archives of Sexual Behavior* 5 (1976): 425–46; Green, *The "Sissy Boy Syndrome" and the Development of Homosexuality* (New Haven, CT: Yale University Press, 1987); Bernard Zuger, "Effeminate Behavior Present in Boys from Early Childhood," *Journal of Pediatrics* 69 (1966): 1098–1107; Zuger, "Effeminate Behavior Present in Boys from Early Childhood: Ten Additional Years of Follow-up," *Comparative Psychiatry* 19 (1978): 363–69; Phil S. Lebovitz, "Feminine Behavior in Boys: Aspects of Its Outcome," *American Journal of Psychiatry* 128 (April 1972): 1283–89; John Money and A. J. Russo, "Homosexual Outcome of Discordant Gender Identity/Role in Childhood: Longitudinal Follow-up," *Journal of Pediatric Psychology* (1979): 29–41; Charles W. Davenport, "A Follow-up Study of 10 Feminine Boys," *Archives of Sexual Behavior* 15 (1986): 511–17.

Homosexuality is the most common outcome of cross dressing as a child. Transsexualism is relatively common, given the fact that it is much more rare in the total population. Transvestites seem to be underrepresented, but cross dressing at a level that is not labeled transvestism probably exists, albeit unreported since it does not assume the attributes of a diagnosis. However, even the boys who later become transvestites could hide their behavior sufficiently well that they would not be brought to psychiatrists for treatment as children. Secret cross-dressing activities relieve their desire for a touch of femininity, and the secret becomes part of the excitement. This leaves them free to play the masculine role to the fullest, and some of them do so, excelling in sports, in school, and at home. They please their rather powerful mothers and never give the family a reason to seek psychiatric counseling for them.

Another interesting facet of the studies of feminine boys is the fact that most of them are not overtly feminine as adults. They apparently go through a defeminization process during adolescence. This process has been particularly well described among homosexual men. Many were overtly cross-gendered as boys, but by the time they became adults most of them were defeminized; they became gender conventional in their behavior, with only a minority of the population remaining feminine.[61] Joseph Harry points out that social class is a major factor in determining which of the feminine boys go through this transition. In his sample of 686 homosexual men, blue-collar class respondents were more likely to remain feminine than were the men from higher socioeconomic levels. The blue-collar respondents were also more likely to have sexual experiences with same-sex persons at a younger age. Harry interprets his data as showing that the early sexual activity, before any defeminization process could take place, was a reinforcing factor for the young blue-collar boys, so they were more likely to remain effeminate as adults.[62]

Tomboys

To date, there has been no study of girls who are tomboys, probably because cross-gender behavior in girls is considered less problematic. Whitam and Mathy have, however, done retrospective studies of homosexual and heterosexual women in four societies: Brazil, Peru, the Philippines, and the United States. All of the groups were volunteers who were located through clubs, bars, professional groups, student groups, or friendships. Childhood behavioral patterns were significantly different. The homosexual woman were much more likely to have been called tomboys, played with boys' toys, and played dress-up in men's clothing. The heterosexual women were more likely to have paid attention to women's fashions and played dress-up in women's clothing. The authors consider the cross-gender childhood behaviors to be precursor patterns for women who later develop a lesbian lifestyle.[63]

Not all cross-gendered children become homosexual. Rather, the data suggest that a childhood cross-gender identity and behavior is the precursor to three types of adult patterns: cross dressing, transsexualism, and homosexuality. The strength of the urge for the cross-gendered behavior and the social learning that takes place help to determine the pattern of adult behavior. The biological factors seem to be strongest in the transsexual children. In a society such as ours, which highly values macho men and feminine women and punishes gentle men and aggressive women, transsexuals are likely to be unhappy children. In our comparative study, only 16 percent of our transsexual sample reported happy childhoods, as compared with 35 percent of the transvestite sample, 64 percent of the homosexual sample, and 61 percent of the undifferentiated control group.[64] Transsexual children know they are deviating from the norms of society; they hear the admonitions of their parents and the taunts of peers, but they are unable to cope in a better way. They do not feel that they belong to their assigned gender group. Psychotherapy may help somewhat, but it is often unsuccessful because the therapist tries to eradicate the cross-gendered behaviors instead of rechanneling them or trying to build up self-esteem.[65]

Girls who feel themselves to be cross-gendered to an extreme degree may have a slightly easier road. Tomboys are not as stigmatized as "sissy" boys. Still parents, teachers, and society will often try to "help" the young girl to learn her place. Historically, that "place" has not only been soft and pretty, it has also been the subordinate position, with lower salaries and more menial work than those of men. Although the situation is improving there is still a long way to go. The cross-gendered girl must not only give up rough-and-tumble play and boys' clothing, she must learn to hide a drive for achievement if she is to adjust to the norms of society. The cross-gendered girl is much less likely to be brought to a psychiatrist, but she is much more likely to be excluded from the professional school of her choice or from the skilled trades.

Children with only a mild deviation from the dimorphic gender norm or those who grow up in a more supportive environment are much less likely to become transsexual. Rather, they find a less stigmatized path by cross dressing or adopting a gay or lesbian life-style. The homosexual outcome was the case for most of the children in Richard Green's study. These children were referred to him because they and their families were suffering. The original contact included testing and therapy, and parents who were unwittingly reinforcing feminine behavior in their sons were helped to stop doing so. In addition, Green probably also unconsciously helped his clients when he interviewed them to collect follow-up data, as is suggested by the verbatim interviews that are included in his book. His clients remember him as a friend, and he comes across as totally accepting of them and their sexual patterns. If the topic of sex reassignment surgery came up, he calmly explained the cross-living that is required. He probably helped some of his cross-gendered clients to choose the homosexual answer to their cross-gender urges rather than the more drastic solution that involves having surgery.[66]

Genesis of Transvestism

If we narrow the focus to heterosexual cross-dressing males who are labeled transvestites, there are some additional studies related to causality. In 1970 H. Taylor Buckner, a sociologist, wrote an article describing what he called the "Transvestic Career Path," in which he outlined the five steps he saw as essential to the development of a transvestite self-identity. Buckner had worked with Bentler and Prince (doing the coding for part of their cross-sectional study of *Transvestia* readers), but most of his generalizations came from an in-depth interview study of seven transvestites. Buckner concluded that a biological etiology for transvestism was not valid; instead, its development was limited to persons who were passive, with a low libido. The five steps are summarized below:

Step 1. Sometime between the ages of five and fourteen, the young boy tries on an article of women's clothing and experiences sexual gratification, usually through masturbation.

Step 2. As a young man the subject experiences some difficulties related to his perception of himself as masculine. The failure can be in any realm: sports, marriage, or occupation, but he interprets it as an indication of inadequate masculinity. His performance may not actually be poor; he may be a perfectionist, and he falls short of his own unreasonable goals.

Step 3. He is blocked from seeking a homosexual outlet. He may have a socialized aversion to homosexuality, or he may not know how to find a homosexual partner.

Step 4. Blocked in both the heterosexual and homosexual directions, he returns to the pleasures of wearing female apparel and masturbating. He elaborates the fantasies surrounding this act. He may learn from the literature that transvestism exists, so he adopts the sexual script that goes with the label.

Step 5. His gratification pattern becomes fixed in the transvestite identity with the development of the other persona, a feminine name, and an elaborate fantasy life. A dyadic relationship is encapsulated in his transvestite activities, and he realizes that he has within himself both a male and female, so he can play out many of the culturally prescribed heterosexual dyadic scripts. He can buy himself gifts and seek comfort from his feminine persona. He may find that his actual marriage is less satisfying for tension release than his internal marriage.[67]

Two decades of research have added significantly to the data base, but the outlines of this pattern after the first cross-dressing episode seem valid at least for some male transvestites.[68] The evidence for a genetic and physiological precursor condition has grown in the last two decades, and a significant body of research literature outlines the parallel socialization process that produces a gay identity,[69] with some research on the socialization process of the male transvestite. An updated scenario for the development of a male transvestite identity can be suggested as follows:

Step 1. A genetic predisposition and physiological factors, including hormonal secretions and neural patterns, combine to produce a boy who is less active and less aggressive than his peers.

Step 2. Family and social factors influence the child: The mother may be the dominant figure in the family. The socioeconomic status of the family may be high. Respectability may be highly regarded by the family and peer group. The culture may stigmatize homosexuality. The family may be homophobic. In addition, various idiosyncratic social forces intervene.

Step 3. The child or adolescent stumbles onto the joy of cross dressing and masturbation. Orgasm occurs and is a reinforcement. The activity remains clandestine and is possible without any loss of respectability or other punishment.

Step 4. Marriage to a conventional partner takes place, and thoughts of any same-sex orientation are suppressed.

Step 5. The sex partner joins in with and supports the cross-dressing activity, or grudgingly accepts it, or leaves. If she leaves or other losses are felt, the activity may well accelerate. A supportive partner also helps the activity to increase. The grudging partner may hamper the activity, but the relationship is probably not a pleasant or lasting one.

Step 6. If the subject discovers the transvestite clubs or publications, his activities are shaped by the norms of the group. His cross dressing escalates, he adopts a female name, and going out dressed in public becomes a valued goal.

Although the psychiatric definitions and most of the research is about male transvestites, the data that have emerged from historical study and other available research leads us to believe that the process by which the cross-gendered woman develops is as follows:

Step 1. A genetic predisposition and physiological factors including hormonal secretions and neural pathways combine to produce a girl who is more active and aggressive than her peers.

Step 2. Family and social factors influence the development of the child. She may find ready playmates who support her rough-and-tumble play patterns and little or no support for the traditionally feminine attributes.

Step 3. At adolescence or young adulthood she realizes that her erotic attachments have a same-sex orientation.

Step 4. She finds a mate and lives a lesbian life-style which may include cross dressing. She may adopt a traditionally male work role and life-style. Although most cross-gendered females are lesbians or bisexual, their endorsement of the other markers for a cross-gendered identity vary significantly.

Throughout history the most attractive aspect of the masculine role has been the male work role and the power and recognition accompanying it, so this has been the area where the breach in the boundaries between the sexes has ordinarily occurred. Women have coveted the work role and status held by men, so cross dressing to achieve those aspects of masculinity has taken on an instrumental characteristic. This, however, is in keeping with the male persona since men, at least in Western society, have not been as interested in clothes as women. Thus, while male cross dressers focus on clothing as a part of the feminine persona, female cross dressers are usually much less concerned about clothing. They dress for comfort, just as their male role models do. There are, however, some women who also enjoy cross dressing in and of itself. These few women may cross dress to the point where they are identified as men, but this is unusual.

Summary

We have studied the evidence for a genetic predisposition for a cross-gendered identity and have found it persuasive. The biological data supporting neurohormonal factors are accumulating. Children who are biologically cross-gendered may act in a variety of ways: they may develop a homosexual identity, which may or may not include cross dressing, or a bisexual identity; or they may struggle to conform and develop a heterosexual identity. Sometimes their heterosexual identity includes a pattern of intermittent cross dressing. A few of the cross-gendered children become transsexuals, who feel that their body and their mind-set do not match. The various outcomes related to a cross-gender identity are related to each other but different, and the differences probably stem from the strength of the cross-gendered identity and the impact of the psychosocial environment.

Notes

1. Eleanor E. Maccoby, ed., *The Development of Sex Differences* (Stanford, CA: Stanford University Press, 1966); Charles J. Lumsden and Edward O. Wilson,

Genes, Mind and Culture: The Evolutionary Process (Cambridge, MA: Harvard University Press, 1981); Alan P. Bell, Martin S. Weinberg, and Sue Kiefer Hammersmith, *Sexual Preference: Its Development in Men and Women* (Bloomington: Indiana University Press, 1981).

2. Frederick Suppe, "Classifying Sexual Disorders: The *Diagnostic and Statistical Manual* of the American Psychiatric Association," *Journal of Homosexuality* 9 (Summer 1984): 9–28.

3. Ira B. Pauly, "Gender Identity Disorders: Evaluation and Treatment," *Journal of Sex Education & Therapy* 16, no. 1 (1990): 1–24.

4. Susan M. Rogers and Charles F. Turner, "Male-Male Sexual Contact in the U.S.A.: Findings from Five Sample Surveys, 1970 to 1990," *The Journal of Sex Research* 28 (November 1991): 491–519.

5. Vern L. Bullough, *Sexual Variance in Society and History* (Chicago: University of Chicago Press, 1976).

6. Frederick L. Whitam, "A Cross-Cultural Perspective on Homosexuality, Transvestism and Trans-sexualism," *Variant Sexuality: Research and Theory,* ed. Glen D. Wilson (London: Croom Helm, 1978).

7. Dennis Werner, "Cross Cultural Perspectives on Theory and Research on Male Homosexuality," *Journal of Homosexuality* 4 (Summer 1979): 345–411; and Bullough, *Sexual Variance,* passim.

8. Edward O. Wilson, *On Human Nature* (Cambridge, MA: Harvard University Press, 1978), 142–48; Elizabeth Rice Allgeier and Albert Richard Allgeier, *Sexual Interactions* (Lexington, MA: D.C. Heath, 1991).

9. T. F. Hoult, "Human Sexuality in Biological Perspective," *Journal of Homosexuality* 9 (Spring 1984): 137–55; D. J. Futuyma and S. J. Risch, "Sexual Orientation, Sociobiology, and Evolution," *Journal of Homosexuality* 9 (Spring 1984): 157–168.

10. Michael Ruse, "Are There Gay Genes? Sociobiology and Homosexuality," *Journal of Homosexuality* 6 (Summer 1981): 5–34; James D. Weinrich, "Homosexuality and Sociobiology: It's Time to Play Fair," unpublished manuscript, 1984.

11. George W. Henry, *Sex Variants: A Study of Homosexual Patterns* (New York: Paul B. Hoeber, 1941).

12. M. S. Margolese and O. Janiger, "Androsterone/Etiocholanolone Ratios in Male Homosexuals," *British Medical Journal* 3 (1973): 207–10.

13. Richard C. Pillard, Jeannette Poumadere, and Ruth A. Carretta, "Is Homosexuality Familial? A Review, Some Data and a Suggestion," *Archives of Sexual Behavior* 19 (1981): 465–75. For a collection of other studies on twins, see Geoff Puterbaugh, ed., *Twins and Homosexuality: A Casebook* (New York: Garland Publishing, 1990).

14. Franz J. Kallman, "Comparative Twin Study on the Genetic Aspects of Male Homosexuality," *Journal of Nervous and Mental Disease* 115 (1952): 283–98.

15. Milton Diamond, "Bisexualities: A Biological Perspective," paper read at the Third International Berlin Conference of Sexology, Berlin, 1990.

16. Judd Marmor, "Overview: The Multiple Roots of Homosexual Behavior," in *Homosexual Behavior: A Modern Reappraisal,* ed. Judd Marmor (New York: Basic Books, 1980), 3–22.

17. John Bancroft, "The Relationship Between Hormones and Sexual Behavior in Humans," *Biological Determinants of Sexual Behavior,* ed. J. B. Hutchison (New York: John Wiley, 1978), 494–519.

18. Jean D. Wilson, Frederick W. George, and James E. Griffin, "The Hormonal Control of Sexual Development," *Science* 211 (20 March 1981): 1278–84.

19. Anke A. Ehrhardt and Heino F. L. Meyer-Bahlburg, "Effects of Prenatal Sex Hormones on Gender-Related Behavior," *Science* 211 (March 1981): 1312–17.

20. Anke A. Ehrhardt, Heino F. L. Meyer-Bahlburg, Laura R. Rosen, Judith F. Feldman, Norma Veridiano, I. Zimmerman, and Bruce S. McEwen, "Sexual Orientation after Prenatal Exposure to Exogenous Estrogen," *Archives of Sexual Behavior* 14 (1985): 57–75.

21. "News and Comment: Is Homosexuality Biological?" *Science* 253 (30 August 1991): 253–59.

22. Gunter Dorner, Wolfgang Rohde, Fritz Stahl, Lothar Krell, and Wolf-Gunther Masius, "A Neuroendocrine Predisposition for Homosexuality in Men," *Archives of Sexual Behavior* 4 (1975): 1–8; Garfield Tourney, "Hormones and Homosexuality," in *Homosexual Behavior: A Modern Reappraisal*, 41–58.

23. A. P. Arnold and R. A. Gorski, "Gonadal Steroid Induction of Structural Sex Differences in the Central Nervous System," *Annual Review of Neuroscience* 7 (1984): 413–22.

24. Milton Diamond, "Human Sexual Development: Biological Foundations for Social Development," in *Human Sexuality in Four Perspectives*, ed. Frank Beach (Baltimore, MD: Johns Hopkins Press, 1977), 22–61.

25. Janet Shibley Hyde, "Gender Differences in Aggression," in *The Psychology of Gender: Advances through Meta-analysis*, ed. Janet Shibley Hyde and Marcia C. Linn (Baltimore, MD: Johns Hopkins University Press, 1986), 51–66.

26. Vern L. Bullough, Brenda Shelton, and Sarah Slavin, *The Subordinated Sex: A History of Attitudes Toward Women*, rev. ed. (Athens: University of Georgia Press, 1988).

27. G. Dorner, *Hormones and Brain Differentiation* (New York: Elsevier, 1976).

28. Richard C. Pillard and James D. Weinrich, "The Periodic Table of the Gender Transpositions: Part 1. A Theory Based on Masculinization and Defeminization of the Brain," *Journal of Sex Research* 23 (November 1987): 425–54.

29. Muriel Wilson Perkins, "Female Homosexuality and Body Build," *Archives of Sexual Behavior* 10 (1981): 337–45.

30. Brian A. Gladue, Richard Green, and Ronald E. Hellman, "Neuroendocrine Response to Estrogen and Sexual Orientation," *Science* 225 (28 September 1984): 1496–99.

31. Garfield Tourney, "Hormones and Homosexuality," 41–58.

32. Eli Coleman, Louis Gooren, and Michael Ross, "Adversaria: Theories of Gender Transpositions: A Critique and Suggestions for Further Research," *Journal of Sex Research* 26 (November 1989): 525–38; Lynda I. A. Birke, "Is Homosexuality Hormonally Determined?" *Journal of Homosexuality* 6 (Summer 1981): 35–49; Wendell Ricketts, "Biological Research on Homosexuality: Ansell's Cow or Occam's Razor?" *Journal of Homosexuality* 9 (Summer 1984): 65–93.

33. Louis Gooren, Eric Fliers, and Keith Courtney, "Biological Determinants of Sexual Orientation," *Annual Review of Sex Research* 1 (1990): 175–96.

34. Stanford Dornbusch, "Afterword," in *The Development of Sex Differences*, ed. Eleanor E. Maccoby, (Stanford, CA: Stanford University Press, 1966), 205–19.

35. John Money, Joan G. Hampson, and John L. Hampson, "An Examina-

tion of Some Basic Sexual Concepts: The Evidence of Human Hermaphroditism," *Bulletin of Johns Hopkins Hospital* 97 (1955): 301–19; Joan G. Hampson, "Determinants of Psychosexual Orientation," *Sex and Behavior*, ed. F. Beach (New York: John Wiley, 1965).

36. Julianne Imperato-McGinley, Ralph E. Peterson, Teofilo Gautier, and Erasmo Sturla, "Androgens and the Evolution of Male-Gender Identity Among Male Pseudohermaphrodites with 5α-Reductase Deficiency," *The New England Journal of Medicine* 300 (31 May 1979): 1233–37.

37. A. K. Cohen, *Delinquent Boys: The Culture of the Gang* (Glencoe, IL: The Free Press, 1974).

38. Kenneth J. Gergen, "The Social Constructionist Movement in Modern Psychology," *American Psychologist* 40 (March 1985): 266.

39. Anselm Strauss, "Interactionism," in *History of Sociological Analysis*, ed. Tom Bottomore and Robert Nisbet (New York: Basic Books, 1978), 456–98; John P. Hewitt, *Self and Society: A Symbolic Interactionist Social Psychology* (Boston: Allyn and Bacon, 1979).

40. Kenneth Plummer, "Symbolic Interaction and Sexual Conduct: An Emergent Perspective," in *Human Sexual Relations: Towards a Redefinition of Sexual Politics*, ed. Miles Brake (New York: Pantheon Books, 1982), 230.

41. Jeffrey Weeks, "Discourse, Desire and Sexual Deviance: Some Problems in a History of Homosexuality," in *The Making of the Modern Homosexual*, ed. Kenneth Plummer (Totowa, NJ: Barnes and Noble Books, 1981), 76–101; Jeffrey Weeks, *Sex, Politics and Society: The Regulation of Sexuality Since 1800* (London: Longman, 1981), 96–121.

42. R. C. Anderson, *Cognitive Psychology* (New York: Academic Press, 1975); V. F. Guidano and G. Liotti, *Cognitive Process and Emotional Disorders: A Structural Approach to Psychotherapy* (New York: Guilford Press, 1983).

43. John Turner, "Toward a Cognitive Redefinition of the Social Group," in *Social Identity and Intergroup Relations*, ed. Henri Taefel (Cambridge: Cambridge University Press, 1982), 18–21.

44. For example, see Frederick Jameson, "Imaginary and Symbolic in Lacan: Marxism, Psychoanalytic Criticism and the Problem of the Subject," in *The Question of Reading: Otherwise*, ed. Shoshana Felman (New Haven, CN: Yale French Studies, 1977); see also Jacques Lacan, *The Four Fundamental Concepts of Psychoanalysis*, trans. Alan Sheridan (New York: W. W. Norton, 1982).

45. Marjorie Garber, *Vested Interests: Cross-Dressing and Cultural Anxiety* (New York: Routledge, 1992).

46. Irving Bieber, Harvey J. Dain, Paul R. Dince, Marvin G. Drellich, Henry G. Grand, Ralph H. Gundlach, Malvina W. Kremer, Alfred H. Rifkin, Cornelia B. Wilbur, and Toby B. Bieber, *Homosexuality: A Psychoanalytic Study*, (New York: Basic Books, 1962).

47. A. P. Bell, M. S. Weinberg, and S. K. Hammersmith, *Sexual Preference, Its Development in Men and Women* (Bloomington: University of Indiana Press, 1981).

48. Neil Buhrich and Neil McConaghy, "Parental Relationships During Childhood in Homosexuality, Transvestism, and Transsexualism," *Australian and New Zealand Journal of Psychiatry*, 12 (1978): 103–8; Michael D. Newcomb, "The Role of Perceived Relative Parent Personality in the Development of Heterosexuals, Homosexuals and Transvestites," *Archives of Sexual Behavior* 14 (1985): 147–64.

49. Vern L. Bullough, Bonnie Bullough, and Richard Smith, "A Compara-

tive Study of Male Transvestites, Male to Female Transsexuals and Male Homosexuals," *Journal of Sex Research* 19 (August 1983): 238–57; Vern Bullough, Bonnie Bullough, and Richard Smith, "Childhood and Family of Male Sexual Minority Groups," *Health Values: Achieving High Level Wellness* 7 (July–August 1983): 19–26.

50. Deborah Heller Feinbloom, *Transvestites, Transsexuals: Mixed Views* (New York: Delacorte Press, 1976).

51. Irving Bieber et al., *Homosexuality: A Psychoanalytic Study.*

52. Frederick L. Whitam and Michael Zent, "Cross-Cultural Assessment of Early Cross Gender Behavior and Familial Factors in Male Homosexuality," *Archives of Sexual Behavior* 13 (1984): 427–39.

53. Michael Newcomb, "The Role of Perceived Relative Parent Personality in the Development of Heterosexuals, Homosexuals and Transvestites," *Archives of Sexual Behavior* 14 (1985): 147–64.

54. Richard Green, "One-Hundred Ten Feminine and Masculine Boys: Behavioral Contrasts and Demographic Similarities," *Archives of Sexual Behavior* 5 (1976): 425–46.

55. Richard Green, *The "Sissy Boy Syndrome" and the Development of Homosexuality* (New Haven, CT: Yale University Press, 1987).

56. Bernard Zuger, "Effeminate Behavior in Boys from Early Childhood," *The Journal of Pediatrics* 69 (1966): 1098–107.

57. Bernard Zuger, "Effeminate Behavior Present in Boys from Childhood: Ten Additional Years of Follow-up," *Comparative Psychiatry* 19 (1978): 363–69.

58. Phil S. Lebovitz, "Feminine Behavior in Boys: Aspects of Its Outcome," *American Journal of Psychiatry* 128 (April 1972): 1283–89.

59. John Money and A. J. Russo, "Homosexual Outcome of Discordant Gender Identity/Role in Childhood: Longitudinal Follow-up," *Journal of Pediatric Psychology* 4 (1979): 29–41.

60. Charles W. Davenport, "A Follow-Up Study of 10 Feminine Boys," *Archives of Sexual Behavior* 15 (1986): 511–17.

61. M. Saghir and W. Robins, *Male and Female Homosexuality* (Baltimore: Williams and Wilkins, 1973), 25; Joseph Harry, "Defeminization and Adult Psychological Well-Being Among Male Homosexuals," *Archives of Sexual Behavior* 12 (1983): 1–19.

62. Joseph Harry, "Defeminization and Social Class," *Archives of Sexual Behavior* 14 (1985): 1–12.

63. Frederick L. Whitam and Robin M. Mathy, "Childhood Cross-Gender Behavior of Homosexual Females in Brazil, Peru, the Philippines, and the United States," *Archives of Sexual Behavior* 20 (1991): 151–70.

64. Bullough et al., "Transvestite, Transsexual and Homosexual Men."

65. Davenport, "A Follow-Up Study of 10 Feminine Boys."

66. Richard Green, *The "Sissy Boy Syndrome" and the Development of Homosexuality.*

67. H. Taylor Buckner, "The Transvestic Career Path," *Psychiatry* 33 (1970): 381–89.

68. Richard F. Docter, *Transvestites and Transsexuals* (New York: Plenum Press, 1988).

69. Eli Coleman, "Developmental Stages of the Coming Out Process," *Journal of Homosexuality* 7 (1981–82): 31–43; Henry L. Minton and Gary J. McDonald, "Homosexual Identity Formation as a Developmental Process," *Journal of Homosexuality* 9 (1983–84): 91–104.

Chapter 14
What To Do About Cross Dressing

Women who cross dress are rarely seen by therapists unless they are considering transsexual surgery. Among male transvestite club members the percentage who have sought therapy varies from 30 to 50 percent. Among closeted male cross dressers the percentage is even lower, and this is probably the largest group of cross dressers. These men cross dress in private; their behavior causes no disturbance or problem for society. Still, some people are either very troubled by their urge to cross dress or—and this is more likely—their families are troubled by it. Since most transvestites as children cross dress only occasionally, parents and siblings are often unaware of the behavior. As the behavior becomes more frequent during the adult years, it is more likely to become problematic, and the usual precipitating cause for seeking psychotherapy is the distress of a wife or potential wife. Consequently, the marriage becomes the focus of much of the therapy related to cross dressing.[1]

As indicated in Chapter 12, many transvestites in the United States and other Western countries identify themselves as heterosexual. Although some of these heterosexual men have homoerotic fantasies or participate in homoerotic activities when they are cross dressed, they tend to discount these attractions and seek a marriage partner. In the Prince and Bentler study of 504 readers of the magazine *Transvestia*, 78 percent had been married, and 74 percent had one or more children. The authors could not be sure of the divorce figure but estimated that between 19 and 29 percent of the study population had been previously divorced. At the time of the study, 20 percent of the married men believed that their wives were totally unaware of their cross-dressing activities. Another 27 percent of the wives who knew at the time of the survey had not been informed before they were married.

Prince and Bentler speculated that the accidental discovery of the husband's cross dressing may have contributed to the marital strain in the group. They reported a wide range of attitudes of the wives to their husbands' cross dressing: 23 percent were characterized as completely accepting and cooperative, 20 percent were antagonistic, and the others fell at various positions in between.[2] These authors did not question the wives but relied on the husbands' reports of their attitudes.

In order to study the marital situation from the wife's point of view, Thomas S. Weinberg and one of us (V.L.B.) did a sociological study of seventy wives of transvestites. Respondents were located through three wives' support and counseling groups and one transvestite club. Only 36 percent of this group of wives knew about their husbands' cross dressing before they were married; 49 percent of the group found out within the first five years after marriage. The earlier the wife knew about the behavior the more positive was her attitude. Women who learned about the behavior well into the marriage felt betrayed. Most of the time the husband himself told the wife, but a few of them found the clothing or surprised their spouse when he was dressed. Some men wore one or two items of clothing at first and then escalated their cross dressing, so the wives came to the realization gradually.

Usually, these wives had known nothing about transvestism until they found out about the practice from their husbands. Some were angry and fearful. Their most common fear was that others would find out (66 percent). Other respondents frequently mentioned concerns that the husband was homosexual (36 percent), that his cross dressing would affect the children (36 percent), that the wife had failed as a woman (22 percent), that she had failed as a wife (16 percent), or that he was mentally ill (18 percent). Despite these negative feelings, the most common reaction of these wives when they discovered their husbands were transvestites was to seek further information. Some husbands had a collection of literature about the phenomenon, which they shared. Some wives sought advice from counselors, therapists, or physicians and looked for information in libraries and bookstores. The information outside of that supplied by the husbands was sparse.

The most common coping mechanism was to try to keep the activity a secret, and 49 percent reported doing so. Some even offered to buy women's clothing for their husbands to keep them from being suspected at clothing stores. Some women initially encouraged their husbands, but this support tended to be half-hearted. Some reluctantly helped their husbands with makeup. At one time or another, 43 percent of the women reported they had sex with their husbands when they were fully cross dressed or in undergarments or nighties; most disliked the experience but tried to tolerate it. Two-thirds of the women had gone out in public with their husbands cross dressed. A few enjoyed the experience, particularly if it took place at Fantasia Fair (an annual meeting in Provincetown, MA) or one of the other safe gatherings of transvestites.[3]

The wives' attitudes changed over time. They became both less fearful and less supportive. The longer the women in the sample were married, the less sympathetic was their attitude toward cross dressing. A common coping mechanism of these women was to set limits on the behavior, and this usually meant that the cross dressing was not carried out in front of them. In 81 percent of the marriages in the study sample, the husbands did not cross dress in front of the wives.[4] Despite the problems of living with a transvestite husband, most of the women (79 percent) indicated that their marriages were happy.

The authors used the theoretical formulations of Erving Goffman to explain this interesting paradox. They suggested that the husbands' transvestism created a problem in the management of stigma, and when the coping mechanism was successful, the situation could be happy. Goffman defined stigma as a deeply discrediting discrepancy between the image the individual wishes his public identity to be and his actual private identity. Goffman divided people with stigma into those whose proclivities were known and those whose stigma was hidden. People with known stigmas developed coping mechanisms such as bravado or humor. A major problem for people with unknown stigmas was loneliness. They often revealed themselves to selected others in order to gain some allies. These persons who were informed were described as "wise" to the stigma.[5]

The wives of transvestites fit this description of the wise outsiders. While the potential husband may not reveal his life-style before marriage because of fear of losing his chosen mate as a candidate for marriage, he may well want the wife to find out after marriage so she can share his stigma and so he will feel less lonely.

J. K. Jackson, who studied the wives of alcoholics who are wise to a similar stigma, developed a series of stages to describe their coping patterns. The wives often denied the problem at first, but when they eventually recognized it, they tried a variety of coping mechanisms until either the marriage broke up or the husband quit drinking.[6] Weinberg and Bullough argued that the stigma of transvestism is more easily managed than that of alcoholism because the alcoholic spouse may well lose his job, his health, or become abusive or violent. This level of dysfunction is difficult to conceal. In contrast, cross dressing is much less dysfunctional and easier to compartmentalize. Transvestite husbands are more willing to compromise and to limit cross dressing to selected times and places. Many of the wives could identify positive qualities of their mates when they are cross dressed (sensitivity and tenderness, for example), while the wives of alcoholics find their mates very abusive when they are drunk. The wives of transvestites can also focus their hostility on the cross dressing but still love their mates, while alcoholics may become so out of control that the wives come to hate both the behavior and the men.

There are some other behavioral science oriented studies of the wives of transvestites. Richard Docter included a survey questionnaire for wives in the packets distributed to his sample of transvestite males. Thirty-five questionnaires (including four from long-term partners who were not married) were returned. The demographic characteristics of the group were similar to those of the Bullough and Weinberg study, with 58 percent married more than ten years. Only 29 percent of the group had been informed of their husbands' cross-dressing activities before marriage; most of the group found out after marriage. Docter used a nine-point scale to measure the attitudes toward the husbands' cross dressing and thus elicited a wide variety of attitudes from positive to negative, with the negative attitude slightly outweighing the positive. The most common concern expressed by the wives was a fear that their husbands' activities would become public and, second, that this would harm the children. These wives believed, and Docter concurred, that the children should not be informed of their fathers' cross dressing.[7]

In his study of fifty-five wives of members of a transvestite organization, Roger Peo found many of the same patterns. In addition to the problems listed above, the women in his study indicated that a cross-dressing mate raised the specter of lesbianism, and many were distressed by these feelings. Peo supported Bullough and Weinberg's conclusion that an early discovery, preferably before marriage, made the relationship more viable in the long run. Peo speculated that the men who were more sensitive to their partners' needs may have been the ones who told them about cross dressing earlier in the relationship. In 44 percent of the relationships, the man's cross dressing dominated the relationship. The men in the study cross dressed often, with one-third doing so daily and another 20 percent dressing once a week or more, making it obvious that these activities could dominate the relationship.

When the women were asked if they ever thought about leaving the relationship because of their partners' cross dressing, thirty-three of the fifty-five women indicated that they had never considered it. When the seventeen who had considered it were questioned as to why they stayed, most of them indicated that they loved their partners; they would rather that he did not cross dress but had come to understand that cross dressing was an unchangeable part of their mate's personality. In addition, their social and economic dependence kept some of them in the relationship.[8]

John Talamani interviewed fifty wives of transvestites from the mid-Atlantic and New England regions; 60 percent were not informed of their husbands' cross dressing before marriage. They explained this failure to Talamani by indicating that the husband was afraid that such a revelation would scare the wife away, or that the husband thought marriage would cure his transvestism. At the time of the interviews, 40 percent of the marriages were strained because of the issue of transvestism. Among the most difficult of the husbands were four men whom Talamani called "princesses" (a term also used by Virginia Prince). When these men cross dressed they spent their time gazing at themselves in the mirror. Their definition of themselves as women did not include their participation in cooking, housekeeping, shopping, or taking care of children.[9]

Deborah Feinbloom also looked at the wives of transvestites when she did her anthropological study of the men involved in a transvestite sorority. Her observations led her to believe that the women who chose to marry transvestites or stay married to transvestites had low self-esteem. They felt they were not worthwhile enough to attract anyone else. Once married, the low self-esteem of these wives made them feel that marriage to a transvestite was better than no marriage at all. They were also vulnerable to competition from their husbands in the area of clothing and appearance. They continually told their husbands that they made the most attractive women. Feinbloom also suggested that some of the transvestite wives and girlfriends who shopped and participated fully in the cross-dressing activities were looking for a girlfriend rather than a lover or they were latent homosexuals.[10]

Annie Woodhouse also used a qualitative methodology to study British transvestite members of the Beaumont Society and a London group called TV/TS. Woodhouse, a feminist, was concerned with the lives of the wives of transvestites, many of whom she felt were victims of the situation. Her interviews, unlike most previous studies, centered on the wives of blue-collar workers, who were housewives or employed themselves. Their worlds were turned on end when they found out about their husbands' cross dressing. They thought of divorce but they were conventional women, and simply putting up with the situation seemed to be a better option. Many of them found the support group set up by TV/TS very helpful, although the group had some difficulty securing its independence from the TV group in the early years. A board member of the male transvestite club felt that he should be able to attend meetings and help set the goals of the group, with a primary focus being to help wives to support their husbands. The wives, on the other hand, were looking for peer support for themselves. The problem finally was resolved, and the support group was able to secure enough autonomy to function independent of the male club members.[11]

The characterization of the wives of transvestites as victims with low self-esteem is not uncommon, and all of us who have observed the transvestite scene have seen some "doormat" wives who cook the food and scrub the floors, worry about the children, then go out to buy some beautiful article of feminine clothing which they give to their husbands. The husband accepts the part of the female role that focuses on leisure-time activities rather than on the drudgery of the role. Consequently, Bullough and Weinberg decided to systematically test the self-concepts of the wives using scales measuring self-esteem and internal versus external control (sometimes called a scale of alienation). Marital happiness was measured on a seven-point scale. One group of women scored low on the scale of self-esteem, and thus this characterization may hold for some wives of transvestites. However, the scores varied widely, and the women who scored higher on self-esteem were the happiest in their marriages. Women with low self-esteem were more likely to feel they had failed in their role as wives than were those with high self-esteem. In addition, self-esteem and marital happiness were also correlated with the sense of internal control. Women who felt they controlled their own lives and did not feel buffeted by fate or controlled by other powerful persons not only had more self-esteem but also coped better with the stress of finding out about their husbands' cross-dressing activities.[12]

A major limitation in all of these studies is the fact that they included only those women who stayed with their transvestite husbands or lovers and who felt good enough about their mate to answer the query. In the Bullough and Weinberg study, six of the questionnaires sent to wives by their husbands were returned unanswered with notes from the husbands saying that the wife was too hostile about transvestism to respond. Missing also are those wives who were divorced. In the Docter study, eight questionnaires were not given to wives by husbands who were convinced their wives would not respond. Consequently, these studies have not included the most distressed wives, including those who were still unhappily married as well as those who were already divorced.

In Brierly's study of the British Beaumont society, only 9.1 percent of his sample indicated they had been divorced. As he suggests, divorce rates were difficult to compare with national averages in Great Britain because of the varying ages of the males and the increasing divorce rate, but he felt this figure was comparable with the general British statistics.[13] As indicated earlier, the divorce rate for the American

Prince and Bentler sample was between 19 and 29 percent, but significantly, 36 percent of the divorces were attributed to the husband's cross dressing. Obviously, there are a number of women who found cross-dressing husbands intolerable.

Some of the more negative women may have been seen by psychiatrists, since studies of the wives of transvestites done by psychiatrists present a more negative picture than the sociological studies. Thomas Wise and his colleagues at Johns Hopkins Hospital Sexual Behaviors Consultation Unit studied eighteen partners of transvestites.[14] The original clients in these cases were the male partners, nine of whom had sought psychotherapy because of their mates' distress, while the other nine were considering sex change procedures. Data for the report were gathered from chart reviews in twelve cases with interviews of six women. Sixteen of the women studied were wives and two were girlfriends of transvestites. The group was well educated, eight having finished college. They had been married or living with the transvestite client for an average of 11.5 years, and twelve of them had children.

Fourteen of the eighteen women indicated they frequently experienced orgasm during intercourse, although none was aroused by her partner's cross dressing. A few had allowed their partner to wear feminine garments during lovemaking, but admitted being angry or disgusted when this occurred. The psychiatric authors characterized the women as "moral masochists," that is, individuals who seek psychic suffering by claiming moral superiority. Half of the women in the group had been neglected or lost a parent as children; most had negative self-images, reported feeling depressed, and felt they deserved to suffer. Case studies were used to illustrate the themes of the article, two of which are summarized here:

MRS. A had a difficult childhood with an alcoholic father who died when she was twelve. Her mother died when she was fifteen, and she lived with her brother until she graduated from high school and married. She found women's clothing in her husband's dresser and assumed he was having an affair with another woman, but she did not mention it. Six years later her husband told her about his cross-dressing activities. She decided to stay with him because of their two children, until one day when he asked her to tie him down while he was cross dressed. She was unable to control her fury and began hitting him; she threatened to leave him unless he sought psychiatric help.

MRS. B had grown up in a home with a promiscuous mother and a depressed father who were divorced when she was nine. She had multiple sex partners until she met Mr. B at age fifteen. She liked him and his warm, friendly family. She knew about his cross dressing but thought he would outgrow it. They dated throughout high school and married in college. Mr. B said he wanted to save her from being a slut. Mrs. B worked while he finished professional school. After six years of marriage she became discontented with his cross dressing (during which he would seek compliments about his appearance), so she insisted on the psychotherapy.

A more pathological view of the wives of transvestites was presented by Robert Stoller, who lumped transvestites' wives and mothers together and claimed that they all took conscious and intense pleasure in seeing males dressed as females. Most of Stoller's hostility is vented against the mothers, whom he divided into two categories: overt "malicious male haters" and "symbiotes" who hid their own homosexuality and hatred for men and effectively crippled their sons by smothering and cross dressing them. He labeled the wives of transvestites as "succorers" who support transvestism with sympathy and enthusiasm. They either knew about their fiancé's cross dressing before marriage or they found out about it after and taught their men how to dress and pass in society. Stoller claimed his conclusions were drawn from eight hundred hours of treatment of thirty-two transvestites and their women.[15] Though Stoller undoubtedly saw the women he described, his psychiatric blinders seemed to have prevented him from seeing a broader spectrum of women. He seemed to believe that transvestism was such a horrible malady that a woman who did not reject a male cross dresser was somehow abnormal. This is, again, a part of the past generation's psychiatric dogma of labeling all sexual activity outside of heterosexual intercourse as a paraphilia and of considering all paraphiliacs abnormal.

The account written by Peggy Rudd, the wife of a transvestite and herself a therapist, is so far removed from the Stoller point of view that it is difficult to believe they are describing the same phenomenon. Rudd is very positive regarding the mental health of the cross-dressing husband and his wife.[16] Rudd is the second wife of a transvestite husband whose first wife left him partly over the issue of cross dressing. Nevertheless, her husband did not tell Rudd about his cross dressing until after the marriage, when he passed her a scholarly article on the subject (which he had coauthored). As she realized the full extent of his cross dressing, she felt angry and rejected. She found his cross dressing a turn-off to lovemaking. She feared that he was gay, that he would want a sex change surgery, and that neighbors and friends would find out.

She read some of the literature on the subject, including Feinbloom's anthropological study, thereby likely gaining a broader perspective on the problem than the ordinary wife. She apparently never urged her husband to seek psychotherapy aimed at changing the behavior. Instead, she came to believe that, despite her first negative emotional response, the reality was that his cross dressing would not go away. It would always be a part of their lives. Therefore, she forced herself to adopt a positive attitude toward both of her husband's personalities. She came to learn to like the feminine persona he presented while cross dressed, and she shared her clothing with him. She has since gone on to conduct workshops and provide counseling for cross dressers and their wives.

In some ways Rudd may have inherited the mantle of advocacy from Virginia Prince, whose classic book for wives, *The Transvestite and His Wife,* was written so it could be presented to wives when they found out about their husband's cross dressing. The book reviewed the literature about transvestism and presented Prince's ideas on the subject. Prince reassured the reader that her husband was not homosexual (and that he was a much nicer person than homosexual men are). She listed the causes of cross dressing as including four needs: (1) to acquire virtue and experience beauty, (2) to gain personality expression, (3) to obtain relief from the requirements of masculinity, and (4) to obtain relief from social expectations. The book also included Prince's well-known system for grading wives from A+ to F. Some of this was presented tongue-in-cheek. The system gave a low rating to the ordinary woman who responds in the expected way to a transvestite husband. The ratings are summarized below:

A+: This wife goes into ecstasy every time her husband cross dresses. She never buys herself anything unless she buys something equally pretty for her husband's femme self.

A: She loves her husband and does not try to change him. She discusses transvestism with him and is fully accepting. She makes a point of meeting other wives and helps them understand and cope with the facts.

B: This wife allows her husband to cross dress but does not look forward to it. She buys him clothes, goes with him to transvestite parties and is polite to the other wives. She does not complain when he wears nightgowns to bed.

C: She is shocked when she finds out about his cross dressing. She wants to accept it but is unable to enjoy it, so she suffers in silence.

D: This level is marked by overt hostility about cross dressing. When she finds him dressed, she suggests he do the housework.

E: This wife will not lift a finger to do anything to help her husband cross dress. She speaks hostilely of him and all his transvestite friends. She tells him she would rather see him drunk than cross dressed.

F: This wife divorces the transvestite husband and takes the children with her. She tells the world about his cross dressing and gets full custody of the children.[17]

This work, first published in 1967 and reprinted several times, was sold to transvestites who were urged to give it to their wives to "educate" them. Its partisan approach certainly made many wives feel guilty, but it also furnished some useful information along with its advocacy. The other literature available in this era was the psychiatric material, which was still painting the transvestite as grossly abnormal and attributing causality to the Oedipus complex. Prince's approach furnished a more positive alternative, but how helpful it was to wives is debatable.

Therapeutic Approaches

There have been a variety of approaches to treatment of male transvestism over time. In the historical approaches discussed in earlier chapters, the treatment methodology was a part of the theoretical thinking about causality. The early twentieth-century psychiatrists used psychotherapeutic models developed by Freud or Jung and carried out therapy aimed at allowing the client to gain insight into the genesis of his problem. This insight was aimed at making him less compulsive about cross dressing, thereby allowing him to feel less guilt and to manage his affairs better. Sometimes this therapy proved helpful. The classic Freudians looked for causality in the Oedipus complex, explaining that the male transvestite needed to create a phallic woman (himself cross dressed) to protect himself from the fear of castration and the guilt surrounding his desire to replace his father as his mother's lover. Female cross dressers represented the reverse situation, with the girl both wanting to replace her mother as her father's love object and envying her father and other people with penises.[18]

When evidence of an Oedipus complex or penis envy was found in the client's childhood (and it seems this always was found), the therapist could not simply tell the client; rather, the client had to stay in therapy until he himself found this evidence and believed it. Only then would he be free of the compulsion to cross dress. As different schools of psychotherapy developed, transvestism often fell under the rubric of either homosexuality or fetishism. Emil Gutheil believed transvestism was caused by homosexual panic, so he looked for evidence of this as well as castration anxiety in the background of his clients.[19] In addition, some analysts looked for other background factors, including traumatic events and forced cross dressing in childhood.[20] While there are still a few traditional Oedipal theorists around, most psychiatrists have moved on to different views of causality, and their insight therapy focuses on traumatic incidents or negative feelings with which they help clients deal.

The practitioners who give counseling and therapy to transvestites and their wives have also broadened their professional ranks to include psychologists, social workers, nurse practitioners, clinical nurse specialists, and other physicians as well as the traditional psychiatrists. None of these practitioners should attempt to do therapy in the sex field unless they have both the basic counseling skills offered by their own discipline as well as knowledge of human sexuality. The basic counseling skills are probably the easiest component of the knowledge base to acquire, since each of these disciplines has such training available for those who seek it out. Obtaining the necessary knowledge of sexology is more difficult, because there are only a handful of graduate programs available (New York University, the University of Pennsylvania, and the Institute for Advanced Study of Human Sexuality in San Francisco). It is possible to gain a knowledge base in sexology after obtaining a professional degree by way of a comprehensive reading program and participation at scholarly meetings. However, the field has changed so rapidly in the last few decades that no one should presume to be well informed unless he or she has kept up-to-date with current scholarship.

Given the basic qualifications, the therapist who counsels transvestites or their spouses should start the process with a careful assessment of the client's goals. In our study of transvestites, transsexuals, and homosexual men, we found that those persons who entered a therapeutic situation with an unclear goal passed through the experience untouched or dissatisfied.[21] This included children who were taken for therapy by parents without any shared perception of why they were there. The first task of the therapist is to find out why the client sought help and what he or she expects to get out of the process. There also must be some consideration as to whether or not the goals are realistic. The lack of a realistic goal often plagues therapists who see transvestites, since many clients enter therapy because their wives were shocked to find them cross dressing; they themselves have no lasting desire to stop cross dressing because it is their chief erotic pleasure. Thomas Wise and his group indicated that in such situations they simply avoid trying to treat the man or the couple and move on to give the wife supportive, insight-oriented therapy.[22]

Still, there are some transvestites who come to therapy with realistic goals, or they can identify such goals with some help from the therapist. These goals tend to fall into three distinct categories: (1) they want to save their marriage, (2) they want to feel better about themselves, or (3) they feel their transvestism has become an unmanageable compulsion they want to control.

The man who wants to save his marriage needs to get a better understanding of how his wife views his cross dressing. He will have to lay aside the partisan writings of Virginia Prince and the other advocates of transvestism and consider the impact of his behavior on his wife. The therapist can help him work through this thought process on an individual basis, but eventually steps must be taken to bring the couple together and to allow them to express their real attitudes and feelings under the supportive sponsorship of the therapist. If the male transvestite really does want to save the marriage, he will probably have to give up his fantasies about the perfect transvestite wife and live with the wife he has. In light of the survey data about real wives, he probably will have to live with limits. He probably will have to realize that his cross dressing is not a sexual turn-on for her and that for some women it is distasteful. This means he may have to take off his regalia for lovemaking. If he is taking estrogen to create feminine curves, he will have to realize that his diminished libido may be a problem for his wife. He will also have to listen to her fears about disclosure and about their children. He may then decide to change his goal and not seek to stay married, but this will then be a reasoned decision.

If his goal is to feel better about himself, the therapy should be supportive. The therapist can listen to his fears and concerns, clear up misinformation in light of current scholarship, and support him as he makes a plan for his life that is functional for him.

If he feels overwhelmed by a compulsion to cross dress and sincerely wants to be free of the compulsion, the therapy should focus on transvestism as an obsessive-compulsive behavior. This will include a combination of supportive and insight therapy and medication. If the therapist is not licensed to prescribe medications, he or she will need to seek the collaboration of a physician because the most promising treatment for obsessive-compulsive behavior is drug therapy accompanied by supportive counseling (discussed in more detail below).

If the client is the transvestite's wife, her goals also need to be assessed. Sometimes she enters therapy with a need for help with a decision-making process. She may want to decide whether or not to stay married to her husband. In the past women often did not have the luxury of this decision. They stayed married even in an unhappy situation. Today, the norms of society and the opportunities for work make divorce possible (although still difficult). The therapist may want to use the following four steps in working with the wife:

1. Listen to her problem, helping her to build up her level of self-esteem and to overcome her feelings of powerlessness.
2. Serve as an educator, helping her to understand cross dressing in light of present scholarship, which makes it a less formidable problem unless it is at the obsessive-compulsive level.
3. Assist her with the decision-making process. Help her to broaden her horizons to consider all available options before she makes a decision.
4. Assist the couple with negotiations for staying together, if that is the option that is being explored. The therapist may need to meet with them as individuals and as a couple to help them open up the communication process. The husband may be willing to limit his activities to a level she can tolerate, and she may be able to live with the limits.

Group therapy or a support group for wives of transvestites can be very helpful. It allows wives to find out that their situation is not unique and that other women are also bothered by their husbands' cross dressing. It allows them to look at alternatives and to find out how other women have coped with the situation. In the end the wife must make her own decision, but she undoubtedly feels less lonely when she knows that others are struggling with the same decision. If the support group is sponsored by one of the transvestite clubs, it should be independently operated so the wives can control the flow of information and the advice they give each other. It is important to remember that transvestites are often very forceful men whose make-believe femininity often does not extend to giving up power and control. The pressure from transvestite organizations is often aimed at trying to remake wives to conform to the model of the "A" or "B" wife, and that may not be possible or even desirable for most wives. The wife who can retain her own self-esteem and have her legitimate concerns recognized will be happier in the long run; and those who have found a support group indicate that it has helped them to achieve these goals.[23]

The issue of whether or not the children should be informed of their father's cross dressing may also be brought to the counselor for advice. Peggy Rudd says that although she ordinarily believes in complete honesty, she can see reasons for not telling the children. She suggests that the couple collect the pro and con arguments and decide on their merits as to whether or not the children should be informed.[24] Most other therapists consider it too much of a burden for children, given the current level of stigma attached to the behavior, so they support not telling them.[25]

Cross Dressing as an Obsessive-Compulsive Disorder

A theme that runs through the literature is that many transvestites feel a compulsion to cross dress. They often describe their feelings as an overpowering need to put on women's clothing. After an episode of cross dressing, they feel relieved; sometimes they are repentant and purge themselves of their finery, planning to never cross dress again. However, often they feel the compulsion again and so acquire new clothes, and the pattern is repeated. This has led many observers to consider transvestism as an obsessive-compulsive disorder. The first to identify it as such may have been John Randall, a British physician-psychologist, who studied fifty cases of transvestism and transsexualism in 1958. He included both males and females in the group and decided that most of the members either were homosexual (including all but one of the women) or they were compulsive.[26] He felt the homosexually oriented group were closer to transsexualism, while the transvestites were most characterized by their compulsiveness. Some contemporary therapists now look upon some levels of cross dressing among both men and women as a compulsion and treat it like other obsessive-compulsive disorders. This diagnosis would not apply to all cross dressers but would include those who cross dress often, feel compelled to do so, and realize their behavior is interfering with their work or their personal lives to an intolerable level. There are other sexual behaviors that are considered obsessive-compulsive, including behaviors which were in the past called nymphomania, satyriasis, or sexual addiction. Eli Coleman defines compulsive sexual behavior as behavior that is driven by anxiety-reduction mechanisms rather than sexual desire. He explains that the obsessive thoughts and compulsive behaviors serve the function of temporarily reducing anxiety, but the relief is only temporary, so the compulsive behavior has to be carried out again and again.[27]

DSM-III-R indicates that one may have an obsessive or compulsive disorder or both. In order to be considered as a psychiatric disorder, the problem must be sufficiently severe to cause marked distress, be time-consuming, or significantly interfere with the individual's life or relationships. An obsession is a persistent idea, thought, or image that cannot be controlled. Compulsions are repetitive, purposeful, and intentional behaviors that are performed in response to an obsession. The individual may realize that the behavior is excessive but cannot resist doing it. Trying to resist the compulsion causes extreme anxiety and a mounting tension until the compulsion is carried out. Frequent hand-washing, counting and recounting, and checking something over and over again are the most common compulsions. Depression and anxiety are commonly seen with obsessive-compulsive disorders. The diagnostic criteria for compulsion include the following:

1. Repetitive, purposeful, and intentional behaviors that are performed in response to an obsession or according to certain rules or in a stereotyped fashion.
2. The behavior is designed to neutralize or prevent discomfort or some dreaded event or situation; however, either the activity is not connected in a realistic way with what it is designed to neutralize or prevent or it is clearly excessive.
3. The person recognizes that his or her behavior is excessive or unreasonable (this may not be true for young children; it may no longer be true for people whose obsessions have evolved into overvalued ideas).[28]

The DSM-III-R definition further indicates that compulsions that fit the criteria cause marked distress, are time-consuming (taking more than an hour a day), or significantly interfere with the person's normal routine, occupational functioning, social activities, or relationships with others.

The life of the obsessive-compulsive person is often filled with idiosyncratic daily rituals or odd habits. The patient, at least early in the history of the problem, is well aware that the impulses are intruding on his or her life—and this differentiates the pattern from schizophrenia—but the patient is unable to control it. The obsession creates anxiety, and the compulsive act is carried out to lessen the anxiety. However, the compulsive act usually has nothing to do with the feared consequence. The act is either unrelated to the anxiety or it is excessive, as in the case of hand-washing routines that are excessive in relation to the danger from microorganisms. Often the dreaded consequence is unknown.[29]

Drug Therapy

John Money, who has described many of the sexual compulsions as paraphilias, treats the disorders using a combination of counseling and medication, usually with an antiandrogenic drug such as medroxyprogesterone acetate (Depo-Provero).[30] In recent years there has been a search for a medication that would control compulsions more effectively. A 1988 case report by John Paul Federoff reported the use of buspirone hydrochloride (BuSpar) for a transvestite patient. Buspirone is an anti-anxiety medication. The patient came to the clinic at the insistence of his wife because he could not become sexually aroused unless he was wearing women's clothing. He was cross dressing and masturbating four times weekly but having sexual intercourse with his wife only once every two to three months. He was very anxious and could control his panic only by cross dressing or with alcohol. He was unable to eat in public or ride in public transportation unless he was seated next to the door. He and his wife were given psychotherapy, and his alcohol intake was tapered. He was given alprazolam (Xanax), and though this decreased his anxiety as well as his need for alcohol, it did not change his sexual interest or frequency of cross dressing. He was switched to buspirone, and nine days after starting the drug, he reported a decrease in his urge to cross dress. He completely stopped cross dressing in three weeks, and he was able to become sexually aroused without cross dressing or fantasizing about cross dressing. Both he and his wife were pleased with the outcome. Federoff commented that the buspirone did more than relieve the anxiety (which was relieved by alcohol and alprazolam); it also facilitated his sexual activities with his wife. Buspirone is also used for patients with inhibited sexual desire, so Federoff speculated that it filled this role with this client.[31]

Eli Coleman and John Cesnik report the successful treatment of two patients with obsessional gender dysphoria using lithium carbonate, a well-known drug used to control depression. It acts at the cellular level in the central nervous system, controlling the levels of norepinephrine and serotonin. The patients who were treated had severe gender dysphoria; they were completely disgusted with their male genitalia to the point that they wanted their penis and testicles removed, and were even considering self-mutilization. Coleman and Cesnik used the term *skoptic syndrome* to describe this phenomenon (a term coined by John Money). Both patients were obsessive-compulsive, cross dressing, but finding no joy in it. They were severely depressed and did not want to be either men or women. Both responded well to treatment with lithium. They lost their obsessive thoughts of castration and mutilation. They are continuing with psychotherapy, and one of them may seek sex reassignment, but he will seek it in a reasoned manner without the pain of his obsession.[32]

Cesnik and Coleman have also used lithium to treat a man with autoerotic asphyxia. This man reported that he had developed a ritualized and compulsive masturbation sequence in which he restricted his air flow by putting a plastic bag over his head, or bound his head with duct tape, or some other such approach. In addition, he sometimes wore a diving suit to further restrict his body. These activities produced a feeling of panic followed by euphoria associated with orgasm. His treatment with lithium carbonate has allowed him to participate in psychotherapy, and he can be maintained on a low dose without significant side effects.[33]

Flouxetine (Prozac), an antidepressant, is a bicyclic inhibitor of serotonin reuptake. It has been successfully used for obsessive-compulsive disorders.[34] However, the drug reported as the most successful in treating obsessive-compulsive disorders is clomipramine (Anafranil).[35] Clomipramine is a tricyclic antidepressive drug similar in some ways to flouxetine in that it is a potent inhibitor of the reuptake of serotonin. Clomipramine was approved by the Food and Drug Administration for general use with obsessive-compulsive disorders in 1989. Based on the effectiveness of these drugs, a neurotransmitter hypothesis for obsessive-compulsive disorders has emerged. This hypothesis suggests that insufficient serotonin in the frontal lobe basal ganglia creates or supports the obsessive-compulsive symptoms, so the problem is at least partly biochemical.[36]

Clinical trials have documented the efficacy of clomipramine in controlling even severe obsessive-compulsive disorders in adolescents[37] and in women who pull out their hair (trichotillomania).[38] The drug is not without side effects, including persistent sedation, nausea, sexual dysfunction, weight gain, and occasional seizures with high doses, so it must be medically monitored.[39]

Apparently, a clinical trial is in progress to test clomipramine (Anafranil) with transvestites. A National Institutes of Health researcher placed an ad in the August 1989 issue of *Femme Mirror* seeking volunteers who considered themselves compulsive cross dressers. In March 1991 one of those volunteers wrote to the editor to tell of his successful therapy with Anafranil. A portion of his letter telling of his experience with the clinical trial is quoted below:

Contact with NIH encompassed a full day of discussion with a male psychiatrist and a female case worker . . . both people were compassionate and understanding. I was accepted for the trial which took place over nine weeks. . . . I was given a placebo; a medication which had little effect and a third medication that proved to be quite incredible. The drug is called Anafranil and its effect is several fold. First it has . . . nearly eliminated the inner anger I constantly had. . . . After a year on the drug I have had all desire to cross dress eliminated. That is not to say I haven't thought about it, but not with the excitement or intensity I once had. I still have full appreciation for everything feminine but the burning need to have it for my own is no longer the driving force to my psyche. In the past I experienced several wardrobe purges, however with this medication I felt no regret about giving up the wardrobe. . . . Now I recognize that many TVs would find what I did . . . opposite to their wishes and desires. For me personally, the cross dressing was a bittersweet event and it was damaging personal relationships with friends and family. I have nothing but compassion for our sisters, because I have been there. But there is an alternative, there is hope and I have elected this course. Perhaps my story should be shared.[40]

A telephone call by the authors to the NIH-sponsored group that is testing clomipramine for various types of obsessive-compulsive behaviors yielded reprints of articles focused on other behaviors but not cross dressing; the cross dressing article had not been published at the time this book was printed.

Summary: Treatment Conclusions

The client who presents for counseling related to cross dressing may be either the husband or the wife. The homosexual and lesbian communities are more tolerant of cross dressing, so members of these groups seldom are seen with cross dressing as a presenting complaint. If the client is a husband, he may want to keep his marriage intact but not want to change his cross-dressing behavior, so the task of the therapist is not easy. Both members of the marriage will need to confront the reality of the situation. The wife needs to realize that her husband will probably continue to cross dress, and the husband needs to realize that he will have to accept some limits if the marriage is to survive. Occasionally, a transvestite who is not yet married but is contemplating such a step presents for counseling. The timing is fortunate because the therapist can assure him that wives who are informed about the situation ahead of time cope much better later.

If the client is the wife, she will need to be supported and her level of self-esteem will probably need to be built up so she can make a decision about her marriage in a more relaxed fashion. Support groups for wives of transvestites have been shown to be helpful.

If the urge to cross dress is so frequent and intense that it interferes with the individual's life-style and relationships, it can be conceptualized as an obsessive-compulsive disorder and treated with drug therapy, either alone or as an adjunct to supportive counseling. Lithium, flouxetine (Prozac), buspirone (BuSpar), and clomipramine (Anafranil) have been used for this purpose. Probably clomipramine, which has been used for a variety of other compulsive disorders, will become the drug of choice, but further research is needed to assess its effectiveness in the control of a compulsion to cross dress. These are all powerful drugs that require medical supervision.

Notes

1. Richard F. Docter, *Transvestites and Transsexuals: Towards a Theory of Cross-Gender Behavior* (New York: Plenum Press, 1988); Thomas Wise, Carol Dupkin, and Jon K. Meyer, "Partners of Distressed Transvestites, *American Journal of Psychiatry,* 138 (September 1981): 1221–24; Deborah Heller Feinbloom, *Transvestites, Transsexuals: Mixed Views* (New York: Delacorte Press, 1976).

2. Virginia Prince and P. M. Bentler, "Survey of 504 Cases of Transvestism," *Psychological Reports* 31 (1972): 903–17.

3. Vern L. Bullough and Thomas S. Weinberg, "Women Married to Transvestites: Problems and Adjustments," *Journal of Psychology and Human Sexuality* 1 (1988): 83–104.

4. Ibid.

5. Erving Goffman, *Stigma: Notes on the Management of Spoiled Identity* (Englewood Cliffs, NJ: Prentice-Hall, 1963).

6. J. K. Jackson, "The Adjustment of the Family to the Crisis of Alcoholism," *Quarterly Journal of Studies on Alcohol* 15 (1954): 564–86.

7. Richard F. Docter, *Transvestites and Transsexuals: Towards a Theory of Cross-Gender Behavior* (New York: Plenum Press, 1988), 167–93.

8. Roger E. Peo, *Wives of Cross-Dressers: Isolated and Misunderstood,* unpublished monograph, original version 1985, revised 1987.

9. John T. Talamani, *Boys Will Be Girls: The Hidden World of the Heterosexual Male Transvestite* (Washington, DC: University Press of America, 1982), 29–35.

10. Feinbloom, *Transvestites, Transsexuals: Mixed Views,* 107–11, 264–66.

11. Annie Woodhouse, *Fantastic Women* (New Brunswick, NJ: Rutgers University Press, 1989), 120–33.

12. Thomas S. Weinberg and Vern L. Bullough, "Alienation, Self-Image, and the Importance of Support Groups for the Wives of Transvestites," *Journal of Sex Research* 24 (1988): 262–68.

13. Harry Brierly, *Transvestism: A Handbook with Case Studies for Psychologists, Psychiatrists and Counsellors* (Oxford: Pergamon Press, 1979), 32–33.

14. Wise et al., "Partners of Distressed Transvestites."

15. Robert J. Stoller, "Transvestite's Women," *American Journal of Psychiatry* 124 (September 1967): 333–39.

16. Peggy J. Rudd, *My Husband Wears My Clothes: Crossdressing from the Perspective of the Wife* (Katy, TX: PM Publishers, 1988).

17. Virginia Charles Prince, *The Transvestite and His Wife* (Los Angeles: Argyle Books, 1967).

18. O. Fenichel, *The Psychoanalytic Theory of Neuroses* (New York: W. W. Norton, 1945); N. Lukianowicz, "Survey of Various Aspects of Transvestism in Light of Present Knowledge," *Journal of Nervous and Mental Disease* 129 (1959): 36–64.

19. Emil Gutheil, "An Analysis of a Case of Transvestism," in *Sexual Aberrations: The Phenomenon of Fetishism in Relation to Sex,* ed. Wilhelm Stekel, trans. S. Parker (New York: Liveright Publishing Co., 1930), 281–318.

20. Robert Stoller, "Pornography and Perversion," *Archives of General Psychiatry* 22 (June 1970): 490–99; N. Lukianowicz, "Survey of Various Aspects of Transvestism."

21. Vern Bullough and Bonnie Bullough, "PNPs, Patients, Parents and Sexuality," *Pediatric Nursing* 8 (May–June 1982): 121–87.

22. Wise, Dupkin, and Meyer, "Partners of Distressed Transvestites."

23. Weinberg and Bullough, "Alienation, Self-Image and the Importance of Support Groups for the Wives of Transvestites."

24. Rudd, *My Husband Wears My Clothes*, 85–100.

25. Docter, *Transvestites and Transsexuals;* JoAnn Roberts, *Coping With Cross-dressing: Tools and Strategies for Partners in Committed Relationships* (King of Prussia, PA: Creative Design Services, 1991), 62.

26. John B. Randall, "Transvestism and Trans-sexualism: A Study of 50 Cases," *British Medical Journal* 2 (25 December 1959): 1448–52.

27. Eli Coleman, "The Obsessive-Compulsive Model for Describing Sexual Behavior," *American Journal of Preventive Psychiatry and Neurology* 2 (May 1990): 9–14; Coleman, "Sexual Compulsivity: Definitions, Etiology and Treatment Considerations," *Journal of Chemical Dependency Treatment* 1 (1987): 189–204.

28. American Psychiatric Association, "Diagnostic Criteria for 300.30: Obsessive-Compulsive Disorder," *Diagnostic and Statistical Manual,* rev. 3d ed. (Washington, DC: American Psychiatric Association, 1987), 245–47.

29. Judith L. Rapoport, "The Waking Nightmare: An Overview of Obsessive-Compulsive Disorder," *Journal of Clinical Psychiatry* 51 (November 1990): 25–28.

30. John Money, "Use of Androgen-depleting Hormone in the Treatment of Male Sex Offenders," Journal of Sex Research 6 (1970): 165–170; John Paul Federoff, "Buspirone Hydrochloride in the Treatment of Transvestic Fetishism," *Clinical Psychiatry* 49 (October 1988): 408–9.

31. John Paul Federoff, "Buspirone Hydrochloride in the Treatment of Transvestic Fetishism."

32. Eli Coleman and John Cesnik, "Skoptic Syndrome: The Treatment of an Obsessional Gender Dysphoria with Lithium Carbonate and Psychotherapy," *American Journal of Psychotherapy* 44 (April 1990): 204–17.

33. John Cesnik and Eli Coleman, "Use of Lithium Carbonate in the Treatment of Autoerotic Asphyxia," *American Journal of Psychotherapy* 44 (April 1989): 277–86.

34. Samuel M. Turner, Rolf G. Jacob, Deborah C. Beidel, and Jonathan Himmelhoch, "Flouxetine Treatment of Obsessive-Compulsive Disorder," *Journal of Clinical Psychopharmacology* 5 (1985): 207–12; Roger B. Granet, "Flouxetine Treatment of Obsessive-Compulsive Disorder," *Clinical Psychiatry* 50 (November 1989): 436.

35. Henrietta L. Leonard, Susan E. Swedo, Judith L. Rapoport, Elizabeth V. Koby, Marge C. Lenane, Deborah L. Cheslow, and Susan D. Hamburger, "Treatment of Obsessive-Compulsive Disorder with Clomipramine and Desipramine in Children and Adolescents: A Double-Blind Crossover Comparison," in *Annual Progress in Child Psychiatry and Child Development, 1990,* ed. Stella Chess and Margaret E. Hertzig (New York: Brunner/Mazel, 1991), 467–80; Michael Jenike, Lee Baer and John H. Greist, "Clomipramine versus Flouxetine in Obsessive-Compulsive Disorder: A Retrospective Comparison of Side Effects and Efficacy," *Journal of Clinical Psychopharmacology* 10 (1990): 122–24.

36. Judith L. Rapoport, "The Waking Nightmare: An Overview of Obsessive-Compulsive Disorder"; Turner et al., "Flouxetine Treatment of Obsessive-Compulsive Disorder."

37. Leonard et al., "Treatment of Obsessive-Compulsive Disorder with Clomipramine and Desipramine in Children and Adolescents."

38. Susan E. Swedo, Henrietta L. Leonard, Judith L. Rapoport, Marge C. Lenane, Erica Goldberger, and Deborah L. Cheslow, "A Double Blind Com-

parison of Clomipramine and Desipramine in the Treatment of Trichotilloma-nia (Hair Pulling)," *New England Journal of Medicine* 32 (24 August 1989): 497–501.

39. Jenike et al. "Clomipramine versus Flouxetine in Obsessive-Compulsive Disorder."

40. Personal letter from Margo (pseudonym) to Eileen, c/o Tri-Ess Chapter Organization, P.O. Box 4067, Visalia, CA (March 1991).

Postscript

One conclusion that can be derived from the material presented in this book is that cross dressing and gender-blending have been ubiquitous throughout human history. Though there are anatomical differences between the sexes, which may reflect physiological differences mediated by hormones and other factors, there is the potential for tremendous physiological and anatomical variation among persons with the same sex organs and a vast area of overlap between the two sexes. Much of what we believe to be feminine or masculine behavior is socially and culturally derived, and it is no exaggeration to state that genitalia alone have never been either a universal or essential insignia of lifelong gender.

Certainly throughout recorded history, having a penis gave a person a higher status than having a vagina, and this has meant that females have often been praised for having a masculine mind or other masculine abilities. By living and passing as men they also gained higher status. Conversely, men who appeared to be effeminate, regardless of how society defined such behavior, have often been denigrated, although many societies have institutionalized roles for such individuals as shamans or berdaches. In many societies gender is an achieved rather than an ascribed characteristic and is based on tasks performed and the significance of clothing rather than on any anatomical factor. This is most evident in the large numbers of women who in the past have lived and worked as men. The fact that in history fewer men in Western culture have lived and worked as women is due not only to the status loss associated with adopting the feminine role but also the very real economic and social difficulties faced by the would-be woman. This was the case because it was almost impossible for a single woman to live independently unless she came from a rich and powerful family;

the usual role for a woman was to be a wife and mother. Traditionally and legally, women have almost always been under the control of some male—father, husband, brother, or son. When women did exist independently as tradespersons, they were usually widows taking over for their husbands. Except for prostitution, occupations where they could earn an independent living were almost nonexistent for much of history.[1]

Still festivals or special holidays allowed some individuals to express their more feminine or masculine side. Sometimes special roles were assigned to them. This is the case in some areas of Myanmar (formerly Burma) where men known as *acaults* wear female clothing (mostly in religious ceremonies), symbolizing that they are representatives of the female spirit god Manguedon.[2] Many more examples appear throughout this book.

Sometimes the women who lived and worked as men were known to be biological women but still had their role defined as a male one. This was the case in northern Albania until at least the end of World War II, where the custom of the "sworn virgin" or "Albanian virgin" allowed certain women to live as men provided they appeared before a council of elders and swore an oath of lifelong celibacy. Such women became men in the sense that they adopted men's clothing, bore arms, and were counted as men in blood feuds. They did all the tasks of men. Why some women did this is not always clear, but at least in some cases, it was because such women had no brothers and needed to be men in order to carry out familial obligations.[3] What the case of the "sworn virgin" emphasizes is that the idea of gender can be defined by interactions between actors, involving negotiation and compromise that occurs in differing contexts of opportunity and constraint. In American history, the case of Dr. Mary Walker emphasizes the ability of a strong-willed person to be accepted on his or her own terms. Often individuals come to be so well known for their "idiosyncracies" that they influence major social changes. Certainly this was true of Marlene Dietrich and Greta Garbo, who made cross dressing a major part of their film images and were important in introducing long pants as part of a woman's costume. No male movie actor contemporary managed to blur the gender role image as effectively. It was not until the appearance of rock groups that similar gender confusion was tolerated for male stars.

One of the major fears that men with any effeminate tendencies had in the past was being labeled homosexual, but with the growing acceptance of homosexuality and lesbianism by the public at large and the lessening of the stigma associated with it, cross dressing among men has become more open. If Hollywood is any indication of changing American culture, then it is obvious there are changes taking place.

Most of the visible changes deal with the formerly inhibited male and cross dressing. Movies such as the comedy *Some Like It Hot* with Tony Curtis and Jack Lemmon blazed a path for more serious fare such as *Outrageous,* featuring professional female impersonator Craig Russell, and *Tootsie,* starring Dustin Hoffman, both of which challenged traditional stereotypes of the masculine role. On the feminine side Julie Andrews in *Victor/Victoria* was more in the tradition of *Some Like It Hot* than *Tootsie* or *Outrageous,* but this film too emphasized just how much we judge people by the clothes they wear. The willingness of the current film industry to deal seriously with lesbianism and homosexuality emphasizes the ongoing challenge to traditional stereotypes. And in fact, the removal of homosexuality and lesbianism from the *Diagnostic and Statistical Manual* of the American Psychiatric Association represents a more or less official break with the past.

In some ways, at least in terms of personal appearance, this break with traditional stereotypes has been easier for women than for men. Historically, women who cross dressed were allowed by society to determine the significance of their cross dressing themselves, since it not only gave them a higher status but greater freedom and income. Even the most macho male recognized that the traditional woman's role was confining, and he could understand why some women wanted to cross dress or even be a lesbian. This was far less threatening to him than male homosexuality or serious female impersonation because he could always rationalize that the woman who passed as a man was too homely or too masculine looking to make it as a "successful" woman. He could even convince himself that a woman might be a lesbian because she had never had sex with a man. In his mind, he believed he could "cure" her if she would only let a "real" man like him show her what sex could mean to a woman. Unfortunately, men sometimes have tried to demonstrate this expertise without bothering to get the consent of their sought-after partner. Still, despite having to deal with machismo, a woman could have a variety of reasons for cross dressing, even simply to gain attention.

No such toleration was extended by the macho male to the feminized male or the male who cross dressed except in comedy impersonations. This meant that male cross dressing, whether or not the person was homosexual, was associated with particular, stigmatizing effeminate behavior, at least until there was greater acceptance of homosexuality itself. It was probably for this reason that the 1987 revised third edition of the *Diagnostic and Statistic Manual* offered the diagnosis of "fetishistic transvestism" to describe the male cross dresser and not the female.[4] Even though psychiatrists had cross-gendered patients of both sexes, they did not conceive of female cross dressers in the same sense they did their male patients. Nor was the female cross dresser likely to have a spouse or parents so distressed by the cross dressing that they were referred for professional treatment. If such women did exist they were not diagnosed as transvestites. Only recently has the possibility of the existence of such individuals been recognized. In the collection of sexual fantasies by Nancy Friday in *My Secret Garden,* she tells of a woman admiring herself in the mirror wearing jockey shorts with a tampon penis protruding from them. Further, Stoller has emphasized that wearing items like denim jeans, engineer boots, and false moustaches can produce orgasmic sensations in women.[5]

What this double standard indicates is that it was the meaning attached to male cross dressing by psychiatrists and the public at large as well as by the individual transvestite and his family that caused it to be recognized as a psychiatric illness. This only emphasizes that cross dressing is not so significant in itself but has a social meaning that both the participants and society attribute to it. Attributing such meaning, however, is a circular process, since it is also influenced by what the professionals say. The professionals originally established the categorization to deal with clients who wanted and needed help or were believed to need help; as the diagnosis became established, it announced to society that the male cross dresser, unlike the female one, was a troubled person. It also tended to reinforce a strict gender separation which, as we have tried to emphasize, is contrary to the findings of current research in both the biological and behavioral sciences. Distinctions between gender are obviously undergoing a change, and inevitably there will be societal changes such as have occurred in attitudes toward homosexuality and lesbianism. It is quite possible that cross dressing as such will be removed in the revised DSM except in those rare instances when it fits the criteria for obsessive-compulsive behavior.

As should be evident from the discussions earlier in this book, we can offer no definitive explanation for why people cross dress. Instead, we believe there are biological, cultural, social, historical, and individual reasons. One of the more interesting findings of our own research into organized "heterosexual" transvestites was that the club members generally were in high-status occupations usually associated with strong male images; they worked as bankers, engineers, pilots, administrators, stockbrokers, or lawyers, or in masculine jobs as mechanics, carpenters, or even professional athletes. In a sense, the individuals had officially repressed a feminine side of their persona in order to succeed in the male world, although they allowed this aspect to appear in private or among other cross dressers. This perceived unwillingness of society to allow males to express what society has labeled a feminine side is more a pathology of our society than of the individual. So serious has this societal pathology been that some individuals, both male and female, feel that it is only by surgically changing their sex that they can truly express their real selves.

We need as a society to continue to explore ways for those who do not fit into the rigid, bipolar gender roles to explore other alternatives. Some might well feel that cross dressing is the only alternative to the masculine or feminine roles they have been obliged to accept. Some males feel guilty enough about their cross dressing to seek the help of a therapist. Others do so because their spouses demand they get help. The task of the therapist then is to find out how to help them and, if continued cross dressing is important, to help them set limits acceptable to themselves and their spouses. If in the near future, society and the various professionals concerned with defining what is normal redefine societal attitudes toward male cross dressing to correspond with attitudes toward female cross dressing, much of the stigma ascribed to cross dressing would disappear and be replaced by greater freedom for personality development. The best model for such redefinition is the removal of homosexuality and lesbianism from the earlier versions of the DSM.

Certainly, there needs to be a rethinking of the whole concept of gender boxes in society and, with this, a recognition of the androgynous or gynandrous tendencies present in all humans. It might then be possible to judge individuals on what they accomplish or do as individuals rather than to restrict them to set gender roles. Both men and women, for example, have strong nurturing tendencies, although women traditionally have been assigned the nurturing role. Both women and men may have leadership qualities, but society in the past has been reluctant to recognize such qualities in women. Some men are quite narcissistic and self-centered, but usually in the past, we have attributed such qualities only to women. Many women have considerable athletic ability, but in the past we have generally ignored this possibility. The list of stereotypical notions could be expanded, but it should be clear that what society has done in the past is to put males in one box and females in another and then try to draw further limitations around the boxes. The box for women was far more restricted than that for men, but perhaps because of this, more encroachments were allowed on male prerogatives for special classes of women. The male role allowed a greater variety of opportunities but was more hostile to anything that smacked of femininity. Girls were "sugar and spice" and boys were "snails and puppy dog tails," and the net result of such cliché oversimplification was to limit the development of the human being as a person. Hopefully, this study of gender behavior, particularly as exemplified by cross dressing, will serve to emphasize the greater potential that exists in each of us and make us far more sympathetic to those men and women who do not quite fit into the gender boxes to which we traditionally have assigned them. A male may have a penis and a female a vagina, but behavior is far more complicated than this simple biological difference.

Notes

1. See Vern L. Bullough and Bonnie Bullough, *Women and Prostitution* (Buffalo: Prometheus Books, 1987).

2. For references, see Eli Coleman, "Expanding the Boundaries of Sex Research," *Journal of Sex Research* 27 (November 1990): 473–80.

3. There is a large corpus of literature reporting the existence of such individuals that dates from the nineteenth and twentieth centuries. Probably the best account surveying all of the literature is by Mildred Dickemann in an as-yet unpublished manuscript. We are indebted to her for sharing her research with us.

4. American Psychiatric Association, *Diagnostic and Statistical Manual of Mental Disorders,* rev. 3d ed. (Washington, DC: American Psychiatric Association, 1987).

5. Robert J. Stoller, *Observing the Erotic Imagination* (New Haven, CT: Yale University Press, 1985), 135–36.

Guide to Further Reading and Research

The endnotes to various chapters are the best guide to further study of cross dressing, and the interested reader should consult them. Some idea of the extent of the rapidly growing literature on the topic is evident from the two existing bibliographical guides. The first attempt at bibliography appears in an added section to Vern L. Bullough, Dorr Legg, Barret Elcano, and James Kepner, *Annotated Bibliography of Homosexuality*, 2 vols. (New York: Garland, 1976), 2 351–84, items 12240–12794. Its listing of approximately 450 items is a good starting point since it includes many of the articles published by Magnus Hirschfeld and his colleagues at the beginning of the twentieth century.

The most comprehensive bibliography of research and writing since that time is a typescript compiled by Dallas Denny, *Annotated Bibliography of Gender Dysphoria,* available through Atlanta Educational Gender Information Service, P.O. Box 33724, Decatur, GA 30033. It was compiled in 1990 but has updates through 1992. Included are nearly three thousand articles and over five hundred books. As of this writing Denny is in the process of updating this work for commercial publication by Garland Publishers in 1993. It casts a broad net and includes books and articles dealing with general sexual topics as well as the more specific items dealing with cross dressing and gender dysphoria. Also helpful is Gilbert Demeyere, *Transvestism and Its Wide Context: A Working Bibliography* (Wijnegem, Belgium: Demeyere, 1992). It is available through G. Demeyere, Turnhoutsebaan 588, B. 2110 Wijnegem, Belgium. Demeyere's book is much more historically oriented than Denny's bibliography but is not as current on journal articles.

The first major study of cross dressing was carried out by Magnus Hirschfeld, who called the phenomenon *transvestism.* Though his book, *Die Transvestiten* (Leipzig: Max Spohr, 1910) was slightly revised and reprinted in 1925 (and was often cited) it was never translated into

English (until recently). Most of the English citations to the book were made by people who had never read it. In fact, some of the English summaries are contrary to what Hirschfeld actually said. Since German research on the topic ended with the Nazis, the distortions of Hirschfeld continued to go unchallenged in the United States, where most of the research on cross dressing came to be centered. Concerned about these distortions, the authors of this book commissioned an English translation by Michael Lombardi-Nash and included it in their edited series of sex classics (Magnus Hirschfeld, *Transvestites: The Erotic Drive to Cross Dress*, trans. Michael Lombardi-Nash [Buffalo, NY: Prometheus Books, 1991]). It has to be called the classic of transvestism, and its findings challenge and undermine much of what was written on cross dressing prior to the 1970s.

The second classic work on cross dressing was written by Havelock Ellis, *Eonism and Other Supplementary Studies* (Philadelphia: F. A. Davis, 1928), and published as volume 7 in his *Studies in the Psychology of Sex*. Though it has long been available, and was often cited for its case studies, the assumptions and theoretical underpinnings were ignored by most American researchers into the topic until the 1970s, when there was a reassessment of his contribution.

Renewed interest in cross dressing came primarily through the great publicity given to the case of Christine Jorgensen in 1952–53. It was not the surgical castration and penectomy that made the Jorgensen transition possible, since these surgical techniques had long existed, but the availability and knowledge of hormone supplements. Though there subsequently was much writing on the topic of transsexualism, the classic work was that of Harry Benjamin, *The Transsexual Phenomenon* (New York: Julian Press, 1966). Research, however, was made easier by the interest of the Erickson Education Foundation set up by Reed Erickson, who was an early female-to-male transsexual. The Erickson Foundation helped sponsor Benjamin and gave funds to John Money and to the authors of this book, among others, before more or less closing its doors in the late 1970s.

John Money was a particularly influential figure. He wrote his doctoral dissertation at Harvard in 1952 on hermaphroditism and from that came to be interested in what the *Diagnostic and Statistical Manual* of the American Psychiatric Association eventually came to call "gender dysphoria" (3rd ed., revised, Washington DC: American Psychiatric Association, 1987). Among Money's publications are *Sex Errors of the Body: Dilemmas, Education, and Counseling* (Baltimore, MD: Johns Hopkins University Press, 1968); *Love and Love Sickness: The Science of Sex, Gender Difference, and Pair-Bonding* (Baltimore, MD: Johns Hopkins University Press, 1980); Money and A. A. Ehrhardt, *Man & Woman,*

Boy & Girl: The Differentiation and Dimorphism of Gender Identity (Baltimore, MD: Johns Hopkins University Press, 1972). Many of Money's graduate and post-doctoral students also published significantly in the field, including Richard Green, *Sexual Identity Conflict in Children and Adults* (New York: Basic Books, 1973) and *The "Sissy Boy" Syndrome and the Development of Homosexuality* (New Haven, CT: Yale University Press, 1987). Green co-authored with Money *Transsexualism and Sex Reassignment* (Baltimore, MD: Johns Hopkins University Press, 1969).

Money was a psychologist and Green a psychiatrist and their collaboration tended to lessen some of the barriers that exist between the two groups in interpreting transsexualism and transvestism. Other psychiatrists such as Ira Pauly also made major contributions to the study of cross dressing, but almost all of his work appears in journal articles, as chapters in books, or in the proceedings of the various meetings of the International Gender Dysphoria Association. His thinking may perhaps best be seen his article "Gender Identity Disorders: Evaluation and Treatment," *Journal of Sex Education and Therapy* 16 (1990): 2–24. Also important in the article literature are Neil McConaghy and Neil Buhrich, two Australian psychiatrists whose articles are listed in the endnotes.

Betty Steiner's edited volume, *Gender Dysphoria: Development, Research, Management* (New York: Plenum Press, 1985) is directed primarily toward transsexualism. See also William A. W. Walters and Michael W. Ross, eds., *Transsexualism and Sex Reassignment* (New York: Oxford University Press, 1986). A more hostile view toward transsexualism is Janice G. Raymond's *The Transsexual Empire: The Making of the She-Male* (Boston: Beacon Press, 1979). She criticizes the surgical solutions to gender dissatisfaction, maintaining that it was a patriarchal society that generated rigid sex roles and that male-to-female surgical transformation is the ultimate step in continuing male domination of the female. She ignores entirely the growing number of female-to-male transsexuals.

The major contribution of a psychologist to the understanding of cross dressing was that of Richard Docter, *Transvestites and Transsexuals: Toward a Theory of Cross-Gender Behavior* (London: Plenum Press, 1988). His work is ongoing and is much more concerned with heterosexual transvestism than many of the other investigators. Also important is Harry Brierly, *Transvestism: A Handbook with Case Studies for Psychologists, Psychiatrists and Counsellors* (London: Pergamon Press, 1979).

Some studies that bear on cross dressing deal with the existence of basic traits of masculinity and femininity. Particularly important in this respect is J. T. Spence and R. L. Helmreich, *Masculinity and Femininity: Their Psychological Dimensions, Correlates, and Antecedents* (Austin: University of Texas Press, 1978). Many others are also working in the area but have not published book-length studies; the interested reader should consult the endnotes for more detailed studies.

Others who made basic contributions to developing the understanding of cross dressing came from outside the fields of psychology, psychiatry, or medicine. In anthropology, for example, are Margaret Mead, *Sex and Temperament in Three Primitive Societies* (New York: William A. Morrow, 1935), and *Male and Female* (New York: William Morrow & Co., 1949). Among the most valuable of recent studies are Walter Williams, *The Spirit and the Flesh: Sexual Diversity in American Culture* (Boston: Beacon Press, 1986); Anne Bolin, *In Search of Eve: Transsexual Rites of Passage* (South Hadley, MA: Bergin and Garvey Publishers, Inc., 1988); and Gilbert Herdt, in various papers and books (a good start is Herdt and Robert J. Stoller, *Intimate Communications: Erotics and the Study of Culture* [New York: Columbia University Press, 1990]). A different kind of anthropological approach is Esther Newton, *Mother Camp: Female Impersonators in America* (New York: Prentice Hall, 1972). Sociologists have also contributed to the studies of gender, and though Fred Whitam is primarily interested in homosexuality, his various cross-cultural studies give important insights to cross dressing. A good example of his work is F. Whitam and R. M. Mathy, *Male Homosexuality in Four Societies: Brazil, Guatemala, the Philippines, and the United States* (New York: Praeger, 1986). Also important is Annie Woodhouse, *Fantastic Women: Sex, Gender, and Transvestism* (New Brunswick, NJ: Rutgers University Press, 1989). Others are listed in the various chapter references.

Historians and other humanities-oriented scholars have also been major contributors to the understanding of cross dressing. One of the pioneering works in this respect was written by one of the authors of this book, Vern L. Bullough, *Sexual Variance in Society and Culture* (Chicago: University of Chicago Press, 1976). Many historians have not yet published books on the topic, but their scholarly efforts thus far are listed in the endnotes. There has, however, been a literal explosion of studies, many of them with a feminist perspective, such as Marjorie Garber, *Vested Interests: Cross-Dressing and Cultural Anxiety* (New York: Routledge, 1992), who argues that there can be no culture without the transvestite. Her book complements this study very well since she amplifies and expands on many of the literary references listed herein, although we probably are not always in agreement on interpretation. There is a growing number of books about women who dressed as men, such as Julie Wheelwright, *Amazons and Military Maids* (London: Pandora, 1989), and many others that are listed in the endnotes.

Approaching the topic from a different angle are such writers as

Carolyn G. Heilbrun, *Toward a Recognition of Androgyny* (New York: Alfred A. Knopf, 1973). In a sense her emphasis on androgyny was a continuation of that pioneered by Edward Carpenter in *The Intermediate Sex: A Study of Some Transitional Types of Men and Women* (New York: Mitchell Kennerley, 1912), which also influenced the work of such writers as Elisabeth Badinter (*Man/Woman: The One Is the Other* (London: Collins Harvill, 1989).

One of the early studies of transvestism was edited by David O. Cauldwell, *Transvestism: Men in Female Dress* (New York: Sexology Corporation, 1956), and included discussion of the origins and natures of transvestism and transsexualism and a number of biographical and autobiographical accounts. These accounts predate much of the scholarly study of cross dressing. An early collection was by C. J. Bulliet, *Venus Castina: Famous Female Impersonators Celestial and Human* (New York: privately printed, 1928; reprinted, New York: Bonanza Books, 1956). Also frequently reprinted, sometimes as one volume and sometimes as two, is C. J. S. Thompson, *Mysteries of Sex: Women Who Posed as Men and Men Who Impersonated Women* (London: Hutchinson & Co., n.d.), and O. P. Gilbert, *Men in Women's Guise* (New York: Brentano, 1926). A more recent study along these lines is Peter Ackroyd, *Transvestism and Drag: The History of an Obsession* (New York: Simon and Schuster, 1979).

Concentrating more on the theater is Roger Baker, *Drag: A History of Female Impersonation on the Stage* (London: Triton Books, 1968). Much more scholarly, but also directed more at homosexuality and including cross dressing only incidentally is John M. Clum, *Acting Gay: Male Homosexuality in Modern Drama* (New York: Columbia University Press, 1992).

A quite different approach is that of Mariette Pathy Allen, *Transformations: Crossdressers and Those Who Love Them* (New York: E. P. Dutton, 1989), which provides pictures of transvestites and their families and brings home the idea that real human beings are involved here.

Much of the current research into the topic, including much of our own, however, appears in professional journals. Journals in all disciplines publish articles on the topic, but those that emphasize sex research should be consulted first, including *Archives of Sexual Behavior, Journal of Sex Research, Journal of Sex Therapy and Counseling, Journal of Psychology and Human Sexuality, Journal of the History of Sexuality, Annual Review of Sex Research, Medical Aspects of Human Sexuality,* and *Journal of Homosexuality.*

There is also a large number of publications sponsored by the cross-dressing community itself which include studies at various levels of scholarship. The first in the field was *Transvestia,* edited and published by Virginia Prince. As of this writing it is no longer published, but it is a valuable guide to changing opinions on the topic. Copies of these issues are not available in every library, but the Vern Bullough and Bonnie Bullough Collection on Sex and Gender in the special collections section of the California University Library in Northridge, CA, has all the issues as well as vast numbers of other periodicals and ephemera on cross dressing and other areas of the study of human sexuality. More recent journals include the *Journal of Gender Studies*, published by the Human Outreach Institute (405 Western Ave., Suite 345, South Portland, ME 04106). Its editor, Ariadne Kane, has long been active in the transgender community and was active in establishing the Fantasia Fair get-together of cross dressers in Provincetown, MA, which held its eighteenth annual event in 1992.

Extremely informative, since it makes an effort to list all the events in the cross-gender community as well as the variety of organizations, is *Tapestry: The Journal for All Persons Interested in Crossdressing and Transsexualism*, a magazine published by the International Foundation for Gender Education (Box 367, Wayland, MA 01778). It is edited by Merissa Sherrill Lyn, a long-time active member in the cross-gendered community who is now a postoperative transsexual. Another group with an active publishing program is Renaissance Education Association (Box 552, King of Prussia, PA 29406); Joan Roberts is the publisher. *Chrysalis Quarterly* is published by American Educational Gender Information Service (P.O. Box 33724, Decatur, GA 30033-0724). The Society for the Second Self (Box 194, Tulare, CA 93275), under Carol Beecroft took over much of the publishing program of Virginia Prince and Chevalier Publications. It publishes a correspondence directory, a directory of commercial services, and a magazine, *Femme Mirror;* it also runs a roster of chapters throughout the country, many of which have their own publications. A listing can be found in *Tapestry*.

Deserving of specific mention, however, is *Female to Male:F2M* (1827 Haight St., No. 164, San Francisco, CA 94117) which was run for many years by Lou Sullivan. Since Sullivan's recent death it has not been clear what will happen to this organization. A similar society for female-to-male cross dressers is the Adam Society (6 Cushing St., 2nd Fl., Waltham, MA 02154). Generally, however, there are fewer support groups for women cross dressers or transgenderists than for men. Almost every state in the United States and the provinces in Canada have some sort of group, as do a large number of foreign countries. Interested readers are advised to look at the updated directory of organizations and services in *Tapestry*, the editors of which make a concerted effort to keep up-to-date on the various organizations.

Index

This book was set in Baskerville and Eras typefaces. Baskerville was designed by John Baskerville at his private press in Birmingham, England, in the eighteenth century. The first typeface to depart from oldstyle typeface design, Baskerville has more variation between thick and thin strokes. In an effort to insure that the thick and thin strokes of his typeface reproduced well on paper, John Baskerville developed the first wove paper, the surface of which was much smoother than the laid paper of the time. The development of wove paper was partly responsible for the introduction of typefaces classified as modern, which have even more contrast between thick and thin strokes.

Eras was designed in 1969 by Studio Hollenstein in Paris for the Wagner Typefoundry. A contemporary script-like version of a sans-serif typeface, the letters of Eras have a monotone stroke and are slightly inclined.

Printed on acid-free paper.